TRANSGENDER JURISPRUDENCE

Dysphoric Bodies of Law

Cavendish
Publishing
Limited

London • Sydney

TRANSGENDER JURISPRUDENCE

Dysphoric Bodies of Law

Andrew N Sharpe
Senior Lecturer in Law, Department of Law
Macquarie University

Cavendish
Publishing
Limited

London • Sydney

First published in Great Britain 2002 by Cavendish Publishing Limited, The Glass House, Wharton Street, London WC1X 9PX, United Kingdom

Telephone: +44 (0)20 7278 8000   Facsimile: +44 (0)20 7278 8080

Email: info@cavendishpublishing.com

Website: www.cavendishpublishing.com

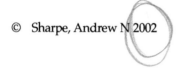

British Library Cataloguing in Publication Data

Transgender Jurisprudence: dysphoric bodies of law

1 Sociological jurisprudence 2 Transsexuals – Legal status, laws, etc

I Title

346'013

ISBN 1 85941 666 7

Printed and bound in Great Britain

[MC Escher's 'Metamorphosis III' © 2001 Cordon BV – Baarn – Holland. All rights reserved.]

I would like to dedicate this book to my mother, Susan Winifred O'Hagan and my father, Neville Tomlinson Sharpe. With love and gratitude.

FOREWORD

It is *de rigueur* for law to draw clear lines between people so that some are 'in' while others are 'not in'. In/out, norm/other: dualistic thought has been naturalised through language and myriad discourses. Male and female is one such dualism, superficially simple, but in fact highly complex. Law both reflects and reifies the ostensible simplicity through countless legislative and adjudicative sites. Heterosexuality is the normative sexual transparency which overlays the sexed pairing, while homosexuality complicates it. Andrew Sharpe's trailblazing study of transgender jurisprudence goes further, putting paid, once and for all, to a two dimensional, anatomical characterisation of sex.

The word 'trailblazing' is not hyperbolic in this case because *Transgender Jurisprudence* is the first full length, scholarly study on the topic. Transgenderism itself is not new, although the scholarly discourses around it did not really develop until well into the 20th century. Such discourses were initially dominated by medical knowledges. The author's jurisprudential focus signals a new sophistication in understandings and theorisation that seek to transcend what he calls '(bio)logic'. The author does not merely replace a medical hegemony with a legal hegemony. Instead, he emphasises the destabilising potential of transgendered bodies, which refuse to be corralled by biologistic binary boxes. 'Dysphoria', the central trope of the book, is defined as 'a state of mutual unease or discomfort'. It applies to the law of bodies, which is discomfited and disrupted by interrogation and critique, as well as to some transgender people.

The legal story is a fascinating one and by no means a linear tale of progress. Transgenderism, has connotations of dangerousness because it evokes fear – fear of the abject – which is why law's conservatising role has to be selectively invoked. This is graphically illustrated by the author through both marriage law and anti-discrimination law, areas of law inherently beset by contradictions. While liberal law purports to operate as a progressive and reformist instrument, law's '(bio)logic' simultaneously operates to reproduce conventional incarnations of sex. Hence, transgender issues have a habit of inducing judicial vertigo, a condition that is apt to be exacerbated by the belief that transgender and homosexuality are synonymous.

To understand how the spectre of homosexuality looms over encounters between law and transgender, I exhort you to read this book. Its elegant arguments and lucid prose are guaranteed to make the task a pleasure.

Margaret Thornton
Professor of Law and Legal Studies
La Trobe University, Melbourne
August 2001

ACKNOWLEDGMENTS

In thinking about transgender/law relations and in the writing of this book I have received the support, encouragement and constructive criticism of many friends and colleagues. In particular, I would like to thank Anne Barron, Margaret Davies, David Fraser, Didi Herman, Desmond Manderson, Gail Mason, Daniel Monk, Les Moran, Wayne Morgan, John Mountbatten, Katherine O'Donovan, Carl Stychin, Margaret Thornton and Stephen Whittle. I would also like to thank two librarians at Macquarie University, Diane Mitchell and Joy Wearne, for their assistance throughout the writing of this book and Maggie Liston for her help with formatting. I would also like to thank Jo Reddy and Cara Annett at Cavendish Publishing for their unwavering support throughout this project. And I would like to thank the Faculty of Law at the University of Sydney where I recently completed a sabbatical and in particular its Dean, Jeremy Weber, for providing me with a room and other resources.

The book has also benefited from the comments of audiences at numerous academic conferences, including the 'Gender, Sexuality and the Law' Conference, Department of Law, University of Keele (1998); the Australian Feminist Law Conference, Faculty of Law, University of Sydney (1999) and Faculty of Law, Queensland University of Technology (2001); the 'Law and Literature' Conference, Department of Law, University of Technology Sydney (2000), as well as at numerous staff seminars, including the School of Law, Flinders University (1999); the Department of Law, Australian National University (1999, 2001); the Department of Law, Macquarie University (1999, 2001); the Faculty of Law, University of Sydney (1999, 2001); the Department of Gender Studies, University of Sydney (2000); the Department of Law, University of Technology, Sydney (2001), and the Department of Sociology, Macquarie University (2001).

Finally, I acknowledge permission to reproduce previously published earlier versions of portions of this book. An earlier version of portions of Chapters 3 and 4 appears as 'Anglo-Australian Judicial Approaches to Transsexuality: Discontinuities, Continuities and Wider Issues at Stake', in *Social and Legal Studies: An International Journal* (1997); an earlier version of portions of Chapters 5 and 6 appears as 'Transgender Jurisprudence and the Spectre of Homosexuality', in the *Australian Feminist Law Journal* (2000), and an earlier version of Chapter 8 appears as 'Transgender Performance and the Discriminating Gaze: A Critique of Anti-Discrimination Regulatory Regimes', in *Social and Legal Studies: An International Journal* (1999). I would also like to acknowledge permission of Kluwer Academic Publishers BV and of Federation Press to reproduce earlier, though as yet unpublished, versions of portions of this book. An earlier version of portions of Chapters 3 and 5 will appear as 'English Transgender Law Reform and the Spectre of *Corbett*', in *Feminist Legal Studies* (2002) while an earlier version of Chapter 9 will appear as 'In the Shadow of Homosexual Anxiety: Transgender Law Reform in Western Australia', in the *Australasian Gay and Lesbian Law Journal* (2001). Chapter 3 appears by permission of Sage Publications Ltd and Kluwer Academic Publishers BV, Chapter 4 by permission of Sage Publications Ltd, Chapter 5 by permission of Kluwer Academic Publishers BV and the Australian Feminist Law Foundation Inc, Chapter 6 by permission of the Australian Feminist Law Foundation Inc, Chapter 8 by permission of Sage Publications Ltd and Chapter 9 by permission of Federation Press.

CONTENTS

PART I

APPROACHING TRANSGENDER BODIES

TABLE OF CASES

TABLE OF LEGISLATION

INTRODUCTION

1.1 TERMINOLOGY

This book is about the relationship between law, politics and transgender people. In exploring, and in order to understand, this relationship it is necessary to identify and pay close attention to the lexicon surrounding transgender, its sources and history. While there is ample evidence for the claim that particular identifications, practices and desires, which we might today call transgendered, have existed transhistorically (see, for example, Green, 1969a; Karlen, 1971; Green, 1974; Warnes and Hill, 1974; Bullough, 1975; Bullough, 1976; Boswell, 1980; Steiner, 1981; Feinberg, 1996; Devor, 1997, Chapter 1), contemporary cultural understandings of this phenomenon can be traced to late 19th century sexological discourse. It is in the writings of early sexologists, men like Karl Heinrich Ulrichs (*third sex*) (1994), Richard von Krafft-Ebing (*psychopathia transexualis*) (1965), Henry Havelock Ellis (*sexual inversion*) (1936a) and Magnus Hirschfeld (*transvestite*) (1910), that a vocabulary first emerged for describing transgender identities and desires. It was within the domain of sexology that transgender bodies were first given both some degree of visibility and subjected to intense institutional scrutiny. These early sexological writings are important because, in setting terms for thinking about sex, gender and sexuality and their interrelationship, they positioned transgender bodies in ways that continue to inform the legal present. Moreover, and as we shall see, subsequent medical and legal discourses generated around transgender bodies have tended to, and do, operate within a frame established by these early sexological forays.

As we will see in Chapter 2, the 'scientific' history of transgender since the late 19th century has, when not erasing transgender people altogether, been one of considerable delimitation. Against this background, and as a political response to it, the term 'transgender' emerged in the 1990s (see, for example, Hale, 1995, p 20; Califia, 1997, p 224; Cromwell, 1999, Chapter 2). The term was used initially in order to distinguish particular identities and practices from the medical terminology of *transsexualism* and *transvestism* (Cromwell, 1999, p 23). It represented a counter-discourse, or a 'reverse-discourse', as Foucault has put it (1981a, p 101), to these terms and their pathological overtones. Moreover, and accordingly, it delineated a position between desire for sex reassignment surgery, which had gradually become the hallmark of transsexuality, and episodic or temporary gender crossings. As Boswell has put it, the term 'transgender' represented a 'viable option between crossdresser [transvestite] and transsexual' (1991, p 31). However, it is important here to resist thinking of transgender as anti-transsexualism, as 'yet another version of the morality tale that condemns the cutting of the flesh' (Stryker, 1998, p 153). On the contrary, the term 'transgender' has come increasingly to function as an umbrella term for a range of trans-subjectivities including people who identify as transsexual and who seek or have undertaken sex (genital) reassignment surgery, people seeking other surgical procedures and/or hormonal treatments, and people whose permanent or temporary gender crossings are unaccompanied by medical intervention (see, for example, Whittle, 1996; Stryker, 1998, p 149; Cromwell, 1999, p 23; Currah and Minter, 2000a, pp 3–4).

Moreover, as transgender communities have grown it has become clear that the term is not exhausted by sex/gender binary crossings. Rather, it has been used increasingly to accommodate people who identify as both, neither, or something other than male or female. That is to say, some self-identified transgender people seek to occupy the position of the 'third' (fourth, fifth ...). Moreover, there is, perhaps, a trend toward this more transgressive stance with a proliferation of terms such as *she-male, pansexual* and *spansexual* (see, for example, Stone, 1991; Feinberg, 1993a, 1993b; Bornstein, 1994; May-Welby, 1994, p 11; Bruce-Pratt, 1995; Nataf, 1996, p 32; Califia, 1997). While transgender is, perhaps, not a term of unlimited scope, it is a term of self-description. Accordingly, it is this term that will be preferred throughout the book. However, other terms such as *transsexual* and *gender dysphoria* will be used at times in order to reflect medico-legal usage and for purposes of clarity. Moreover, in using the dyad 'pre/post-operative' the book again reflects medico-legal usage that equates post-operative status with sex (genital) reassignment surgery, specifically, vaginoplasty/phalloplasty.[1] However, it should be borne in mind that this usage of the distinction is problematic in that persons classified as pre-operative frequently undergo, or have undergone, invasive surgical procedures, including castration and penectomy,[2] in the case of (male-to-female) transgender women, and mastectomy and hysterectomy in the case of (female-to-male) transgender men. Moreover, the term 'pre-operative' proves problematic in that it suggests a particular and teological relationship between 'authentic' transgender identity and sex reassignment surgery. In these and in other ways transgender jurisprudence emerges as an important site for contestation over the meaning and ownership of terms.

1.2 A TRANSGENDER JURISPRUDENCE

In writing this book it is not my intention to speak for transgender communities nor to critique transgender understandings of sex, gender and sexuality. Rather, in thinking through transgender bodies of law this book offers some critical insights into the nature and practices of law and situates legal doctrine and law reform within the context of transgender politics. The transgender/law nexus has been the site for a number of critical interventions at the level of legal doctrine in recent years (see, for example, Muller, 1994; Mountbatten, 1994; Collier, 1995; Franke, 1995; Pearlman, 1995; Whittle and McMullan, 1995; Sharpe, 1996, 1997a, 1997b, 1998, 2000; Shafiqullah, 1997; Storrow, 1997; Holt, 1997; Cain, 1998; Coombes, 1998; Whittle, 1998, 1999; Keller, 1999), as well as for some earlier forays (Gould, 1979; O'Donovan, 1985). These interventions have produced important and valuable contributions to a critical transgender jurisprudence. However, in interrogating legal reasoning, within primarily North American, United Kingdom and Australasian legal contexts, this book offers, for the first time, a sustained, integrated and comparative critique of transgender/law relations across common law jurisdictions and legal subject matters and situates those relations within contexts of law's relationship

---

1   'Vaginoplasty' refers to the construction of a vagina and 'phalloplasty' to the construction of a penis.
2   The term 'penectomy' refers to the removal of the penis (see Koranyi, 1980, p 127).

with medicine. It aims, through taking legal doctrine seriously, to tease out, map and make (non)sense of the multiple themes and subtexts that comprise this nascent jurisprudence.

This is in contrast to the more general legal literature in the area, a literature that is characterised by more traditional forms of legal scholarship and which dates from the early 1970s (see, for example, Green, 1970; van Niekerk, 1970; Note, 1971; Smith, 1971; Walton, 1974, 1984; David, 1975; Lupton, 1976; Finlay, 1980, 1989, 1995, 1996; Graham, 1980; Richardson, 1983; Pace, 1983; Samuels, 1984; Hurley, 1984; Dewar, 1985; Wilson, 1985; Taitz, 1986, 1987, 1988, 1992; Kirby, 1987; Bailey-Harris, 1989; Otlowski, 1990; Andrews, 1991; Bates, 1993; Johnson, 1994; Bourke, 1994). Transgender jurisprudence has emerged in the context of the practice and legitimisation of sex reassignment surgery in the West. Against this backdrop traditional legal scholarship has tended toward preoccupation with legal determination of the sex of post-operative transgender persons for purposes such as marriage, gendered criminal offences, sex discrimination and social security claims. More particularly, this scholarship has adopted a fairly consistent stance regarding the question of legal sex. Thus there has been widespread condemnation of the 1970 English decision of *Corbett v Corbett*[3] which decided that *sex is determined at birth*, and of the line of authority which has followed in its wake.[4] Conversely, decisions that have departed from the 'disaster' of *Corbett* (David, 1975, p 340) have been widely, yet uncritically, accepted. We will see that in a number of jurisdictions, particularly in the United States, Australia and New Zealand, courts have abandoned chromosomes and birth as the governing moment in determining sex for legal purposes, preferring instead to articulate a test of *psychological and anatomical harmony* whereby the fact of sex reassignment surgery assumes cardinal importance.[5] In other words, and in these jurisdictions, law's response to reformist calls for the re-sexing of transgender bodies has tended to be confined to the post-surgical body. This has had the effects of delimiting transgender as a category of legal analysis and encouraging a view of the transgender body as 'an esoteric subject for legal study' (Collier, 1995, p 114).

Moreover, while reformulations of the test for determining sex for legal purposes and the surrounding legal commentary can be situated within a legal framework of reform, this impulse to reform has proved largely unconcerned with the medico-legal modes of regulation it instantiates or the discursive effects it produces. Rather, much of the existing legal scholarship has tended to highlight only law's repressive power which, of course,

---

3   *Corbett v Corbett* [1970] 2 All ER 33.

4   *Re T* [1975] 2 NZLR 449; *W v W* [1976] 2 SALR 308; *Dec CP 6/76 National Insurance Commissioner Decisions*; *EA White v British Sugar Corporation* [1977] IRLR 121; *K v Health Division of Human Resources* 560 P 2d 1070 (1977); *Anonymous v Irving Mellon as Director of Bureau of Vital Records, Department of Health of the City of New York* 398 NYS 2d 99 (1977); *Social Security Decision Nos R(P) 1 and R(P) 2* [1980] National Insurance Commissioner Decisions; *R v Tan* [1983] QB 1053; *Peterson v Peterson* (1985) *The Times*, 12 July; *Re Ladrach* 32 Ohio Misc 2d 6 (1987); *Franklin v Franklin* (1990) *The Scotsman*, 9 November; *Lim Ying v Hiok Kian Ming Eric* (1992) 1 SLR 184; *Collins v Wilkin Chapman* [1994] EAT/945/93 (Transcript); *Re P and G* [1996] FLR 90; *S-T (Formerly J) v J* [1998] 1 All ER 431; *Littleton v Prange* [1999] 288th Judicial District Court, Bexar County, Texas (www.4thcoa.courts.state.tx.us/opinions/9900010.htm); *W v W* (2000) *The Times*, 31 October (Transcript); *Bellinger v Bellinger* (2000) *The Times*, 2 November.

5   See *Re Anonymous* 293 NYS 2d 834 (1968); *MT v JT* 355 A 2d 204 (1976); *R v Harris and McGuiness* [1989] 17 NSWLR 158; *Secretary, Department of Social Security v HH* [1991] 13 AAR 314; *Secretary, Department of Social Security v SRA* (1993) 118 ALR 467; *M v M* [1991] NZFLR 337; *Attorney-General v Otahuhu Family Court* [1995] 1 NZLR 603.

the reform movement has sought to contest. Accordingly, the focus of legal inquiry has tended to be decision-oriented. Drawing upon poststructural thought, the book seeks to move beyond this preoccupation with legal decision and repressive legal power (Foucault, 1981a) so typical of traditional legal analyses and reform agendas. Rather, recognising law as a site of cultural production, the book aims to take law reform activism into the very texts of law itself, where legal decision or legal ruling represents only one portion of those texts. Moreover, in emphasising law as a site of cultural production the book serves to heighten what is at stake politically when the choice is made to engage law. The book aims, therefore, not merely to render transgender people more visible within the domain of law but also to contest and problematise the medico-legal conditions upon which transgender people have been granted a limited presence within law and to consider their discursive effects.

Transgender people represent for law a challenge to the notion of sex as naturally immutable, and therefore serve to problematise the basis of gendered and heterosexual subjectivities. In response to this challenge we shall see that law, in a number of different contexts, deploys pre/post-operative, transgender/cross-dresser, transgender/homosexual, natural/unnatural, sexual/non-sexual and sexually functional/dysfunctional dyads as regulatory strategies around bodies. Traditional legal scholarship has omitted to explore these attempts to defuse the transgender challenge and has therefore been blind to the wider connections and intersections of transgender jurisprudence. This has served to conceal the ways in which medico-legal discourse has deployed transgender people in furtherance of much wider regulatory strategies around sexual practice and gender performance. In this regard the book will, in considering the excessive work that law requires transgender people to perform, situate the transgender/law relation within a much broader sexual political field, thereby informing feminist and gay and lesbian legal theory and practice.

Moreover, the book will argue that in the process of seeking to contain the threat that the transgender body is considered to pose, law destabilises and 'denaturalises' hegemonic understandings of sex, gender and sexuality, thereby opening up spaces for disruption and rearticulation. While law portrays itself as certain, predictable, coherent and ordered and views the transgender body as the locus of dissonance, ambiguity and contradiction, the book will argue it is the body of law, not transgender bodies, that more accurately fits that description. It is this claim that leads, through a play on words, to the book's subtitle. In opposition to the contemporary medical view of transgender people as suffering from *gender dysphoria*, a phrase which the book will critique, it is bodies of law which are viewed as dysphoric in the sense that disruption to the legal categories of sex, gender and sexuality is internal to law. The book will map the particular fractures, fissures and gaps which are opened up by forms of legal reasoning that attempt to maintain a particular constellation of sex, gender and sexuality in the face of transgender trouble.

1.3 THEMES

The chapters of the book deal with different areas of law. While significant discontinuities will be seen to emerge across these areas of law as well as across legal cultures, a number of common and intersecting themes will be seen to emerge. It is, perhaps, the figure inside/outside (Fuss, 1991, p 1) which best captures what links these themes together. First, it will be argued throughout the book that transgender bodies of law are important sites for the production and non-production (Butler, 1993, p 22) of sexed, gendered and sexual identities. That is to say, law, in coming up against transgender bodies, and through different regulatory strategies across and within different legal cultures, aims to reproduce medico-legal binary understandings of sex, gender and sexuality as well as a particular interrelationship of that constellation.

A connected theme relates to the need to consider and emphasise the wider discourse of law; that is to say, to emphasise law as a site of cultural production. Traditional legal analyses of transgender bodies of law have tended to be decision-oriented. That is to say, they have tended to be preoccupied with the instrumental question: what is the legal test for determining sex for legal purposes? While this is an important question, and one which lawyers and some transgender litigants need to know, the chapters of this book are more concerned to understand the discourses, including medical discourses, which inform legal tests and to consider their discursive effects. In these latter senses the book aims to deepen and broaden inquiry into transgender bodies of law. Connected to this theme is the book's aim of contesting the notion of transgender as an esoteric subject for legal study. Rather, the book aims to demonstrate how the impact of transgender bodies of law greatly exceeds the transgender body itself. In particular, legal discourse will be seen to have significant and confronting implications for feminist and gay and lesbian politics. This negative discursive fall-out, which the book will detail, points to the need for the transgender/law relation to be placed more firmly upon a range of sexual political agendas.

Thus the book will highlight how judicial anxiety over the homosexual body proves to be a consistent and central feature of transgender jurisprudence. It is fear over an imagined proximity of transgender bodies and sexual practices to homosexuality, especially in relation to particular areas of law such as marriage, which generates this anxiety. The homophobia of law will be seen to manifest itself both in terms of conflation of transgender and homosexual bodies and desires and a somewhat contradictory medico-legal insistence on viewing those bodies and desires as incommensurate. In both instances homosexuality will be seen to function as a sign of 'inauthentic' transgender identity and desire. Thus transgender bodies of law will be seen both to negate homosexuality in the biological sense, and to preclude it in the psychological and transgender sense. In this respect, the book traces one relatively recent 'route by which the unthinkability of homosexuality is being constituted time and again' (Butler, 1991, p 20). Moreover, because the figure of the homosexual serves in important respects to structure transgender jurisprudence, medico-legal formulations of homosexual/transgender relations become of tremendous significance for possibilities of transgender and gay and lesbian coalitional politics. That is to say, it is important to appreciate how tensions within and across transgender and gay and lesbian communities regarding identity and political action are themselves structured, at least in part, by the categorical imperatives of law and medical science. Moreover, the book will draw attention to the ways in which traditional legal scholarship is implicated in the cultural 'unintelligibility' of non-heterosexual transgender desire, thereby problematising uncritical reformism.

A connected theme will be to chart the negative discursive effects of transgender jurisprudence for women, including transgender women. It will become apparent that legal discourse around (male-to-female) transgender bodies reproduces phallocentric and performativist assumptions about women. In this context medico-legal constructions of the 'passing' woman, the deployment of the active/passive dichotomy, the distinction between the pre-operative and post-operative body and the privileging of male-to-female capacity for penetrative heterosexual sex in legal determinations of sex all serve to confront feminist politics. Of further concern to feminist politics is law's differential treatment of male-to-female and female-to-male transgender bodies. It will become clear that the (female-to-male) transgender man who makes claims upon law encounters greater difficulties than the (male-to-female) transgender woman. While this is, in part, due to the current state of the surgical techniques of vaginoplasty and phalloplasty, it is also, and importantly, an effect of the legal construction and valuation of the vagina and penis. That is to say, while the penis is viewed as a complex anatomical organ, difficult to replicate, the vagina is, within a liberal legal gaze, viewed as a mere cavity, absence or lack (Naffine, 1997, p 88) and therefore relatively easy to create. Moreover, this view is, as we will see, replicated even within a more recent strain of reform jurisprudence that purports to privilege the aesthetics over the functionality of the vagina. Another important theme containing obvious implications for feminist politics is that of reproduction. While the treatment of reproduction or procreation in transgender jurisprudence lacks consistency, several strands of the discourse deploy procreative capacity in styles that reproduce a notion antithetical to feminism, namely, that anatomy determines destiny (de Beauvoir, 1953).

Another theme relates to the act/identity dyad. Foucault has argued that over the last two centuries we have witnessed a gradual shift in concern away from action toward identity (1981a). As a general proposition, it would seem that this description of the changing operation of power can be mapped onto law. As Foucault has argued, law functions less and less as a juridical entity and more and more in order to constitute the norm around which bodies are to be regulated and distributed (1981a, p 144). This observation would seem perhaps to be especially apposite in the present context given the symbiotic relationship between transgender jurisprudence and medical science. Nevertheless, it is important to recognise that law continues to deploy both sides of the act/identity dyad in the regulation of bodies, a point rendered abundantly clear by Moran in relation to the gay male body (1996, Chapter 2). Indeed, law's straddling of the act/identity dyad around the gay male body is exemplified by the reasoning of the United States Supreme Court in *Bowers v Hardwick* (Stychin, 1995, p 150),[6] a case concerning a constitutional challenge to the validity of state sodomy laws, and by the reasoning of the House of Lords in the infamous sado-masochism case, *R v Brown* (Stychin, 1995, Chapter 7).[7]

This book will draw attention in specific contexts to the ways in which transgender emerges as both act and identity in medico-legal reasoning. Thus, and in a number of different legal contexts, law, drawing selectively on medical knowledge, will be seen to oscillate between a search for a core 'truth' of transgender subjectivity on the one hand, and a preoccupation with sex reassignment surgery as well as pre/post-operative sexual

---

6   *Bowers v Hardwick* 478 US 186 (1986).
7   *R v Brown* [1993] 2 All ER 75 (HL).

and gender practice on the other. However, identity and practice, which law views as distinct, are not necessarily treated as mutually exclusive within transgender jurisprudence. Rather, we will see that they are capable of bearing, and frequently do bear, a mutually reinforcing relation. That is to say, particular acts are viewed through the lens of law as confirming transgender 'authenticity'. Moreover, we will see that this legal concern over 'authenticity' is inextricably bound up with perceived proximity to the homosexual body. In this regard the themes of act/identity and homophobia evident within transgender jurisprudence inform one another. However, the relationship between act and identity in law is complex and it should not be thought that acts serve only to demonstrate identity, thereby privileging the latter term. On the contrary, we will see in Chapters 7 and 8 that legal developments in the field of anti-discrimination law have, in important respects, reworked the act/identity dyad so as to foreground performance, thereby uncoupling legal protection, and therefore rights, from the notion of 'coherent fixed identity'.

Another theme which the book will explore is that of law's bodily aesthetics. In particular it will be argued that legal reasoning around the pre/post-surgical dyad cannot be accounted for solely by reference to a concern over procreative and/or heterosexual capacity. Rather, while judicial emphasis is placed on heterosexual functioning and the absence of procreative capacity post-surgically, it will become clear that legal preoccupation with sex reassignment surgery is also an effect of law's inability to reimagine bodies. In this regard, the pre-operative or non-surgical transgender body emerges as 'monstrous'. Law's concern over bodily aesthetics, while a consistent theme within transgender jurisprudence, tends to be masked by concerns over functionality. However, as we will see, morphological considerations become explicit in some of the most 'progressive' cases where concerns over sexual functioning are abandoned, displaced or backgrounded. Accordingly, it may be that the re-sexing of the bodies of pre- or non-surgical transgender people, the overwhelming proportion of transgender communities (Cromwell, 1999), will ultimately depend on contestation and rearticulation in terms of bodily aesthetics. Moreover, as we will see in Chapter 6, the foregrounding of law's bodily aesthetics serves to re-emphasise the homophobia of law given that post-operative sexual capacity can no longer provide a rationale for law's insistence on sex reassignment surgery.

While recognising the dangers inherent in any engagement with law from the margins the book will explore the theme of resistance. It will be argued that in the process of seeking to contain the threat that the transgender body is considered to pose to the heterosexual matrix, law destabilises and 'denaturalises' hegemonic understandings of sex, gender and heterosexuality. That is to say, as legal reasoning has become increasingly strained in attempting to contain troublesome transgender bodies, fissures have opened up in legal texts. In this regard, and because these disruptions to legal categories are internal to law, the book will contest law's depiction of the transgender/law relation. While law presents itself as certain, coherent, predictable and ordered, and transgender bodies as the locus of dissonance, ambiguity, and contradiction, the book will argue for a reversal of this view. The book will delineate the precise ways in which the destabilisation of legal categories has occurred across a range of legal subject matters. In particular we will see that legal reasoning reveals the imitative or performative structure of gender and indeed anatomical sex. Further, we will see that heterosexuality, though importantly not homosexuality, is 'denaturalised' in law's 're-sexualisation' and re-sexing of transgender bodies. In these and other respects transgender jurisprudence creates spaces for the articulation of alternative sexed, gendered and non-heterosexual transgender subjectivities.

Moreover, this jurisprudence which confronts feminist and gay and lesbian politics in so many respects offers such politics, through these very same gaps in legal reasoning, possibilities for challenge. That is to say, arguments developed from legal reasoning around the sex, gender and sexuality of transgender people might be deployed in order to challenge negative representations of women and of gay men and lesbians produced by transgender jurisprudence. Moreover, the contradictory forms of legal reasoning within transgender jurisprudence might be redeployed on other sexual political terrains. However, this might require abandoning, or at least reconceptualising, notions of identity as fixed and coherent. Indeed, as we shall see, it is precisely thinking of this type that has served to foreclose particular kinds of transgender subjectivity within medicine and law as well as within some gay and lesbian communities (Stone, 1991; Rubin, 1992; Califia, 1997). On the other hand, law's treatment of homosexuality as the more stable sexual category might be viewed as inviting forms of 'strategic essentialism' (Spivak, 1990, p 51). In this sense, thinking through transgender bodies of law serves to draw attention to, and perhaps heighten, the existing tension between assertion and deconstruction of identities (Weeks, 1991, pp 84–85; Seidman, 1993; Stychin, 1995, p 8).

A final and crucial theme that ties the chapters together involves consideration of the interrelationship of medical science and law That is to say, the book will map the medical knowledges that have informed transgender jurisprudence. The need to foreground this relation is heightened by the fact that in transgender contexts legal claims are processed through the lens of medical science to an extraordinary degree, a fact which draws attention to specific dangers transgender people face when invoking law. That resort to law has this effect is due to a number of factors. First, many transgender people remain dependent upon physicians and/or surgeons to the extent that they desire sex reassignment surgery, other surgical procedures, and/or regulated hormone treatments. Indeed, and as we will see when we consider the case law, the overwhelming majority of transgender people making claims before law have undertaken surgical and/or hormonal procedures. Moreover, we will see that within transgender jurisprudence, genital surgery functions as a threshold requirement for legal recognition of sex claims. Further, unlike homosexuality, which is no longer officially considered to be a mental disorder in the West,[8] transgender people continue to be pathologised within ever burgeoning psychiatric discourses. While it would be mistaken to reduce legal decision to medical knowledge, or refuse to acknowledge, and in the context of transgender politics exploit, tensions that exist between medicine and law, it will be argued that reliance upon the scientific power of medicine has proved a consistent feature of transgender jurisprudence across legal cultures. Moreover, the coupling of these two powerful and privileged discourses, and their inscription on transgender bodies, is significant. That is to say, the special power enjoyed by law, an effect of the institutional, political and moral authority it commands (Cover, 1986; Sarat and Kearns, 1992), is, in transgender contexts, bolstered by

---

8   The American Psychiatric Association (APA) voted in 1973 to remove homosexuality from the *Diagnostic and Statistical Manual of Mental Disorders* (DSM III).

a particularly intimate relationship with medical science. In this regard, there is a strengthening of the 'truth' claims thereby generated. Accordingly, the encounter between transgender and law is one of both possibility and considerable risk.

1.4 CHAPTER OUTLINES

In Part I, 'Approaching Transgender Bodies', which comprises Chapters 2–4, the book will offer an analysis and critique of the medical history of transgender as a prelude to mapping judicial approaches to transgender bodies each of which translates medical dialogue over sex into legal monologue. Chapter 2 will provide an account of the emergence of transgender as an object of scientific study. It will trace contemporary (mis)understandings of transgender bodies to late 19th century sexological discourse. It will also pay particular attention to more contemporary attempts by medical science to lay claim to transgender bodies. In the process the chapter will map the changing nature of scientific knowledge about transgender bodies in order to better understand legal approaches to those bodies. That is to say, the chapter will chart the medical knowledges that inform, or have informed, legal discourse. Subsequent chapters will reveal how law has deployed these medical knowledges in specific legal contexts as well as emphasising the ways in which legal desire differs from, or exceeds, that of medical science. In tracing contemporary understandings of transgender to 19th century sexology the chapter will highlight in particular how at the moment of sexology's entry into discourse transgender and homosexuality were utterly conflated. This conflation has, in different ways, been reproduced by subsequent medical knowledges into the present. In this regard, the chapter will lay a foundation for comprehending the degree of homophobia evident within transgender jurisprudence. Finally, the chapter will detail contemporary counter-discourses of transgender people who have sought to challenge, in a number of respects, medical orthodoxy regarding their bodies.

In Chapter 3 the book will introduce the transgender/law relation through an analysis of (bio)logical approaches to transgender bodies. That is to say, the chapter will consider case law that deploys (bio)logic in constructing sex. While more generally adopted, this judicial practice has been particularly noticeable in the English context. While such approaches have consistently articulated a *sex is determined at birth* narrative whereby sex precedes, and therefore provides an apparent foundation for, gender, the precise configuration of legally relevant factors to be considered at birth will be seen to vary. Moreover, and in a manner that questions legal fidelity to science, we will see that genitalia are privileged over other factors irrespective of the specificity of (bio)logical approach. In laying bare the genitocentrism of law that is masked, at least partially, by the language of (bio)logic the chapter lays a foundation for linking (bio)logical approaches to the reform jurisprudence to be examined in Chapter 4. In addition to highlighting law's selective use of biology the chapter will problematise the wisdom of appealing to (bio)logic as a litigation strategy, given its restriction of legal claims to particular (bio)logical factors and one temporal moment. Further, while (bio)logical approaches to transgender sex claims locate the 'truth' of sex in the past it will become evident that a focus on 'truth' and the past is not confined to biology. That is to say, a concern over transgender 'authenticity' is also apparent. This dimension of the (bio)logical approach, one that will be pursued further in Chapter 5, is highlighted in Chapter 3 through consideration of a number of appeals to the European Court of Human Rights, primarily against the United Kingdom. Moreover, European transgender jurisprudence, while upholding Member State decisions based on the *sex is determined at birth* narrative, has tended to place more emphasis on a State's 'margin of appreciation' than (bio)logical concerns. In this respect, and in view of the increasing vulnerability of the 'margin of appreciation' argument, consideration of the European case law anticipates reform jurisprudence to be considered in Chapter 4.

In Chapter 4 (bio)logical approaches to transgender sex claims, considered in Chapter 3, will be contrasted with reformist approaches. Reform jurisprudence has so far generated two alternative legal tests for determining sex. The first test, which has been privileged, constructs sex as being premised on *psychological and anatomical harmony*. This test has its common law origins in the United States but has been pursued more consistently in Australia and New Zealand. The second test constructs sex as premised on *psychological, social and cultural harmony*. This approach, dispensing with anatomical considerations as it does, has so far received only limited judicial support. Indeed, apart from a few obiter statements, it has been confined so far to Australian and Canadian social security decisions emphatically overturned on appeal.[9] In contrasting these reformist legal constructions of sex to a (bio)logical account the chapter will emphasise continuity over discontinuity. That is to say, it will resist the temptation to characterise reform jurisprudence as unproblematically 'progressive'. Rather, as with (bio)logical approaches, reform jurisprudence will be seen to reproduce the gender order through constructing sex, albeit differently, as gender's 'foundation'. There is no question here of gender floating free from sex within reform jurisprudence. Moreover, similarities across approach become apparent once an insistence on saying 'no' to the sex claims of transgender persons, an insistence that characterises a (bio)logical account, is considered alongside the exclusionary and negative discursive effects produced by reform jurisprudence. Thus we will see, for example, that the construction of the male-to-female transgender body as female within reform jurisprudence is premised on the exclusion of sexed, gendered and sexual difference. That is to say, attention will be drawn to the constitutive outside of the legally recognised subject. With regard to sexed difference the chapter will reveal how the instantiation of a pre/post-operative dyad serves to mirror the genitocentrism evident within legal approaches to sex that resort to (bio)logic. Further, reform jurisprudence will, like (bio)logical approaches, be seen to entail an interrogative mode of regulation whereby transgender 'authenticity,' which law locates in the past, assumes importance. Finally, the interweaving into legal discourse of homophobic, sexist and phallocentric assumptions evident within approaches that deploy (bio)logic will be seen to be replicated within reform jurisprudence.

In Part II, 'Homophobia as Subtext', which comprises Chapters 5 and 6, the book will develop many of the themes articulated in Chapters 3 and 4, but will do so within the specific context of marriage. In particular, this Part, in developing the idea of continuity across approach, will foreground the homophobia of law. While homophobia may itself represent displaced anxiety, a symptom of something else, the book will suggest that it

---

9   *Secretary, Department of Social Security v SRA* (1993) 118 ALR 467; *Canada v Owen* (1993) 110 DLR (4th) 339.

appears to occupy a pivotal place within transgender jurisprudence, akin to a structuring principle. In Chapter 5 it will be argued that at the heart of transgender marriage jurisprudence lies a tension in legal desire. On the one hand, law desires to incorporate transgender people within an existing gender dichotomy so that transgender difference and 'ambiguity' disappear. On the other hand, typically, law proves unable to satiate this desire, even in the context of post-operative transgender people, checked as it is by a contradictory desire to privilege, and preserve a space for, 'natural' heterosexual intercourse. While this tension in legal desire is not confined to marriage, it will become apparent that it becomes particularly acute in the marriage context. Accordingly, it will be argued that legal discourse with regard to the transgender/marriage relation is likely to, and does, magnify the nature, significance and value of legal treatment of the sex claims of transgender persons more generally. That is to say, it is at the site of marriage that the 'truth' of sex in law is, perhaps, most likely to be glimpsed. For it is in relation to marriage that legal understandings of sex, gender and sexuality, which the transgender body would appear to threaten, are most entrenched. The chapter will contend that legal anxiety over the 'naturalness' of heterosexual intercourse is an effect of perceived proximity of transgender to homosexuality. In the marriage context it will become apparent that homophobic anxiety serves typically to set a (bio)logical 'limit' to the effective incorporation ('normalisation') of transgender people within the existing gender order. In this regard, judicial defence of marriage serves, somewhat ironically, to hinder the reformist project of heterosexualising 'ambiguous' bodies.

In Chapter 6 we will consider primarily recent case law that has recognised the sex claims of post-operative transgender persons for marriage purposes, thereby exceeding the 'limit' of marriage. While homophobia does not operate to preclude legal recognition in these decisions it will become apparent how it continues to structure the reform moment. In the first place, a certain ambivalence about the coupling of transgender and heterosexuality will be seen to be evident in the marriage context. Of more significance, perhaps, is the fact that the positioning of post-operative transgender bodies within the sanctity of marriage relies on homophobia as its foundation. That is to say, inclusion of the post-operative body within the realm of marriage proves possible only because of the 'renaturalising' efforts law expends around that body. In particular, this legal work requires that the 'naturalness' of included bodies be mirrored. It is the pre-operative body, a body that law conflates utterly with homosexuality, which is employed to this end. Accordingly, homosexuality is both coded as 'unnatural' and distanced from the institution of marriage. Further, homophobia is evident in another regard. Thus we will see anxiety expressed over the possibility of 'gay' and 'lesbian' transgender people already being located within marriage. In this regard it is clear that transgender marriage jurisprudence seeks to resist homosexuality from both inside and out. In highlighting how the homosexual body serves as a 'limit' to reform, Chapters 5 and 6 emphasise how possibilities for future transgender and gay and lesbian political alliance are constrained by law. In addition to mapping the complex manifestations of homophobia within reform jurisprudence, Chapter 6 will issue a cautionary note lest it be thought that a (bio)logical understanding of sex has been expunged within reform jurisprudence. Thus we will see that, irrespective of legal recognition for marriage purposes, a number of reform decisions to be considered in Chapter 6 simply postpone the question of the 'truth' of sex. In particular, it will be seen to be displaced on to other legal terrain, namely competitive sport, which, much like marriage, functions to 'naturalise' sexed difference (Cole and Birrell, 1990, p 18). Thus, even in the moment of recognising transgender sex claims for the purposes of marriage, law attempts to control and limit the meaning of that recognition. In this regard a view of reform jurisprudence as having transcended the (bio)logic of law may prove somewhat premature.

In Part III, 'Sex: From Designation to Discrimination', comprising Chapters 7–9, the book will consider the transgender/law relation in contexts of discrimination rather than, as in Chapters 3–6, in the context of legal issues requiring a legal determination as to male/female status. In view of the fact that discrimination against transgender people tends to be activated by transgender, not male/female status, it might be thought that inclusion of transgender people within the anti-discrimination law protected category sex would require an interpretation of sex that is unconstrained by binary thinking. In Chapter 7, however, we will see that much of the analysis in preceding chapters, including its homophobic content, is replicated through legal interpretation of the anti-discrimination law protected category sex. That is to say, while the concept of anti-discrimination law sex contains the potential for an expansive interpretation that moves beyond an understanding grounded in the male/female dyad, the courts have, in transgender contexts, limited sex to precisely this understanding, or have positioned transgender in such a way as to reproduce the male/female dyad. In other words, interpretations of sex have, until recently, been confined to either a (bio)logical account, as has been particularly evident regarding interpretation of Title VII of the United States Federal Civil Rights Act 1964, or have endorsed a narrative of *psychological and anatomical harmony*, as has been the case in New York,[10] Canada[11] and before the European Court of Justice.[12] Thus, as in earlier chapters, it would appear that law attempts to regulate transgender bodies through incorporation within the gender order. The limits to this strategy will, as in earlier chapters, be seen to be informed by homophobic anxiety. However, recent reform within United States federal transgender jurisprudence has interpreted prior case law equating sex with gender stereotyping[13] to cover (trans)gender performance.[14] This legal move, while still requiring a comparator and thereby reproducing in some measure sex/gender 'normality', differs from prior transgender jurisprudence in that it backgrounds, if not dispenses with, ontological inquiry. In this regard the development is a significant one opening up possibilities both for greater protection of transgender people against discrimination as well as perhaps encouraging a retreat from identity-based politics in favour of the adoption of shared political strategies with other minority groups. In particular, the shift away from ontology perhaps renders irrelevant, or at least less important, legal constructions of the transgender/homosexual relation.

This legal development also represents a challenge to critical legal thinking as to the relationship between law, rights and subjectivity. That is to say, a view of rights as

---

10 *Richards v United States Tennis Association* 400 NYS 2d 267 (1977); *Maffei v Kolaeton Industry Inc* 626 NYS 2d 391 (1995); *Rentos v Oce-Office Systems* US Dist LEXIS 19060 (1996).

11 *Commission des Droits de la Personne et des Droits de la Jeunesse v Maison des Jeunes* [1998] Quebec Human Rights Tribunal (www2.lexum.canlii.org/qc/cas/ qctdp/1998/1998qctdp236.html).

12 *P v S and Cornwall County Council* [1996] 2 CMLR 247.

13 *Price Waterhouse v Hopkins* 490 US 228 (1989).

14 *Schwenk v Hartford* 204 F 3d 1187 (2000); *Rosa v Park West Bank* 214 F 3d 213 (2000).

dependent on the 'fixed coherent identity' of rights-bearers (Bumiller, 1988; Iyer, 1993, Herman, 1994; Morgan, 1996) is problematised, if not obliterated, by such a development. This theme will be explored in Chapter 8 through an analysis and critique of Australian anti-discrimination law legislative frameworks. In contrast to reform jurisprudence that seeks to accommodate transgender through an expansive interpretation of sex, Australian anti-discrimination laws have introduced transgender either as an independent legal category or as a subcategory within the protected head of sexuality. In considering the entry of transgender into the lexicon of Australian anti-discrimination law, the chapter will first draw attention to the different ways in which law delimits this category. Then, in furtherance of a more nuanced understanding of legal regulation of transgender bodies within anti-discrimination law contexts, the chapter will consider the potential for interplay between the categories of sex, sexuality and transgender. The need to consider how these categories intersect is heightened by the fact that in several Australian jurisdictions individuals discriminated against because they are perceived to be members of a protected category are protected irrespective of whether they are legally considered to be members of that category. Such 'deeming provisions', like the view that Title VII sex means gender, to be considered in Chapter 7, serve to uncouple legal regulation from ontological considerations, thereby opening up spaces for the disruption of legal categories. That is to say, in a number of Australian jurisdictions (trans)gender performance and discriminating gaze serve to trump more recognisable forms of regulation premised on interrogative and genitocentric preoccupations. Such developments might be viewed as inciting the practice of '(tres)passing' as a member of the 'opposite' sex thereby reproducing the gender order through rendering transgender invisible. In this sense, the reproduction of gender becomes uncoupled from sex as foundation. However, it may be that the homophobia of law provides a 'limit' to legal strategies of regulation around appearance, as it has in relation to the re-sexing of bodies to be considered in Chapters 3–6. Thus, and in a way that suggests legal anxiety over proximity to the homosexual body, we will see that in some Australian jurisdictions incitement to '(tres)pass' as a member of the 'opposite' sex refuses to traverse the pre/post-operative divide.

In Chapter 9 the theme of homophobia will be pursued in the context of recent West Australian legislation, the Gender Reassignment Act 2000, and surrounding parliamentary debates. In drawing attention to this theme and to the interrelationship between transgender and homosexuality in law, the chapter builds on earlier chapters. Moreover, it situates transgender/homosexual relations and their '(un)intelligibility' within a specific political context and draws attention to the potential dangers of a legislative approach to transgender rights claims. The selection of West Australian legislation is informed by the fact that transgender and gay and lesbian law reform coincide in time. Thus we shall see that the passage of the legislation, and the pre/post-operative distinction which serves as its trigger, were mediated by another Bill introduced at the same time, namely the Acts Amendment (Sexuality Discrimination) Bill, and its pre-history. In other words, West Australian anxiety over the possibility of gay and lesbian law reform serves to bring to the fore a pre-existing cultural conflation. As will become apparent, passage of the Gender Reassignment Act proved possible only through constituting post-operative transgender persons in opposition to homosexuality. This is particularly observable in the West Australian parliamentary debates that approach the subject-matter through a series of interrelated dyads: pre-operative/post-operative, act/identity, deserving/undeserving, visibility/invisibility, sexual/non-sexual. In highlighting how the homosexual body serves as a 'limit' to reform, the chapter re-emphasises how possibilities for future transgender and gay and lesbian political alliance are constrained by law.

Finally, the concluding chapter will bring the chapters and their subject-matters together and will offer some directions for the future in terms of any engagement with law. In particular, the chapter will highlight the theme of resistance and the possibilities for disruption of heterosexual hegemony that lie within the proliferating cracks of transgender jurisprudence.

PART I

APPROACHING TRANSGENDER BODIES

CHAPTER 2

SCIENTIA (TRANS)SEXUALIS

> Through sexual inversion sexologists sought to describe not homosexuality but a broad transgendered condition of which same-sex desire was but one symptom ... as a consequence there is substantive gendered material in inversion that exceeds homosexual identity (Prosser, 1998, p 138).

This chapter aims to provide an account of the emergence of transgender as an object of scientific study. In the process it will map the changing nature of scientific knowledge about transgender people as a prelude to understanding legal approaches to their legal claims. The chapter will trace contemporary medico-legal and wider cultural understandings of transgender people to sexological discourses of the late 19th century. This is not to suggest that transgender, as a phenomenon, did not exist prior to sexology. On the contrary, there is ample evidence for the claim that identifications, practices and desires, which we might today call transgendered, have existed transhistorically (see, for example, Green, 1969a; Karlen, 1971; Green, 1974; Warnes and Hill, 1974; Bullough, 1975, 1976; Boswell, 1980; Steiner, 1981; Feinberg, 1996; Devor, 1997, Chapter 1). Rather, the contention here is that discourses generated by sexual science have, in large measure, created the terms for comprehending (trans)sexual desire and (trans)gender identification in the legal present. That is to say, judicial reasoning, as well as contemporary law reform arguments, around transgender bodies operate within a frame established by the imprint of sexual science.

The various 19th century ideas expounded about sexuality and gender, and which inform our understandings of transgender, were not novel ones. Rather, those ideas came to enjoy greater credibility once inflected through the prism of sexual science. Moreover, the significance of these ideas was heightened in the 19th century as concerns over health, prostitution and the growing visibility of same-sex subcultures in European cities began to take hold (Weeks, 1985, p 73, 1991, Chapter 3). While sexological research would trigger a discursive explosion, an ever-burgeoning taxonomy of 'deviant' sexual desires and practices, it was the study of same (bio)logical sex desiring subjects, and their characterisation as inverts, that marked sexology's entry into discourse. This trope of inversion, premised on disembodiment as it is, illustrates how the mapping of transgender bodies was at the heart of sexological discourse from the beginning (Prosser, 1998, p 138). That is to say, transgender operated as the structuring principle for comprehending same (bio)logical sex sexual desires. Through this figure of the invert, what would later come to be understood as homosexuality and transgender came to be inextricably linked in medical, legal and cultural terms.

Of course, in conflating axes of gender and sexuality sexologists were, no doubt, informed by existing cultural assumptions as to, and misreadings of, cross-dressing practices of same-sex desiring persons, such as those occurring in the Molly Houses of 18th century London (Bloch, 1965; Trumbach, 1977, 1987; Bray, 1982; Davenport-Hines, 1990). Indeed, over the preceding centuries cross-dressing had changed in character in the popular imaginary. From being perceived as disguise or masquerade and as associated with the theatre, albeit with occasional overtones of sodomy, it had come to be seen as the signifier of a form of sodomite (Trumbach, 1977).

From the outset sexological research was marked by a tension between sexual libertarianism and excessive social classification and control (Weeks, 1985, Chapter 4). Accordingly, consideration of debates which animated sexual science from the late 19th century onwards offers to inform reformist strategies in the legal present. Thus we shall see that aetiological explanations of inversion involved appeals to biology, ones premised on natural theory as well as pathology, and to inheritance as well as to congenital factors and degeneracy. As for diagnosis, somatic accounts, whereby inversion was to be read off the body, vied with psychological accounts whereby the subject was required to speak, to announce itself. Later, with the advent of psychoanalysis and prior to the development of endocrinology and sex reassignment surgical techniques, there was a dramatic devaluation of (bio)logical explanations as well as transgender narratives. Crucially, the ideas at the heart of these sexological debates would recur over time, and into the medico-legal present, both as strategies of regulation and liberation.

2.1 THE BIRTH OF THE INVERT

Prior to the mid-19th century, the idea of sexually deviant action as explicable in terms of identity had yet to fully materialise. Up to that time, the notion of volitional action continued to structure understandings of sexual transgression within discourses of forensic medicine.[1] In 1849 a French physician, Claude Francois Michea, hypothesised that feminine habits and preferences of same-sex desiring subjects were rooted in biology (Greenberg, 1988, p 406). In this regard, his work represents an attempt to revive the notion that 'Greek love' was an instinctive passion with a somatic basis (Plato, 1951). Michea was the first to develop fully the theory that sexual desire between men was an inborn phenomenon, thereby 'providing an identity and physiologically explain[ing] the effeminacy' of these males (Hekma, 1996, p 216). From the mid-19th century the medical literature on what would later come to be termed 'homosexuality' began to proliferate with many authors supporting Michea's (bio)logical theory. In the 1850s Johann Ludwig Casper, a German medico-legal expert, renewed discussion about the 'hermaphrodisy' of the pederast's mind which he believed could explain a minority of same-sex behaviour (1852). Hekma has claimed that the writings of Casper 'marked the beginnings of forensic psychiatry' as distinct from forensic medicine (1996, p 217). The work of Michea and Casper is significant for the study of transgender because, in moving from the 'pleasures of the flesh' (Foucault, 1981, p 108) to the mysteries of the mind, it involved, and encouraged, paying greater attention to the effeminacy of some same-sex practitioners.

---

1   However, it should be noted that in an 1824 report on the state of French prisons the physician, Louis-Rene Villerme, distinguished between inmate 'pederasts' who assumed the 'male' role, whom he described as 'circumstantial', and those who adopted the role of their 'female' partners (*gironds* or *petits jesus*) whose involvement he considered to be instinctive or preferential (Greenberg, 1988, p 404). While Villerme's report may indicate some support for the view that same-sex desires/practices were hereditary, it does not appear to have had any real impact upon thinking about aetiology. Interestingly, Villerme's essentialisation of gender, rather than sexual, transgression would later be reversed by Richard von Krafft-Ebing (1965).

This focus on effeminacy was taken up in the work of the German sexual liberationist and lawyer, Karl Heinrich Ulrichs in the 1860s and 1870s. Drawing on Plato's *Symposium*, Ulrichs postulated his theory of 'Uranian' love (1994). He sought to vindicate love between men 'by insisting on the congenital, as distinct from the hereditary, nature of the Urning's desires' (Bristow, 1997, p 21). Moreover, he claimed to have identified, within the parameters of normal sexual variation, the existence of 'a class of born Urnings, a class of individuals who are born with the sexual drive of women and who have male bodies' (Ulrichs, 1994, p 36). For Ulrichs, the Urning was 'not a man, but rather a kind of feminine being when it concerns not only his entire organism, but also his sexual feelings of love, his entire natural temperament, and his talents' (1994, p 36). Indeed, he described his own male inversion as an authentic womanly identification concealed by a male body: '... [h]ave I a masculine beard and manly limbs and body;/Yes, confined by these: but I am and remain a woman' (1898, cited in Kennedy, 1988, p 56).

This articulation of inversion, centred on disembodiment as it is, anticipates and gives life to transgender narratives that would later receive medical sanction in the mid-20th century. Jay Prosser has noted that Ulrichs' description of inversion effectively commenced 'the mapping of transgender as an identity in the West' (1998, p 143). In opposition to Foucault's view that inversion marked homosexuality's origins as 'a species' (1981, p 43), a view well rehearsed in much gay and lesbian historiography (see, for example, Katz, 1976; Williams, 1986; Wheelright, 1989; Califia, 1997, Chapter 4), it seems more convincing, as Prosser contends, that 'sexologists sought to describe not homosexuality but a broad transgender condition of which same-sex desire was but one symptom, and not vice versa' (1998, p 138). Sexual inversion, as Chauncey has pointed out, 'did not denote the same conceptual phenomenon as homosexuality' but rather 'referred to a broad range of deviant gender behavior, of which [same (bio)logical sex] desire was only a logical but indistinct aspect' (1982–83, p 116).

Ulrichs defended his theory by asserting that Uranism had a similar origin to hermaphrodisy of the body, which other researchers had claimed originated in the first three months of pregnancy (Hekma, 1996, p 220). The soul rather than the body became hermaphroditic in the case of the Uranian fetus. The first important case study following Ulrichs' work was an article published in 1869 about 'kontrare Sexualempfindung' by Carl Westphal (1869), the physician often given credit for placing the study of stigmatised sexual behaviour on a 'scientific' basis (Bullough and Bullough, 1993, p 203). The literal translation of the article's title is 'contrary sexual feeling' but it was more often interpreted as 'sexual inversion' (Hekma, 1996, p 224).

The article describes the cases of two persons who cross-dressed. The first, a young woman, experienced pleasure in dressing like a boy and playing boy's games from early childhood. She was sexually attracted only to women. The second case involved a man who desired to dress and live as a woman on a permanent basis. His sexual orientation is unclear from Westphal's study (Bullough and Bullough, 1993, p 203). In each of these cases Westphal diagnosed 'contrary sexual feeling'. In other words, the lexicon of contrary sexual feeling or sexual inversion served, as in Ulrichs' work, to capture not homosexuality, but the phenomenon of transgenderism. Indeed, many of the fullest autobiographical accounts of inversion within sexology prove, when considered from the present, to be the most transgendered (Prosser, 1998, p 144).

The study by Westphal is particularly significant because it inaugurates the pathologising of bodies ascribed inverted status. While Ulrichs had sought to explain Uranism in terms of normal sexual variation, Westphal insisted that his case studies revealed either a neuropathic or psychopathic condition (Hekma, 1996, p 224). While somatic and (bio)logical understandings of inversion would persist throughout the remainder of the late 19th century, Ulrichs' natural theory of Uranian desire would be challenged increasingly by scientific endeavours that sought to recouple sexual transgression with disease.[2] In this regard, the appeal to biology as a law reform strategy proved from its inception to be both unpredictable and dangerous for intended beneficiaries. While Ulrichs' formula of a 'female soul in a male body' continued to be cited by numerous authors, his natural theory succumbed increasingly to a rivalry between neuropathology and psychopathology as causal explanations for 'sexual' inversion (Hekma, 1996, p 224).

In this climate of pathologising desire, Richard von Krafft-Ebing (1877) considered all published cases and claimed that 'sexual inversion was both a neuropathic and psychopathic condition, hereditary and coexistent with other insanities' (Hekma, 1996, p 225). The Darwinian-influenced suggestion that inversion was explicable in hereditary terms was quite contrary to Ulrichs' congenital explanation and damaging in terms of prospects for social and legal change. Moreover, Krafft-Ebing mixed hereditary explanations with ones based in degeneracy theory. Drawing on the work of Morel (1857, 1860) he argued that pathologies brought about by poverty, alcohol and poor diet could be transmitted genetically to offspring resulting in progressive degeneracy (Greenberg, 1988, p 414). In response to the argument that parents of homosexuals are rarely homosexual, and never exclusively so, Krafft-Ebing contended:

> In almost all cases where an examination of the physical and mental peculiarities of the ancestors and blood relations has been possible, neuroses, psychoses, degenerative signs, etc, have been found in the families (1965, pp 223–24, quoted by Greenberg, 1988, p 414).

His argument, like many of his contemporaries (see, for example, Charcot and Magnan, 1882; Tarnowsky, 1886; Moreau, 1887; Moll, 1891; Fere, 1899; Forel, 1905), was that it was degeneracy that was inherited and homosexuality was but one manifestation of degeneracy. However, while the pathologising trajectory of Krafft-Ebing's work differs from the law reform motivated identity-based contentions of Ulrichs, his writings and case studies, like those of Ulrichs, served to foreground transgender. Thus, in listing the 'remarkable features' of sexual inversion, Krafft-Ebing ranked attraction to the same sex as only the sixth item of indication (1877, pp 307–08). In other words, in Krafft-Ebing's early work same-sex sexual preference was only an aspect of a more generalisable transgender phenomenon.

That Krafft-Ebing, like Westphal, was describing transgender, and not homosexuality, is particularly apparent from many of his case studies, referred to in his major tome, *Psychopathia Sexualis* (1965), 'probably the most widely read and influential medical work on sex prior to the Kinsey reports' (Bullough and Bullough, 1993, p 204). For example,

---

2   The coupling of sexual transgression of dominant moral codes and dis-ease has a long history (see Dollimore, 1999).

case 129 offers an account of a Hungarian male who felt as though s/he had already undergone a sex change. As the patient put it:

> I feel like a woman in a man's form; and even though I am often sensible of the man's form, yet it is always in a feminine sense. Thus for example, I feel the penis as clitoris; the urethra as urethra and vaginal orifice, which always feels a little wet, even when it is actually dry; the scrotum as *labia majora*; in short I always feel the vulva (Krafft-Ebing, 1965, p 207).

Significantly, there is nothing homosexual about sexual practice in this case of inversion. Rather, heterosexual practice is structured through an embodied transgender identification. During coitus with his/her female partner 's/he inverts genital morphologies, imagining him/herself to have a vagina penetrated by the penis of the (other) woman' (Prosser, 1998, p 145).

In another case, that of Count Sandor V (Countess Sarolta V) (case 166), Krafft-Ebing details the narrative of a female invert who lived as a man, married twice, had several female lovers and visited brothels. Yet, Sandor refused mutual sexual relations as well as mutual or solitary masturbation. Like menstruation, which s/he found to be 'a thing repugnant to ... masculine consciousness and feeling' (1965, p 289), Sandor considered the sexual use of her genitals to be 'disgusting' and 'not conducive to manliness' (Krafft-Ebing, 1965, p 289). This case is significant, not only for rendering visible transgender identification, but because of its promulgation of the notion of a refusal of sex through sexuality (Prosser, 1998, pp 146–47). This idea, one which Pauly has suggested separates transgender from homosexuality (1969, p 83), would emerge later to problematise identity claims made within the arenas of medicine and law. The foregrounding of transgender is also apparent in the writings of Havelock Ellis. In his book, *Sexual Inversion*, published in 1897, Ellis details the case of D (History 39) a female invert:

> Ever since I can remember anything at all, I could never think of myself as a girl ... When I was 5 or 6 years old I began to say to myself that whatever anyone said, if I was not a boy at any rate I was not a girl. This has been my unchanged conviction all through my life. When I was little, nothing ever made me doubt it, in spite of external appearance. I regarded the conformation of my body as a mysterious accident (1936a, p 235, quoted by Prosser, 1998, pp 147–48).

Despite their differences Ulrichs, Westphal, Krafft-Ebing, Ellis and other sexologists of the late 19th century relied on autobiographical narratives in producing their diagnoses of inversion (Prosser, 1998, p 152). That is to say, they allowed subjects to speak for themselves and that speech profoundly influenced sexological discourse. This willingness to take personal narratives literally was, as we shall see, something that distinguished these sexologists from the psychoanalysts who would later gain ascendancy over the field.

However, while sexologists listened to their subjects they also sought to read inversion off bodies, influenced as they were, in different ways, by causal explanations rooted in biology. Thus Ulrichs himself, while articulating the idea of a 'female soul in a male body', had brought into question the 'maleness' of that body. After listing what he considered to be nine specifically 'male' features: '... male organs, lack of breasts, Adam's apple, male body and voice, beard, manly habitus, male inclinations and sexual love drive ('geschlechtliche Liebestrieb') for women,' (Hekma, 1996, p 219) Ulrichs contended that some, and perhaps most, of these traits were absent in the Uranian (1899, p 59). A focus on cross-sexed characteristics as inversion's somatic markers was pursued by

Krafft-Ebing, who emphasised the 'deep voice, manly gait [and] small mammae' of a female invert (1894, p 410), and by Havelock Ellis, for whom symptoms of inversion in the case of the female invert ranged from 'slight' hirsutism of the body and face, to more 'genuine approximations to the masculine type' in which 'the muscles tend to be everywhere firm, with a comparative absence of soft connective tissue', to genitalia which are 'more or less undeveloped' (1936a, p 255). The focus on specific physical manifestations of inversion is again apparent in the work of Iwan Bloch. In speaking of male inversion Bloch stated:

> Still more importantly for the determination of a feminine habitus are direct physical characteristics. Among these there must be mentioned a considerable deposit of fat, by which the resemblance to the feminine type is produced, the contours of the body being more rounded than in the case of the normal male. In correspondence with this the muscular system is less powerfully developed than it is in heterosexual men, the skin is delicate and soft, and the complexion is much clearer than is usual in men (1908, pp 498–99).

2.2 DISSECTING INVERSION

While gender inversion was central to most theories articulated in the wake of Ulrichs' Uranian, it became necessary to acknowledge, as Ulrichs himself had,[3] that the figure of the gender invert failed to exhaust the phenomenon of same-sex desire and practice.[4] The attempt to subdivide and reclassify same-sex desires and practices led over time to the foregrounding of sexuality and to the use of the term 'homosexual', a term first coined by Karl Kertbeny (1869), in preference to inversion. In *Psychopathia Sexualis*, Krafft-Ebing subdivided same-sex desires and practices into eight pathological types of what he described in that book as homosexuality. Of these types he distinguished between four types of congenital or inborn homosexuality: *psychical hermaphroditism; homosexual/Urning; effemination; androgyny,* and four types of learned or acquired homosexuality: *simple reversal of sexual feeling; eviration and defemination; stage of transition to change of sex delusion; delusion of sex change* (Krafft-Ebing, 1965, pp 186–291). Hekma has argued that 'the learned-behavior types were strongly coloured by effeminacy, but the four innate types were not' (1996, p 226). However, a close reading of Krafft-Ebing's commentary and the case studies he cites to illustrate each type suggests that effeminacy straddles the inborn/acquired distinction in more complex fashion. Nevertheless, effeminacy does receive more emphasis as a characteristic of acquired homosexuality. More particularly, for present purposes, two of the four acquired types of homosexuality deal with what later will come to be described as 'transsexualism' (*stage of transition to change of sex delusion/delusion of sex change*) (Krafft-Ebing, 1965, pp 200–21).

---

3   Thus Ulrichs' analysis was not confined to effeminate same-sex desiring men ('*weiblings*'). He also included 'mannlings' (virile same-sex desiring men) and 'intermediaries' within his complex typology (1994, p 314).

4   Indeed, there existed opposition to the idea of the invert or 'third sex' among many same-sex desiring/practising men. In particular, considerable hostility was generated in response to the coupling of homosexuality with effeminacy. In contrast to Ulrichs' 'Uranian', proponents of the 'movement for masculine culture' in Germany, eg, sought to emphasise a virile homosexuality of (bio)logical origin (see Friedlander, 1904).

This subdivision of what Krafft-Ebing describes as homosexuality is significant in two respects. First, it had the effect of separating out, in some measure, (trans)gender from (homo)sexuality, something that would be pursued further in the work of Havelock Ellis and Magnus Hirschfeld, but which would later be reconflated with the rise of psychoanalysis. Secondly, in broad terms, Krafft-Ebing's reclassification positioned gender 'anomalies' on the acquired side, and sexual 'anomalies' on the inborn side, of the split. The effect of this was to uncouple inversion (and therefore transgender) from a (bio)logical account while portraying homosexuality, now to be understood primarily through sexual desire and practice, as grounded in biology. While psychoanalysis would later detach homosexuality from biology, Krafft-Ebing's classification anticipated Freud through foregrounding object choice in the analysis of sexual deviation.

The separation of (trans)gender from (homo)sexuality was taken up in the work of Ellis and Hirschfeld, who sought to rescue the invert from the acquired side of Krafft-Ebing's dyad and to resist psychoanalytic attempts to reduce (trans)gender to (homo)sexuality. Drawing on the earlier work of Ulrichs, Hirschfeld, in his major work, *The Transvestites: An Investigation of the Erotic Desire to Cross Dress*, suggested a theory of 'intermediaries' (1910, pp 215–36) whereby he sought to capture the complexity of gender and sexual roles and identities and to distinguish the practice of cross-dressing from homosexuality. While Hirschfeld classified transvestites as heterosexual, bisexual, homosexual, narcisstic and asexual, he concluded from his studies that most cross-dressers were heterosexual:

> How in fact are we to understand this peculiar urge to cross dress? ... Is it perhaps only a matter of a form of homosexuality? ... However, more accurate testing revealed that this was not the case because the main marker of homosexuality ... is the sex drive towards persons of the same sex. We saw in most of our cases there was not a trace of it ... To be sure some of them had homosexual episodes, which is not unusual for heterosexuals, but they were so transient and superficial that truly inborn homosexuality – and only congenital homosexuality can be true – is not a question here (1910, pp 147–48, quoted by Bullough and Bullough, 1993, p 208).

While this passage is problematic in terms of its characterisation and circumscription of homosexuality it is clear that Hirschfeld resists the slide, which was becoming increasingly apparent, from inversion to homosexuality. Moreover, Hirschfeld's study revealed that subjects typically started cross-dressing early in life (1910, p 125). This temporal aspect served to challenge a view of male effeminacy as acquired rather than inborn. Moreover, as we will see, early onset of (trans)gender identity would emerge later, in the mid-20th century, as a key trope within medical (mis)understandings of transgender 'authenticity' upon which law would draw. Further, despite coupling cross-dressing practices with erotic desire in the subtitle to his major work, Hirschfeld's data emphasised gender role over clothing in the cross-dressing experience (Bullough and Bullough, 1993, p 212). Ellis agreed with this finding, and in order to communicate it introduced the term *sexo-aesthetic inversion* in preference to the term 'transvestite' (1913). However, because the term 'inversion' had come increasingly to signify homosexuality Ellis later coined the term *Eonism* to describe a gender role-based phenomenon in which cross-dressing and erotic pleasure were incidental and inessential (1936b).[5] This

---

5   The term 'Eonism' was coined after the the 18th century French nobleman, Chevalier d'Eon (contd)

uncoupling of gender role from erotic pleasure would later acquire significance in the context of medical 'diagnosis' of transsexuality, access to sex reassignment surgery and, therefore, legal recognition.

2.3 ERASING THE INVERT

While Ellis and Hirschfeld sought to carve out a discursive space, separate from that of homosexuality, for pronounced cases of cross-dressing they ultimately failed to provide a lexicon for the desire to transform sex. Indeed, Ellis carefully divided Eonists (primarily heterosexual cross-dressers) from those whose desires were more transformative in nature and whom today we might describe as transgender. He located the latter group under the head of 'sexual inversion' (Chauncey, 1982–83, p 122; Prosser, 1998, p 151), thereby (re)conflating transgender with homosexuality. In any event, the ideas that Hirschfeld and Ellis sought to develop, and which were routed in the work of Ulrichs, had increasingly come under challenge since the turn of the 20th century.

After that period the medical hegemony of congenital theories of inversion, to which both Hirschfeld and Ellis subscribed, began to decline. The challenge to congenital theories was led most forcibly by Freud, who reintroduced and privileged an acquired theory of homosexuality, a term which, after 1900, would replace increasingly the language of inversion (Chauncey, 1982–83, p 124). While Krafft-Ebing's subdivision of 'homosexuality' into inborn and acquired types foreshadowed Freud's differentiation between sexual aim and sexual object in his *Three Essays on Sexuality* (1905), for Freud, and more especially those who followed Freud, biology was to be increasingly marginalised in aetiological accounts of homosexuality.[6] Moreover, Freud's distinction between sexual aim and object and his foregrounding of the latter in the classification of sexuality was a pivotal moment in the history of transgender, and one that would lead to a hiatus in its telling. It amounted to what Prosser has described as 'a massive discursive loss' (1998, p 151).

For Freud, 'sexual aim' referred to mode of sexual behaviour, orifice preference and/or active/passive roles, while 'sexual object' referred to the target of sexual desire (1962, pp 1–2). In the late 19th century, active/passive *aim*, to use Freud's term, was considered at least as important as sexual object choice in the social classification of sexuality (Chauncey, 1982–83, p 123). From the beginning of the 20th century, however, a focus on sexual object was to channel, in the main, subsequent inquiry. The emergence, and later the dominance, of the psychoanalytical model led to the erasure of transgender. The gradual replacement of sexological research with psychoanalytic 'therapy' forestalled further illumination of transgender. This was due largely to the fact that psychoanalysts stopped listening to their transgender patients. In short, Freud rescripted gender identities into 'phantasmatic and transitory sexual identifications, moments on route to

---

5   (contd) (see Cox, 1966; Nixon, 1965). In a sense, the choice of the Chevalier is perhaps unfortunate in that, in addition to cross-dressing, his fame extended to spying in England and Russia (Califia, 1997, p 11), thereby perhaps consolidating a view of gender-crossings as fraud, masquerade and a threat to the social body.

6   Freud himself never abandoned the possibility that homosexuality was at least partially explained by constitutional (bio)logical factors (see Lewes, 1995, p 17).

the development of sexual identities' (Prosser, 1998, p 150). Within the psychoanalytic perspective, sexual inversion is scripted as myth, 'sexology's false construction of homosexuality' (Prosser, 1998, p 150).

For Freud, transgender narratives cannot be taken literally. They are to be decoded by the analyst who must interpret their meaning. In this respect, the movement from sexology to psychoanalysis entails an important shift in power relations as between speaking subject and expert, one that constrains the ability of the former to participate in the generation of 'truth'. Thus, in his most overtly transgender case, that of *Schreber*, Freud interprets a clear narrative premised on imagined sex change as a case of repressed homosexuality (1964b). Similarly, another early psychoanalyst, Karl Abraham, scripted as homosexual a man who desired to be a woman and in his daydreams imagined himself so transformed (1910).

Later the coding of transgender as homosexual would be influenced by Freud's writings on fetishism, which other psychoanalysts, such as Stekel (1922) and Gutheil (1922), applied to practices of cross-dressing (Bullough and Bullough, 1993, p 214). This led to a view of cross-dressing as a flight from homosexuality caused by some childhood event that created castration anxiety. While Gutheil distinguished between (genuine) fetishism and transvestism (1922), the linkage of cross-dressing to castration anxiety served to consolidate further a view of cross-dressing as (homo)sexual in nature. Accordingly, the (trans)gender dimension of the phenomenon receded further from view. Moreover, as Bullough and Bullough have noted, Gutheil criticised Hirschfeld 'for overlooking the importance of latent homosexuality as an important causal factor in transvestism' (1993, p 215). He claimed to have identified homosexual tendencies in most of Hirschfeld's case studies, and explained his [Hirschfeld's] failure to do so as an inability to use deep psychoanalytical techniques, itself an effect of his over-reliance on constitutional factors (1922, pp 312–13).

Indeed, Gutheil and other analysts saw homosexuality everywhere. It was apparent in dreams, in admissions and in denials. As for 'so-called heterosexual transvestites', they had 'only masked their homosexuality' (pp 312–13). Thus, over time, cross-dressing behaviour came to be conflated more and more with homosexuality. Moreover, the notion of castration anxiety as an explanation for cross-dressing served to eroticise the practice. This view of cross-dressing as erotic practice would, as already mentioned, later resurface as an obstacle to transgender persons seeking sex reassignment surgery and making claims in law. The psychoanalytic view of cross-dressing as inextricably tied to homosexuality would retain hegemony through to the 1950s and persist into the 1970s and beyond (see, for example, Randall, 1959; Socarides, 1969, 1970; Ostrow, 1974; Meyer, 1974, 1982). Indeed, in the late 1960s Meerloo popularised Freud's reading of *Schreber* as delusional and homosexual (1967). However, from the 1950s a degree of medical disillusionment with psychotherapy coincided with advances in endocrinology and sex reassignment surgical techniques. In that context, the language of transsexualism emerged to describe a desire for sex transformation as something distinct from, though not necessarily unrelated to, transvestism. The disembodied narrative of the invert, so evident in the sexological writings of the late 19th century, was about to be recuperated.

2.4 RECUPERATING TRANSGENDER NARRATIVES

From the 1950s onwards it became increasingly apparent that cross-gender behaviour, for some individuals, included a desire to change sex. This (re)discovery and the appearance of a new diagnostic category, *transsexual* (Cauldwell, 1949), to capture this desire was not the result of a theoretical breakthrough. Rather, it represented a response to the development of surgical treatments for the extreme form of 'transvestism', as the phenomenon of transsexualism had previously been described.[7] While Cauldwell opposed surgery for transsexuals, and viewed transsexuals as 'products, largely of unfavourable childhood environment' (1949, p 280) his definition of *psychopathia transexualis*, as an independent sexological category, was an important moment in transgender history. In particular, he contended that while '[many] individuals have an irresistible desire to have their sex changed surgically' such persons were 'not necessarily homosexual' (1949, p 274).

While the psychoanalytic conflation of transgender and homosexuality would persist well into the 1970s, and in some quarters beyond, physicians examining the desire for sex reassignment surgery from the 1950s onward would distinguish, increasingly, transsexuality from transvestism and homosexuality. However, as we shall see, this recuperation of the transgender narrative of inversion unfolded in complex and often competing taxonomies within which these three categories became reconflated, and in ways which would have significance for later engagements with law. The medical history of transgender from the 1950s on might be described as a series of attempts to legitimise sex reassignment surgery, and the doctors who practised it, in the face of considerable medical opposition (Benjamin, 1966; Green, 1969b),[8] including the charge of 'palliative collusion with symptomology' (Meyer, 1982, p 401).

While Cauldwell is usually given the credit for introducing the term' transsexual',[9] it was an endocrinologist, Doctor Harry Benjamin (the so-called 'father' of transsexualism) (King, 1993, p 46), more than any other, who pioneered the case for sex reassignment surgery. Benjamin had been using the term 'transsexualism' from the early 1950s, though it would not be until the end of that decade that the term would be distinguished from transvestism in the wider medical literature (King, 1993, 44). In explaining the term, he distinguished heterosexual transvestites from transsexuals. For Benjamin, transvestites

---

7   While it was not until 1952 that sex reassignment surgery came to world attention through the case of Christine Jorgensen (Meyerowitz, 1998, pp 171–75; see, also, Jorgensen, 1968), and not until the 1960s that it was publicly practiced in the United States, surgical attempts to re-sex bodies can be traced to the late 19th and early 20th centuries (Bullough and Bullough, 1993, p 255; Meyerowitz, 1998, p 161).

8   In his book, *The Transsexual Phenomenon* (1966), Benjamin speaks of the condemnation that sex reassignment surgeons provoked within the wider medical community. Indeed, at one point in his career he was threatened with revocation of his medical licence when one of his patients, while in the process of transitioning, was convicted for 'female impersonation' (p 67). In Green's study, published in 1969, four-fifths of his approximately 400 clinician respondents indicated that they would refuse a request for sex reassignment surgery, even if the patient was judged non-psychotic by a psychiatrist, had undergone two years of psychotherapy, had convinced the treating psychiatrist that surgery was indicated and would probably commit suicide if the request for surgery was denied (1969b, p 241). While the stigma associated with working with transgender people has lessened within medicine it should not be thought that it has disappeared (King, 1993, p 79).

9   In fact, Magnus Hirschfeld had described one of his patients as a 'psychic transsexual' in 1910 (Bullough and Bullough, 1993, p 257).

were primarily heterosexual men who could appease feelings of gender role disharmony by cross-dressing, from which they usually derived erotic pleasure. In Benjamin's view these men led reasonably normal lives and had no need to resort to psychiatrists. He did, however, view psychiatry and endocrine therapy as appropriate for more emotionally disturbed transvestites. The transsexual, on the other hand, wanted to be a woman in every sense (Benjamin, 1966, pp 18–19). While Benjamin's understanding of transsexuality is, in some respects, more fluid than some later conceptualisations, it is important to recognise how his initial framing of the phenomenon helped establish an orthodoxy that continues to support and undermine claims of transgender people within medicine and law. First, Benjamin refused to define as a 'true transsexual' a person who wished to retain their male genitals (p 54), and the early focus was almost entirely on the male-to-female subject. The neglect of female-to-male transsexualism is, perhaps, to be explained by 'puritanical beliefs regarding female sexuality' which had 'a pervasive influence on clinical practice', as Lothstein has suggested (1983, p 7). For Benjamin, the desire to have the penis removed emerges as a key diagnostic criterion:

> For them [transsexuals], their sex organs, the primary (testes) as well as the secondary (penis and others) are disgusting deformities that must be changed by the surgeon's knife (1966, pp 13–14).

The emphasis on hatred of one's genitals as a key diagnostic criterion for transsexuality, and as a precondition of sex reassignment surgery, had legitimising effects. First, it brought the practice of orchidectomy (castration) and/or penectomy (removal of the penis) into greater proximity to the medical edict 'first do no harm' through emphasising the absence of penile pleasure. The view that (male-to-female) transsexual women do not enjoy erections or penile stimulation was supported by Money and Primrose, who contended that 'none of their patients expressed any regret at the functional loss of his penis in erection and ejaculation through hormone treatment' (1969, p 122). Moreover, it would seem that this view of (male-to-female) transsexual women as unconcerned with sexual pleasure has influenced research into transsexual aetiology. Thus it has been argued that temporal lobe abnormalities cause hyposexuality (low sex drive) and that 'lack of normal genital sexual arousal and orgasm may provide the substrate for abnormal sexual tendencies' such as transsexualism (Blumer, 1969, p 281). However, the finding (autobiographical account) of hyposexuality in transsexuals may be an effect of patient conformation to a set of gendered and sexual assumptions associated with a particular medical model which views genital pleasure as anathema to transsexual 'truth'.[10] Secondly, the screening out of sexual pleasure served, as Califia has noted, to sanitise transsexuality, to 'raise [transsexuals] above the rest of sex deviates' (1997, p 58). Another key aspect of Benjamin's characterisation of transsexuality relates to the sexual trajectory of the transsexual journey. That is to say, sexual desire for a male post-surgically and the absence of sexual desire for a female pre-surgically were, in the case of the (male-to-female) transsexual woman, scripted as essential (Benjamin, 1966, p 126). Indeed, it was an 'unambiguous' heterosexual past that led Benjamin to refuse to authorise surgery for Renee Richards (Prosser, 1998, p 108), a transgender figure we shall encounter in Chapter 4. The emphasis on desire for surgical intervention and the heterosexualisation of

---

10 Some researchers have argued that low sex drive is associated with the administration of oestrogen rather than the transsexual syndrome itself (Terzian, 1958).

the transsexual phenomenon has, as we shall see throughout this book, served to render inauthentic the legal claims of transgender persons whose autobiographies fail to follow these particular narrative lines.

The attempt to legitimise sex reassignment procedures also led, in ways which parallel 19th century sexological understandings of sexual inversion, to increased emphasis being placed on aetiological factors located in biology. Influenced, as he was, by Hirschfeld and Eugen Steinach's work with animal hormones (1940), and utterly opposed to the psychiatric view that transsexuality was a mental disorder caused by childhood trauma that could be cured by psychoanalysis, Benjamin contended that transsexuality was explicable in terms of an as yet unknown 'constitutional factor' (1966, p 9). He later speculated about pre-natal exposure to hormones (Bullough and Bullough, 1993, p 257). This view echoed the work of Ellis in that it was prompted by the fact that of his first 91 patients, 28 had exhibited hypogonadism (small genitals) even though he could detect no current hormonal abnormalities (1964).

While no consensus regarding transsexual aetiology has emerged in the medical literature to date, a plethora of (bio)logical explanations have been, and continue to be, presented. Thus transsexualism has been framed as a cerebral (and particularly temporal lobe) pathology, a cytogenetic disorder, an enzyme defect, and a neurohormonal disorder (Lothstein, 1983, p 164). Currently, the most favoured (bio)logical explanation is a hormonal one, a view with some history having already been expounded by Ulrichs, Ellis, Hirschfeld and Benjamin. In its most up to date and 'scientific' version, the contention is that genetically male transsexuals possess a female brain structure, which supports the hypothesis that gender identity develops as a result of an interaction of the developing brain and sex hormones. The tiny region of the brain that has been scrutinised is the central subdivision of the bed nucleus of the *stria terminalis*, known as BSTc. It is part of the hypothalamus which helps to keep the different systems of the body working in harmony and which is viewed as essential for sexual behaviour. This area of the brain is ordinarily larger in men than in women, while in transsexuals studies suggest that size corresponds with assumed gender (Gooren *et al*, 1995; Kruijver *et al*, 2000). We will see in Chapter 3 that much reliance has been placed on this type of research in making claims about sex within legal forums, particularly within the United Kingdom context, where legal resistance to such claims has proved to be the most marked.

Despite the growing body of literature around (bio)logical aetiology, and perhaps because of its failure to consolidate into any kind of consensus, psychoanalytical accounts have tended to have more impact on the assessment and categorisation of persons requesting sex reassignment surgery. While many psychoanalysts continued to link the desire for sex reassignment surgery with homosexuality and transvestism, and therefore opposed the practice, Robert Stoller, like Benjamin, sought to distinguish these categories, which he viewed as forms of perversion (1975), from transsexuality. In doing so he presented a carefully delineated profile of what he considered to be the 'true' or 'primary' transsexual (Stoller, 1968, p 251; 1973, 1975, pp 49, 139–40). It was this figure, and this figure alone according to Stoller, that should have access to sex reassignment surgery. According to Stoller, 'true' transsexuals are the product of a particular family constellation in which a gender-disturbed mother and a father uninvolved in her son's upbringing succeed in providing only feminising influences for the young boy and thus produce a son, who from the earliest age that gender differences appear, behaves in a cross-gendered manner and identifies as a girl. As he explained:

> From those days of childhood when any sort of gender behavior makes its first appearance, this boy has appeared as if he believed himself a girl (not a female but a girl). His behavior has always been feminine; and in it there has been no more quality of imitating or acting than in undeniably feminine girls ... As childhood progresses and passes into adolescence and adulthood, the femininity does not diminish, the desire to have a female body persists, and no amount of threat can make the transsexual able even to imitate a masculine person for a few moments (1975, pp 139–40).

Adding that:

> Almost all men have profound feelings for, concern about, and pleasure from their genitals. These organs are both a direct source of sensations and a confirmation that one's sex assignment is correct, his gender identity inevitable, and his masculinity valuable. If these positions are threatened, almost all males will set up defenses – but not true transsexuals. They simply do not want, need or cherish their male genitals, and they make no effort to preserve these organs in reality or symbolically (1975, p 140).

The latter passage, like Benjamin's transsexual profile, codes sexual pleasure as a sign of 'inauthenticity'. Indeed, Stoller insisted that any kind of evidence whatsoever of having had gratification from male genitals, whether through heterosexuality, homosexuality, or through the practice of 'perversions' such as fetishism and transvestism, precluded the diagnosis of 'primary' transsexualism. He also insisted, as the first passage makes clear, that early onset of feminine gender identity in the male-to-female subject was crucial to the diagnosis, as he viewed core gender identity as consolidating around the age of two-and-a-half (1968, p 65). The insistence that 'true' transsexualism developed prior to the onset of adolescent sexuality served also, at least in some measure, to insulate the phenomenon from homosexuality and transvestism (to the extent that transvestism is linked to sexual gratification). Over time, however, it became increasingly apparent that those requesting sex reassignment surgery were an extremely varied group. Moreover, few conformed to Stoller's picture of the 'primary', 'true' or 'classic' transsexual (King, 1993, p 63). While Stoller continued to insist that departure from this type provided evidence of 'inauthenticity' and unsuitability for surgery, others working in the area began to provide new taxonomies and rationales for surgical intervention, which had the effect of expanding the group to whom sex reassignment procedures might be made available.

In the early 1970s, Person and Ovesey identified another group of 'primary' transsexuals (1974a). In addition to Stoller's figure, they characterised as 'primary' transsexuals, individuals whose core gender identity was ambiguous at an early age but had never been effeminate in childhood, their feminine gender identity only solidifying in late adolescence (1974a, p 7). They also drew attention to what they described as two kinds of 'secondary' transsexualism, where sex reassignment would be inappropriate (1974b, p 191). The individuals to be filtered out were those whose ambiguous gender identity in childhood had been resolved through transvestism or homosexuality. Such individuals, Person and Ovesey contended, might, under conditions of extreme stress, gravitate toward a desire for sex reassignment surgery (1974b, p 181).

In 1973 Fisk introduced the term *gender dysphoria* to capture the diverse group of persons requesting sex reassignment surgery and to suggest, consistent with Stoller, that the primary transsexual narrative was but one manifestation of an underlying condition. In contrast to Stoller, however, Fisk did not confine access to sex reassignment surgery to persons relaying that particular narrative. Moreover, in suggesting that some non-primary transsexuals, specifically 'effeminate homosexuals' and 'atypical transvestites', might benefit from surgery, Fisk moved beyond the position advocated by Person and Ovesey (1978). The language of gender dysphoria gave expression to a more liberal and pragmatic approach, already adopted in practice by some clinicians, toward requests for sex reassignment surgery. This approach was adopted in 1979 by the founding committee of the Harry Benjamin International Gender Dysphoria Association (the *Benjamin Standards*) (Walker *et al*, 1979) and by the American Psychiatric Association (APA) when transsexualism was formally recognised for the first time in the third edition of the *Diagnostic and Statistics Manual of Mental Disorders* (APA, 1980).[11] The term 'transsexualism' was chosen by the APA despite the emergence of the language of gender dysphoria because it had become the most commonly accepted and widely used in the medical literature (Lothstein, 1983, p 59). The essential features of transsexualism were defined as:

> A persistent sense of discomfort and inappropriateness about one's anatomic sex and a persistent wish to be rid of one's genitals and to live as a member of the other sex. The diagnosis is made only if the disturbance has been continuous ... for at least two years (American Psychiatric Association (APA), 1980, pp 261–62).

The fourth edition of the DSM replaced the term 'transsexualism' with the phrase *Gender identity disorder* (GID), thereby bringing the lexicons of the DSM and the *Benjamin Standards* into closer proximity (APA, 1995). This change in terminology reflected wider recognition of the heterogeneous quality of applicants who presented for sex reassignment surgery and the fact that, despite extensive research into transsexual aetiology, no consensus had been established (King, 1993, p 63). The new terminology also served to emphasise that it was gender, rather than sexuality, which lay at the core of the phenomenon (King, 1993, p 63). While the change in language may have occasioned/reflected the liberalisation of access to sex reassignment surgery, it also produced negative discursive effects. While the term 'transsexualism' has a relation to ontology, where sex reassignment surgery might be viewed as a route to the realisation of being, the language of gender dysphoria serves to translate desire into need and disorder. In abandoning the term 'transsexualism' we witness the loss of its connotation of 'intermediate sex' and the capacity for self-definition that inheres within 'states of being' (King, 1993, p 64). In its wake identity gives way to 'dis-ease' and the propertied claims of medicine consolidate around transgender bodies. Moreover, as Cromwell has pointed out, the language of gender dysphoria is simply inaccurate. If transgender persons requesting sex reassignment surgery are to be described as dysphoric, then surely it is 'body dysphoria' or 'body-part dysphoria' rather than any confusion about gender (1999, p 135). Indeed, it is typically certainty about gender that leads to the request for surgery.

---

11 The *Diagnostic and Statistics Manual of Mental Disorders* was first published by the American Psychiatric Association (APA) in 1952 and again in 1968. In 1980 transsexualism appeared under the head of 'Psychosexual Disorders'.

It has been suggested that the more expansive gender dysphoria perspective, in contrast to earlier medical approaches, eschewed the search for 'truth', preferring instead to ascertain the sex in which it is best for a person to live (King, 1993, p 63). That is to say, while earlier approaches sought to discover some 'truth' of transgender 'authenticity' located in the past, the gender dysphoria model looks forward to post-surgical well-being. However, while these medical epistemologies can be differentiated along temporal lines, medical concern over post-surgical well-being continues to be informed by transgender autobiographical accounts. In short, access to surgery and, as we shall see in subsequent chapters, therefore legal recognition, remain, in important ways, tied to transgender pasts. The difference is that in the *discovery story of transsexuality* (King, 1993, pp 45, 63) transgender narratives are interpreted for signs of 'truth' which reside in the past, while in the gender dysphoria model those same narratives are scrutinised for their capacity to predict the future. While diagnosis remains important in categorising surgical candidates within complex taxonomies that typically invoke the primary/secondary transsexual distinction, the 'truth' diagnosis produces lies not in the past but in the future. In other words, it is prognosis that has become crucial in assessing requests for sex reassignment. What is significant here, however, is that it is the narrative promulgated by the discovery story, the narrative of Stoller's 'classic' transsexual, which most points to good prognosis. Thus it is precisely the tropes of early onset of gender identity, absence of erotic arousal and the presence of heterosexual desire (in the psychological sense) that structure 'best' prognostic practice. It is the relaying of these privileged historical fragments of pleasure, identity and desire which medicine incites and 'good' prognosis demands be recounted. Accordingly, and irrespective of medical epistemology, a transgender person must be a skilled narrator of his/her own life. For if s/he should 'falter, repeat, disorder, omit, digress ... you've had it, however "authentic" a transsexual you are' (Prosser, 1998, p 108).

A clinical concern to distinguish between primary and secondary transsexualism gained in significance as the number of persons requesting such procedures continued to grow and the medical literature relating to post-surgical outcomes revealed significant levels of dissatisfaction with surgical procedures and 'poor adjustment' (see, for example, Lundstrom, Pauly and Walinder, 1984; Lindemalm, Korlin and Uddenberg, 1986). The more recent literature has tended to stress positive surgical outcomes in the overwhelming number of cases (Walters and Ross, 1986; Kuiper, and Cohen-Kettenis, 1988; Green and Fleming, 1990) and has explained dissatisfaction as incorrect diagnosis of 'primary transsexualism' (Lothstein, 1982), a strategy which has sought to insulate the practice of sex reassignment surgery from more trenchant criticism. Thus Lundstrom and others have concluded that surgery is appropriate only for 'carefully evaluated, genuine primary transsexuals' and should not be offered to 'secondary gender dysphoric patients' (Lundstrom, Pauly and Walinder, 1984, p 293). This concern has led clinicians increasingly to employ a 'hermeneutics of suspicion' in evaluating candidates for surgery. Indeed, Tully has called for detailed 'authenticity checks' with regard to transgender autobiographies (1992, p 24). Thus at the moment of epistemological 'change' – the movement from the *discovery story of transsexuality* toward the gender dysphoria perspective – a privileged transgender narrative acquires a premium in the service of the legitimation of medical practice.

In particular, interpretative medical practice has fixated upon sexuality. While sexuality is not the only factor utilised to distinguish between primary and secondary transsexualism, it operates as a key sign (Pauly, 1990). Thus in order to assist in the diagnosis of individuals requesting sex reassignment surgery DSM III specified three specific subtypes of transsexualism, namely, *asexual*, *homosexual* and *heterosexual* (APA, 1980, p 262). Significantly, these subtypes correspond to predominant sexual history prior to the request for sex reassignment surgery. The 'asexual' subtype is described as typically never having had strong sexual feelings, sexual activity or genital pleasure (APA, 1980, p 262) and accordingly corresponds closely to accounts of primary transsexualism proferred by Benjamin and Stoller. The 'homosexual' subtype is portrayed as an individual who is, pre-surgically, erotically attracted to members of his or her own anatomical sex (APA, 1980, p 262). The (female-to-male) transsexual man is viewed as falling almost exclusively into this category (Steiner, 1985, p 353; Blanchard, 1985, p 234). The 'homosexual' transsexual might also be characterised as primary, though not in Stoller's sense (Fisk, 1973; Person and Ovesey, 1974a, 1974b). The 'heterosexual' subtype is presented as an individual, almost exclusively male, who is sexually attracted to females at least until the gender 'disorder' is well established (APA, 1980, p 262). The 'heterosexual' subtype is viewed as a form of secondary transsexualism. This subtype has been described in the literature as 'transvestitic (secondary) transsexualism' (Person and Ovesey, 1974a, 1974b) and 'heterosexual-fetishistic transsexualism' (Blanchard, 1985, p 229). Some clinicians have offered more simple typologies. Thus Blanchard has divided 'gender dysphoric' male-to-female subjects into two types, 'homosexual' (primary transsexuals) and 'non-homosexual' (secondary transsexuals) (1989).[12] While DSM IV replaces the terms 'homosexuality' and 'heterosexuality' with 'sexually attracted to males' and 'sexually attracted to females' (APA, 1995, p 547), and while this new language represents an improvement over the quite inappropriate usage of the former terms in transgender contexts, it holds in place the coupling of primary transsexualism with heterosexual desire (in the psychological sense) on the one hand, and secondary transsexualism with homosexual desire (in the psychological sense) on the other.

Thus in the case of (male-to-female) transgender women the medical script requires that desire be directed toward a (bio)logical man. While clinicians seek to distinguish this figure from the gay man who might seek out sex reassignment surgery in order to escape the stigma of homosexual identification, my aim here is to highlight how definitions of primary transsexualism erase homosexuality in the sense of male-to-female sexual desire for women and especially female-to-male sexual desire for men. In other words, transgender people who identify as lesbian or gay or as non-heterosexual are likely to be positioned outside the category of primary transsexualism. This positioning serves to problematise access to surgery and therefore, and as we will see in subsequent chapters, legal recognition of sex claims.

In many clinics heterosexual orientation, in the psychological and transgender sense, has operated as a requirement of surgery (see, for example, Denny, 1992, p 14; Lewins, 1995, p 94; Califia, 1997, p 209). Moreover, past 'heterosexual' practice, in the (bio)logical sense, is viewed as contra-indicative of surgery (Walinder, Lundstrom and Thuwe, 1978;

---

12 On the basis of research done at the Clarke Institute in Toronto, Blanchard estimated the 'homosexual' group at 55% and the 'heterosexual' group at 45% (1989).

Denny, 1992, p 13). By the same token present lesbian identity or anticipated future lesbian practice is, in the case of (male-to-female) transgender women, viewed unfavourably in prognostic terms (Kando, 1973; Pomeroy, 1975; Bolin, 1988, p 63; Ross and Need, 1989; Blanchard, Steiner, Clemmensen and Dickey, 1989; Lewins, 1995, p 95; Denny, 1996, p 40; Cromwell, 1999, pp 110–12). Indeed, some medical experts have viewed lesbian desire as indicative of transvestism and/or impotence in the 'heterosexual' male (Koranyi, 1980, p 89). Further, the absence of present sexual relations with a male is, for (male-to-female) transgender women, viewed by some medical practitioners as an adverse sign (Koranyi, 1980, p 31). Indeed, it has been argued that the primary motive for seeking surgery is, in the case of (male-to-female) transgender women, a desire to attract gynephilic (women-loving) male partners (Freund, Langevin, Zajac, Steiner and Zajac, 1974), a view we will see replicated within reform jurisprudence. The view of lesbian desire as 'inappropriate' finds further expression in medical reluctance to refer for surgery persons who are still lawfully married (Hastings, 1969, pp 243, 248–51; Smith, 1971, p 973; King, 1993, p 83; Bolin, 1996, p 454). This resistance to the idea of transgender and homosexuality residing in the same body is, of course, consistent with the earlier views of Benjamin and Stoller. While, more recently, some clinicians have recognised lesbian desires of transgender people, they have tended to code such desires as 'rare', 'unusual' or as 'not unknown' (Feinbloom, Fleming, Kijewski and Schulter, 1976; Casey, 1981; Blanchard, Clemmensen and Steiner, 1987).

The heterosexualisation of the transgender phenomenon is even more pronounced in the case of (female-to-male) transgender men who are viewed as almost exclusively attracted to women (Steiner, 1985, p 353; Pauly, 1974, p 502). Thus Fleming *et al* have argued that (female-to-male) transgender men 'form stable and enduring intimate relationships with biological women',[13] and consider 'their relationships heterosexual' (Fleming, MacGowan and Costos, 1985, pp 47–48) while Stoller insisted that they are 'repelled by the idea of sexual relations with males' (1973, p 386). More recently, the existence of gay (female-to-male) transgender men has received some acknowledgment, though their rarity and characterisation as secondary transsexuals have been emphasised (Blanchard, Clemmensen and Steiner, 1987; Coleman and Bockting, 1988; Clare and Tully, 1989; APA, 1995, p 548; Pauly, 1998, p 243). Moreover, the medical coupling of transsexuality with heterosexuality has operated as a self-fulfilling prophesy. That is to say, because clinicians have consistently underestimated and marginalised non-heterosexual transgender desires and practices, and because any suggestion of lesbianism has, in the words of one transsexual, served to place surgical possibilities 'under a cloud' (Lewins, 1995, p 94), transgender people seeking sex reassignment surgery or other medical procedures typically provide clinicians with unproblematic heterosexual narratives. In this regard, the 'fact' that transsexuals 'distort their autobiographies' and 'tend to be less than honest about their personal histories' (Lothstein, 1983, pp 46, 160) proves, at least in part, to be an effect of homophobic medical practice.

---

13   The reference to the enduring nature of the sexual relations of (female-to-male) transgender men contrasts with medical characterisations of the sexual relations of (male-to-female) transgender women (see, eg, Green, 1974, p 129; Millot, 1990, pp 106–07). In this regard stereotypes about gay men and lesbians are replicated and applied to transgender people.

It is therefore apparent that medicine and, as we shall see in subsequent chapters, law deploy (bio)logical and psychological understandings of sexuality differentially across the hetero/homo divide. Sex reassignment surgery proceeds on the basis of a reimagined heterosexuality, a heterosexuality uncoupled from its biological referent. That is to say, heterosexuality is reinvented in the transgender context so that it no longer signifies desire for persons of the opposite (bio)logical sex. Rather, it is rendered intelligible through recourse to a psychological understanding of sexuality. In contrast, medicine has resisted a parallel reconceptualisation of homosexuality. In this regard, sex reassignment surgery emerges as a practice concerned to facilitate one-way sexual traffic. That is to say, 'good' prognosis implies a particular gendered relationship between the re-sexed body and sexual preference.

Another key trope in the narrative of 'primary' transsexualism is early onset of gender identity in childhood or early adolescence (APA, 1995, p 549). While articulation of heterosexual desire is read as consistent with this trope, late onset of feminine gender identity in (male-to-female) transgender women is linked to 'lesbian' desire (Blanchard, 1989; APA, 1995, p 549). Here, lesbian desire comes to function as a sign of secondary transsexualism or non-transsexualism (Pauly, 1992, pp 7–9) and therefore serves to problematise the request for sex reassignment surgery. That is to say, lesbian desire and late onset of gender identity are viewed as mutually reinforcing. Further, lesbian desire not only serves to call into question the suitability and legitimacy of surgery but also the 'authenticity' of sexual desire and transsexual identity.

The importance of gender to 'good' prognostic practice is not, however, confined to medical assumptions about the relevance of early onset of gender identity. Rather, the medical gaze appears to be traversed by a range of somatic and gender performance-based assumptions. Thus, sex reassignment surgery is conditional upon a candidate living in the gender role opposite to their sex designated at birth for a lengthy period, usually two years (APA, 1980, p 261).[14] This has been referred to as a 'real life test' (Money and Walker, 1977, p 1292) in which performance is directed toward 'passing'. Thus, in the case of the (male-to-female) transgender woman she is required to 'do gender' successfully enough to convince, predominantly male, medical experts that she will blend into society post-surgically (Kessler and McKenna, 1978). The successful accomplishment of gender would seem to require a presentation of self that, amongst other things, is feminine in physique, dress and demeanour, attractive, more concerned with giving than receiving sexual pleasure and preferably working in a 'suitable' occupation for a woman (see, for example, Raymond, 1979, Chapter 3; Koranyi, 1980, pp 27, 84; Billings and Urban, 1982, p 275; Bolin, 1988, pp 107–08; Cole and Birrell, 1990, p 5; King, 1993, p 85; Lewins, 1995, pp 103, 116; Griggs, 1998, pp 31, 62; Kaveney, 1999, p 151). While 'too conspicuous physical characteristics and behaviour' (Reid, 1995, p 34) appear relevant to clinical decisions, Lewins found that clinical assessments of 'convincing' or 'reasonably convincing' feminine performance had more to do with 'manner' than 'appearance' (1995, p 116). The further a candidate departs from this feminine 'ideal' the less chance she has of obtaining reassignment surgery, or the longer she will have to wait (King, 1993, p 85). Moreover, while a medical concern over transgender performance precedes the gender dysphoria perspective, the shift from a

---

14 The required period of living in the opposite gender role varies to some degree across clinics.

search for 'origins' to the contemporary emphasis on future 'well-being' and psycho-social adjustment has perhaps served to intensify the medical gaze in this respect.

While transgender narratives have been recuperated from the 1950s onward the recuperative process has, at the same time, served to circumscribe and diminish the richness of transgender. In the early period, through to the 1970s, the discovery story dominated as medical epistemology thereby restricting transgender to a single narrative, that of the 'true' transsexual. After that time the gender dysphoria perspective gradually assumed hegemony. This more contemporary medical epistemology envisioned several narrative lines culminating in the request for sex reassignment surgery. However, these narrative lines have not been thought in terms of equivalence. On the contrary, they have been hierarchialised in such a way as to privilege one story, that of the 'true' transsexual, albeit that her/his truth is now projected into the future in terms of 'good' prognosis. It is to the contestation of the privileging of this narrative, and the relevance of sex reassignment surgery to the 'authenticity' of transgender status, that attention now turns.

2.5 A TRANSGENDER POLITICS

While there were clearly forerunners (see, for example, Prince, 1971, 1976; Beaumont Society, 1975, 1983; SHAFT, 1981), the modern transgender movement can be dated to the early 1990s. While the politicisation of transgender at this historical moment reflects a series of intersecting factors, including marginalisation within gay, and especially lesbian, communities (Rubin, 1992; Wilchins, 1995; Nataf, 1996; Califia, 1997, p 223), it was directed to the failure of medicine to accommodate the rich diversity that is transgender (Hale, 1995, p 20; Califia, 1997, p 224; Cromwell, 1999, Chapter 2). The term 'transgender', while initially denoting a cultural space between *transsexual* and *transvestite* (Boswell, 1991, p 31; Cromwell, 1999, p 23), has come to operate as an umbrella term for a multiplicity of trans-subjectivities (Whittle, 1996; Stryker, 1998, p 149; Cromwell, 1999, p 23; Currah and Minter, 2000a, pp 3–4) that, as already explained, have been variously located within complex and ever burgeoning medical taxonomies. It encompasses numerous, including non-surgical, ways of 'being' male or female as well as positions which problematise binary understandings of sex (Stone, 1991; Denny, 1991, p 6; Boswell, 1991; Feinberg, 1993b; Bornstein, 1994; May-Welby, 1994, p 11; Hooley, 1994; Bruce-Pratt, 1995; Nataf, 1996, p 32; Califia, 1997; Wilchins, 1997).

Transgender politics has challenged medicine's reduction of an 'authentic' transgender state to the desire for sex reassignment surgery. That is to say, there has been opposition to the 'wrong body' stories propounded by medicine (Cromwell, 1999, p 23). Thus, while the term 'pre-operative' identifies anatomical (genital) and psychological 'disharmony' residing in a subject to whom medicine claims to offer a solution, many transgender people refuse to bow to this knowledge, considering their anatomy and psychology to be harmoniously male or female even though, and precisely because, it is located outside either sphere of medico-legal binary constructions of sex.[15] Moreover,

---

15 It is important to stress that my usage of the pre-/post-operative distinction throughout this book reflects that of medicine and law. That is to say, post-operative status denotes and requires that vaginoplasty/phalloplasty has been undertaken. There are many other surgical procedures that many transgender persons undertake, including castration, penectomy (in the case of (contd)

medicine's privileging of a single transgender narrative as either diagnostically or prognostically significant has been challenged. In particular, counter-discourses have been generated around the medical assumptions of hatred of genitalia (Nataf, 1996; p 25; Califia, 1997, pp 185–86; Cromwell, 1999, pp 112–13) and heterosexual desire (Bolin, 1988, p 63; Lewins, 1995, p 95; Nataf, 1996, p 32; Cromwell, 1999, pp 110–12). Thus in relation to sexuality, for example, both Bolin (1988, p 63) and Lewins (1995, p 95) found approximately one-third of their respective male-to-female transgender samples to be lesbian identified, while in relation to their female-to-male transgender samples Stuart found 10–17% (1991) and Whittle 25% (Nataf, 1996, p 30) to identify as gay men. In the same vein some transgender people and their partners, who are themselves increasingly transgendered (Califia, 1997, Chapter 6), refuse to identify sexually in terms of the hetero/homo dyad (see, for example, Nataf, 1996, pp 32–33; Califia, 1997, p 196).

Moreover, as part of the challenge to medical orthodoxy an alternative set of standards to the *Benjamin Standards*, the *Health Law Standards*, were adopted in 1993 by the Second International Conference on Transgender Law and Employment Policy, a group of, primarily transgender, people in the fields of law and health care policy (Nelson, 1998, pp 221–24). These alternative standards are predicated on the view that most transgender people seeking sex reassignment surgery, hormonal treatments or other medical services do not require psychological services. Further, the standards deem it unethical to discriminate in the provision of sex reassignment services on the basis of sexual orientation, marital status or physical appearance (Nelson, 1998, p 221). It is important to articulate this challenge to medical orthodoxy and the alternative transgender positions that it implies for, as we will see in the following chapters, transgender jurisprudence has drawn heavily upon medical, to the detriment of 'other', knowledges.

2.6 CONCLUSION

This chapter has provided an account of the emergence of transgender as an object of scientific study. It has traced contemporary medical approaches to transgender people to sexological discourses of the late 19th century. While present medical understandings of transgender differ in many respects from earlier attempts to map this phenomenon, they nevertheless operate within a frame established by sexual science. In particular, assumptions about gender and sexuality that proved formative for early sexual science continue to inform medical understandings of transgender. While these assumptions are clearly interrelated, this chapter has placed particular emphasis on the conflation of transgender with homosexuality. While neither category today is subsumed by the other, as in earlier epochs, their very differentiation has exacerbated conflation. That is to say, while transgender has been gradually recuperated from the 1950s onwards, the 'recuperative' process has privileged a linear transgender narrative. For those transgender people whose autobiographies depart from this account, proximity to homosexuality has been more readily concluded.

---

15 (contd) (male-to-female) transgender women), hysterectomy and mastectomy (in the case of (female-to-male) transgender men), procedures which lead to the continued characterisation of such persons as pre-operative within medicine and especially law.

While legal concerns cannot be reduced to those of medicine we will see in the following chapters that law draws heavily, though selectively, on medical knowledge in support of its, often conflicting, propositions. In more consistent fashion we will see that law has functioned as yet another locale for the repetition of the particular transgender narrative privileged within medicine and in which the past assumes significance. In this, and in other regards, the richness of transgender will be seen to appear only as absence, as the necessary 'outside' to that which is constructed as male or female in the context of sex designation, or as sex or transgender in the context of anti-discrimination law protected categories. However, while medicine's concern with transgender pasts is, at least ostensibly, directed toward predicting future well-being, it is not possible to account for law's preoccupation with the past in this way. For in contrast to medicine, which considers the past in the context of decisions surrounding sex reassignment surgery, law typically is confronted by transgender people who have not only undertaken surgery but did so years, sometimes decades, earlier and where, therefore, well-being is already established. Accordingly, it is hard to avoid the conclusion, at least in relation to interrogation of the past, that it is the *discovery story of transsexuality* to which law appeals. Thus, while ontological questions may have been backgrounded within medical practice this does not prove to be the case with regard to law, especially in relation to its re-sexing practices. We will see that law's concern over transgender 'authenticity' bears a particular and strong relation to the primary theme explored in this chapter, namely, homosexual/transgender conflation. Indeed, and irrespective of legal approach, we will see that the homosexual body, and its legal imagining, operate as a structuring principle within transgender jurisprudence, making (non)sense of the case law.

Further, and as should be clear from this chapter, medical treatment of transgender people cannot be confined in its effects to transgender. In addition to, and through, circumscribing transgender, medical knowledge quite clearly confronts feminist and gay and lesbian politics. That is to say, medical discourse and practice incite gender conformity, heterosexual desire and reproduce the view, antithetical to feminism, that anatomy determines destiny (de Beauvoir, 1953). We will see that in ratifying medical knowledge law recites, and thereby 'naturalises', these practices. In this regard, our attention is drawn to the excessive work law requires transgender people to perform in furtherance of much wider regulatory strategies around gender and sexuality. Accordingly, the intersection of law and transgender should be viewed as a locus or site for wider political contestation where, perhaps, the anatomical, sexual and gender specificity of re-sexed bodies, as well as the reasoning adopted in cases of legal denial, might be subjected to disruption and radical re-articulation (Butler, 1993). Indeed, given the multiple effects produced, transgender bodies of law, to which we now turn, may properly be regarded as a strategic field.

CHAPTER 3

THE (BIO)LOGIC OF LAW

> It is time to assert that there is no 'wrong body' and that all bodies are alright, whatever their shape or genital status. It is the power of the norm, and of medicine and law, which take the cultural meanings made of biology as ultimate truth, that sustains our deviant status, body regulation and discrimination (Hooley, 1994).

This chapter introduces the transgender/law relation through an analysis of judicial approaches that have consistently refused to recognise the sex claims of transgender people at large. These approaches to transgender, through which law's repressive legal power (Foucault, 1981a) has been displayed, have been articulated in terms of (bio)logic. That is to say, the chapter will consider case law that deploys (bio)logic in constructing sex. While more generally adopted, this judicial practice has been particularly noticeable in the English context. While such approaches have consistently articulated a *sex is determined at birth* narrative whereby sex precedes, and therefore provides, an apparent foundation for gender, the precise configuration of legally relevant factors to be considered at birth will be seen to vary. Moreover, and in a manner that questions legal fidelity to medical science, we will see that genitalia are privileged over other factors irrespective of the specificity of (bio)logical approach. In laying bare the genitocentrism of law that is masked, at least partially, by the language of (bio)logic, the chapter lays a foundation for linking (bio)logical approaches to the reform jurisprudence to be examined in Chapter 4. In addition to highlighting law's selective use of biology the chapter will problematise the wisdom of appealing to (bio)logic as a litigation strategy, given its restriction of legal claims to particular (bio)logical factors and one temporal moment. Further, while (bio)logical approaches to transgender sex claims locate the 'truth' of sex in the past, it will become evident that a focus on 'truth' and the past is not confined to biology. That is to say, a concern over transgender 'authenticity' is also apparent. This dimension of legal reasoning evident within (bio)logical approaches which, as we will see in the next chapter, demonstrates further continuity with reform jurisprudence, will be highlighted through consideration of a number of appeals to the European Court of Human Rights, primarily against the United Kingdom. In considering the (bio)logic of law the chapter will pay close attention to the relationship between law and medical science, thereby building on the previous chapter.

3.1 A PREFERENCE FOR CHROMOSOMES

The lead decision within, and indeed the decision that has become most associated with, a (bio)logical approach is the English decision of *Corbett v Corbett*.[1] It is important to consider *Corbett* not only because of its considerable impact on judicial thinking, but because it provides a context in which to both understand and gauge subsequent reform jurisprudence to be considered in Chapter 4. However, before turning to *Corbett* it is first

---

1   *Corbett v Corbett* [1970] 2 All ER 33.

necessary to make mention of earlier common law cases denying transgender sex claims. As early as 1957, the *Corbett* approach appears to have been anticipated in some respects in the Scottish case of *Re X*.[2] In rejecting a (male-to-female) transgender woman's application to have her birth certificate altered to reflect her change of sex, the court stated: '... skin and blood tests still show X's basic sex to be male and that the changes have not yet reached the deepest level of sex determination.'[3] Here it is the chromosomal factor that appears decisive in sex determination. In two subsequent New York decisions it is again the chromosomal factor that assumes significance. In the cases of *Anonymous v Weiner*[4] and *Anonymous v Hartin*,[5] Sarafite J and Helman J respectively dismissed the applications of post-operative (male-to-female) transgender women to change birth certificates so as to reflect their female sex. In each case, emphasis was placed on a 1965 report by the New York Academy of Medicine's Public Health Committee titled *Change of Sex on Birth Certificates for Transsexuals*. The report, which was very unfavourable to the legal sex claims of transgender persons,[6] concluded 'male-to-female transsexuals are still chromosomally males while ostensibly females',[7] and in a reference to subsequent commentary on the issue by the New York Board of Health, Helman J noted that surgery 'does not change the body cells governing sexuality'.[8] The linkage of sex to the birth moment evident in these decisions was to undergo complexification in the 1970 English decision of *Corbett v Corbett*.

3.2 THE (BIO)LOGIC OF *CORBETT*

In *Corbett*, a case concerning the validity of a marriage between a (bio)logical male petitioner, Arthur Corbett, and a post-operative (male-to-female) transgender woman respondent, April Ashley, Ormrod J stated the primary issue to be the determination of the 'true' sex of the latter.[9] In addressing the matter, Ormrod J recognised that law alone could not decide the issue. He was 'assisted', however, by no fewer than nine medical expert witnesses who gave evidence as to the 'truth' of the respondent's sex.[10] While the expert witnesses for the petitioner emphasised chromosomal, gonadal and genital factors as crucial in sex determination, psychology was also recognised, though attributed less

---

2   *X, Petitioner* [1957] Scot LT 61; 73 Scot L Rev 203.

3   *Ibid*, p 62.

4   *Anonymous v Weiner as the Director of the Bureau of Records and Statistics of the Department of Health of the City of New York* 270 NYS 2d 319 (1996).

5   *Hartin v Director of the Bureau of Records and Statistics, Department of Health of the City of New York* 347 NYS 2d 515 (1973).

6   Indeed, the report's claim 'that surgery for the transsexual is an experimental form of psychotherapy by which mutilating surgery is conducted on a person with the intent of setting his mind at ease' serves to highlight the considerable opposition that existed in the United States regarding the practice of sex reassignment surgery during this period (see Green, 1969b, p 241).

7   *Anonymous v Weiner as the Director of the Bureau of Records and Statistics of the Department of Health of the City of New York* 270 NYS 2d 319 (1996), p 321; *Hartin v Director of the Bureau of Records and Statistics Department of Health of the City of New York* 347 NYS 2d 515 (1973), p 516. The 1965 New York medical report was invoked as recently as 1987 in an Ohio decision (see *Re Ladrach* 32 Ohio Misc 2d 6 (1987)).

8   *Ibid*, p 518.

9   *Corbett v Corbett* [1970] 2 All ER 33, p 35.

10   *Ibid*.

weight. Conversely, the expert witnesses for the respondent placed considerably greater emphasis upon psychological and hormonal factors. Indeed, four of the nine medical expert witnesses argued that April Ashley was intersexed due to psychological and/or hormonal factors.[11] While the emphasis upon psychological and hormonal factors proved to be an unsuccessful litigation strategy in *Corbett*, the manner in which they were deployed raises a major concern for transgender politics. It appears that counsel for April Ashley effectively argued, particularly with regard to 'hormonal sex', that she was female and had been so prior to birth. This argument is potentially damaging to future litigation claims of persons who might wish to contest their sex categorisation because it concedes birth as the critical moment for legal determination of sex, and thereby detracts from subsequent psychological, gonadal and/or genital change. This strategy, one we will see recur in subsequent cases and which continues to receive the support of some legal scholars (see, for example, Armstrong and Walton, 1992, p 96), is typical of identity-based law reform agendas which rely on assertions of 'coherent fixed identity' to achieve legal recognition (Morgan, 1996, p 129). This is not to legislate against instrumental uses of 'identity' in all law reform contexts, nor is it to mask law's categorical imperative which provokes, if not compels, such strategies. Rather, it is to echo Butler's concern that instrumental uses of identity should 'not become regulatory imperatives' (1991, p 16). This danger is particularly apparent in strategies that resort to (bio)logic.

The notion of sex as cultural production remains unacknowledged in the *Corbett* decision. Yet, while Professor Dewhurst suggested 'we do not determine sex ... in medicine we determine the sex in which it is best for the individual to live',[12] the various medical experts in *Corbett* were quite clearly engaged in differential constructions of sex, specifying which factors are to be taken into account and the relative weight to be given to each. After emphasising the high quality of the medical evidence and its 'intellectual and scientific objectivity'[13] Ormrod J, mindful that law, unlike medicine, is a binary system (Ormrod, 1972, p 78), ignored important portions of that evidence. In particular, he dismissed the idea that transgender might have an organic or hormonal basis:

> This hypothesis is based on experimental work ... which suggests that the copulatory behaviour of ... adult animals may be affected by the influence of certain sex hormones on particular cells in the hypothalamus ... At present the application of this work to the human being is purely hypothetical and speculative ... The use of such phrases as 'male or female brain' in this connection is apt to mislead owing to the ambiguity of the word 'brain' ... In my judgment these theories have nothing to contribute to the solution of the present case.[14]

In the final analysis, Ormrod J held that *sex is determined at birth* and by a congruence of chromosomal, gonadal and genital factors.[15] Accordingly, and despite the claim that it 'cannot be doubted' that his decision was 'based on apparently logic grounds' (van Niekerk, 1970, p 240) it is clear that Ormrod J's choice of factors is highly selective. Indeed, in view of his selectivity regarding the criteria for determining sex and his insistence upon birth as the governing moment, there is no shortage of irony in Ormrod

11 *Ibid*, pp 43–46.
12 *Ibid*, p 44.
13 *Ibid*, p 35.
14 *Ibid*, p 43.
15 *Ibid*, p 48.

J's assertion that '[transsexuals] are said to be "selective historians" tending to stress events which fit in with their ideas and to suppress those which do not'.[16] In constructing sex in the particular (bio)logical and temporal fashion that he did, Ormrod J reduced the diversity of medical expertise to legal monologue (Foucault, 1981b). Accordingly, the legal sex of April Ashley was scripted as male. In contrast to genetic woman she is located outside the boundaries of law, for her present reality lies in opposition to a 'truth' that resides in the past. The decision asserts that there exists an immutable, binary and oppositional division of sex that precedes, and therefore provides an apparent foundation for, gender.

However, while Ormrod J emphasised the need for congruence of chromosomes, gonads and genitalia at birth his judgment belies a preoccupation with genitalia. It is genital insignia, rather than chromosomes or gonads, which underscores the judgment. This is implicit in the use of male and female pronouns, which Ormrod J claimed to use 'as seems convenient in the context'.[17] The use of female pronouns, however, was only considered 'convenient' once the respondent, April Ashley, had undergone genital surgery. An explicit concern with genitalia is revealed in the following passage:

> The real difficulties, of course, will occur if these criteria [gonadal, chromosomal and genital] are not congruent. This question does not arise in the present case and I must not anticipate, but it would seem to follow from what I have said that the greater weight would probably be given to the genital criteria than to the other two.[18]

It is not at all clear why sex should be read at birth rather than at some later date, or why the genital factor should be privileged in legal determinations of sex:

> ... especially as the sexual condition of an individual is determined by several factors (vis chromosomal factors; gonadal factors; genital factors; psychological factors) nearly all of which are (more or less) capable of changing.[19]

The privileging of the genital factor in Ormrod J's analysis is particularly revealing in a number of respects. First, the fact that the genital factor should trump gonadal and chromosomal factors in the event of 'incongruence' serves to detract from the ostensibly scientific-based nature of Ormrod J's reasoning. In this regard, the grounding of the decision in (bio)logic emerges as rhetorical trope rather than fidelity to science. Moreover, in formulating his test Ormrod J insisted that he was not determining the 'legal sex' of the respondent at large,[20] but only within the context of marriage. Indeed, Ormrod J addressed the possibility that sex might be determined outside the specific (bio)logical and temporal framework constructed for the purposes of marriage. He expressed the view that in the context of certain legal relationships, for example, most contractual, employment, pensions, social security and national insurance matters, as well as the

---

16   *Ibid*, p 42. It should be pointed out that a view of transgender people as 'selective historians' is an effect of a desire for sex reassignment surgery and the fact that a pre-condition of surgery is conformity to rigid gender and sexual stereotypes that comprise the narrative lines of transgender biography constructed within medicine. Moreover, this medically induced 'selective amnesia' is hardly consistent with the future well-being of transgender persons (see Califia, 1997, p 59).

17   *Ibid*, p 35.

18   *Ibid*, p 48.

19   *Cossey v UK* [1991] 13 EHRR 622, p 657, *per* Martens J dissenting.

20   *Corbett v Corbett* [1970] 2 All ER 33, p 48.

greater part of the criminal law, a person (bio)logically male at birth might be treated as a woman.[21] Indeed, more recently, Ormrod J expressed the view that '[t]he law can accommodate the transsexual in almost all of its other aspects' (Finlay, 1996, p 508).[22] This distinction between marriage and other subject matters is important in understanding both *Corbett* and, as we shall see in Chapter 4, many of the decisions departing from it within reform jurisprudence. For present purposes, it is clear from his judgment that Ormrod J viewed any recognition of sex claims for non-marriage purposes to be based on gender rather than sex. In this way, psychology and/or post-surgical anatomy, which might be viewed as overriding criteria, or at least be accorded greater weight in sex determination, are assigned to the category of gender. In other words, the possibility of an alternative test for determining sex for legal purposes is rendered inauthentic. Ultimately, despite purportedly confining the judgment to the issue of marriage, Ormrod J insists implicitly upon the universal 'truth' of sex, which is, of course, (bio)logically and temporally specific. When we consider reform jurisprudence in Chapter 4 we will see that departure from *Corbett* is inextricably tied to the legal reimagination of the relationship between sex and gender.

Despite Ormrod J alluding to the possibility of an alternative legal test for determining sex for non-marriage purposes, many, and all English, common law cases after *Corbett* have applied (bio)logical criteria. Thus the *sex is determined at birth* story has been affirmed in common law cases concerning birth certificates,[23] social security,[24] sex discrimination, unfair dismissal,[25] equal pay,[26] criminal law[27] and marriage.[28] In *R v Tan*, which saw the extension of Ormrod J's (bio)logical test to English criminal law, counsel for the defence submitted that a person should not be held to be a man for the purposes of certain sexual offences 'if the person had become philosophically or psychologically or socially female'.[29] In dismissing the submission without hesitation the court took the view that both 'commonsense and the desirability of certainty and consistency'[30] demanded that *Corbett* be followed. In the most recent English decision, that of *Bellinger v Bellinger*,[31] the court, while recognising that there had been a marked change in social

---

21   *Ibid*, p 48.

22   This statement is contained in a letter from Sir Roger Ormrod to Dr Henry Finlay dated January 1989 (Finlay, 1996, p 508) and written in response to a publication co-authored by Dr Finlay and Dr WAW Walters (Finlay and Walters, 1988).

23   See *Re T* [1975] 2 NZLR 449; *K v Health Division of Human Resources* 560 P 2d 1070 (1977); *Anonymous v Irving Mellon as Director of Bureau of Vital Records, Department of Health of the City of New York* 398 NYS 2d 99 (1977); *Re P and G* [1996] 2 FLR 90.

24   *Dec CP 6/76 National Insurance Commissioner Decisions*; *Social Security Decision Nos R(P) 1 and R(P) 2* [1980] National Insurance Commissioner Decisions.

25   *EA White v British Sugar Corporation* [1977] IRLR 121; *Re P and G* [1996] FLR 90.

26   *Collins v Wilkin Chapman* [1994] EAT/945/93 (Transcript).

27   *R v Tan* [1983] QB 1053.

28   See *W v W* [1976] 2 SALR 308; *Peterson v Peterson* (1985) *The Times*, 12 July; *Re Ladrach* 32 Ohio Misc 2d 6 (1987); *Franklin v Franklin* (1990) *The Scotsman*, 9 November; *Lim Ying v Hiok Kian Ming Eric* [1992] 1 SLR 184; *S-T (formerly J) v J* [1998] 1 All ER 431; *Littleton v Prange* [1999] 288th Judicial District Court, Bexar County, Texas (www.4thcoa.courts.state.tx.us/opinions/9900010.htm); *W v W* (2000) *The Times*, 31 October (Transcript); *Bellinger v Bellinger* (2000) *The Times*, 2 November.

29   *R v Tan* [1983] QB 105, p 1064.

30   *Ibid*.

31   *Bellinger v Bellinger* (2000) *The Times*, 2 November.

[handwritten margin notes: "more concerned with precedent than doing the right thing!"]

attitudes since the *Corbett* decision, insisted that Ormrod J's triumvirate still governed the legal determination of sex, a conclusion shared by the Attorney-General who intervened in the case. While the desirability of certainty and consistency, and indeed fidelity to *Corbett*, have proved important within English transgender jurisprudence, two recent decisions, *S-T (formerly J) v J*[32] and *W v W*,[33] ones which address the question of 'legal sex' in some detail, represent subtle, though different, kinds of departure from *Corbett*. However, while imagining or producing reform these decisions reproduce the *sex is determined at birth* narrative, guided as they are, in different ways, by (bio)logic. Moreover, they serve to highlight how the *Corbett* decision continues to structure the development of transgender jurisprudence and the possibility of reform in the UK context.

3.3 RECONFIGURING THE (BIO)LOGIC OF *CORBETT*

The legal reasoning in *S-T (formerly J) v J* raises the possibility that the re-sexing of transgender bodies may occur at English common law, rather than requiring statutory intervention or successful appeal to the European Court of Human Rights. This is perhaps especially significant given that common law resistance to recognition of transgender sex claims has been particularly pronounced in relation to marriage. However, the judicial reimagination of transgender bodies that is apparent in *S-T (formerly J) v J* is, as we shall see, not without its own difficulties. The facts of the case were that J, a (female-to-male) transgender man, who had undergone a bilateral mastectomy and had received hormone injections, went through a ceremony of marriage with a (bio)logical woman, S-T. After 17 years, and on the application of S-T, the marriage was declared null and void under s 11(c) of the Matrimonial Causes Act 1973 on the ground that at the time of the marriage the parties were not respectively male and female.[34] The finding that J was female and the characterisation of his marital union with S-T as a 'legal impossibility'[35] appears to be premised on a view of J's body as pre-operative, or as still in transition. That is to say, it is the fact that J's body lacked a penis that assumes importance in law's characterisation of his relationship with S-T as a 'single sex union'.[36] This theme, and the homophobia of law that underwrites it, will be explored in depth in Chapter 5. For present purposes, it is sufficient to point out that J did not challenge the court's finding as to 'legal sex'. Rather, it was the merits of his application for ancillary relief that the Court of Appeal had to determine. In view of the absence of any challenge by J as to the finding that he was female, the majority of the court took the view that it was 'neither necessary nor appropriate ... to rule or even to speculate whether *Corbett v Corbett* remains good law'.[37] Nevertheless, and particularly in the judgment of Ward LJ, the court did speculate and, indeed, reimagined sex along lines somewhat different to Ormrod J. Thus, in referring to the New Zealand marriage case of *Attorney-General v Otahuhu Family Court*, and in contrast to the trial judge in *S-T (formerly J) v J*, Ward LJ expressed the view:

---

32   *S-T (formerly J) v J* [1998] 1 All ER 431.
33   *W v W* (2000) *The Times*, 31 October (Transcript).
34   *S-T (formerly J) v J* [1998] 1 All ER 431.
35   *Ibid*, p 450.
36   *Ibid*, p 465.
37   *Ibid*.

For my part, I find myself unable lightly to dismiss it. Taken with the new insight into the aetiology of transsexualism, it may be that *Corbett v Corbett* would bear re-examination at some appropriate time. For present purposes, it should, however, be stressed that ... declaration of validity will only apply in a case where there has been 'physical conformation' to the desired sex by full reconstructive surgery, including in the case of a female-to-male transsexual, surgical construction of a penis. For that reason the decision does not assist [J].[38]

This passage is revealing in a number of respects. First, it is perhaps significant that a superior English court, against the backdrop of *Corbett* and while not being required to determine the question of sex, proved capable of reimagining sex uncoupled from chromosomes and did so within the marriage context. However, and while Ward LJ appears to entertain the possibility of endorsing the test of *psychological and anatomical harmony*, a legal test already adopted in common law jurisdictions of the United States, Australia and New Zealand and to be considered in Chapter 4, the passage makes clear that prospects for reform are tied to an additional factor. That is to say, Ward LJ's view 'that *Corbett v Corbett* would bear re-examination at some appropriate time' was due not only to the persuasiveness of the reasoning of Ellis J in *Attorney-General v Otahuhu Family Court*. Rather, Ward LJ placed considerable emphasis on 'new insight into the aetiology of transsexualism', a concern that was absent in the judgment of Ellis J and given little weight within reform jurisprudence generally. Indeed, considerable weight was placed on contemporary scientific studies conducted post mortem on male-to-female transsexuals suggesting they possess a female brain structure (Gooren *et al*, 1995; Kruijver *et al*, 2000).[39] Such studies support the hypothesis that gender identity develops as a result of an interaction of the developing brain and sex hormones.[40] Such a view serves to problematise Ormrod J's analysis, predicated as it is on the reduction of sex to a triumvirate of chromosomes, gonads and genitalia and the rejection of the view that transgender might have an organic basis.

The emphasis on 'new insight into the aetiology of transsexualism' is significant in a number of respects. In the first place, a judicial focus on 'advances' in medical science enabled Ward LJ to characterise an anticipated future departure from *Corbett* as consistent with the underlying scientific tenor of that landmark decision, rather than as a fundamental and violent departure from it. That is to say, the deployment of science assisted in the portrayal of law as logical, rational and coherent. The emphasis on new research regarding the aetiology of transsexualism is also significant in that it is indicative of a persistent, yet troublesome, approach to transgender law reform in the UK context. While, in a jurisdiction that has consistently refused to recognise transgender sex claims,

---

38 *Ibid*, p 447.

39 *Ibid*, p 451.

40 The tiny region of the brain that has been scrutinised is the central subdivision of the bed nucleus of the *stria terminalis*, known as BSTc. It is part of the hypothalamus which helps to keep the different systems of the body working in harmony and which is essential for sexual behaviour. This area of the brain is ordinarily larger in men than in women, while in transsexuals, according to Professor Gooren's studies, size corresponds with assumed gender. It should be noted that this area of the brain has also been targeted in accounting for gay and lesbian desires (see Levay, 1991, 1993).

it is understandable that law reform has relied heavily on the legitimising effects of (bio)logical science, there is a danger in this strategy, one already outlined in relation to litigation strategies pursued in *Corbett*. The difficulty with an approach that privileges hormones is that it concedes birth as the governing moment in sex determination. Reform on these terms seeks to reimpose 'the ideal of Being on the fact of becoming' (Booth, 1985, p 132). That is to say, it maintains the temporal specificity of *Corbett* intact, thereby circumscribing the future legal possibilities of transgender persons who are unable to link their sex claims to the womb. Thus, while transgender law reform is imagined, though not realised, in *S-T (formerly J) v J* the imaginative exercise is one which continues to ground sex in the birth moment. In short, Ward LJ imagines hormonal sex coupled with sex reassignment surgery to be determinative of the issue. While this represents a departure from *Corbett* it is one which is entirely consistent with that decision's emphasis on (bio)logic and temporality. The refusal, and the nature of the refusal, of the English judiciary to depart from these key dimensions of *Corbett* receives particular clarification in *W v W*, a case in which the sex claims of a post-operative (male-to-female) intersexed woman were recognised for the purposes of marriage.

However, before turning to *W v W* it is instructive to consider a prior Australian decision in which the sex claims of a post-operative (female-to-male) intersexed man were rejected for marriage purposes. In *Re the Marriage of C v D (falsely called C)* Bell J had to consider the validity of an 11 year marriage between a (bio)logical wife and an intersexed husband.[41] At birth Mr C possessed 'external male genitalia, an ovary and a uterus and a normal female sex chromosome complement'.[42] Prior to the marriage he underwent a double mastectomy, a hysterectomy and 'corrective' surgery in relation to his external sex organs[43] so that at the time of the marriage he 'exhibited as a male in two of the three criteria'.[44] Nevertheless, and in purporting to follow the reasoning in *Corbett*, Bell J, in a much criticised judgment (Bailey-Harris, 1979, p 660; Finlay, 1996, p 516), held the marriage to be void on the basis that Mr C was 'a combination of male and female'.[45] While referring to Ormrod J's observation that 'real difficulties ... will occur if these three criteria [chromosomes, gonads and genitalia] are not congruent',[46] Bell J, in contrast to Ormrod J who had indicated a clear preference for genitalia in such circumstances, refused to make any choice. Accordingly, the decision in *Re the Marriage of C v D (falsely called C)* failed to exploit the possibilities for reform left open by Ormrod J, an omission that would not be repeated in *W v W* despite 'ambiguity' regarding Mrs W's genitalia. While the effect of the decision in *Re the Marriage of C v D (falsely called C)* is to render Mr C 'a non-person so far as marriage is concerned' (Finlay, 1996, p 516), and therefore to produce a situation where 'he can marry no one' (Bailey-Harris, 1979, p 660) it nevertheless, and precisely because of these facts, contains disruptive potential. That is to say, while the decision is clearly unsatisfactory for Mr C, and while Foucault's characterisation of intersexed experience as 'a happy limbo' (1980, p xiii) clearly lacks

---

41 *Re the Marriage of C v D (falsely called C)* [1979] 35 FLR 340.
42 *Ibid*.
43 *Ibid*, p 342. For greater detail concerning the medical history of Mr C see Fraser and O'Reilly (1966).
44 *Ibid*, p 344.
45 *Ibid*, p 341.
46 *Ibid*, p 344.

pathos, Bell J's refusal to locate Mr C within a male/female dichotomy might be viewed as a point within legal discourse from which to challenge the certainty, indeed the inevitability, of that dyad. In Chapter 4, however, we will see that *Re the Marriage of C v D (falsely called C)* has been treated as something of an anomaly by the courts, which have otherwise consistently and emphatically rejected any argument regarding the possibility of a 'third sex'.

In *W v W*, counsel for Mrs W and Charles J sought to position the facts in relation to the reasoning adopted in *Corbett*. However, in contrast to an emphasis on sex hormones so evident in the judgment of Ward LJ in *S-T (formerly J) v J*, the approach adopted in *W v W* finds consistency with Corbett elsewhere. While Charles J, in alluding to debate over issues of hormonal sex, expressed the view that 'in my judgment I should bear in mind the points made in *S-T v J* in respect of the medical advances that have been made',[47] it is clear that hormonal factors are de-emphasised and ultimately considered irrelevant in the determination of Mrs W's legal sex. Rather than seek to revisit Ormrod J's analysis of legal sex in the light of scientific advances, the court in *W v W* preferred to reason from the fact that Mrs W's morphology exceeded, and therefore could not be determined by, the *Corbett* test. That is to say, and in contrast to J, Mrs W's chromosomes, gonads and genitalia lacked 'congruence' in terms of a binary understanding of sex. It is precisely this fact that distinguishes, and of course links, *W v W* with *Corbett*.[48]

In order to understand fully the somewhat spurious reasoning of the court, it is necessary to specify precisely the nature of Mrs W's body. According to the medical evidence, which Charles J accepted, Mrs W had XY (male) chromosomes.[49] In relation to the other two factors in Ormrod J's triumvirate it proved 'extremely difficult to be conclusive',[50] given a lack of medical records and the fact of subsequent sex reassignment surgery. Nevertheless, on the basis of the medical evidence it was concluded that Mrs W's gonadal sex was likely to have been male and her genitalia 'ambiguous' at birth.[51] In other words, it was the genital factor that placed the facts of *W v W* and the body of Mrs W beyond Ormrod J's test. Moreover, it was genital 'ambiguity' that led to her characterisation as intersexed. Considerable attention was paid to Mrs W's genitalia in the judgment of Charles J. Thus we learn that her external genitalia prior to surgery were 'extremely small',[52] that her 'penis' was 'definitely abnormal',[53] and that she had 'no vaginal opening'.[54] Indeed, in giving evidence as to the pre-surgical state of Mrs W's genitalia, Dr Conway expressed the view that it was 'a close call'[55] as to whether the flap of skin that existed should be described as 'a micro penis or a mini clitoris'.[56] He

---

47 *W v W* (2000) *The Times*, 31 October (Transcript), p 7.
48 While it might be thought that an important distinction between the two decisions lies in the degree of financial hardship likely to be suffered upon annulment of marriage (Mrs W's marriage lasting three years in contrast to April Ashley's marriage of 14 days) the English courts possess considerable discretion with regard to distribution of property in the event of a nullity decree (Matrimonial Causes Act 1973, ss 23–25).
49 *Ibid*, p 5.
50 *Ibid*.
51 *Ibid*.
52 *Ibid*.
53 *Ibid*.
54 *Ibid*, p 6.
55 *Ibid*, p 5.
56 *Ibid*.

concluded that if he had to classify Mrs W's genitalia as either male or female he would locate them on the male side.[57] The medical evidence also indicated 'some spontaneous female breast development'[58] and tended toward a diagnosis of 'partial androgen insensitivity'.[59]

It is clear from the judgment and the medical evidence that Ormrod J's test could not resolve the question of Mrs W's sex at the moment of birth. However, Ormrod J had alluded to the possibility of 'incongruence' in formulating his triumvirate test. In a move that evinces a concern to limit departure from *Corbett* Charles J turned to the obiter, as well as subsequent extra-judicial, statements of Ormrod J. In his judgment, as already noted, Ormrod J expressed the view that in the event of 'incongruence', 'the greater weight would probably be given to the genital criteria than to the other two'[60] and later in an address to the Medico-Legal Society he elaborated the point:

> I was fortunate enough to find myself faced with a transsexual ... The difficulty would be acute in the cases of testicular feminization and testicular failure. In these cases the genital sex is unalterably female or approaching female in character yet the gonads and the chromosomes are male ... If the decision ever had to be made in a matrimonial situation I think that the genital sex would probably be decisive (Ormrod, 1972, p 86).[61]

Each of these passages and the interpretation placed on them by Charles J is significant. First, it seems clear from Ormrod J's reasoning that any warrant for characterising as female a person whose chromosomes and gonads are male is dependent on the presence of genitalia that are 'unalterably female or approaching female in character'.[62] The importance of these words seems to be underscored by Ormrod J's distinction between the 'abnormal' vagina of a (bio)logical woman and April Ashley's lack of a vagina pre-surgically.[63] Yet it is far from clear that Mrs W's genitalia, the pre-surgical state of which was traced to 'partial androgen insensitivity', met this test. Rather than requiring medical assessment of genitalia as female, Charles J preferred to reason from the 'fact' of 'ambiguity', expressing the view that 'to determine the sex of [Mrs W] for the purpose of marriage by reference to the fact that [her] ambiguous genital sex prior to the operation fell on the male side of the line' would be 'an incorrect application of [Ormrod J's] test'.[64]

---

57 *Ibid.*

58 *Ibid.*

59 *Ibid.*

60 *Corbett v Corbett* [1970] 2 All ER 33, p 54.

61 In his judgment Ormrod J explained that a person with testicular feminisation syndrome appears to be 'a more or less normal female with well formed breasts and female external genitalia but with an abnormally short vagina, ending blindly, no cervix and no uterus' while in a person with testicular failure syndrome 'the appearance of the external genitalia may be more doubtful, with a phallic organ which could be either a small penis or an enlarged clitoris and a short vagina' (p 47).

62 However, Ormrod J commented in his 1972 Address to the Medico-legal Society that 'these cases of testicular feminization or failure, I suspect, account for at least some of the cases where a marriage is annulled on the ground of physical incapacity on the part of the "woman"' (Ormrod, 1972, p 86). It is unclear therefore whether Ormrod J's reimagination of sex in these contexts overcomes potential problems associated with consummation.

63 *Corbett v Corbett* [1970] 2 All ER 33, p 50.

64 *W v W* (2000) *The Times*, 31 October (Transcript), p 17.

In other words, the 'ambiguity' of genitalia on this account trumps the fact that the medical evidence located Mrs W's genitalia on the male side. This coupling of 'ambiguous' genitalia with the female sex is, perhaps, an effect of the cultural and liberal legal construction of the female body as amorphous, unbounded, lacking in clear definition. On this reading Mrs W, despite being chromosomally male, gonadally male, and genitally more male than female, can be viewed as female. A feminist politics is clearly confronted by this idea that the category 'woman' should function to name persons whose genitalia are 'imperfectly' formed. This move is, however, entirely consistent with the tendency within liberal legalism to regard women's bodies 'as non-standard or aberrant (not-male) bodies' (Naffine, 1997, p 88).

The references to testicular feminisation and testicular failure by Ormrod J and the diagnosis of Mrs W as being 'partially androgen insensitive' are also of interest because they direct our attention to hormonal factors. The fact that Ormrod J envisaged the re-sexing of bodies in cases of testicular feminisation and testicular failure and that Charles J re-sexed the body of a partially androgen insensitive person in W v W, might be viewed as providing a link between these cases and the judgment of Ward LJ in S-T (formerly J) v J. That is to say, and while this argument is clearly problematic as already explained, hormonal factors may help to explain, in each instance, gender identity and the desire for sex reassignment surgery. Moreover, an emphasis on hormones perhaps serves to undermine the clarity of any distinction between intersex and transgender, a distinction, I might add, that proves important in grounding the reform moment in W v W.[65] On this account any distinction becomes an effect of the degree, nature, manifestation and temporality of the influence of sex hormones. However, it is precisely at the moment of recognising this potential continuity, and its concealment in W v W, that it becomes clear that the decisions in W v W and Corbett as to 'legal sex' have nothing, or little, to do with the development of the human body and its scientific verification. On the contrary, the concern over (bio)logic evident in these decisions proves to be a rhetorical device serving to mask what is really at stake in transgender jurisprudence, particularly in the marriage context. The argument here, which will be explored more fully in Chapter 5, is that transgender jurisprudence, particularly around issues of marriage, is largely explicable in terms of judicial anxiety over the 'naturalness' of heterosexual intercourse. For the difference between the bodies of Mrs W and April Ashley appears to lie in the relationship between sex reassignment surgery and 'nature'. That is to say, while Mrs W's surgery is viewed in terms of a process of 'naturalisation', predicated upon a problematic view of the intersexed body as nature's 'mistake', post-operative status in the case of April Ashley is viewed as a flight from 'nature'.

Thus while W v W represents a departure from the Corbett test it is entirely consistent with Ormrod J's underlying concerns. Moreover, both W v W and S-T (formerly J) v J, while representing moments of departure from Corbett, reproduce the (bio)logic and temporality of that landmark decision. If the sex is determined at birth narrative is to be departed from in the UK context it is perhaps toward Europe that we must cast our gaze.

---

65 It should be emphasised that the court's instantiation of an intersex/transgender dyad also belies the capacity of the term 'transgender', and a developing transgender politics, to include non-binary sex differences. For a discussion of trans terminology in the 1990s see, eg, Bolin, 1988; Feinberg, 1992, 1993; Bornstein, 1994; Nataf, 1996; Wilchins, 1997; Califia, 1997; Cromwell, 1999; Whittle and More, 1999.

In view of the consistently repressive approach of English courts to transgender sex claims there has been a steady stream of appeals to the European Court of Human Rights. While the European Court has so far upheld the legal interpretation of sex adopted by the English courts for the purposes of English law, the reasoning of the European Court and the increase in dissenting judgments perhaps signal a shift toward reform from without. These decisions of the European Court are of interest because of their treatment of (bio)logical arguments and their deployment of contradictory medical epistemologies.

3.4 BEYOND (BIO)LOGIC AND TOWARD SUBSTANTIVE REFORM

In a number of European cases appellants have argued unsuccessfully that the UK had violated Art 8 and/or Art 12 of the European Convention on Human Rights, which guarantee respectively the 'right to respect for private and family life' and the 'right to marry and to found a family, according to the national laws governing the exercise of this right'.[66] In furtherance of these contentions litigants have, not unproblematically, relied increasingly on the legitimising effects of (bio)logical science.[67] In particular litigants have pointed to contemporary scientific evidence concerning hormonal research which suggests that 'transsexuality [is] not merely a psychological disorder, but [has] a physiological basis in the structure of the brain'.[68] Indeed, Dr Swaab and other medical experts engaged in this type of research have concluded that 'transsexuals are right in their belief that their sex was wrongly judged at the moment of birth' (Gooren et al, 1995).[69] In consistently rejecting this medical research as determinative of sex, the European Court has placed emphasis on continuing uncertainty as to transsexual aetiology.[70] In the most recent case of Sheffield and Horsham v UK the majority of the European Court expressed the view that:

> ... the applicants have not shown that since the date of adoption of its Cossey judgment in 1990 there have been any findings in the area of medical science which settle conclusively the doubts concerning the causes of the condition of transsexualism. While Professor Gooren's research into the role of the brain in conditioning transsexualism may be seen as an important contribution to the debate in this area, it cannot be said that his views enjoy the universal support of the medico-scientific profession.[71]

---

66 Violation of Art 8 has typically involved State refusal to amend birth certificates to reflect post-surgical status. Violation of other Articles of the European Convention on Human Rights has been alleged by transgender litigants but Arts 8 and 12 feature most frequently and have received the greater attention of the European Court.

67 Thus this strategy is more discernable in P v S and Cornwall County Council [1996] 2 CMLR 247; X, Y and Z v UK (1997) 24 EHRR 143 and Sheffield and Horsham v UK (1998) 27 EHRR 163 than it is in the earlier European Court decisions of Rees v UK (1986) 9 EHRR 56 and Cossey v UK (1991) 13 EHRR 622. This strategy was also apparent in an unsuccessful attempt to get Alex Carlile's Private Members Bill (the Gender Identity (Registration and Civil Status) Bill 23) through the British parliament in 1996 (see the Hon Mr Alex Carlile, Parliamentary Debates of the House of Commons, 2 February 1996, pp 1282–83).

68 X,Y and Z v UK (1997) 24 EHRR 143, p 167.

69 See the Hon Mr Alex Carlile regarding the failed Gender Identity (Registration and Civil Status) Bill, Parliamentary Debates of the House of Commons, 2 February 1996, p 1283.

70 See X,Y and Z v UK (1997) 24 EHRR 143, pp 171–72; Sheffield and Horsham v UK (1998) 27 EHRR 163, p 192.

71 Ibid.

Indeed, and as the court noted, the UK government disputed the significance of the alleged 'medical developments'.[72] In particular, it drew attention to an article by Dr Breedlove (1995) in the prestigious scientific journal *Nature*, the same journal in which Professor Gooren's findings had been published, who commented that:

> ... the difficulties inherent in studying the diverse sexual behaviour of humans ensures that this will be far from the final word on the subject and that it could not be excluded that the differential brain sizes found in the study derived from external causes such as oestrogen treatment of transsexuals or development and social influences.[73]

In addition to this possibility that (bio)logical science may not deliver on its promise there is the very real danger that it will. That is to say, reliance on (bio)logic may serve to fuel a desire to eradicate 'deviant' people altogether. While the idea of fixed identity is seen by some as offering 'resistance to the social-engineering momentum apparently built into every one of the human sciences' (Sedgwick, 1990, p 42; see, also, Sedgwick, 1993) it is increasingly as Sedgwick notes:

> ... the conjecture that a particular trait is genetically or biologically based, *not* that it is 'only cultural', that seems to trigger an estrus of manipulative fantasy in the technological institutions of the culture. A relative depressiveness about the efficacy of social-engineering techniques, a high mania about biological control: the Cartesian bipolar psychosis that always underlay the nature/nurture debates has switched its polar assignments without surrendering a bit of its hold over the collective life (1993, p 43).

In any event, the need to resort to (bio)logic, with all its attendant problems, would appear to be less pressing in the European context given that the European Court's reluctance to rule against the UK has had less to do with causal questions than with the 'margin of appreciation' enjoyed by States. That is to say, the court has been concerned to ensure that the correct balance between community and individual interests has been struck.[74] In other words, the court has endeavoured to identify the boundary beyond which allowing States to regulate their own internal affairs would undermine fundamental human rights guaranteed by the European Convention. While this balancing exercise has so far favoured the UK, the trend has been in the opposite direction, especially in relation to Art 8.[75] In *Cossey v UK* Martens J, dissenting, contended that 'a margin of appreciation' is less 'a matter of right' than of 'judicial self-restraint'[76] and does not permit a Member State to avoid its obligations under Art 8 but is, rather, limited to a discretion as to the form and manner of meeting those obligations.[77] He insisted that for the purposes of Arts 8 and 12, where a (male-to-female) transgender woman has undergone 'long, dangerous and painful medical treatment to have his sexual organs, as far as is humanly feasible, adapted to the sex he is convinced be belongs' it is

---

72 *Ibid*, p 175.
73 *Ibid*, pp 175–76.
74 *Ibid*, p 193. See, also, *X, Y and Z v UK* (1997) 24 EHRR 143, pp 169–72.
75 That is to say, a 12–3 split in *Rees v UK* (1986) 9 EHRR 56 has been recast at 11–9 in the most recent case of *Sheffield and Horsham v UK* (1998) 27 EHRR 163. In relation to Art 12 the European Court has exhibited more marked reluctance to recognising violation. This is an issue to be explored in Chapter 5.
76 *Cossey v UK* (1991) 13 EHRR 622, p 652.
77 *Ibid*, p 653.

EU helping move away more so than national law!

right and proper for her new identity to be recognised not only by society but also in law and that 'refusal [of such recognition] can only be qualified as cruel'.[78]

This view, which has been taken up by a growing number of dissenting European court judges, de-emphasises (bio)logic. As Bernhardt, Thor, Vilhjalmsson, Spielmann, Palm, Wildhaber, Makarczyk and Voicu JJ explain, in their joint dissenting judgment in *Sheffield and Horsham v UK*, it is not a sufficient answer to say 'that the scientific community cannot agree on the explanation of the causes of transsexualism or that surgery cannot – and perhaps will never be able to – lead to a change in biological sex'.[79] It is less scientific, than medical and social, developments that prove important in this move toward reform. It is the fact that 'the medical profession has reached a consensus that "gender dysphoria" is an identifiable medical condition, in respect of which gender re-assignment surgery is ethically permissible and may be recommended for the purpose of improving the quality of life',[80] in conjunction with the fact that 'there has been a steadily increasing trend in Member States of the Council of Europe to adopt legislation which permits changes to be made to the birth certificate to recognise, in one form or other, the new sexual identity of the gender re-assigned transsexual'[81] that lies at the heart of a shift toward legal recognition. Indeed, the UK now appears to be the only Member State that permits sex reassignment surgery while refusing to give legal effect to its consequences.[82]

It should be borne in mind, however, that while the European Court may eventually re-sex transgender bodies for the purposes of English law, somatic boundaries to that imagined reform are clearly envisaged. That is to say, it seems extremely unlikely that reform will extend to pre- or non-surgical transgender people. In other words, while the legal script for sex might change the underlying text that anatomy determines destiny, one antithetical to feminism (de Beauvoir, 1953), is unlikely to do so (Stone, 1991, p 297). Thus, in his much-applauded dissenting judgment in *Cossey* Martens J, while contesting birth as the critical moment, and the relevance of chromosomes in determining sex, placed considerable emphasis upon gonadal (removal) and genital (reconstruction) change.[83] Indeed, in the context of marriage, and while irrelevant to contracting a valid marriage under English law,[84] Martens J made clear that physical reconstruction required the creation of a capacity for heterosexual intercourse, a capacity, he noted, that might be lacking in the case of a post-operative (female-to-male) transgender man, like Mr Rees,[85] due presumably to the difficulties associated with phalloplastic surgery (see, for example, Noe *et al*, 1978; Steiner, 1985, pp 338–39; Walters, Kennedy and Ross, 1986, p 151; Walters and Ross, 1986, pp 112–13). In the following chapter we will see that this concern over

---

78 *Ibid*, p 648.

79 *Sheffield and Horsham v UK* (1998) 27 EHRR 163, p 202.

80 *Ibid*, p 204, *per* Casadevall J partly dissenting.

81 *Ibid*, p 201, *per* Bernhardt, Thor Vilhjalmsson, Spielmann, Palm, Wildhaber, Makarczyk and Voicu JJ joint partly dissenting.

82 *Ibid*, p 206, *per* Van Dijk J dissenting.

83 *Cossey v UK* (1991) 13 EHRR 622, p 657.

84 While a marriage may be voidable under English law for non-consummation there is no question that an unconsummated marriage remains valid if neither party seeks a nullity decree (see Cretney and Mason, 1997, p 54). This point will receive elaboration in Chapter 5.

85 *Cossey v UK* (1991) 13 EHRR 622, p 657.

must be able to perform as a married couple!

heterosexual function has proved to be an important and persistent theme within reform jurisprudence.

While the European Court's approach to transgender sex claims has been influenced more by the 'margin of appreciation' enjoyed by Members States than (bio)logic, it should not be thought that concerns over transgender 'authenticity' have been absent. On the contrary, a number of European court judges willing to re-sex bodies have evinced precisely this concern. That is to say, while placing emphasis on present anatomical form, a number of reform judges have cast more than a glance toward the past. In this regard, the gender dysphoria medical perspective (Fisk, 1973; Laub and Gandy, 1973), upon which reformist approaches ostensibly draw, and which is apparently indifferent to any deep 'truth' residing in the body, becomes conflated in legal discourse with the contradictory *discovery story of transsexuality* (Benjamin, 1953, 1966; Stoller, 1968, 1975),[86] a conflation we shall see reproduced in Chapter 4. Thus, in *Rees v UK*, Bindschedler-Robert, Russo and Gersing JJ, in their dissenting judgment, took the view that the operations Mr Rees had undergone and the anguish and suffering that accompanied them were 'evidence of the genuineness and the depth of his urge at the earliest possible moment to take on a new sexual identity'.[87] In drawing attention to the 'genuineness' of Mr Rees' desire these dissenting judges sought only to endorse issuing him with 'an extract of the [birth] register showing only his sexual identity which could thus better guarantee respect for his private life',[88] for they were firmly of the view that there was 'no question of correcting the register by concealing the historical truth'.[89] It is precisely because their judgment is marked by a concern over 'authenticity', despite the fact that it divorces the possibility of a remedy under Art 8 from the question of legal sex itself, that serves to foreground the persistence of an interrogative mode of regulating transgender bodies within transgender jurisprudence irrespective of epistemological change within medicine.[90]

While the judgment seems implicitly to uncouple the possibility of a remedy under Art 8 from the need to undergo full sex reassignment surgery, given that Mark Rees had not undergone phalloplastic procedures (Rees, 1996, p 32), it is clear that the concern of Bindschedler-Robert, Russo and Gersing JJ extends to the 'depth' as well as the surface of Mark Rees' body. That is to say, there is a concern to know the 'truth' of Mark Rees' sexual/gender identity. In essence, reassurance is sought that Rees is a transsexual and it is found in his willingness to undergo painful and complex surgical procedures. In this way the 'authenticity' of transgender identity becomes tied to bodily change, and those

---

86   The phrase 'discovery story of transsexuality' is attributable to Dave King (1993, pp 45, 63).
87   *Rees v UK* (1986) 9 EHRR 56, p 69.
88   *Ibid.*
89   *Ibid*, p 70.
90   I am not suggesting here that the gender dysphoria perspective lacks this interrogatory element. However, a concern with transgender pasts, evident within this medical approach, is directed toward prognosis of future well-being. While the projection of the past into the future might be viewed in much the same terms as a concern that simply looks to the past, the difference lies in the fact that the 'discovery story of transsexuality' excavates the past in search of transgender 'being'. Conversely, the gender dysphoria model utilises (constructs) fragments of the past in order to predict post-surgical adjustment and well-being. While both approaches privilege a particular and highly circumscribed narrative account of transgender as we saw in Chapter 2, and while they both produce regimes of 'truth', it is only the discovery story that couples 'truth' with ontology.

unwilling and/or unable to undergo surgical procedures are depicted as 'inauthentic' and, therefore, undeserving. In other words, surgical intervention is important not only for the bodily changes it effects in the present but also for what it signifies about the past.

This concern over the 'authenticity' of transgender identity in European transgender jurisprudence, however, is not necessarily satiated by the fact of surgery, including full sex reassignment surgery. Indeed, in his powerful dissenting judgment, Martens J made it clear that legal recognition of post-operative transgender persons proceeded on the assumption not merely that surgery would promote patient 'well-being' but that 'doctors were satisfied' such persons were *'bona fide* transsexual[s]'.[91] This severance of well-being from a concern over a truth that resides in the past renders particularly explicit the conflation in legal discourse of medical epistemologies. For within the gender dysphoria perspective the past has no relevance beyond its capacity to predict future well-being. The fact that Martens draws attention to the 'authenticity' of Caroline Cossey's transsexuality 16 years after her sex reassignment surgery (Cossey, 1992) serves to illustrate that in law the past signifies more than the (im)probability of post-surgical well-being. Rather, post-surgical concerns over transgender pasts suggest anxiety over proximity to, and the re-sexing of, non-transsexual bodies. In short, and irrespective of the 'success' of surgical intervention, the conflation of transgender and homosexuality continues to structure legal thinking.

This concern over 'authenticity' is perhaps rendered most explicit in the dissenting judgments in *B v France*, a case in which the European Court held that Art 8 had been violated.[92] These judges raised a question mark over B's status as a transsexual. It was suggested that B was not a 'true'[93] or 'genuine transsexual',[94] that her present state was not the result of irreversible innate factors and that she had undertaken surgery 'lightly'[95] and 'voluntarily'.[96] Indeed, in emphasising that there are 'numerous types of transsexuals' Valticos J invoked a distinction between 'natural' and 'acquired' types, reminiscent of Krafft-Ebing's late 19th century sexological dissections of 'homosexuality' (1965).[97] In short, surgical intervention in B's case had not led to the disclosure of a 'hidden true sex'[98] but rather amounted to little more than dabbling in an unusual sexual

---

91   *Cossey v UK* (1991) 13 EHRR 622, p 645.

92   *B v France* (1993) 16 EHRR 1. It should be noted that the decision did not involve recognition of sex claims. Rather the European Court's departure from its previous decisions in *Rees v UK* (1986) 9 EHRR 56 and *Cossey UK* (1991) 13 EHRR 622 hinged on significant differences between French and English law with regard to civil registration, change of forename and use of identity documents. For a discussion of the case, see Millns (1992). Moreover, resort to (bio)logic, so characteristic of recent litigation brought before the European court, finds expression in *B v France* in counsel's introduction of new scientific findings suggesting that 'the ingestion of certain substances at a given stage of pregnancy, or during the first few days of life, determined transsexual behaviour, and that transsexualism might result from a chromosome anomaly' (p 28).

93   *B v France* (1993) 16 EHRR 1, p 37, *per* Pinheiro Farinha J and p 39, *per* Pettiti J.

94   *Ibid*, p 46, *per* Morenilla J. Indeed, in considering B to be an 'inauthentic' transsexual Morenilla J placed emphasis on the Court of Cassation's view that B 'continued to show the characteristics of a person of male sex' (p 46). This reference clearly confronts a feminist politics, suggesting as it does B's gender performance and/or morphology to be of relevance in the consideration of her claims.

95   *Ibid*, p 36, *per* Matscher J.

96   *Ibid*, p 43, *per* Valticos J.

97   *Ibid*. As explained in Chapter 2 Krafft-Ebing's typology of 'homosexualities' encompassed both homosexuality and transgender.

98   *Ibid*, p 5.

experiment (Millns, 1992, p 565) which had served only to 'trivial[ise] ... irreversible surgical operations'.[99] It is precisely because of these concerns that B's 'change of sex'[100] was viewed as 'incomplete'.[101] Of particular significance, the dissenting judges agreed with the Bordeaux Court of Appeal that amendment to civil status can only be made 'after a long period of observation and reflection prior to the operation stage, during which a qualified medical team can gradually reach the conclusion that the situation is genuine and irreversible'.[102] In relation to B, the Bordeaux court and the dissenting European Court judges placed emphasis upon the fact that 'no form of psychological or psychiatric treatment was tried',[103] that 'the first doctor who prescribed hormone treatment did not carry out any protracted observation'[104] and that 'no guarantee of such observation was given before the surgical operation carried out abroad'.[105]

It would seem that the French court's disqualification of the fact of B's surgery, and the sympathy for that view shared by the dissenting European Court judges, arises out of the fact that B bypassed pre-surgical medical regulation. Thus, the suggestion that B is not a 'true transsexual' is not based on any medical diagnostic evidence. Rather, it is attributable to the very absence of such evidence. It is clear in *B v France* that the 'truth' of B's gender identification must be established irrespective of sex reassignment surgery and that this can only occur through examination and observation by those with the requisite medical expertise. Moreover, it is significant that, given a focus upon the 'truth' of transsexuality in *B v France*, 'homosexuality' emerges in opposition to that 'truth'. Thus B's pre-operative sexual behaviour is described, and indeed in the majority judgment, as 'noticeably homosexual'.[106] This concern over transgender 'authenticity' and its relationship with anxiety over homosexuality, that is to say, the conflation of transgender with homosexual bodies, is a recurring theme with transgender jurisprudence, one which traverses judicial approach, thereby linking opposition to transgender sex claims with reformism. We will explore this legal coupling more fully in Chapters 5 and 6.

3.5 CONCLUSION

This chapter introduced the transgender/law relation through an analysis of (bio)logical approaches to the sex claims of transgender persons. That is to say, it considered, primarily English, case law that has approached sex through the language of (bio)logic. While the grounding of legal decision in (bio)logic suggests fidelity to science, thereby

---

99 *Ibid*, p 37, *per* Pinheiro Farinha J. In view of such judicial attitudes toward transgender people it is perhaps not surprising, albeit highly problematic, that B contended before the French Court of Cassation, and on an application for rectification of her civil status, that '[i]t is humanly necessary in order for people who are not medically perverted but are merely victims of aberrations of nature finally to be able to live in harmony with themselves and with the whole of society' (*ibid*, p 6).

100 *Ibid*, p 43, *per* Valticos J.

101 *Ibid*.

102 *Ibid*, p 6.

103 *Ibid*.

104 *Ibid*. It is perhaps also of relevance to note that 'exhaustive pre-operative evaluation and diagnosis was lacking in *Corbett*' (Smith, 1971, p 1007).

105 *Ibid*.

106 *Ibid*, p 5. As we shall see in Chapter 5 this is precisely the view of April Ashley's pre-operative sexual practice adopted by Ormrod J in *Corbett*.

masking law's construction of sex, it becomes clear from a close reading of the decisions that law draws selectively on medical science. Thus Ormrod J in the landmark decision of *Corbett v Corbett* ignored psychological and hormonal factors, reducing the concept of sex to a 'congruence' of chromosomal, gonadal and genital factors and at one temporal moment, birth. Of more significance, perhaps, is the fact that Ormrod J privileged the genital factor in the event of 'incongruence'. In doing so he rendered clear not only that law draws selectively on medical science but that resort to (bio)logic is no more than a rhetorical move. Moreover, while some decisions following in the wake of *Corbett* have revisited Ormrod J's triumvirate they have reproduced the notion that sex is to be comprehended in terms of (bio)logical factors at birth, and that in the event of 'incongruence' the genital factor is to prevail.

Accordingly, a so-called (bio)logical approach to sex determination not only serves to reproduce the view that there exists an immutable, binary and oppositional division of sex which precedes, and therefore provides an apparent foundation for, gender. It also serves to reveal how 'coherent' gender identity in law is linked to the state of genitalia, thereby demonstrating that this approach to bodies is founded on phallocentric and aesthetic concerns. While (bio)logical approaches differ from reform jurisprudence in terms of the temporal moment for assessing genitalia, as we will see in the following chapter, it is precisely in the genitocentric logic of law that an important continuity between approaches manifests itself. In Chapters 5 and 6 we will see how these approaches are further linked through an analysis and critique of the homophobia of law, which will emerge as a key subtext of genitocentric legal thinking. Further, while (bio)logical approaches to transgender bodies locate the 'truth' of sex in the past, the chapter revealed how the search for 'truth' within this approach is not confined to biology. That is to say, a concern over transgender 'authenticity', a concern that proves capable of conflating transgender with homosexuality, and one that will be explored in depth in Chapters 5 and 6, also emerged within decisions upholding this approach. In the following chapter we will consider reform jurisprudence that has moved 'beyond' (bio)logic. Despite obvious differences between (bio)logical approaches and reform jurisprudence, which the chapter will map, it is continuity rather than discontinuity that will be seen to characterise the relationship between approaches.

CHAPTER 4

REFORM JURISPRUDENCE

> It would be very simple to state that the gender of an individual has always been that which society says it to be. But to so state would be to disregard the enlightenment of our times.[1]

This chapter will consider reform jurisprudence that has sought to accommodate transgender people within the existing gender order and the disruptive effects thereby produced. That is to say, in contrast to approaches framed in terms of (bio)logic, which have consistently denied transgender sex claims, the chapter will interrogate the medico-legal conditions which make possible the moment of recognition. Reform jurisprudence recognising transgender sex claims has so far generated two narratives, both of which can be described as 'wrong body' stories. First, the courts have articulated a test of *psychological and anatomical harmony* whereby the undertaking of sex reassignment surgery proves to be an essential legal condition. This approach, which has been preferred within reform jurisprudence, has been adopted in some United States jurisdictions and followed in Australia and, more recently, New Zealand. While not abandoning concerns that lie in the past, the approach places emphasis on post-surgical reality. More recently, a second judicial test, one requiring *psychological, social and cultural harmony* has received judicial expression. However, articulation of this test has so far been confined to obiter statements of the New Zealand High Court, and Australian and Canadian social security decisions unanimously overturned on appeal. In mapping this jurisprudence attention will again be drawn to the relationship between law and medicine.

While reform jurisprudence can, when compared with a (bio)logical account, be characterised by a greater preparedness to say 'yes' to the sex claims of transgender persons, it is important to resist the temptation to simply characterise reform as 'progressive' in contrast to a repressive (bio)logical scenario (Foucault, 1981a). For in legal recognition of sex claims sex continues to function as 'a regulatory ideal' (Butler, 1993, p 22). Thus we will see that the re-sexing of bodies has served to reproduce, as well as disrupt, gender roles and sexual hierarchies. In other words, reform jurisprudence, like its (bio)logical counterpart, strives to contain the challenge that transgender represents to dominant social relations. Moreover, it may be that ossification of the gender order is being achieved more effectively through recognition of sex claims than it is through denial. In other words, it may be that the reproduction of gender polarity is better achieved through giving legal effect to the medical incorporation ('normalisation') of sexed 'ambiguity', thereby blocking off individuality and difference (Foucault, 1982, p 216), than it is through blanket opposition, a point which will become clearer once the conditions of, and the exclusions generated by, judicial recognition are detailed.

The reproduction of the gender order represents a key theme in the continuity that characterises the relationship between reform jurisprudence and (bio)logic. Thus we will see that although the concept of sex is reworked, it continues to provide a foundation for, and to make sense of, the gender order. Moreover, continuity between legal approaches

---

1   *Re Anonymous* 293 NYS 2d 834 (1968), p 836, *per* Pecora J.

that re-sex bodies and those that refuse to do so again becomes apparent once, instead of juxtaposing productive to repressive legal power (which seeks to 'prohibit or control socially constructed desires' (Sawicki, 1991, p 39) and therefore presupposes the prior operation of productive power), the exclusionary effects of the deployment of productive power are clearly delineated. I use the term 'exclusionary', which could also be described as 'repressive', though in a different sense, to capture precisely that which is not produced other than as the constitutive and abjected 'outside' of a legally produced subject, and it should therefore be understood as both internal to, and 'a modality of, productive power' (Butler, 1993, p 22).

It is important to consider the exclusionary effects of legal recognition of the sex claims of transgender persons for, as Butler points out: '... it is not enough to claim that human subjects are constructed, for the construction of the human is a differential operation that produces the more and the less "human", the inhuman, the humanly unthinkable' (1993, p 8), those 'who are neither named nor prohibited within the economy of the law' (Butler, 1991, p 20). The chapter will place particular emphasis on the exclusionary effects of legal recognition, effects that remain hidden if one merely seeks to ascertain in any given instance whether sex claims are denied or recognised. The characterisation of the relation between denial and recognition as oppositional, and therefore the dramatisation of discontinuity in approach so evident in reformist legal scholarship (see, for example, Green, 1970; van Niekerk, 1970; Smith, 1971; Note, 1971; Walton, 1974, 1984; David, 1975; Lupton, 1976; Finlay, 1980, 1989, 1995, 1996; Graham, 1980; Richardson, 1983; Pace, 1983; Samuels, 1984; Hurley, 1984; Dewar, 1985; Wilson, 1985; Taitz, 1986, 1987, 1988, 1992; Kirby, 1987; Bailey-Harris, 1989; Otlowski, 1990; Andrews, 1991; Bates, 1993; Johnson, 1994; Bourke, 1994), becomes problematised once the constitutive 'outside' of the legally recognised subject, where law locates possible alternative sexed, gendered and (homo)sexual subjectivities, is factored into our analysis. It is to the first of the two narratives that reform jurisprudence has so far produced that our attention now turns.

4.1 A JUDICIAL STORY OF 'PSYCHOLOGICAL AND ANATOMICAL HARMONY': THE PREFERRED VERSION

This approach has its common law origins in United States case law[2] but has received more sustained judicial endorsement in Australia and New Zealand.[3] The approach can be dated to the 1968 New York case of Re Anonymous.[4] In that case, which involved an application by a (male-to-female) transgender woman to have her birth certificate changed to reflect her post-operative status, Pecora J held the applicant to be female because her anatomy had been brought into conformity with her psychological sex.[5] For

---

2   However, in 1945 a Swiss court concluded that psychological sex was the criterion for determining the sex of the post-operative transsexual (Re Leber, Neuchatel Cantonal Court, 2 July 1945).

3   R v Harris and McGuiness (1989) 17 NSWLR 158; Secretary, Department of Social Security v HH [1991] 23 ALD 58; Secretary, Department of Social Security v SRA [1993] 118 ALR 467; M v M [1991] NZFLR 337; Attorney-General v Otahuhu Family Court [1995] 1 NZLR 603.

4   Re Anonymous 293 NYS 2d 834 (1968).

5   Ibid, p 838.

Pecora J the difficulty of the case lay not in the post-operative transgender body but in the application of 'static rules of law to situations ... which perhaps merit new rules and/or progressive legislation'.[6] Accordingly, he rejected a (bio)logical analysis. In response to the suggestion that 'male-to-female transsexuals are still chromosomally males while ostensibly females',[7] Pecora J expressed the view that the question of a person's identity should not be limited by 'the results of mere histological section or biochemical analysis'.[8] Rather, and in refusing to 'sweep the problem under the proverbial rug',[9] Pecora J insisted that 'once surgical intervention has taken place, whereby ... anatomical sex is made to conform with ... psychological sex' the position is 'identical to that of the pseudo-hermaphrodite who has been surgically repaired'.[10]

This refusal to instantiate a transgender/intersex dyad for the purposes of determining sex, a distinction that would, as already discussed, become central to English judicial thinking as evidenced by *Corbett* and *W v W*, highlights that at the heart of this reform approach lies a concern to acknowledge post-surgical reality. This emphasis on post-surgical reality is also evident in Pecora J's treatment of a concern over 'fraud'. In rejecting the view that legal recognition of post-surgical reality is 'outweighed by the public interest for protection against fraud',[11] he expressed the view that 'the probability of so-called fraud, if any, exists to a much greater extent when the birth certificate is permitted ... to classify this individual as a "male"'.[12] It is far less clear whether anxiety over 'fraud' is assuaged in relation to the pre-operative body, given that Pecora's judgment, while heralding a temporal shift away from (bio)logic at birth, distinguishes between post- and pre-operative transgender bodies: '... [a]bsent surgical intervention, there is no question that his social sex must conform with his anatomical sex, his mental attitude notwithstanding.'[13] Moreover, we shall see, particularly in Chapters 5 and 6, that concerns over 'fraud' have persisted in relation to the pre-surgical body.

Further, the requirement of surgery appears to be based on more than its 'harmonising' effects. Thus the judgment appears to understand 'harmony' as dependent on post-operative vaginal capacity for heterosexual intercourse. While legal concern over the adequacy of the vagina would seem to be explicable only in terms of phallocentric and performativist assumptions about the female body, thereby demonstrating one of the ways in which transgender jurisprudence confronts a feminist politics, it is especially difficult to account for this requirement in a case concerning an application to change a birth certificate. The court also paid attention to the fact that after surgery the petitioner

What has it got to do with anything?

---

6   *Ibid*, p 836.
7   *Ibid*, p 838. This is a reference to a 1965 report by the New York Academy of Medicine's Public Health Committee titled '*Change of Sex on Birth Certificates for Transsexuals*', one relied on by Sarafite J in *Anonymous v Weiner* 270 NYS 2d 319 (1966) and Helman J in *Hartin v Director of the Bureau of Records and Statistics, Department of Health of the City of New York* 347 NYS 2d 515 (1973).
8   *Ibid*.
9   *Ibid*, p 836.
10   *Ibid*, p 837.
11   *Ibid*, p 838.
12   *Ibid*.
13   *Ibid*, p 837.

Many couples don't have children?

could no longer function as a male for <u>sexual or procreative purposes</u>.[14] However, because such concerns are assuaged by the fact of sex reassignment surgery the concern over post-operative heterosexual functioning has, as we shall see, assumed <u>greater</u> <u>prominence in judicial discourse</u>. Accordingly, for the purposes of this chapter it is this requirement which will be emphasised. However, as we shall see in Chapter 6, judicial emphasis on the heterosexual capacity of the post-operative transgender body has <u>served</u> <u>to mask or blur the relationship</u> between the requirement for sex reassignment <u>surgery</u> and the homophobia of law.

The *psychological and anatomical harmony* test formulated by Pecora J in *Re Anonymous* appears to have been endorsed implicitly, and sometimes explicitly, in much academic legal writing. Thus, and in a passage that has <u>proved influential</u> within reform jurisprudence,[15] Smith expressed the view that:

> ... factors other than a person's psychological sex <u>cannot be ignored</u>. In fact, they must be held to be <u>controlling if</u> overwhelmingly contrary to the assumed sex role. Thus, a pre-perative transsexual would have to be <u>classified according</u> to his anatomical sex. Society would consider a fully anatomical male to be male <u>regardless of</u> a convincing feminine appearance or the individual's inner beliefs (1971, p 969).

More recently, it has been contended that 'it is <u>hard to see</u> an earlier point at which legal sex reassignment could take place' (Dewar, 1985, p 63) <u>given 'the need for "objective"</u> evidence of a subjective state of mind, and the need for a clear-cut point at which the legal sex-change takes place' (Dewar, 1985, p 62).

The test was consolidated in *MT v JT*, a Superior Court of New Jersey decision that has served as something of a rallying point for departure from *Corbett*.[16] Here Handler, Carton and Crahay JJ held a post-operative (male-to-female) transgender woman to be female for the <u>purposes of marriage</u>.[17] In doing so they <u>rejected Ormrod J's</u> view in Corbett that sex and gender were <u>disparate phenomena</u>, a view reiterated in *MT v JT* by a certain Dr T.[18] Rather, relying on the preponderance of the medical evidence, and the fact that 'the evidence before this court teaches that there are several criteria or standards which may be <u>relevant in determining the sex of an individual</u>',[19] the court considered that there could be <u>movement between the categories of sex and gender</u>. However, and while viewing a chromosomal test as '<u>inhumane</u>'[20] and recognising that '[legal] recognition will <u>promote the individual's quest for inner peace</u> and personal happiness',[21] the court <u>limited movement to those persons whose quest led through sex</u> <u>reassignment surgery to the establishment of *psychological and anatomical harmony*.</u>

---

14 *Ibid*, p 836. This concern over procreation serves to highlight a particularly disturbing theme within transgender jurisprudence. It would seem that legal recognition, premised as it is on sex reassignment surgery, effectively requires sterilisation of transgender persons. For a discussion of this theme, see Whittle (1998).

15 See, eg, *Secretary, Department of Social Security v HH* [1991] 13 AAR 314, p 320; *Secretary, Department of Social Security v SRA* [1993] 118 ALR 467, p 495.

16 *MT v JT* 355 A 2d 204 (1976).

17 *Ibid*, p 210. Handler J delivered the judgment of the court.

18 *Ibid*, p 207.

19 *Ibid*, p 208.

20 *Ibid*, p 210.

21 *Ibid*.

Accordingly, the pre-operative transgender body continued to be conceived of only in terms of gender. Thus reform is, as in *Re Anonymous*, directed toward post-surgical 'reality'. While 'the entire area of transsexualism is repugnant to the nature of many persons within our society' the court insisted that 'this should not govern the legal acceptance of a fact'.[22] Thus, and in contrast to approaches premised on (bio)logic, it would seem that in the face of post-surgical 'facts' reform jurisprudence proves able to forget (amnesia) and forgive (amnesty) the 'disharmony' of the past (Fraser, 1995, p 86). However, facticity proved to be based on more than the 'mere' undertaking of sex reassignment surgery. Thus, as in *Re Anonymous*, while reference was made to the fact that MT could no longer 'function as a male sexually either for purposes of recreation or procreation',[23] particular emphasis was placed on post-operative capacity:

> Implicit in the reasoning underpinning our determination is the tacit but valid assumption of the lower court and the experts upon whom reliance was placed that for purposes of marriage under the circumstances of this case, it is the [post-operative] sexual capacity of the individual which must be scrutinized.[24]

As in *Re Anonymous* the capacity to be vaginally penetrated assumes particular significance in enabling law to read the male-to-female transgender body as female. Indeed, this type of analysis had, in the marriage context, received prior endorsement within reformist legal scholarship. Thus it had been contended that '[t]he standard that Judge Ormrod suggested, absent the element of biological determinism, is sound. The marriage should be valid if the transsexual is found capable of fulfilling the essential marriage role of the sex he or she has assumed' (Smith, 1971, p 1007), a role which requires 'the ability to engage in sexual intercourse' (p 1008). While this view might be thought to be dated, it has been reproduced more recently and in almost identical terms within legal scholarship as noted by Muller (1994, p 109). Thus Otlowski has contended that 'there are strong arguments in favour of giving legal recognition to a surgically reassigned transsexual for the purposes of marriage' provided that 'the individuals can fulfil the role of the sex in which they have been assigned' (1990, p 72).

While such a requirement serves to highlight the phallocentricism of law, it might be thought that such an analysis is necessitated in *MT v JT* by the relevance of consummation to marriage law in New Jersey. Certainly, this is the conclusion drawn by Storrow (1997, p 291). However, while New Jersey law makes clear that a marriage is voidable where '[t]he parties, or either of them, were at the time of marriage physically and incurably impotent',[25] a provision which replicates the position at common law, this is subject to the proviso that 'the party making the application shall have been ignorant of such impotency or incapability at the time of the marriage, and has not subsequently ratified the marriage'.[26] The facts of *MT v JT* reveal that the husband was aware of MT's transgender status, 'there being no fraud' on her part. Accordingly, a finding that MT was incapable of consummating a marriage could not have rendered it void from the

---

22   *Ibid.*
23   *Ibid*, p 206.
24   *Ibid*, p 209.
25   See STAT ANN 1987 (NJ), S 2A:34-1.
26   *Ibid.*

beginning.[27] Only a finding that she was 'male' could have led to that eventuality. In other words, legal concerns over MT's sexual capacity have no prior relevance to the determination of her sex for marriage purposes. Rather, a requirement of sexual capacity for the purpose of re-sexing bodies is one generated within reform jurisprudence.

In pursuing this concern the court explored MT's genital topography in some detail, noting she had 'a vagina and labia which were adequate for sexual intercourse and could function as any female vagina, that is, for traditional penile/vaginal intercourse'.[28] There is no reference in the judgment or the medical evidence as to any sexual pleasure that MT might derive from her vagina, an omission consistent with medico-legal discourse on marital sex more generally (Collier, 1995, p 159).[29] Rather, law seeks reassurance that MT's vagina can function as a site of heterosexual male pleasure. Indeed, the following year, in the case of *Richards v United States Tennis Association*,[30] Ascione J, in expressing the view that transsexuals 'desire the removal of [their sexual] apparatus and further surgical assistance in order that they may enter into normal heterosexual relationships',[31] made clear that vaginal capacity is both the aim of, and the outcome which confers meaning upon, sex reassignment surgery. In accounting for this feature of law reform it should be recognised that it is the centrality of genitalia and the capacity for heterosexual intercourse in the legal reformulation of sex which ensures that a dichotomous notion of gender is reproduced. While the (bio)logical and temporal specificities of *Corbett* are abandoned the commonsensical and genitocentric notion that women are persons with functional vaginas and men are persons with functional penises is reaffirmed. In this way sex, albeit in refashioned form, continues to provide a foundation for, and to make sense of, the social system of gender. In other words, only one body per gendered subject is 'right' (Stone, 1991, p 297) and the 'rightness' of that body is to be understood in relation to heterosexual function. In this regard, the view that anatomy determines destiny is taken to somatic limits.

However, while post-operative capacity for sexual intercourse is a crucial requirement within reform jurisprudence it is important not to reduce legal analysis to this moment. Thus the view of one critical scholar that 'transgender cases ... illustrate that legal marriage depends on conduct (penis/vagina/penetration) rather than heterosexual status' and that the ability of transgender persons to marry rests on 'their physical ability to perform one particular sex-act: PVP' (Robertson, 1998, p 1400) needs to be treated with some caution. Thus, while professing to 'do no more than give legal effect to a *fait accompli* based upon medical judgment and action which are irreversible',[32] the court

---

27 It would seem therefore that New Jersey laws dealing with consummation are directed more toward the question of 'fraud' or 'deceit' than to incapacity, in and of itself, given that absence of the former trumps the presence of the latter in the determination of whether a marriage contract is, on the application of either/both of the parties, to be treated as void from the beginning. This issue of interpersonal 'fraud' is one that will be pursued in Chapters 5 and 6 where it will be seen to be inextricably tied to legal anxiety over perceived proximity to the homosexual body.

28 *MT v JT* 355 A 2d 204 (1976), p 206.

29 Indeed, a concern with one's own sexual pleasure is not typically read as a sign of 'authentic' transgender identity within the medical arena (Benjamin, 1966, pp 13–14, 54; Money and Primrose, 1969, pp 121–22; Stoller, 1973).

30 *Richards v United States Tennis Association* 400 NYS 2d 267 (1977).

31 *Ibid*, p 271. Drawing on the evidence of Dr Money the court noted that '[f]or all intents and purposes, Dr Richards functions as a woman' (p 271).

32 *MT v JT* 355 Ad 204 (1976), p 210.

in *MT v JT* was concerned to explore pre-surgical 'facts'. In this regard, the court is seen to deploy an interrogative mode of regulating MT's body, one that draws on medicine's *discovery story of transsexuality* (King, 1993, pp 45, 63). Accordingly, a view of the decision as a 'departure' from *Corbett* needs to be tempered by recognition that it is structured through reference to the past. As the court explained:

> It is the opinion of the court that if the psychological choice of a person is medically sound, *not a mere whim*, and irreversible sex reassignment surgery has been performed, society has no right to prohibit the transsexual from leading a normal life.[33]

The surgery performed on MT apparently was 'medically sound', rather than being undertaken on a 'mere whim', as she was considered to be, as the court pointed out, a 'genuine transsexual'.[34] Indeed, evidence given by Dr Ihlenfeld and MT's own autobiographical account mapped in many respects Stoller's profile of the classic transsexual (1968, p 251; 1973; 1975, pp 49, 139–40). Thus we learn, and the court accepted, that 'as a youngster [MT] did not participate in sports and at an early age became very interested in boys. At the age of 14 she began dressing in a feminine manner and later began dating men. She had no real adjustment to make because throughout her life she had always felt that she was a female'.[35] What is significant here is that legal recognition of MT as female depended on more than the 'fact' of her post-surgical status and newly acquired capacity for heterosexual intercourse. The court was concerned to know that MT's psychological sex matched her present anatomical form and required assurance on this point from medical experts. In this regard, the court not only pursues a logic of identity but refuses to divorce that logic from a 'truth' that resides in the past. That is to say, the court exhibits reluctance to comprehend the re-sexing of bodies solely in relation to present surgical facts. While those facts are, in and of themselves, crucial to the prospects for legal recognition, and while they function as a sign offering some confirmation of transgender 'authenticity', the court looks for further evidence of 'authenticity' and finds it in pre-surgical autobiography.

Moreover, the concern over 'authenticity' in *MT v JT* bears a clear relation to heterosexual desire. This is rendered explicit in the court's insistence that '[s]exual capacity or sexuality' which 'must be scrutinized' requires 'the coalescence of both the physical ability and the psychological and emotional orientation to engage in sexual intercourse as either male or female'.[36] Thus the creation of a 'functional' vagina proves, in and of itself, to be insufficient for the purposes of legal recognition of sex claims. For law also desires to know MT's desire, to know that it is heterosexual, and to be assured through that knowledge as to the 'authenticity' of her transgender status. Moreover, this approach to law reform, in serving to problematise sex reassignment surgery as a sufficient condition for legal recognition, has the effect of consolidating the dependency of many transgender people on the psychiatric community, a community that has, as we saw in Chapter 2, reduced transgender ontology to mental disorder (King, 1993, p 64). This will to know the 'truth' about transgender pasts proves, as we will see, to be a

---

33 *Ibid*, p 209 (my emphasis).
34 *Ibid*.
35 *Ibid*, p 204.
36 *Ibid*, p 209.

persistent feature of reform jurisprudence, thereby linking reform to (bio)logical approaches considered in Chapter 3. It might be wondered why, in an era of gender dysphoria, where medical intervention is directed toward post-surgical well-being rather than the realisation of some deep 'truth' residing in transgender bodies, that the *discovery story of transsexuality* continues to have such purchase in legal discourses of reform. In Chapters 5 and 6 it will be contended that this interrogation of transgender pasts is driven, at least in part, by legal anxiety over the perceived proximity of transgender to the homosexual body.

Though in a quite different context, the decision of Ascione J in *Richards v United States Tennis Association* provided further support for a reform approach that gives legal effect to post-surgical 'reality'. In this case Renee Richards, formerly Richard Raskind, an accomplished male tennis player, claimed a violation of the New York State Human Rights Law on the basis that she was prevented from qualifying and/or participating in the United States Tennis Open as a woman since the USTA had instituted a chromosomal test for women players in 1976 after, and in consequence of, a former application to participate by Richards herself. In finding that a requirement that Richards pass a chromosomal test in order to be eligible to participate in the US Open to be 'grossly unfair, discriminatory and inequitable, and violative of her rights under the Human Rights Law of this State',[37] Ascione J insisted that 'the only justification for using a [chromosomal] test in athletic competition is to prevent fraud, that is, men masquerading as women, competing as women. This court rejects any such suggestion as applied to the plaintiff ... When an individual ... finds it necessary for his own mental sanity to undergo a sex reassignment, the unfounded fears and misconceptions of defendants must give way to the overwhelming medical evidence that this person is now female'.[38]

While this analysis perhaps reproduces the coupling of the pre-operative body with 'fraud', it is clear that legal sex is constructed as an effect of present bodily form. Indeed, in *Richards* an emphasis on the present is particularly noticeable. For while Renee Richards propounded the *'woman trapped inside the body of a man'* narrative[39] she did not, unlike MT, fit classic understandings of transsexuality. As a person who had undertaken sex reassignment surgery at 41 years of age, after a period of marriage and having produced offspring as a man, she clearly fell outside Stoller's profile (1968, p 251; 1973; 1975, pp 49, 139–40). In this regard, Ascione J's judgment de-emphasises 'truth' that resides in the past in favour of present *'psychological and anatomical harmony'*. While this may be partly attributable to a displacement of the *discovery story of transsexuality* by the medical model of gender dysphoria by the time of the decision, it is perhaps also due to the way that the facts of the case serve to intensify a concern over human rights. That is to say, the USTA's decision to institute a chromosomal test was a direct result of Richards' application to the 1976 United States Open. While the USTA contended that 'the question at issue transcends the factual background or medical history of one applicant',[40] Ascione J concluded that the effect, as well as the design, was to specifically target Richards: '... [i]t seems clear that [the] defendants knowingly instituted this test for the sole purpose of

---

37 *Richards v United States Tennis Association* 400 NYS 2d 267 (1977), p 272. See Human Rights Law Exec (NY), ss 290 and 297, subd 9.
38 *Ibid.*
39 *Ibid*, p 268.
40 *Ibid*, p 269.

preventing [the] plaintiff from participating in the tournament ... This court is totally convinced that there are very few biological males, who are accomplished tennis players, who are either preoperative or postoperative transsexuals.'[41]

However, while representing something of a departure from judicial preoccupation with transgender 'authenticity', the decision does not abandon concern over the past. Rather, a concern with the past presents itself through resort to (bio)logic. Thus, and guided by a concern over 'fairness' in the sporting context, Ascione J, drawing on medical evidence, noted that Renee Richards had 'no unfair advantage when competing against other women' as '[h]er muscle development, weight, height and physique fit within the female norm'.[42] In this regard, legal recognition of Richards as female within the sporting arena is premised on more than *psychological and anatomical harmony* in the present. Rather, it proves contingent on somatic requirements, the 'origins' of which reside in the past, that some post-operative transgender persons might be unable to meet. Moreover, it is significant that consideration of sex claims in the context of sport produces a more complex somatic analysis of sex. In Chapter 6 we will see that sport has functioned to equate sex with biology, thereby serving to 'naturalise' sexed difference even, and precisely, when transgender sex claims have been recognised for marriage purposes. In this regard, the *Richards* decision represents something of an anomaly within transgender jurisprudence.

While a reformist approach to transgender sex claims originated in the United States, and while New Jersey is the first common law jurisdiction in the world to recognise sex claims for marriage purposes, it should not be thought that the *psychological and anatomical harmony* test enjoys wide judicial support in the United States (Hurley, 1984, p 653; Storrow, 1997, p 291).[43] On the contrary, United States transgender jurisprudence, especially since the 1970s, and particularly with regard to marriage,[44] has, if anything, tended to endorse the (bio)logical approach traceable to *Corbett*. Indeed, Storrow considers *MT v JT* to be 'an anomaly among American jurisdictions' (1997, p 291).[45] It is, perhaps, curious that transgender sex claims have not met with greater success judicially in the United States, the paradigm 'culture of rights'. While the factors that account for this deficit in law reform are, no doubt, complex and varied, it may be that they are inflected through the coupling of transgender with homosexuality, which is a consistent theme of transgender jurisprudence. This legal and cultural conflation is perhaps of special significance in the United States given the highly politicised atmosphere, and contemporary backlash, that surrounds gay and lesbian rights claims (Herman, 1994, 1997), a backlash which is, perhaps, most evident in the passing of the Defense of

---

41 *Ibid*, p 272.

42 *Ibid*, p 271.

43 Indeed, Donaldson J expressed the view that *MT v JT* represented a 'complete departure from all reason and logic' adding that '[p]erhaps the ultimate indignity that might be inflicted was the award of alimony to a former "wife", a person born male but denominated a transsexual having undergone surgical alteration' (*Olsen v Olsen* 557 P 2d 604 (1976), p 610).

44 See *Re Ladrach* 32 Ohio Misc 2d 6 (1987); *Littleton v Prange* [1999] 288th Judicial District Court, Bexar County, Texas (www.4thcoa.courts.state.tx.us/opinions/9900010.htm).

45 Recently, however, two United States decisions (*Vecchione v Vecchione* No 95D003769 (Orange County, Calif, filed 23 April 1996); *Re the Estate of Marshall G Gardiner* Kan App LEXIS 376 (2001)) have recognised sex claims for marriage purposes. We will consider these decisions in Chapter 5 in the context of reform jurisprudence pertaining to marriage.

Marriage Act by Congress in 1996 in response to recognition of same-sex marriages in Hawaii.[46] Reform jurisprudence has, however, received more sustained judicial support from the Australian and New Zealand judiciary.

In the Australian context, the reception of the legal reasoning advocated in *MT v JT* occurred in the case of *R v Harris and McGuiness*.[47] In this case the New South Wales Court of Criminal Appeals was required to consider whether a (male-to-female) transgender woman was a male person within the meaning of (the now repealed) s 81A of the Crimes Act (NSW) 1900. By virtue of s 81A it was an offence for 'a male person, whether in public or private, to procure or attempt to procure the commission by any male person of any act of indecency with another male person'. At trial Lee Harris, a post-operative (male-to-female) transgender woman,[48] and Phillis McGuiness, a pre-operative (male-to-female) transgender woman who proposed to undergo surgery, had been convicted of soliciting an undercover Vice Squad officer. In the case of Lee Harris, she had allegedly offered to perform oral intercourse. The majority of the appeal court (Street CJ, Mathews J), following the legal reasoning adopted in *Re Anonymous* and *MT v JT*, held that a male-to-female transsexual who has undergone full sex reassignment surgery to align her genital features with her psychological sex is to be regarded as a female for the purposes of the criminal law.[49] Accordingly, the court did not confer general legal recognition and, in fact, specifically drew a distinction between criminal law and the issue of marriage, a theme to be explored in Chapter 5. The majority decision led to the conclusion that Lee Harris fell outside the ambit of the legislation, while the conviction of Phillis McGuiness was upheld. In enunciating the narrative of *psychological and anatomical harmony* as the test for determining sex for the purposes of the criminal law, a departure from the *Corbett* test, which had been applied in the context of sexual offences in the English decision of *R v Tan*,[50] was required.

In rejecting *Corbett*, Mathews J aligned herself with the view expressed by an academic legal commentator that '[r]efusal to reclassify the sex of a postoperative transsexual seems inconsistent with the principles of a society which expresses concern for the privacy and dignity of its citizens' (Note, 1971, p 253).[51] In a similar vein, and in emphasising the importance of post-operative reality to their respective analyses, Street CJ and Mathews J quoted the eminent Australian jurist, and at the time of the decision justice of the Australian High Court, Sir Ronald Wilson, who made the following comments in a paper delivered to the Australian Academy of Forensic Sciences:

> Medicine has outstripped the law. April Ashley represented as successful a change of sex as can be imagined yet any legal significance attaching to her post-surgery condition was denied. No doubt the court [in *Corbett*] was bound to come to the decision that it did but nevertheless the decision signals the need for a greater flexibility in the law to enable it to

---

46 *Baehr v Lewin* 852 P 2d 44 (1993).

47 *R v Harris and McGuiness* (1989) 17 NSWLR 158.

48 It appears that Lee Harris was also T in the earlier New Zealand case *Re T* [1975] 2 NZLR 449, *per* Mathews J, p 175.

49 *Ibid*, p 193.

50 *R v Tan* [1983] QB 1053.

51 *R v Harris and McGuiness* (1989) 17 NSWLR 158, p 190.

come to grips with *current reality* freed from bondage to displaced historical circumstances.[52]

This assessment is not only endorsed by the majority judges in *R v Harris and McGuiness* but is afforded greater weight due to the fact that the case fell within the purview of criminal law, where a determination that Lee Harris was male would provoke criminal sanctions. Thus Street CJ emphasised that 'there is a public issue at stake which extends more widely than the issues arising out of the special personal relationship between the two people who had gone through a ceremony of marriage in *Corbett*'.[53] Moreover, he cast doubt as to whether the state had a legitimate interest in 'probing behind the physical attributes of an individual, who is to all intents and purposes a woman, with a view to having her clinically classified as a male person for the purposes of fixing her with guilt'.[54] Ultimately, however, as in the United States case law already considered, it is the need 'to come to grips with [the] current reality' of a surgically altered body that serves to ground the decision. As Mathews J explained:

> Criminal law is concerned with the regulation of behaviour. It is the relevant circumstances at the time of the behaviour to which we must have regard. And I cannot see that the state of a person's chromosomes can or should be a relevant circumstance in the determination of his or her criminal liability. It is equally unrealistic, in my view, to treat as relevant the fact that the person has acquired his or her external attributes as a result of operative procedure. After all, sexual offences – with which we are particularly concerned here – frequently involve the use of the external genitalia. How can the law sensibly ignore the state of those genitalia at the time of the alleged offence, simply because they were artificially created or were not the same at birth?[55]

In echoing the view that chromosomes should be considered irrelevant to determining criminal liability, Street CJ contended that 'Mr Bumble would give chromosomes short shrift'.[56] The calling forth of this particular Dickensian character, whereby sex is translated into lay sense, serves to add emphasise to the court's matter-of-fact or pragmatic approach to post-operative transgender bodies. That is to say, if the law thinks sex is chromosomes then 'the law is an ass' (Dickens, 1892). However, and while Bailey-Harris stated that the court's approach 'is to be applauded in the interests of social justice' (1989, p 360), Street CJ, Mathews J and apparently the proverbial Mr Bumble were not prepared to give genitalia short shrift in the legal (re)construction of sex. In other words, while the court was prepared to abandon the *Corbett* test it shared the English court's preoccupation with genital insignia apparent in Ormrod J's analysis of sex 'incongruence'. That is to say, genitalia emerge, once again, as a limit to reform. It would seem that humanitarian and libertarian concerns expressed by the majority judges arise only in relation to prosecutions of persons falling on one side of the pre/post-operative dyad.

Moreover, it is important to emphasise that legal recognition of Lee Harris as female proved dependent upon more than genital surgery. While Mathews J pointed out that

---

52 *Ibid*, p 160, *per* Street CJ and p 190, *per* Mathews J (my emphasis). See Wilson, 1985. See, also, Kirby, 1987.
53 *Ibid*, p 161.
54 *Ibid*.
55 *Ibid*, p 192.
56 *Ibid*, p 161.

surgery had deprived Lee Harris of 'the capacity to procreate or to have normal heterosexual intercourse in her original sex',[57] and while the prospect of having a sexually/procreatively functional male classified as female concerned the court, these forms of irrevocable loss do not ground the decision. Rather, it is the capacity for post-operative heterosexual intercourse which proves crucial. In this regard, the legal reasoning in Re Anonymous and MT v JT is replicated. Thus while Mathews J refused to treat as significant Lee Harris' 'temporary inability to have intercourse as a female'[58] caused by a closing-up of her vagina post-surgically, it would seem that a permanent inability to do so would serve to problematise the characterisation of post-operative transgender people as psychologically and anatomically harmonious. It should be borne in mind that the type of operation for transgender people intent on surgery, as made clear by Carruthers J in his dissenting judgment, 'is not uniformly a reassignment procedure and may amount to little more than full castration'.[59] It would seem that (male-to-female) transgender women undergoing this latter type of procedure would fall outside the scope of the decision as it would fail to produce a capacity for heterosexual intercourse as a female. Accordingly, and while criticising Ormrod J for his reference to 'the essential role of a woman in marriage',[60] Mathews J reproduces in law precisely this 'essential role' while simultaneously extending it beyond the confines of marriage. It is, perhaps, curious that capacity for heterosexual intercourse should have any bearing upon determining sex for the purposes of the criminal law. This is especially so given the facts of, and the charges brought, in R v Harris and McGuiness. That is to say, it is difficult to see the relevance of vaginal capacity in relation to the practice of fellatio. Indeed, such a requirement would be curious even in the context of marriage in Australia, given that since the Family Law Act 1975 (Cth) consummation of marriage has been irrelevant to nullity proceedings (Dickey, 1997, pp 140–41).[61]

However, it should not be thought that legal regulation of transgender people is exhausted in R v Harris and McGuiness by insistence on sex reassignment surgery and medical production of post-surgical vaginal capacity. Rather, as in MT v JT, the court proved concerned to interrogate the past for signs of transgender 'authenticity'. In doing so the court satisfied itself regarding the bona fides of Lee Harris, noting that '[f]or as long as she remembers, [Lee Harris] has felt like a woman trapped in a man's body'.[62] Nevertheless, a concern over 'fraud' is apparent. Thus the submission that the court should treat (bio)logical factors as entirely secondary to psychological ones, made of course with the appellant Phillis McGuiness in mind, provoked the following response from Mathews J: '... it would be vulnerable to abuse by people who were not true transsexuals at all. To this extent it could lead to a trivialisation of the difficulties genuinely faced by people with gender identification disharmony.'[63] While this passage interweaves and confuses two different medical knowledges, failing to recognise that gender dysphoria syndrome incorporates persons who do not conform to the picture of

57 Ibid, p 192.
58 Ibid, p 193.
59 Ibid, p 168, per Carruthers J.
60 Ibid, p 189.
61 The Family Law Act 1975 (Cth), s 23B(1). See Najjarin v Houlayce [1991] 104 FLR 403, pp 404–05.
62 Ibid, p 172.
63 R v Harris and McGuiness (1989) NSWLR 158, p 193 (my emphasis).

the classic or 'true' transsexual as espoused by Stoller, it becomes clear both that sex reassignment surgery proves crucial in demonstrating 'authenticity' and that post-operative status does not serve as guarantor of 'authenticity' thereby precluding investigation into the past.

The test of *psychological and anatomical harmony* received further judicial endorsement in Australia in *Secretary, Department of Social Security v HH*.[64] In this case, the Administrative Appeals Tribunal upheld a decision of the Social Security Appeals Tribunal that a post-operative (male-to-female) transgender woman was female for the purposes of s 25(1) of the Social Security Act 1947 (Cth) and was therefore entitled to an age pension at 60, rather than 65. While unanimous that the sex of HH was female for the purposes of s 25(1), the panel of three (O'Connor J, Muller and Brennan) produced two distinct judgments. However, for present purposes it is sufficient to point out that the primary judgment (O'Connor J and Muller) served to endorse the approach taken in *R v Harris and McGuiness*. As with previous reform jurisprudence, the judgment foregrounded post-surgical reality. Thus O'Connor J and Muller expressed the view that 'Australian society has permitted sex reassignment surgery to take place. The law, in its turn, must acknowledge this fact and accept the medical decisions which have been made'.[65]

However, as in the previous decisions discussed, the 'mere' fact of sex reassignment surgery proved an insufficient condition for legal recognition. That is to say, an emphasis on heterosexual capacity loomed large in the primary judgment. This finds expression in the assertions of O'Connor J and Muller that anatomy must be the overriding factor in sex determination if 'overwhelmingly contrary to the assumed sex role',[66] and that after reassignment surgery the (male-to-female) transgender woman is 'functionally ... a member of her "new" sex'.[67] This contention that the female sex role can only be properly fulfilled with the 'right' anatomical parts, specifically a vagina, assumes that the role requires penetrative sex. While this analysis is problematic for a feminist politics, irrespective of legal subject matter, its application in the context of an age pension is particularly revealing. That is to say, a concern over vaginal capacity in this context serves to highlight the excessive work occasioned through transgender jurisprudence in furtherance of reproducing the gender order.

The judgment of O'Connor J and Muller also maps prior reform jurisprudence both in terms of a (mis)understanding of medical knowledge and in terms of perpetuating the *discovery story of transsexuality*. Thus sex reassignment surgery was, once again, viewed not only in terms of a legal requirement as to present reality. It also, having been preceded by 'a long period of psychological and other assessment'[68] by the 'Transsexual Evaluation Committee',[69] functioned to affirm 'authenticity' residing in the past, thereby reassuring the tribunal regarding the dangers of 'fraud'.[70] The importance of the past is particularly apparent in the court's statement: '... the transsexual syndrome begins long before the

---

64   *Secretary, Department of Social Security v HH* [1991] 13 AAR 314.
65   *Ibid*, p 64.
66   *Ibid*.
67   *Ibid*.
68   *Ibid*, p 60.
69   *Ibid*, p 59.
70   *Ibid*.

individual is aware of what homosexuality or genital sexuality is.'[71] This statement which, importantly, distances transgender from (homo)sexuality, makes clear that the court's understanding of the phenomenon draws on the *discovery story of transsexuality*, as concern over the past evident within the gender dysphoria perspective is exhausted with surgical intervention. Yet, in another regard, the tribunal misunderstood the knowledge to which it resorted. Thus while the *discovery story of transsexuality* views 'authenticity' independently of the request for sex reassignment surgery (Stoller, 1968), O'Connor J and Muller insisted, and in a manner that again perhaps suggests anxiety over perceived proximity of transgender to homosexuality, on describing pre-operative transgender people as 'female impersonators'.[72]

A concern to discover the 'truth' of HH's body is also apparent in the legal treatment of scientific evidence concerning chromosomal analysis. Thus Professor Walters informed the tribunal that 'chromosomal analysis can be faulty',[73] that 'conventional analysis does not reveal where a genetic problem may lie'[74] and that 'to look at only a particular part of the X or Y chromosome may not be sufficient'.[75] It is significant that it was '[f]or these reasons' that 'the Tribunal [did] not regard evidence of chromosome constitution as decisive in determining the sex of [HH]'.[76] While a willingness to read the uncertainty of medical science in favour of HH is perhaps, in contrast to the approach of the European Court of Human Rights, to be welcomed, this aspect of the tribunal's analysis, one absent in prior reform jurisprudence, serves to reintroduce (bio)logic as legally relevant to sex determination. In contrast to prior reform jurisprudence, where the abandonment of chromosomes occurs irrespective of any explanatory power they might have, the retreat from chromosomes in *HH* occurs precisely because of the tribunal's acceptance of scientific uncertainty regarding genes. Thus, while adopting the test of *psychological and anatomical harmony*, the tribunal's decision might be viewed as postponing rather than dispensing with the question of chromosomes. Accordingly, the decision creates legal space for future arguments around chromosomes and therefore for the reintroduction of birth as the critical moment in sex determination.

Reform jurisprudence in Australia received further judicial endorsement on appeal to the Federal Court in *Secretary, Department of Social Security v SRA*.[77] In confirming the decision in *R v Harris and McGuiness* the court (Black CJ, Lockhart and Heerey JJ) unanimously rejected a view that legal sex could be determined on the basis of *psychological, social and cultural harmony*, a set of considerations upon which the Administrative Appeals Tribunal had decided that a pre-operative (male-to-female) transgender woman was entitled to a wife's pension.[78] While expressing the view that reform jurisprudence constitutes 'a compassionate and humane approach to the

---

71   *Ibid*, p 61.

72   *Ibid*.

73   *Ibid*, p 63.

74   *Ibid*.

75   *Ibid*.

76   *Ibid*.

77   *Secretary, Department of Social Security v SRA* [1993] 118 ALR 467.

78   *Secretary, Department of Social Security v SRA* [1992] 28 ALD 361. The term 'wife' is defined to mean 'a female married person' and the expression 'married person' is defined to include a *de facto* spouse (Social Security Act 1947 (Cth), s 3(1)).

sensitivities of human sexuality,'[79] and while at least one legal commentator considered the judgment of Lockhart J to represent 'a masterly overview of the evolution of an aspect of the law that shows that the law is a living construct and capable of moving with the times, in accordance with the views and social attitudes of the society which it serves' (Finlay, 1995, p 36), the Federal Court refused to countenance a mixing of body genres (Derrida, 1980). That is to say, while stressing the need for understanding, compassion and a humane approach to transgender people, the court proved unable to display any of these qualities in relation to pre-operative transgender people (Mountbatten, 1994, p 175). Further, as in previous decisions, judicial anxiety extended beyond concerns over bodily aesthetics and the possibility of procreation in the 'original' sex. Thus the court noted that '[t]he requirement of reassignment surgery ... has the benefit of society acknowledging that an irreversible medical decision has been made, confirming the person's psychological attitude'.[80] It also, perhaps, would have served to assuage judicial anxiety over the nature of the sexual relationship between SRA and B, a biological man with whom SRA had been in a *de facto* relationship for 10 years.[81] In addition to displaying anxiety over transgender 'authenticity', the court exhibited a concern over capacity for heterosexual intercourse noting that, unlike a post-operative (male-to-female) transgender woman, SRA was not '[f]unctionally ... a member of her new sex and capable of sexual intercourse'.[82]

However, unlike previous decisions, the Federal Court's emphasis on heterosexual capacity in *SRA* did not amount to a legal requirement. This is rendered particularly clear in obiter statements of Lockhart J concerning the post-operative female-to-male body. While making it clear that a (female-to-male) transgender man who undertakes sex reassignment surgery is to be considered male for the purposes of social security provisions, his Honour explained that 'even successful surgery cannot cause him to be a fully functional male, although he can be given the appearance of male genitals'.[83] In other words, legal recognition of transgender sex claims, at least for the purposes of social security law, appears to be uncoupled from a requirement regarding heterosexual capacity. The de-emphasis of sexual capacity by the Federal Court in *SRA* serves to bring to the fore law's concern over bodily aesthetics. While this concern is a consistent theme within transgender jurisprudence it is usually masked by judicial emphasis on heterosexual capacity. In *SRA* however, rather than merely co-existing in legal understandings of sex, form trumps function, a step we shall see replicated in the later New Zealand decision of *Attorney-General v Otahuhu Family Court*. Thus while uncoupling legal determination of sex from sexual capacity Lockhart J placed emphasis on the view that 'society would ... regard an anatomical male as male regardless of the feminine appearance of the person or the inner beliefs and convictions of the person'.[84]

This de-emphasis of (hetero)sexual capacity in *SRA*, albeit limited to an area of law beneficial in character, is, in an obvious sense, a welcome one for transgender, feminist

---

79 *Secretary, Department of Social Security v SRA* [1993] 118 ALR 467, p 493, *per* Lockhart J.

80 *Ibid*, p 494.

81 *Ibid*, p 476.

82 *Ibid*, p 493.

83 *Ibid*.

84 *Ibid*, p 495.

and gay and lesbian politics. However, a feminist politics is confronted by legal comparison of the (male-to-female) transgender vagina and the (female-to-male) transgender penis and their respective capacity for sexual intercourse. While the court conceived of differences in this regard in terms of unequal technological development in the field of sex reassignment surgery, it is apparent that other factors are at play. In particular, characterisation of the (male-to-female) transgender vagina as 'functional' and the (female-to-male) transgender penis as 'dysfunctional' is premised on an active/passive sexual dichotomy. That is to say, the 'inadequacy' of the (female-to-male) transgender penis, an 'inadequacy' that law reads off a lack of capacity for erection, is inextricably tied to a legal assumption about the penetrative heterosexual practices it is to perform. Conversely, judicial readiness to view the transgender vagina as 'functional' flows from a legal view of the vagina as mere absence or lack (Naffine, 1997, p 88). Compared to the 'complex' male sexual organ the vagina is viewed in law as more easily replicated. Indeed, Garber has suggested that some of the resistance to, and neglect of, (female-to-male) transgender men is an effect of the view 'that it should not be so easy to "construct" a "man" – which is to say, a male body' (1993, p 102).

In the more recent Australian decision of Re SRDD v Secretary, Department of Family and Community Services, the Administrative Appeals Tribunal resisted counsel's attempt to reconstitute the pre-/post-surgical dyad, thereby denying a (male-to-female) transgender woman's claim under s 23(5C) of the Social Security Act 1991 (Cth) for an age pension at 60 rather than 65.[85] It was contended that the case differed from SRA because, unlike SRA, SRDD had undergone an orchidectomy (castration).[86] While the tribunal recognised that the procedure undertaken was 'irreversible' and that SRDD 'could never function as a male',[87] it insisted that the decision of the Federal Court in SRA was predicated on 'three-step surgery'.[88] According to McMahon, the Deputy President of the tribunal, the three steps 'involve the removal of the penis, the removal of the testicles and the construction of an artificial vagina'.[89] Thus, as in previous decisions, law's bodily aesthetics conceive of 'anatomical harmony' only in terms of a particular genital configuration.

This strain of reform jurisprudence has also been adopted in New Zealand. In M v M,[90] the first decision in Australasia to extend the analysis to marriage, Aubin J upheld the validity of a 12-and-a-half year marriage between a post-operative (male-to-female) transgender woman and a biological male. In considering M to be female, Aubin J declined to follow Corbett. In rejecting (bio)logical factors as determinative of the issue,

---

85 Re SRDD v Secretary, Department of Family and Community Services [1999] 56 ALD 777.
86 Ibid, p 779.
87 Ibid, p 777.
88 Ibid, p 780.
89 Ibid.
90 M v M [1991] NZFLR 337. The test of 'psychological and anatomical harmony' has also received some support in Canada (see M v M (A) [1984] 42 RFL 2d 55; B v A [1990] 29 RFL 3d 262; C(L) v C(C) [1992] 10 OR 3d 254; Canada v Owen (1993) 110 DLR 4th 339). However, in Canadian jurisdictions sex claims have tended to be made by (female-to-male) transgender men who have not undertaken phalloplasty. Accordingly, the cases have not led to legal recognition on the facts. Moreover, the implication that sex reassignment surgery would have led to recognition of transgender sex claims is problematised in several of these decisions. Most of these cases, dealing as they do with denial of sex claims for the purposes of marriage, will be considered in Chapter 5.

and in allusions to the judgments of Ormrod J in *Corbett* and Nedstadt J in the South African case of *W v W*,[91] Aubin refused to view M as a 'pseudo-woman',[92] as a 'pastiche'[93] or as an 'imitation'.[94] Rather, and in purporting to follow the judgment of Mathews J in *R v Harris and McGuiness*, which he found 'to be cogent and compelling',[95] Aubin J placed emphasis on post-surgical reality, insisting that although the question of sex cannot be decided 'merely upon sympathetic or compassionate grounds ... a change of sex in a real sense'[96] had occurred in the case of M. However, and again consistent with previous reform jurisprudence, post-surgical reality is viewed as speaking for more than itself. Thus Aubin J stressed how 'an irreversible medical decision' had the effect of 'affirming the patient's psychological sex choice',[97] thereby assuaging the court's anxiety over 'fraud'. Further, sex reassignment surgery proves to be a necessary rather than a sufficient condition. Thus Aubin J also exhibits a preoccupation with heterosexual capacity, stating that 'as a result [of surgery] sexual intercourse is possible and [M] states that she actually achieves a sexual orgasm on occasion'.[98] Moreover, while the medical report on which he relied was five years old Aubin J found that there was 'nothing in the evidence to suggest that there was any change' and concluded that 'sexual intercourse was possible throughout this marriage'.[99] Further, while the marriage ultimately failed, hence the proceedings, Aubin J noted that 'Mr M [the respondent] did not attribute its failure ... to sexual difficulties within the marriage' and that, had that been the case, 'it seems very improbable that the marriage would have lasted as long as it did'.[100] In view of the fact that '[a] valid marriage in New Zealand law does not require that sexual intercourse takes place'[101] and that '[t]here is now no legal means of ending a marriage merely for non-consummation'[102] the significance of Aubin J's multiple references to heterosexual capacity cannot be accounted for by their legal relevance. Rather, they point, once again, to the centrality of heterosexual function in judicial attempts to comprehend the re-sexing of bodies.

The case of *M v M* prompted an application by the New Zealand Attorney-General on behalf of the Registrar of Marriages for 'a declaration as to whether two persons of the same genetic sex may by the law of New Zealand enter into a valid marriage where one of the parties to the proposed marriage has adopted the sex opposite to that of the proposed marriage partner through sexual reassignment by means of surgery or hormone administration or both or by any other medical means'.[103] In that case, *Attorney-General v Otahuhu Family Court*, Ellis J purported to follow the approaches in *MT v JT*, *Harris and*

---

91   *W v W* [1976] 2 SALR 308.
92   *M v M* [1991] NZFLR 337, p 344.
93   *Ibid.*
94   *Ibid.*
95   *Ibid*, p 348.
96   *Ibid.*
97   *Ibid*, p 349.
98   *Ibid*, p 340.
99   *Ibid.*
100   *Ibid*, p 339.
101   *Attorney-General v Otahuhu Family Court* [1995] 1 NZLR 603, p 612.
102   *Ibid.*
103   *Ibid*, p 604.

McGuiness and *M v M*, three decisions which he found 'to be compelling',[104] insisting that legal recognition of sex claims for marriage purposes flowed from the fact of sex reassignment surgery. However, while Ellis J took the view that '[a] liberal egalitarian jurisprudence justifies legal recognition of sex reassignment as being an issue of freedom and equality',[105] it would seem that the pre-operative body was located outside the realm where freedom and equality might apply. Rather, the court made clear that bodily change brought about through hormone administration or other medical means was insufficient for the purposes of legal recognition:

> There is clearly a continuum which begins with the person who suffers from gender dysphoria (a state of mental unease or discomfort) but who has not chosen to cross-dress on a regular basis and has embarked on no programme of hormonal modification or surgery, through to the person who has embarked on hormone therapy and perhaps had some minor surgical intervention such as removal of gonads, through to the person who undergoes complete reconstructive surgery ... in order for a transsexual to be eligible to marry in the sex of assignment, the end of the continuum must have been reached and reconstructive surgery done.[106]

However, as in prior reform jurisprudence, it is clear from the judgment of Ellis J that the 'mere' fact of surgical intervention does not satiate legal desire. Rather, as Ellis J explains 'persons who have undertaken such procedures will have already had the social and psychological disposition of the chosen sex'.[107] In this regard, the judgment serves not only to redraw attention to legal anxiety over transgender 'authenticity' but also renders explicit a concern to delimit (trans)gender performance. That is to say, the legal production of the post-surgical male-to-female transgender body as female entails the exclusion of gender difference, as it presupposes successful accomplishment of gender within the medical arena. Thus, in addition to its insistence on post-operative status and heterosexual function, reform jurisprudence confronts a feminist politics through retrospective legitimation of medically produced gendered rites of passage (Billings and Urban, 1982, p 275; Bolin, 1988, pp 107–08; Cole and Birrell, 1990, p 5; King, 1993, p 85; Lewins, 1995, pp 103, 116; Griggs, 1998, pp 31, 62; Kaveney, 1999, p 151).

However, while replicating the main body of reform jurisprudence in many respects the judgment of Ellis J differs from that body in that, while stating that in order to be capable of marriage two persons 'must present themselves as having what appear to be the genitals of a man and a woman',[108] he insisted that they did not 'have to prove that each can function sexually'[109] for 'there are many forms of sexual expression possible without penetrative sexual intercourse'.[110] While this analysis is to be preferred to one that evinces a preoccupation with heterosexual capacity, it serves, like the Federal Court's decision in *SRA*, to foreground the bodily aesthetics of law whereby the monstrosity of the pre-operative transgender body is made manifest. We will see in Chapter 6, where the

---

104 *Ibid*, p 607.
105 *Ibid*, p 617.
106 *Ibid*, pp 614–15.
107 *Ibid*, p 607.
108 *Ibid*, p 612.
109 *Ibid*.
110 *Ibid*, p 615.

decision will be explored in more depth, that this move serves to (re)draw our attention to the homophobia of law. Moreover, while this aspect of Ellis J's judgment might be viewed as ameliorating the position of (female-to-male) transgender men for whom surgical techniques are unable to produce a 'functional' penis, it should be recognised that it does not address adequately the gender differential in legal treatment of male-to-female and female-to-male transgender people. As Ellis J himself noted, 'the construction of any kind of artificial penis involves difficult plastic surgery and requires the use of tissues from other parts of the body which means the surgery is more complicated and intrusive. Some female-to-male transsexuals will therefore choose not to undertake a phalloplasty'.[111]

Indeed, many, if not most, (female-to-male) transgender men decline procedures (Devor, 1997, p 447) that are 'not accomplished easily', 'fraught with rather serious hazards', and 'still quite primitive and experimental' (Garber, 1989, p 148). Walters, Kennedy and Ross have noted that 'phalloplasty is a complex multi-stage operative procedure with universally unsatisfactory results' (1986, p 151). Not only is it difficult to produce a penis that can become erect without mechanical aid but it is also difficult to produce a penis that is functional in urinary terms (Walters, 1986, p 112). These matters have led Walters to conclude: '... until surgical techniques improve, phalloplasty should be avoided in female-to-male transsexuals' (1986, p 113).[112] Accordingly, even the few 'progressive' decisions that render post-operative sexual capacity irrelevant to the legal determination of sex are of little practical value to many, if not most, (female-to-male) transgender men. We now turn to consider reform jurisprudence that has moved 'beyond' a preoccupation with anatomy.

4.2 A JUDICIAL STORY OF 'PSYCHOLOGICAL, SOCIAL AND CULTURAL HARMONY': THE UNCUT VERSION

An approach that abandons sex reassignment surgery as a requirement of legal recognition has so far been confined to Australia and Canada, although there are, as we will see, obiter statements to this effect in *Attorney-General v Otahuhu Family Court*. Moreover, the approach has been limited to social security decisions overturned on appeal. Nevertheless, it reveals much about the possibilities for reimagining the transgender/law relation. For we will see that the approach shares much with reform jurisprudence more generally and therefore with (bio)logical approaches considered in Chapter 3. In particular, it serves to reproduce the gender dichotomy through the articulation of a 'wrong body' story. The approach has its origins in the lone judgment of Brennan in *Secretary, Department of Social Security v HH*. In drawing upon Ormrod J's analysis in *Corbett* that legal relations can be classified into those in which the sex of the individuals concerned is irrelevant, relevant or an essential determinant of the nature of the relationship, Brennan took the view that in relation to age pension policies:

---

111 *Ibid*, p 614.
112 Walters suggests that '[a]n acceptable alternative to most patients is the wearing of a phalloscrotal prosthesis, or model of the penis and scrotum, constructed out of suitable pliable plastic material. Such prostheses can look quite realistic, and each patient can be provided with two, one with a non-erect phallus for wearing inside the clothing and one with an erect phallus for coital purposes' (1986, p 113; see, also, Noe *et al*, 1978; Steiner, 1985, pp 338–39).

... the respondent's psychological and social/cultural gender identity are the matters of primary importance not sex chromosomal configurations or gonadal or genital factors ... The age pension does not give rise to any matters where the sex of the individual is a cardinal factor in determining the nature of a relationship eg Wife's Pension.[113]

While the privileging of psychological, social and cultural factors over anatomical, as well as (bio)logical, ones is perhaps to be welcomed, Brennan's judgment raises a number of concerns. First, it is clear from her analysis that departure from the test of *psychological and anatomical harmony* is premised on the view that sex is 'irrelevant' to the legal subject matter of the case. In other words, the articulation of an alternative test is divorced from sex where sex continues to be read as (bio)logical sex. In this regard, Brennan's approach to the pre-operative body mirrors the approach of Ormrod J to its post-operative counterpart in *Corbett*. This becomes especially evident in Brennan's insistence that, on the evidence before the tribunal, she would have found HH to be a male person for the purposes of the Act generally despite reassignment surgery. It would seem that in relation to other provisions of the Social Security Act Brennan viewed sex, which she clearly equated with biology, as a relevant, and perhaps even a cardinal, factor in determining the nature of relationships. Accordingly, Brennan's judgment transcends existing reform jurisprudence while simultaneously reinstantiating *Corbett*. In this regard, transgender's encounter with law produces the potential for differential treatment of sex claims within the context of a single subject matter.

The test of *psychological, social and cultural harmony* was applied for the first time in *Secretary, Department of Social Security v SRA*.[114] Here the Administrative Appeals Tribunal (O'Connor J, Barbour and Grimes) upheld a decision of the Social Security Appeals Tribunal that a pre-operative (male-to-female) transgender woman was female for the purposes of s 37(1) of the Social Security Act 1947 (Cth) and was therefore entitled to a wife's pension. In rejecting the distinction drawn in its own previous decision in *HH* between post- and pre-operative transgender people (O'Connor J and Muller), the tribunal took the view that anatomical, as well as (bio)logical, considerations could be overridden when presented with *psychological, social and cultural harmony*, thereby confirming and expanding the scope of the legal test formulated by Brennan in *HH*. In adopting *psychological, social and cultural harmony* as the legal test for sex, for the purposes of the Social Security Act, the tribunal endorsed its own view in *HH* that the Social Security Act was beneficial in character, dealing as it did with an area of social policy, and could therefore be interpreted more liberally, thereby distinguishing its decision from *R v Harris and McGuiness*. However, unlike O'Connor J and Muller in *HH*, the tribunal in *SRA* did not consider as too liberal an interpretation one that dispensed with anatomical considerations. While the decision was overturned on appeal to the Federal Court, and emphatically so, it is instructive to consider the reasoning adopted by the Administrative Appeals Tribunal.

Importantly, while a requirement for surgical intervention was dispensed with the judgment was nevertheless constructed in such a way that the gender dichotomy remained tied to 'coherent' bodies. Thus considerable emphasis was placed upon the fact that SRA had been approved for, but due to financial constraints had been unable to

---

113 *Secretary, Department of Social Security v HH* [1991] 13 AAR 314, p 323.
114 *Secretary, Department of Social Security v SRA* [1992] 28 ALD 361.

undergo, surgery (Muller, 1994, p 115).[115] Here willingness to undergo surgery supplanted the surgery itself as the appropriate criterion for the legal determination of sex. While desire for surgery and actual surgery differ as criteria for determining sex, they both serve to reproduce gender as binary and polar through the construction of 'wrong body' stories. Ultimately, legal recognition of SRA proved contingent upon her acceptance of a medico-legal 'wrong body' story and the adoption of an apologetic stance toward her own 'wrong body'. Accordingly, the discursive production of SRA as female clarifies the 'unknowability' of the pre-surgical body even as it enables SRA to assume a presence within the law. What unites the *psychological and anatomical harmony* and the *psychological, social and cultural harmony* stories is that they both insist upon the 'wrongness' of the pre-operative transgender body and require the confession of this legal 'truth'. The process of confession complete, and the all-important 'truth' about the 'correctness' of bodies established, the tribunal proved able to develop amnesia with regard to SRA's continued possession of a 'wrong', and therefore transgressive, body and granted legal absolution (Fraser, 1995, p 86). Accordingly, the decision might be viewed as a form of 'repressive tolerance' (Marcuse, 1965).

Moreover, it is important to recognise that the test of *psychological, social and cultural harmony* is not one premised on transgender autonomy. That is to say, while surgical intervention is dispensed with, the approach does not otherwise loosen medicine's hold over transgender bodies. Rather, the tribunal made clear that 'in the case of a pre-operative transsexual medical reports from relevant psychiatrists involved in the management of the person's case ... need to be obtained'.[116] Thus 'psychological sex', which the court noted 'distinguishes the transsexual from the homosexual',[117] remains to be established within the medical arena through observation, assessment and calibration. This emphasis on medical surveillance of the transgender body serves to redraw our attention to law's concern over transgender 'authenticity' and therefore to the homophobia of law which informs that concern. Thus despite recognising that '[t]he aim of surgery is to make somebody feel more comfortable with their body, not to turn them into a woman'[118] the tribunal's concern clearly extended beyond future well-being characteristic of the gender dysphoria perspective. In giving voice to this concern the tribunal noted that SRA, from an early age believed herself to be 'a female trapped in a male body',[119] had 'never deviated from her desire to be a woman',[120] and was described

---

115 *Ibid*, p 367. The cost of sex reassignment surgery was estimated to be AUS$10,000. The costs can be considerably higher in other countries and particularly in relation to more complex phalloplastic procedures. Indeed, in the United States phalloplastic surgery has been estimated to be as high as US$150,000. For a discussion of the relative costs of surgery see (Griggs, 1998, pp 81–86). While surgical procedures would now seem to be available under the National Health System in the UK (*R v North West Lancashire Health Authority ex p A and Others* [2000] 1 WLR 977) this is not the case elsewhere. Accordingly, in other jurisdictions legal recognition of sex claims, and therefore of self-identification, is, in part, an effect of economic wealth.

116 *Ibid*.

117 *Ibid*, p 366.

118 *Ibid*.

119 *Ibid*, p 365.

120 The claim that SRA 'had never deviated from her desire to be a woman' is contained within a doctor's report referred to by the Administrative Appeals Tribunal but not quoted in the judgment. It is however referred to by the Federal Court on appeal (*Secretary, Department of Social Security v SRA* [1993] 118 ALR 467, p 477).

by one medical expert as 'a classic male-to-female transsexual'.[121] The tribunal's emphasis on 'authenticity', which is perhaps heightened by the abandonment of anatomical factors, leads to further exploration into SRA's past:

> From an early age [SRA] felt significantly different from other children which caused her to feel isolated and lonely ... she felt confused about her identity from the age of three or four. These feelings have remained with her throughout her life. There was a sharp distinction between what she felt she was like on the 'inside' and how she appeared on the 'outside'. She experienced difficulty in relating to other children from the time she started school at four years of age. She recalls the games and play of boys and girls being quite segregated. Not being a girl she could not join in with the girls; however she did not enjoy the boys games, was never really accepted by them, and was a target for 'bullies'. This resulted in her feeling even more 'different' than her peers and increased her feelings of loneliness and isolation. By the time she was 11 years old, she felt that her physical body should have been female, not male, and that how she dressed, acted and behaved should have been as a girl.[122]

Further, to the extent that abandonment of anatomical factors divests medicine of control over transgender bodies, the legal analysis adopted by the Administrative Appeals tribunal in *SRA* simply transfers control to another locale. Nominally, the satisfaction of the 'social' and 'cultural' elements of the new test requires judicial consideration of community attitudes toward, and perceptions of, transgender people. Indeed, the court insisted that 'supporting material relating to how the person lives and is accepted by the community should be obtained to ascertain whether the person's social and cultural identity conforms to their psychological sex'.[123] While the tribunal noted that SRA had been 'accepted as a woman in her community for a number of years'[124] the presence of 'social' and 'cultural' elements raises a serious issue regarding the test. That is to say, reform is potentially undermined in *SRA* by rendering legal recognition dependent on community considerations. While SRA was 'accepted as a woman in her community' the possibility of hostile or intolerant community attitudes toward transgender people remains. Indeed, in *MT v JT* Handler J recognised that 'the entire area of transsexualism is repugnant to the nature of many persons within our society'.[125] In reality, perhaps, given that the test was limited to social security law and the irrelevance of juries in that regard, a conclusion as to community attitudes is perhaps more likely to be an effect of the sitting judge's perception of community attitudes rather than any empirical evidence as to the matter. This becomes particularly clear in the appeal to the Federal Court where, despite evidence that her community 'accepted SRA as a woman over a number of years',[126] Lockhart J expressed the view that '[s]ociety would ... regard an anatomical male as male regardless of the feminine appearance of the person or the inner beliefs and convictions of the person'.[127] On the other hand, and irrespective of the position from which the 'social' and 'cultural' are to be known, the potential for variability and uncertainty implicit in

121 *Secretary, Department of Social Security v SRA* [1993] 118 ALR 467, p 468, *per* Black CJ.
122 *Ibid*, p 475.
123 *Secretary, Department of Social Security v SRA* [1992] 28 ALD 361, p 367.
124 *Ibid*.
125 *MT v JT* 355 A 2d 204 (1976), p 207.
126 *Secretary, Department of Social Security v SRA* [1993] 118 ALR 467, p 476.
127 *Ibid*, p 495.

these elements of the test might be viewed as strategically useful in offering to disrupt further the category of sex. Moreover, the dangers of resort to community need to be weighed against the fact that the abandonment of anatomical factors has been so clearly resisted by the judiciary.

In the same year that the Federal Court of Australia handed down its decision in *SRA*, the Federal Court of Canada arrived at the same conclusion in *Canada v Owen*.[128] In this case an Appeals tribunal found Lillian Owen, a pre-operative (male-to-female) transgender woman, to be a woman for the purposes of receiving a Widowed Spouse's Allowance under Pt III of the Old Age Security Act[129] 'on the grounds that she has lived as a female since 1951 and married in 1955, remain[ing] married until the death of her husband in 1964'. As in *SRA*, the Federal Court of Canada insisted that the word 'spouse' in the Act did not apply to same-sex relationships, taking the view that Lillian Owen's nine year 'marriage' to a (bio)logical man constituted just that as she had not undertaken sex reassignment surgery. Most recently, the abandonment of anatomical factors in legal determinations of sex was entertained by the New Zealand High Court in *Attorney-General v Otahuhu Family Court*.[130] In departing from the main body of transgender jurisprudence, Ellis J expressed the opinion that for purposes other than marriage:

> ... a transsexual who has not had reconstructive surgery or only minimal surgical intervention (such as removal of testes) could be classified in his or her chosen sex for certain purposes such as employment law, criminal law and the law of inheritance.[131]

While only an obiter statement, and while it is unclear from his Honour's judgment what 'social', 'cultural' or other factors, if any, are to apply to such a reimagining of sex, it is significant that a superior court within a common law jurisdiction was able to conceive of severing the couplings man/penis and woman/vagina. Moreover, in contrast to *SRA* and *Canada v Owen*, where de-emphasis of anatomy is limited to legislation of beneficial character, Ellis J's judgment appears to expand the scope for possible future reform. For the time being, however, transgender people remain subject to the genitocentric logic of law. Moreover, this logic not only serves to deny male/female status to pre-operative transgender people. It also, through setting limits to the 'harmony' of bodies, precludes legal recognition of sexed positions lying outside of that binary (Feinberg, 1992, 1993a, 1993b; Bornstein, 1994; May-Welby, 1994, p 11; Hooley, 1994; Nataf, 1996, p 32; Denny and Roberts, 1997; Wilchins, 1997; Devor, 1997, pp 447–58; Califia, 1997; Cain, 1998, pp 1350–51). Thus, in *MT v JT* the suggestion that there might be 'some middle ground between the sexes, a "no-man's land" for those individuals who are neither truly "male" nor truly "female"'[132] led the court to declare that 'the standard is much too fixed for such far-out theories'.[133] Again, in *R v Harris and McGuiness* the suggestion that Lee

---

128 *Canada v Owen* (1993) 110 DLR (4th) 339.

129 RSC 1985, c 0–9, s 2.

130 *Attorney-General v Otahuhu Family Court* [1995] 1 NZLR 603.

131 *Ibid*, p 615.

132 *MT v JT* 355 A 2d 204 (1976), p 210.

133 *Ibid*. Here Handler J appears to quote directly from, and endorse, the view of Pecora J in *Re Anonymous* 293 NYS 2d 834 (1968), p 837.

Harris and Phillis McGuiness might constitute a 'third sex'[134] or 'third state'[135] for legal purposes was described as 'novel',[136] 'lacking in substance'[137] and was roundly dismissed, while in *M v M* Aubin J baulked at the prospect that M might occupy 'some kind of sexual twilight zone'.[138] This legal attitude toward the possibility of a 'third sex', as well as the instantiation of a pre/post surgical dyad, highlights how '[l]aw's power is not found in the outcomes achieved through law reform but in law's claim to speak the "truth" and to disqualify the "truth" of other knowledges' (Morgan, 1995, pp 36–37; see, also, Smart, 1989, Chapter 1). However, law's 'truth' claims can have unintended consequences.

4.3 REFORM JURISPRUDENCE AS DYSPHORIC

It should not be thought that the relation between reform jurisprudence and the gender order is merely one of recuperation, simply a 'safety valve in the service of dominant ideology' (Epstein, 1995, p 9). On the contrary, and because transgender 'exceeds and refuses that ideology' (Epstein, 1995, p 9), law's engagement with transgender serves to disrupt the gender order and create legal spaces for further challenge. Thus in contrast to gender theorists (see, for example, Raymond, 1979; Eichler, 1980; Billings and Urban, 1982; Bolin, 1988; Cole and Birrell, 1990, p 1) who conceive of the transgender body as heterosexual prop, as a body that 'renaturalises the relationship' (Note, 1995, pp 1992–93) between the body and gender identity, it is important to appreciate transgender's other effects. Thus while reform jurisprudence, through its genitocentric logic, represents a present 'limit' to a more transgressive politics, the instantiation of a test of *psychological and anatomical harmony*, and its endless citation within reform jurisprudence, serves nevertheless to destabilise gender through uncoupling it from its anchor in (bio)logical sex. In other words, while law continues to tie gender to a notion of sex as foundation, the shift to anatomy introduces malleability. Accordingly, a view of sex reassignment surgery as 'renaturalising' the relationship between the body and gender identity misses the fact that the undertaking of surgery demonstrates the radically performative nature of anatomical sex (Shafiqullah, 1997, p 221), a fact that might, perhaps, be redeployed in other sexual political contexts. Moreover, because reform jurisprudence writes transgender men and women into legal existence for the first time it provides a place within law from which to articulate reverse-discourses about the re-sexing of bodies (Butler, 1991, p 20). Thus in addition to the need to take seriously the desire for, and the practice of, sex reassignment surgery (Kogan, 1997, p 1234), thereby avoiding reproducing 'yet another version of the morality tale that condemns the cutting of the flesh' (Stryker, 1998, p 153), it must be recognised that the relationship between transgender jurisprudence and the gender order is a complex one containing disruptive as well as recuperative possibilities.

---

134 *R v Harris and McGuiness* (1989) 17 NSWLR 158, p 194, *per* Mathews J.

135 *Ibid*, p 170, *per* Carruthers J.

136 *Ibid*, p 194, *per* Mathews J.

137 *Ibid*, p 170, *per* Carruthers J.

138 *M v M* [1991] NZFLR 337, p 347. This incredulity in the face of challenge to a binary notion of sex is a consistent theme within transgender jurisprudence irrespective of judicial approach.

The contradictory effects produced by attempts to shore up the gender order through legal recognition of transgender sex claims are again apparent in legal insistence on viewing transgender and homosexuality as mutually exclusive. This view, one replicated in uncritical legal scholarship (see, for example, Smith, 1971, p 963; Walton, 1974, p 502; Graham, 1981, p 120; Hurley, 1984, p 643; Taitz, 1987, p 54) has proved to be a consistent feature of reform jurisprudence, one evident in legal concern over transgender pasts. By way of example, in *R v Harris and McGuiness* Mathews J asserts that '[t]ranssexuality is quite different from homosexuality which relates to sexual preference rather than gender identity'.[139] Again in *Secretary, Department of Social Security v HH* O'Connor J and Muller, quoting Ascione J from *Richards v United States Tennis Association*, assert that '[t]ranssexuals are not homosexual. They consider themselves to be members of the opposite sex burdened with the wrong sexual apparatus. They desire the removal of this apparatus and further surgical assistance in order that they may enter into heterosexual relationships',[140] and in an attempt to distinguish transsexuals from homosexuals contend that 'homosexuals are satisfied with their anatomical sex and are only attracted to people of the same [by which they mean (bio)logical] sex'.[141] While these statements may seem axiomatic on first reading, they serve to foreclose the possibility of transgender homosexualities. That is to say, lesbian and gay (trans)sexualities are scripted as 'impossible', entailing as they do both anatomical dissatisfaction and sexual desire for persons of the 'opposite' (bio)logical sex.

This view of transgender and homosexuality as incommensurate arises due to legal insistence on a particular gendered relationship between the re-sexed subject and sexual preference. Butler has described this logic as 'one of the most reductive of heterosexism's psychological instruments' (1993, p 239). It is a logic which attempts to erase a figure whose existence, much like the macho gay or lesbian femme, serves to demonstrate the imaginary logic of the heterosexual matrix (Butler, 1993, p 239). However, this attempt to facilitate one-way sexual traffic, to render transgender a 'compulsory heterosexuality' (Rich, 1980), produces another and disruptive effect. That is to say, law's differential deployment of biology and psychology across the hetero/homo divide serves to call into question the priority of heterosexuality. In other words, the uncoupling of heterosexuality from biology destabilises and 'denaturalises' that category within law. Ironically, legal insistence on an opposition between transgender and homosexuality ensures that homosexuality remains anchored in biology and therefore emerges as a more stable and 'natural' category. In a somewhat strange twist of legal reasoning, it is homosexuality that becomes the very ground of 'sex', its most concrete materialisation. The legal reasoning that produces this effect might not only be the subject of challenge in transgender contexts but might also be exploited on other sexual political terrains. Indeed, if 'it is not possible, within discourse, to escape essentializing somewhere' (Spivak, 1990, p 51) then this 'somewhere' may, as Robson notes (1998, p 63), contain particular strategic possibilities. That is to say, this legal move, which subverts the priority or 'originality' of heterosexuality, might be exploited through repetition (Butler, 1991, p 23).

---

139 *R v Harris and McGuiness* (1989) 17 NSWLR 158, p 173.
140 *Secretary, Department of Social Security v HH* [1991] 13 AAR 314, p 317.
141 *Ibid.*

The possibility of/for a transgressive politics around sex is apparent in yet another regard. While articulating a test of *psychological and anatomical harmony* common law courts have exhibited some uncertainty as to whether determination of sex involves a question of law or fact. While the courts have tended to assume, if not render explicit, the view that sex determination is a question of law, doubt has been cast on the correctness of that view. In the Victorian decision of *R v Cogley*[142] the defendant appealed against a conviction for assault with intent to commit rape of a post-operative (male-to-female) transgender woman on the grounds that the victim was not a woman. At the trial both defence (relying upon *Corbett*) and prosecuting counsel (relying upon the majority in *R v Harris and McGuiness*) had accepted that the question for determination was one of law. The trial judge, Cummins J, accepted the prosecution argument, holding that the complainant was a woman as a matter of law. His direction to the jury included the statement: 'Miss A in law is a woman and for the purpose of assault with intent to rape, that count, she is a woman and must be treated by you as such.'[143] However, the Victorian Court of Criminal Appeals (Crockett, Gray and McDonald JJ), while upholding the conviction upon other grounds,[144] unanimously held that the determination of the complainant's sex was 'a question of fact to be determined by the jury',[145] a determination which the jury would have been required to make had the defendant been charged with the completed act of vaginal rape. The court did not, however, confine itself to stressing that the question was one ultimately for the jury. Rather, it took the view that no question of law was involved in the determination at all (Bailey-Harris, 1989, p 360). Thus in response to a request by prosecuting counsel that the court lay down a 'test', or at least 'guidelines', upon which a jury could be directed it was stated:

> This we decline to do. There is, in our view, no legal test that can be applied to the question whether, a person is a man or a woman in a particular context.[146]

Uncertainty over the relationship between law and fact and the determination of sex was compounded further by the Federal Court of Australia in *Secretary, Department of Social Security v SRA*.[147] In *SRA* the court was required to consider whether the question whether a person was a 'woman', a 'female' or a member of the 'opposite sex', words and phrases appearing in relevant provisions of the Social Security Act 1947 (Cth), was one of law or fact. Counsel for SRA argued that the words 'woman' and 'female' and the phrase 'opposite sex' are ordinary English words, not technical terms, and therefore their meaning is a question of fact, and that accordingly the appeal must fail as no question of law arose for decision. While accepting that where a particular word or phrase in a statute is used as an ordinary English word or phrase then it is a question of fact as to the common understanding of the word or phrase, Lockhart J argued:

---

142 *R v Cogley* [1989] 41 A Crim R 198.

143 *Ibid*, p 202.

144 On the particular facts of the case it was unnecessary to quash the conviction and order a new trial because had the jury considered the complainant not to be a woman the defendant could still have been convicted, legal impossibility being no defence to a criminal attempt (*Britten v Alpogut* [1987] VR 929 applied).

145 *Ibid*, p 198.

146 *Ibid*, p 204.

147 *Secretary, Department of Social Security v SRA* [1993] 118 ALR 467.

... the crucial question for present purposes is ... whether or not the evidence before the court *reasonably admits of different conclusions* as to whether certain facts or circumstances fall within the ordinary meaning of the relevant word or phrase. That is a question of law. If different conclusions are reasonably possible, it is necessary to decide which is the correct conclusion and that is a question of fact.[148]

The court took the view that on the facts of the case only one conclusion was reasonably open, namely that a pre-operative, as distinct from a post-operative, (male-to-female) transgender woman was not female for the purposes of the legislation and therefore no question of fact arose for decision. Yet, the court's reasoning around the law/fact distinction is, at best, dubious. The claim that only one conclusion was reasonably open regarding the sex of SRA is hardly persuasive. After all the Social Security and, on appeal, the Administrative Appeals tribunals had concluded that SRA was a woman. Equally unpersuasive is the suggestion that post-operative (male-to-female) transgender women are female because alternative factual conclusions are precluded. Thus the Victorian Court of Criminal Appeals in *R v Cogley* expressed the view:

> We certainly do not think that it can be asserted that the arbitrary selection of satisfaction as to the existence of two factual requirements, viz, 'core identity' and 'sexual re-assignment surgery' thereupon necessarily determines as a matter of law the sex of a transsexual.[149]

Thus legal reasoning around the law/fact distinction offers to disrupt the category of sex. In a sense, the Federal Court in *SRA* invite the assertion of alternative factual conclusions regarding the sex claims of transgender people. An appeal to 'fact', especially in jury contexts, like resort to 'social' and 'cultural' elements, serves to divest medicine and law of their monopoly over sex determination. On the other hand, an appeal to 'fact' reproduces the dilemma evident in resort to 'social' and 'cultural' elements. That is to say, a shift from expert to lay knowledge promises to constrain as well as enable sex claims. Indeed, appeals to 'fact' add a further dimension to this dilemma whenever a jury is empanelled. This is because jury reasoning is not put into public discourse. While this might be viewed as a drawback, precluding the emergence of affirmative stories in moments of reform, it might also be viewed as strategically useful, serving to inhibit repetition of hegemonic understandings of sex which always produce a 'wrong body'.

4.4 CONCLUSION

This chapter has considered reform jurisprudence that has sought to move 'beyond' the (bio)logic of *Corbett*. In doing so it has emphasised continuity over discontinuity of approach. In particular, reform jurisprudence was found to share with (bio)logical approaches a particular relation to the gender order. Thus while the test of *psychological and anatomical harmony* reconstitutes sex temporally and in terms of the criteria to be applied, it nevertheless positions sex as gender's ground. This version of sex entails a construction of sex/gender relations whereby gender roles flow from the present state of genitalia rather than prior (bio)logical factors. Thus, the female gender role continues to

---

148 *Ibid*, p 480.
149 *R v Cogley* [1989] 41 A Crim R 198, p 204.

be confined to women whose ranks are to be determined by the possession of a vagina. The difference then between this approach to transgender and the *Corbett* approach lies not in the relation between sex as 'foundation' and gender as 'edifice', but rather in alternative legal constructions of sex as foundation. Therefore, contrary to the view that the maintenance of gender is occurring through its detachment from sex (Shapiro, 1991, p 272), what we are witnessing, in the context of reform jurisprudence, is a process whereby one notion or fantasy of sex (Butler, 1993, p 6) is being replaced by another. In other words, there is no suggestion of gender floating free from sex in legal discourse. Rather, gender remains very much tied to the notion of sex, albeit a notion of sex which has undergone judicial reformulation. Indeed, this particular characterisation of sex/gender relations holds even in relation to reform that ostensibly abandons anatomical factors. That is to say, the *psychological, social and cultural harmony* test also serves to reproduce the gender dichotomy through linking legal recognition to willingness to undergo sex reassignment surgery. In other words, like the narrative of *psychological and anatomical harmony*, this version of reform requires that a medico-legal 'wrong body' story be voiced.

Thus reform jurisprudence, like its (bio)logical counterpart, continues to deploy repressive legal power in relation to people with 'incorrect' bodies. Conversely, once those bodies have been surgically 'corrected' it resorts to productive, and its correlative exclusionary, legal power. That is to say, while judicial recognition discursively produces the post-surgical male-to-female transgender body as female, this is made possible only through the simultaneous production of a constitutive and abjected 'outside' – a domain of 'unimaginable' bodies (Butler, 1993, p 8), 'incoherent' gender performance and 'impossible' sexual desire. Moreover, the grounding of gender in a reformulated understanding of sex proves to require more than the 'mere' fact of sex reassignment surgery. Rather, the preferred version of reform jurisprudence has, with few exceptions, enshrined a requirement of capacity for heterosexual intercourse. In the following chapter it will become apparent that a concern over the nature of heterosexual intercourse proves to be central to an approach that articulates itself in the language of (bio)logic, thereby demonstrating further continuity across approach. A further point of unity proved to be judicial concern over transgender 'authenticity' which, irrespective of approach, law locates in the past. Thus, and despite contemporary medical understandings that confine inquiry into the past to the question of post-surgical well-being, transgender jurisprudence as a body proves to be preoccupied with pre-surgical 'facts', irrespective of subsequent surgical intervention. That is to say, the *discovery story of transsexuality* (King, 1993, pp 45, 63) proves to be an important narrative informing law, one that requires close scrutiny of transgender histories. In the next chapter this concern over transgender 'authenticity' will be seen to bear a close relation to anxiety over legal perception of proximity to the homosexual body.

However, attempts within reform jurisprudence to contain transgender within an established gender order have produced unintended consequences. Thus the test of *psychological and anatomical harmony*, and its endless citation within reform jurisprudence, while reinscribing sex/gender relations through its genitocentric logic, serves simultaneously to destabilise gender through adopting a more malleable concept of sex as foundation. That is to say, law's equating of sex with anatomy enables the demonstration, quite literally, of its radically performative nature. Moreover, the legal reasoning adopted within reform jurisprudence fails to limit the concept of sex to anatomical form. Judith Butler has asked if sexuality is to be disclosed 'what will be taken as the true determinant of its meaning: the phantasy structure, the act, the orifice, the gender, the anatomy?' (1991, p 17). In the context of reform jurisprudence, the 'true' determinant of the meaning of sex and heterosexuality proves to be not one thing, but rather all the things Butler identifies and more. This 'surfeit of truths' (Moran, 1990, p 158) includes fantasy structure (psychological sex), act/orifice (the capacity for heterosexual intercourse), gender (pre-surgical medical rites of passage) and anatomy (sex reassignment surgery). However, the notion of sex is not exhausted by these factors.

Rather, determination of sex within reform jurisprudence sometimes proves contingent upon legal subject matter. Moreover, the 'social' and 'cultural' elements of the *psychological, social and cultural harmony* test, as well as the law/fact distinction, serve to supplement the 'what' with the 'who' of sex(uality). That is to say, not only does reform jurisprudence produce a multiplicity of legal sex but there is no single stable point definitively established from which determinations can be made. By the same token, legal attempts to maintain the gender order serve to destabilise heterosexuality through uncoupling it from its (bio)logical referent. The importance of this effect is heightened by law's dissimilar treatment of homosexuality, treatment that positions homosexuality as a more grounded category. The fact that legal reasoning can produce such disruptive effects around so 'foundational' a category as sex points to the need to view transgender jurisprudence not only as a site for rearticulating transgender but as a locale for wider political contestation. That is to say, and while any engagement with law from the margins contains dangers, the considerable disruption to the category sex that is internal to transgender jurisprudence invites legal argument across a range of sexual political terrains designed to accelerate and proliferate the meanings of sex(uality) (Fuss, 1991, p 7).

Law's capacity to disrupt sex will be pursued in the following chapter, where the particularity of legal subject matter as a further contingency will be developed. This theme, which was touched upon lightly in this chapter, establishes another point of continuity across legal approaches to sex determination. Thus, while English courts have been consistent in their denial of transgender sex claims, judicial recognition which has been forthcoming in some Australian and United States contexts can be juxtaposed with Ormrod J's view in *Corbett* that a different legal test for determining sex might apply in areas other than marriage. Indeed, judicial recognition in Australia has been confined to precisely the types of subject matter identified by Ormrod J as capable of different legal treatment. Similarly, the judicial concerns that led to the approach in *Corbett* will be seen in the following chapter to be mirrored in the Australian context. Specifically, we will see that Australian decisions that have recognised transgender sex claims have insulated the institution of marriage from the effects of that recognition. Thus, in opposition to the view that reform jurisprudence 'show[s] how easy it is to overcome a decision [*Corbett*] that, while once authoritative, has been shown to be no longer serviceable or appropriate in modern social conditions' (Finlay, 1996, p 530), it would seem that the ghost of *Corbett* is not so easily banished from law. Rather, the decision, and the concerns which inform it, continue to operate as a key subtext within reform jurisprudence. It is the body of marriage law which provides the best site for accurate characterisation of the relation between (bio)logical approaches to sex determination and reform jurisprudence, and for locating the 'truth' of sex in law, because it is at the site of marriage that a tension in legal desire is most apparent. It is therefore to marriage that we turn in the next chapter.

PART II

HOMOPHOBIA AS SUBTEXT

CHAPTER 5

MARRIAGE LAW AS 'LIMIT'

[Q]uestions relating to transsexualism arise in a variety of contexts and different answers may be required. For example the law relating to marriage may require different tests ... the law of marriage may involve special considerations with many factors to be considered by the court and carefully weighed.[1]

In Part I of the book we considered different common law approaches to transgender bodies. In particular, (bio)logical approaches were contrasted with reform-based approaches. While there are obvious differences between, as well as, in some instances, within, these approaches, continuity was emphasised over discontinuity. It was suggested that continuity in approach is, at least in part, explicable in terms of a legal desire to reproduce the gender order in the face of transgender trouble. This is not to suggest that this desire is achieved or, given the 'imaginary logic' which structures it (Butler, 1993, p 239), is even possible to achieve in any absolute sense. Indeed, and while reformist jurisprudence, premised, as it is, on 'normalisation', may be more effective in bolstering the gender order than its (bio)logical counterpart, reformist legal (re)constructions of sex have served, as we saw in Chapter 4, to disrupt and problematise the notions of sex and sexuality, and therefore gender's 'foundation', in a variety of ways.

In this part of the book, which will focus exclusively on marriage law, the theme of continuity of approach will be developed through consideration of the relationship between transgender jurisprudence and the homophobia of law. Moreover, it will be contended that the homophobia of law serves not only to link approaches but is central to an adequate understanding of transgender jurisprudence, irrespective of whether sex claims are denied or recognised. Of course, homophobia is, as we have already seen, an important trope within transgender jurisprudence more generally. In the context of marriage, however, it assumes special significance, manifesting itself through legal desire to privilege, and preserve a space for, 'natural' heterosexual intercourse. For as Butler has pointed out, what stabilises the association and keeps the terms female/femininity/woman and male/masculinity/man discrete and antithetical is the apparent 'naturalness' of heterosexual desire (Prosser, 1998, p 31). Thus we will see judicial mapping of the genital topography of transgender bodies, and analysis around the practice of heterosexual intercourse, intensify in marriage contexts.

In this chapter we will consider case law denying transgender sex claims for marriage purposes. In these decisions the homophobia of law will be seen to have the effect of setting a 'limit' to the effective incorporation ('normalisation') of transgender people within the existing gender order. In this regard, judicial defence of marriage will, somewhat ironically, be seen to hinder the reformist project of heterosexualising 'ambiguous' bodies. Thus, in these decisions, refusal of sex claims is, perhaps, to be comprehended in terms of an unresolved tension between reproducing the gender order and insulating the institution of marriage from 'unnatural' homosexual incursion. Accordingly, in marriage law we will see that, irrespective of sex reassignment surgery,

---

1 *Secretary, Department of Social Security v SRA* [1993] 118 ALR 467, p 495, *per* Lockhart J.

the transgender body is presented as bearing a much more proximate relation to homosexuality. Moreover, because it functions to set a 'limit' to legal recognition of sex claims, marriage offers to provide a glimpse into the 'truth' of sex in law. That is to say, an analysis of marriage law, perhaps, reveals much about the value, nature and significance of legal recognition in other contexts. In other words, the relationship between the 'surfeit of truths' (Moran, 1990, p 158) produced about sex within transgender jurisprudence is, perhaps, not one of equivalence, but rather one of hierarchy in which (bio)logic is privileged. In this regard, the chapter serves to problematise further the tendency within uncritical legal scholarship to characterise (bio)logical and reformist judicial approaches as discontinuous.

In the following chapter we will consider case law that has recognised transgender sex claims for marriage purposes, thereby seemingly resolving this tension in legal desire. We will see, however, that while homophobia does not preclude legal recognition in these decisions it continues to structure the reform moment, thereby linking this body of reform jurisprudence to *Corbett*. Moreover, we will see that even within this body of law (bio)logic is not expunged. Rather, the question of the 'truth' of sex will be seen to be postponed, displaced on to other legal terrain, namely competitive sport, which, much like marriage in the decisions to be considered in this chapter, functions to 'naturalise' sexed difference (Birrell and Cole, 1990, p 18). Before turning to consider case law denying the sex claims of transgender persons for marriage purposes, and as a prelude to Chapter 6, it is first necessary to articulate the definition of marriage in order to highlight the specific legal issues arising at this particular intersection of transgender and law.

5.1 MARRIAGE: 'BETWEEN A MAN AND A WOMAN'

The classic legal definition of marriage was stated by Lord Penzance in *Hyde v Hyde and Woodmansee* to be 'the voluntary union for life of one man and one woman, to the exclusion of all others'.[2] This common law definition of marriage contains five distinct elements. A marriage must be (a) voluntary, (b) a union, (c) for life,[3] (d) between a man and a woman, and (e) to the exclusion of all others.[4] For the purposes of the present chapter it is the first, second and fourth of these elements which fall to be considered. Moreover, we will see that they assume particular interrelationships within transgender jurisprudence. Thus while it is the interpretation of the meaning of the words 'man' and 'woman' that ultimately determine the marriage possibilities of transgender people, we will see that judicial understandings of these terms prove inextricably tied to concerns over the nature of the marital 'union'. This translates into a concern over transgender capacity for heterosexual intercourse, a concern that is not necessarily assuaged by evidence of 'functionality'. By the same token, judicial concerns over 'voluntariness', which, as we will see, have led to the characterisation of non-revelation of transgender status as 'fraud' or 'deceit', connect, in some common law jurisdictions, to the question of

---

2   *Hyde v Hyde and Woodmansee* [1866] LR 1 PD 130; [1861–73] All ER Rep 175.

3   This is no longer a legal requirement in common law jurisdictions.

4   There are, of course, various prohibitions pertaining to age and consanguinity (see, eg, Cretney and Masson, 1997, pp 43–51) as well as procedural requirements in relation to solemenisation and registration (Cretney and Masson, 1997, Chapter 1).

'incapacity' and therefore to the requirement of marital 'union'. All of these points, which marry in the homophobia of law, require further explanation.

First, while the relevant legislative enactments in each of the jurisdictions under study, and a line of judicial statements,[5] emphasise that marriage involves the union of a man and a woman there is no attempt to define either term. In the absence of statutory clarification, the determination of the meaning of these terms has been left to the interpretative practices of the judiciary, practices that have, in different ways, sought to insulate the institution of marriage from the homosexual body and the 'unnatural' practices law maps onto that body. Moreover, while sex claims of transgender people have been recognised legislatively in a number of jurisdictions, this does not necessarily amount to recognition for the purposes of marriage. In Australia, for example, no State can grant conclusively legal recognition to transgender people for the purposes of marriage because marriage law falls under a federal head of power under the Australian Constitution (Otlowski, 1990).[6] Speaking more broadly, however, and in a jurisdiction which lacks such constitutional difficulties, Ellis J recently pointed out in the New Zealand decision of *Attorney-General v Otahuhu Family Court*:

> ... [e]ven if a birth certificate was issued for a person in the alternate sex, that would not automatically allow a person to marry as a member of that sex unless the Courts were willing to endorse such a marriage. It is possible that even though a person has a birth certificate as a female, for example, pursuant to such legislation, a Court could still hold that the person did not have the attributes to marry in that sex.[7]

In other words, determination of sex for marriage purposes may involve a different set of considerations than for other purposes. While Ellis J delivered a 'progressive' judgment on this point, as we saw in Chapter 4, the reference to 'attributes' which transgender people may lack for marriage purposes has assumed significance in other common law decisions. The attribute that the post-operative transgender body has been considered to lack is the capacity for 'natural heterosexual intercourse'. Thus, and despite the rhetoric of (bio)logic, explored in Chapter 3, refusal of sex claims for marriage purposes proves to be tied less to (bio)logic than to judicial anxiety over the nature of the marital union. This anxiety is evident in the intricate mapping of transgender genital topographies and their frequent characterisation as sites of the 'unnatural' within transgender marriage jurisprudence. In this regard, it might be thought that legal exclusion of transgender people from the institution of marriage is explicable in terms of established legal doctrine concerning consummation rather than an effect of anxiety in the legal present.

However, while common law rules of consummation precipitate inquiry into the nature and practice of (hetero)sexual intercourse, it is difficult to account for the exclusion

---

5   See *Khan* [1962] 3 FLR 496, p 497; *Re the Marriage of C and D (falsely called C)* [1979] 35 FLR 340, p 345; *Re the Marriage of S* [1980] 42 FLR 94, p 102. In the US context see, eg, *Baker v Nelson* 291 Minn 310 (1971); *Jones v Hallahan* 501 SW 2d 588 (1973); *Singer v Hara* 522 P 2d 1187 (1974); *B v B* 355 NYS 2d 712 (1974).

6   Australian Constitution, s 51(xxi). Moreover, s 109 of the Constitution makes clear that any Federal Act would override inconsistent State law.

7   *Attorney-General v Otahuhu Family Court* [1995] 1 NZLR 603, p 616. This point is also rendered clear by Nedstadt J in the South African decision of *W v W* [1976] 2 SALR 308 (see Lupton, 1976, p 386) and more recently by Hardberger J in *Littleton v Prange* [1999] 288th Judicial District Court, Bexar County, Texas (www.4thcoa.courts.state.tx.us/opinions/9900010.htm).

of transgender people from the institution of marriage through reference to these rules. A number of points need to be made here. In the first place, in two of the jurisdictions under study, Australia[8] and New Zealand,[9] sexual consummation is completely irrelevant to nullity of marriage (Dickey, 1997, p 141). Elsewhere, a marriage that has not been consummated is voidable, a legal position traceable to the English Reformation (Cretney and Masson, 1997, p 54). This means that it remains valid until such time as one of the parties take steps to have it brought to an end. In other words, it is only at the election of the parties to a marriage that the 'fact' of non-consummation assumes any legal relevance. Thus if, for example, a (male-to-female) transgender woman were to be considered female in law, the rules of consummation would not affect her ability to enter and remain in a lawful marriage. Moreover, where one or both of the parties seek a nullity of the marriage the effect of the proceedings, if successful, is no longer to render the marriage void from its inception. Rather, the marriage is treated as having existed up until the time of the *decree absolute*.[10] Accordingly, a legal view of the post-operative (male-to-female) transgender woman as incapable of consummating a marriage does not serve to locate her outside of the institution of marriage. It should be noted, however, that at earlier historical moments the *decree absolute* did operate retrospectively and that this was the case in England at the time *Corbett* was decided.[11]

However, and irrespective of variation in its effect, common law courts will not necessarily grant a nullity decree on the grounds of non-consummation. That is to say, an application will not be granted in certain circumstances. Under the old law of approbation[12] ecclesiastical courts refused a nullity decree where conduct on the part of the petitioner 'so plainly implied a recognition of the existence and validity of the marriage as to render it inequitable and contrary to public policy that the validity of the marriage should subsequently be questioned' (Cretney and Masson, 1997, p 70). In more recent times, legislation has been enacted in common law jurisdictions barring relief in circumstances of inequity. Thus, for example, in England a court may not grant a decree of nullity where the petitioner, knowing 'that it was open to him to have the marriage avoided, so conducted himself in relation to the respondent as to lead the respondent reasonably to believe that he would not do so'[13] and 'where it would be unjust to the respondent to grant the decree'.[14] In other words, and for present purposes, a decree of nullity may not be granted where a petitioner was aware of the respondent's 'inability' to consummate a marriage or where the petitioner has subsequently ratified the marriage. Thus, it is the knowledge and consent of the parties rather than the presence/absence of heterosexual intercourse, or its characterisation as 'unnatural', which ultimately determines the question of nullity.

---

8   Family Law Act 1975 (Cth), ss 48, 51. See, also, *Najjarin v Houlayce* [1991] 104 FLR 403, pp 404–05.

9   Family Proceedings Act 1980. See *Attorney-General v Otahuhu Family Court* [1995] 1 NZLR 603, p 612.

10   See, eg, Matrimonial Causes Act 1973 (UK), s 16.

11   Prior to the Nullity of Marriage Act 1971 UK the effect of a decree absolute in the context of a voidable marriage was to treat the marriage has having never existed. However, such marriages were still treated as valid for purposes of contracts negotiated while the marriage subsisted (see *R v Algar* [1954] 1 QB 279; *Re Eaves v Eaves* [1939] 4 All ER 260).

12   For a discussion of the old law of approbation see Lasok (1963) and Jackson (1969).

13   Matrimonial Causes Act 1973, s 13(1)(a).

14   *Ibid*, s 13(1)(b). Moreover, by virtue of s 13(2)(b) the court 'shall not grant a decree of nullity ... unless it is satisfied that proceedings were instituted within three years from the date of the marriage'.

In the transgender context, however, the linking of nullity of marriage to states of knowledge amounts to a requirement to disclose transgender status. For the 'incapacity' which law inscribes onto the post-operative transgender body is nothing less than the adoption of a particular attitude toward the surgically constructed vagina. Accordingly, the possibility of invoking equitable protection proves dependent on disclosure of the 'facts' of 'incapacity', namely transgender status. This problematic requirement placed on transgender persons to 'out' themselves also serves to redraw our attention to the temporal relationship between transgender and 'truth' in legal discourse. That is to say, and even within reformist jurisprudence that focuses ostensibly on post-surgical 'reality', the 'truth' of transgender, a 'truth' which must be disclosed, resides in the past. This temporal understanding of transgender will be seen to manifest itself in the case law as anxiety over 'actual' or imagined inter-personal 'fraud'. This concern, which is also voiced by some legal scholars (see, for example, van Niekerk, 1970, p 241; Smith, 1971, pp 970–71; Kennedy, 1973, pp 131–32; Lupton, 1976, p 387; Samuels, 1984, p 166; Finlay, 1988, p 121; Otlowski, 1990, pp 73–74; Finlay, 1996, p 533), is somewhat curious given that non-revelation of transgender status cannot, of itself, provide grounds for the vitiation of a contract of marriage. That is to say, and while Finlay has advocated that non-disclosure should be made a ground for nullity of marriage (1988, p 121) and Otlowski has expressed the view that '[t]his proposal certainly has merit' (1990, p 74), it is clear at common law that, with the exceptions of mistake as to identity and mistake as to the nature of the marriage ceremony, the courts have not been prepared to invalidate a marriage (Cretney and Masson, 1997, p 66).

In accounting for judicial preoccupation with non-disclosure of transgender status prior to marriage, it will be contended that such anxiety is inextricably linked to a perception of proximity to the homosexual body. To reiterate then, laws pertaining to consummation and/or pre-marital 'fraud' have no, or little, relevance to the question of the validity of marriages involving transgender people. Rather, the location of transgender outside of the institution of marriage is an effect of denying sex claims. However, denial, and as we will see in Chapter 6, recognition, of sex claims within transgender marriage jurisprudence is clearly informed by concerns over 'fraud' and the nature of heterosexual intercourse. In trying to understand the relationship between the legal production of sex and these concerns, however, we should not look to the past in the form of legal doctrine surrounding consummation and/or pre-marital 'fraud'. Indeed, as we saw in Chapter 4, judicial preoccupation with heterosexual capacity is far from confined to the issue of marriage. Rather, the relationship between sex, heterosexual capacity and 'fraud' within transgender marriage jurisprudence is constructed in the legal present and finds its point of intersection in the homophobia of law.

5.2 MARRIAGE AS LOCUS OF THE 'NATURAL'

In mapping common law approaches to the sex claims of transgender people for the purposes of marriage, it is necessary to begin by returning to the landmark English decision of *Corbett v Corbett* that we considered in Chapter 3.[15] In *Corbett*, Ormrod J held

---

15   *Corbett v Corbett* [1970] 2 All ER 33.

that sex is determined at birth and by a congruence of chromosomal, gonadal and genital factors.[16] He made it clear, however, that he was not determining the sex of the respondent, April Ashley, at large, but only within the context of marriage. Crucially, it was within the context of marriage that the *Corbett* test came to be formulated in the (bio)logically and temporally specific fashion that it did. Indeed, as we saw in Chapter 3, Ormrod J had addressed the possibility that sex might be determined outside this specific (bio)logical and temporal framework for purposes other than marriage. The test was to be applied wherever sex was considered to be an essential determinant of a legal relationship. In Ormrod J's view the test could have no more obvious application than to marriage:

> [S]ex is clearly an essential determinant of the relationship called marriage, because it is and always has been recognised as the union of man and woman. It is the institution on which the family is built, and in which the capacity for natural heterosexual intercourse is an essential element. It has, of course, many other characteristics, of which companionship and mutual support is an important one, but the characteristics which distinguish it from all other relationships can only be met by two persons of opposite sex.[17]

This passage is revealing. It suggests that the capacity for heterosexual intercourse, and perhaps the capacity to procreate, are requirements of a lawful marriage. Yet there is no, nor has there ever been, a requirement to procreate in English common law,[18] or indeed ecclesiastical law. Moreover, the suggestion that 'the capacity for natural heterosexual intercourse is an essential element' of a marriage is also false in the sense that since the time of the Reformation an unconsummated marriage remains lawful until such time that a decree of nullity is granted, a legal step which, as already explained, is not automatic. However, prior to the Nullity of Marriage Act 1971, and therefore at the time of the Corbett decision, the granting of a decree of nullity did produce the effect of putting the parties retrospectively in the position of never having been married to each other. In other words, interpretation of the English law of consummation at the time of *Corbett* had the potential to invalidate marriages entered into by transgender people from their inception. That is to say, irrespective of any finding as to April Ashley's legal sex, it was open to Ormrod J to find, as he did in fact find,[19] that she was not a woman for the purposes of marriage due to her 'incapacity' to consummate a marriage. However, despite the apparent relevance of non-consummation to the validity of a challenged marriage at the time of *Corbett*, it is clear from the facts that April Ashley's marriage partner, Arthur *Corbett*, knew of her transgender status prior to the marriage. Accordingly, he was aware of the 'facts' from which Ormrod J deduced 'incapacity', a fact that serves to raise a question as to the equity of granting a nullity decree. Moreover, and of greater significance, Ormrod J's view that April Ashley was incapable of consummating a marriage is far from self-evident. Indeed, the facts before the court suggested otherwise.

Prior to the marriage April Ashley had undergone full sex reassignment surgery so that at the time of her marriage she possessed female genitalia and the capacity for heterosexual intercourse. Indeed, according to medical evidence there was 'no

---

16 *Ibid*, p 48.
17 *Ibid*.
18 See *Baxter v Baxter* [1948] AC 274; *B v B* [1954] 3 WLR 237; 2 All ER 598; [1955] P 42.
19 *Corbett v Corbett* [1970] 2 All ER 33, pp 49–50.

impediment on "her part" to sexual intercourse' her vagina being 'of ample size to admit a normal and erect penis'.[20] In seeking to understand why Ormrod J should wish to invalidate the respondent's capacity for heterosexual intercourse for the purposes of marriage, one need only focus on the word 'natural' in the above passage. In describing the respondent's vagina as an 'artificial cavity'[21] Ormrod J considered its use for sexual intercourse impossible to describe as 'ordinary and complete intercourse'[22] or, and in a reference to Dr Lushington's famous 19th century *dictum*,[23] as *'vera copula* of the natural sort of coitus'.[24]

It is the construction of April Ashley's vagina as the locus of the 'unnatural' which is perhaps the most revealing aspect of Ormrod J's judgment. The coding of April Ashley's vagina as 'unnatural' is, perhaps, especially curious given Ormrod J's willingness to assume her to be a woman for the purpose of considering the question of consummation.[25] The implication of this move appears to be that the vagina of the chromosomal female might also be a locus for the 'unnatural'.[26] However, in order to consign April Ashley's body to the realm of the 'unnatural' Ormrod J had first to distinguish the English Court of Appeal's decision in *SY v SY (orse W)*.[27] In *SY v SY* the court had held that where a wife lacked a natural vagina but could be given an artificial one by surgical intervention then coitus by means of that artificial vagina constituted *vera copula*, so as to consummate a marriage.[28] Indeed, and importantly, Wilmer LJ went so far as to state: '... [f]or myself I find it difficult to see why the enlargement of a vestigial vagina should be regarded as producing something different in kind from a vagina artificially created from nothing. The operation involved in either case is substantially the same.'[29] In coming to these conclusions Wilmer LJ took the view that Dr Lushington's famous dictum, while being a statement of commanding authority, had to be interpreted in the context of considerable 20th century advances made in medical science. Indeed, Dr Lushington himself had in 1845 been reluctant to pronounce a marriage void where there exists 'a reasonable probability that the lady can be made capable of a *vera copula* – of the natural sort of coitus'.[30] This willingness to take cognisance of contemporary surgical possibilities is, of course, consistent with the common law of consummation that has exhibited a reluctance to arrive at a conclusion of incapacity (Moran, 1990) preferring instead to explore the possibilities of 'cure'.[31]

---

20 *Ibid*, p 41.
21 *Ibid*, p 49.
22 *Ibid*.
23 *Ibid*. See *D-e v A-g (orse D-e)* [1845] 1 Rob Eccl 279; 163 ER 1039; 27 Digest (Repl) 273, p 2187.
24 *Ibid*.
25 *Ibid*.
26 Indeed, *B v B* [1954] 3 WLR 237; 2 All ER 598; [1955] P 42 would appear to provide some authority for that proposition.
27 *SY v SY (orse W)* [1962] 3 All ER 55.
28 *Ibid*, p 60.
29 *Ibid*, p 59.
30 *Ibid*, p 54.
31 See *Welde (alias Aston) v Welde* [1731] 2 Lee 580, p 586; *Brown v Brown* [1828] 1 Hag Ecc 523; *W v H (falsely called W)* [1861] 2 Sw and Tr 240, pp 244–45; *S (falsely called E) v E* [1863] 3 Sw & Tr 240; *G v G* [1871] LR 2 P and D 287, p 291; *L v L (falsely called W)* [1882] 7 PD 16; *T v M (falsely called T)* [1865] LR 1 P and D 31; *M (falsely called H) v H* [1864] 3 Sw & Tr 517, p 523; *WY v AY* [1946] SC 27; *S v S (otherwise C)* [1954] 3 All ER 736.

In a far from satisfactory manner, especially given that the medical evidence revealed that SY had 'no, or virtually no vagina',[32] Ormrod J exhibited no reluctance in arriving at a conclusion of incapacity, distinguishing the facts of *SY v SY* from those of *Corbett* on the basis that SY's vagina was abnormal rather than wholly absent. It would seem, therefore, that Ormrod J comprehended the 'naturalness' of the vagina in terms of degree. Yet, perceiving that such an understanding of the vagina posed a threat to the institution of marriage, he expressed the view:

> [B]y over-refining and over-defining the limits of 'normal' one may, in the end, produce a situation in which consummation may come to mean something altogether different from normal sexual intercourse.[33]

This differentiation of forms of 'unnaturalness' for the purposes of assessing the possibility of consummation in law is revealing. That is to say, it is not the 'unnatural' state of genitalia *per se* that renders a person incapable of consummating a marriage in Ormrod J's judgment. Rather, it is the fact that April Ashley is viewed as a male person from birth that leads to her vagina being viewed as an 'impossible' site of/for consummation. It is this 'fact' that places her vagina beyond the limits of the 'unnatural' that the law can accommodate. It is this 'fact' that enables Ormrod J to distinguish April Ashley's post-operative sexual practice from that of a (bio)logical woman who possessed 'a vagina artificially created from nothing'. In this regard, Ormrod J's 'willingness' to assume April Ashley to be a woman for the purpose of considering the question of consummation[34] proves unconvincing. It has been suggested that, while it is difficult to account for the discrepancy between *SY v SY* and *Corbett*, 'what marks out the naturalness, or otherwise, of the genitals is not so much their relation to transformative surgery as something much more subjective and difficult to quantify: male sexual pleasure' (Collier, 1995, p 157). I would put it rather differently. What is really significant in making (non)sense of the two decisions is a view of SY's transformative surgery in terms of a process of 'naturalisation' to be contrasted with the process of 'denaturalisation' which culminated in the construction of April Ashley's vagina. Of course, a view of April Ashley's vagina as 'unnatural' perhaps presupposes that male sexual pleasure ought not to be derived at this genital site. In my view, however, it is less a matter of the mere absence of male sexual pleasure than the presence of judicial horror at the prospect of intercourse on account of the fact that Ormrod J always codes April Ashley's body as male. In other words, the overriding concern in Ormrod J's judgment is to insulate marriage, the institution of 'natural' heterosexual intercourse, from perceived 'homosexual' practice. In view of this anxiety it is, perhaps, hardly surprising that Ormrod J conflates April Ashley's desires, practices and body with homosexuality. In the first place, he expressed the following view of April Ashley's vagina:

---

32 *SY v SY (orse W)* [1962] 3 All ER 37, p 38. Indeed, while one of the medical inspectors appointed by the court in *SY v SY* found the respondent's vagina to be 'two inches from the orifice', a consulting specialist, who had treated the respondent for some years, described her vagina as being 'no more than the beginning of a vaginal passage of about one inch long' (Taitz, 1986, p 145).

33 *Corbett v Corbett* [1970] 2 All ER 33, p 50.

34 *Ibid*, p 49.

> When such a cavity has been constructed in a male, the difference between sexual intercourse using it, and anal or intra-crural intercourse is, in my judgment, to be measured in centimetres.[35]

Lest the significance of this reference to anal intercourse be underestimated, consider the following rhetorical flourishes offered more recently by Ormrod J regarding post-operative transgender sexual practice:

> Would anyone regard intercourse per pouch as better than intercourse per annum? ... Can it seriously be argued that penetration of a surgically constructed pouch is any nearer consummation than penetration of the anus? (Finlay, 1996, pp 508–09).[36]

In juxtaposing use of April Ashley's vagina/pouch, a term that suggests her marsupial 'otherness', with the practice of anal intercourse, the judgment brings into view the homosexual body and its assumed practices. Indeed, use of the term 'pouch' might be viewed as reinforcing that coupling. The term refers to a part of the female marsupial body where newly born offspring complete their development. Clearly, the post-operative transgender body lacks procreative capacity. Yet the term might be read as the repository of a secret, specifically of homosexual desire. In a number of other respects, and informed by prevailing medical knowledge, Ormrod J's judgment further inscribes homosexuality onto the body of April Ashley. The nature and importance of the references to homosexuality in the judgment must be understood in the context of prevailing medical knowledge. It must be recognised that in 1970, the contemporary medical perspective of gender dysphoria had not yet displaced the *discovery story of transsexuality* (King, 1993, pp 45, 63) as the dominant medical paradigm for understanding transgender bodies. While legal reasoning cannot be reduced to medical knowledge, and while legal preoccupation with the *discovery story of transsexuality* has, as we saw in earlier chapters, outlived that story's era of dominance within medicine, it is important to appreciate that Ormrod J wrote his judgment at a time when medical knowledge placed a premium on transgender 'authenticity'. In contrast to the gender dysphoria perspective, which seeks to ascertain the sex in which it is best for a person to live and which is therefore capable of considering suitable for sex reassignment surgery 'effeminate homosexuals' and 'atypical transvestites' (Koranyi, 1980, p 156) the *discovery story of transsexuality* views these categories as anathema to the 'truth' of transsexuality. Accordingly, surgery is deemed appropriate only for:

> ... those males who are the most feminine, have been expressing this femininity since earliest childhood, have not had periods of living accepted as masculine males, have not enjoyed their penises and have not advertised themselves as males (for example, by female impersonation) (Stoller, 1968, p 251).

In various portions of the judgment April Ashley is contrasted with this picture of the classic or 'true' transsexual. It is made clear that she worked as a 'female impersonator' in Paris for a four-year period from 1956.[37] This theme, which draws on cultural conflation of homosexuality and transgender, was pursued by Ormrod J who considered the

---

35   *Ibid.*

36   These questions were put to Dr Finlay in a letter written by Sir Roger Ormrod in January 1989 in response to Dr Finlay's co-authored publication with Dr WAW Walters (Finlay and Walters, 1988).

37   *Corbett v Corbett* [1970] 2 All ER 33, p 36.

respondent's outward appearance at first sight to be 'convincingly feminine'.[38] However, closer and longer examination in the witness box revealed her 'voice, manner, gestures and attitudes (to be) increasingly reminiscent of the accomplished female impersonator'.[39] While this judicial postulation of a 'natural' femininity confronts a feminist politics and perhaps implicates a middle-class gaze, (Tyler, 1991, p 57)[40] it is the homophobia of law that is most apparent in Ormrod J's judgment. Indeed, homophobic anxiety is, perhaps, evident in fear over inadvertent proximity to the male body suggested by Ormrod J's reading of April Ashley's gender performance as 'convincingly feminine'.

Moreover, Ormrod J noted that April Ashley was asked in cross-examination 'whether she had ever had an erection, and whether she had had ejaculations'.[41] While she, understandably, refused to answer this question, its purpose seems to have been to establish homosexuality over transsexuality, as in the *discovery story of transsexuality* erotic pleasure in the penis does not exist in the 'true' transsexual (Stoller, 1973). Indeed, it was the use of homosexuality, primarily, which served to demonstrate the respondent's departure from the 'truth' of transsexuality. Thus in a doctor's letter of 1953, a time prior to sex reassignment surgery, the respondent was described as a 'constitutional homosexual'.[42] This view was shared by two of the medical experts called for the petitioner, who described April Ashley as a 'male homosexual transsexualist',[43] the import of which was that she was a male homosexual who had undergone surgical reassignment. In other words, the judgment, in addition to denying April Ashley female status, casts doubt upon the 'authenticity' of her transsexuality on account of her 'homosexuality'.

The construction of the respondent's 'homosexuality' calls for closer attention. The characterisation of April Ashley as homosexual appears to be based on hospital records compiled in 1953 and containing summaries of 'therapeutic' interviews in which she allegedly 'gave some account of various homosexual experiences' had on board a ship while employed by the Merchant Navy.[44] Yet, it is highly unlikely that April Ashley would view these experiences as homosexual, as she viewed herself as a woman. Rather, it is more plausible that April Ashley's account referred to pre-operative sexual experiences with men upon which numerous doctors, and at least one legal commentator (Taitz, 1986, p 146)[45] subsequently inscribed homosexuality. Moreover, given Ormrod J's penchant for highlighting absence of anal intercourse in discussions of homosexual behaviour, it would appear that this practice was either performed, or imagined to have

---

38 *Ibid*, p 47.

39 *Ibid*.

40 Thus Carole-Anne Tyler has argued that '[i]t is only from a middle-class point of view that Dolly Parton looks like a female impersonator; from a working-class point of view she could be the epitome of genuine womanliness' (1991, p 57).

41 *Corbett v Corbett* [1970] 2 All ER 33, p 37.

42 *Ibid*, p 36.

43 *Ibid*, p 43.

44 *Ibid*, p 36.

45 Thus Jerold Taitz, while recognising homophobia as a possible explanation for some of Ormrod J's rather colourful descriptions of April Ashley's genital region, refers to the 'admitted homosexual appetites of the parties to the case' (1986, p 146).

been performed, on the body of April Ashley. In this regard, the scripting of April Ashley as homosexual is an effect of the inability of medicine and law to read anal intercourse as anything other than the locus of homosexual activity. The practice can signify only a particular desire, a particular relation of bodies (Moran, 1996, Chapter 2).

The concern over the proximity of homosexuality to marriage is also apparent in Ormrod J's commentary upon the petitioner, Mr Arthur Corbett. In the witness box Corbett had apparently informed the court that from a comparatively early age, he had experienced a desire to dress up in female clothes, a desire that had persisted into adult life.[46] As this narrative unfolds in the judgment, Ormrod J's anxiety becomes more evident:

> From about 1948 onwards his interest in transvestism increased; at first it was mainly literary, attracting him to pornographic bookshops, but gradually he began to make contact with people of similar tendencies and associated with them from time to time in London. This led to frequent homosexual behaviour with numerous men, stopping short of anal intercourse. As time went on he became more and more involved in the society of sexual deviants, and interested in sexual deviations of all kinds.[47]

This passage is revealing for reasons other than the obvious revulsion that this history provoked and the fact that it was through this world of 'sexual deviation' that April Ashley and Arthur Corbett had first met. It is unclear how much of the passage is directly attributable to Corbett and how much reflects Ormrod J's interpretation of the facts. The assertion that Corbett engaged in 'frequent homosexual behaviour with numerous men', a view reproduced within legal scholarship (Smith, 1971, p 1007; David, 1975, p 319; Taitz, 1987, p 146; MacKenzie, 1992, p 561), is, perhaps, not the most persuasive reading of the facts. After all, the passage makes clear that Corbett's 'homosexual behaviour' occurred only after he had met, and by implication with, persons of similar 'transvestic' tendencies. Accordingly, a more convincing reading of the facts would be that the (trans)gender identities of the parties to the 'homosexual behaviour' preclude, or at least problematise, viewing that behaviour as homosexual. Moreover, Ormrod J, in suggesting that contact with people of similar 'transvestic' tendencies 'led to frequent homosexual behaviour', creates the impression of a causal link between, as well as conflating, the two phenomena. In the final analysis, any distinction is consumed by Ormrod J's deployment of the all-purpose category for the 'unnatural', 'sexual deviant'. The reference to 'frequent homosexual behaviour', in Ormrod J's judgment, is of interest in another regard. We are told that Arthur Corbett's 'homosexual behaviour', frequent though it was, 'stopped short of anal intercourse'. That Ormrod J brings this fact into play reveals a phallocentric judicial assumption that anal sex is the logical end of same-sex sexual activity. In this regard his judgment, even while narrating the absence, and the frequency of the absence, of anal intercourse, couples homosexuality with anal intercourse (Moran, 1996, p 95), and through the figure of Arthur Corbett links both the identity and the practice with transgender.

In another passage of the judgment Ormrod J struggles to comprehend Arthur Corbett's stated desire to both be (like) April Ashley ('[she] was so much more than I

---

46   *Corbett v Corbett* [1970] 2 All ER 33, p 37.
47   *Ibid.*

could ever hope to be. The reality was far greater than my fantasy') and to have sexual relations with her, a desire which Ormrod J described as 'essentially pathetic'.[48] His difficulty arises out of the fact that law assumes a particular, and binary, gendered relationship between the parties to sexual desire. This assumption of an oppositional relation between sexual 'having' and gendered 'being', as both 'natural' and appropriate, is, of course, one that continues to problematise gay and lesbian identities and desires within legal discourse. Indeed, one suspects that the spectre of homosexuality again looms large in Ormrod J's problematisation of Arthur Corbett's masculinity on account of his cross-dressing practices. In contrasting the love of a male transvestite for a transsexual with 'the feelings of a full man in love with a girl',[49] Ormrod J emasculates the body of Arthur Corbett and juxtaposes it to the 'pastiche of femininity'[50] which he inscribed onto the body of April Ashley. In summing up each of their stories, Ormrod J expressed the view:

> Listening to each party describing this strange relationship, my principal impression was that it had little or nothing in common with any heterosexual relationship which I could recall hearing about in a fairly extensive experience of this court.[51]

Thus rejection of April Ashley's sex claims is tied, importantly, to Ormrod J's analysis of her pre-operative sexual practice, gender performance and post-operative heterosexual capacity, an analysis that ultimately conflates transgender with homosexuality. This conflation is, as Majorie Garber has suggested, fuelled by 'a desire to tell the difference, to guard against a difference that might otherwise put the identity of one's own position in question' (1992, p 130). Moreover, it is exacerbated, and indeed replicated, through Ormrod J's problematic reading of the sexual practice and desire of April Ashley's marriage partner, Arthur Corbett. This is not to reduce the decision, or its rationale, to the gender, sexual and/or bodily specificities of April Ashley or Arthur Corbett. Rather, it is to highlight how, especially in a case about marriage, the facts of the case serve to dramatise judicial anxiety over an imagined proximity to the homosexual body. While Ormrod J's (bio)logical test has been subject to sustained criticism (see, for example, Green, 1970; Smith, 1971; Walton, 1974, 1984; Finlay, 1980; Samuels, 1984; Dewar, 1985; Taitz, 1986, 1987, 1988, 1992; Kirby, 1987; Mountbatten, 1991, 1994, 1996; Muller, 1994) the suggestion here is that there is more to the *Corbett* decision than (bio)logic. Indeed, it is perhaps especially significant that homophobia is so evident in a case which, more than any other, inaugurated transgender jurisprudence in the common law world.

More recently, in *S-T (formerly J) v J* the English Court of Appeal had to consider the transgender/marriage relation in a case involving a pre-operative (female-to-male) transgender man.[52] We considered this case in Chapter 3 largely in the context of Ward LJ's imaginative 'flight' from *Corbett*. Here the case is revisited as evidence of the homophobia of law. Thus while Ward LJ contemplated the adoption of the test of *psychological and anatomical harmony*, and therefore gravitated toward reform

---

48 *Ibid.*
49 *Ibid*, p 38.
50 *Ibid*, p 47.
51 *Ibid*, p 38.
52 *S-T (formerly J) v J* [1998] 1 All ER 431.

jurisprudence, that step was premised on an uncoupling of the post-operative transgender body from homosexuality. That is to say, the prelude to the moment of 'departure' from *Corbett* involved not only negation of the sex claims of J, but also the homosexualisation of his body. In other words, it is not merely the depiction of the pre-operative body as monstrous, as an 'ambiguous condition to which [J] is condemned',[53] that serves to reduce judicial anxiety regarding the re-sexing of the post-operative body that the court subsequently imagines. Rather, the homosexual sign that law perceives this 'monstrous' body to emit proves important in law's reappraisal of the post-operative body. While not challenging a finding that he was female, J applied for ancillary relief under the Matrimonial Causes Act 1973.[54] It was the merits of this application that both the trial judge and, on appeal, the Court of Appeal, had to determine. In dismissing the defendant's appeal, the Court of Appeal held that:

> [J] had committed a serious crime: he had deceived the plaintiff into the marriage and, in doing so, had placed himself in a position where he had the opportunity to apply for a wide range of relief which would not otherwise have been open to him. His conduct at the time of the marriage, when judged by principles of public policy, brought down the scales overwhelmingly against the grant of relief.[55]

In evaluating J's conduct in public policy terms, and in concluding that J's act of 'perjury' had crossed the threshold of seriousness, thereby invoking the principle of public policy and barring ancillary relief, the Court of Appeal noted that there was 'a present public interest in buttressing and protecting the institution of marriage'.[56] Like the trial judge, Hollis J, the Court of Appeal took the view that the 'deception' perpetrated by J against S-T, one 'as profound a betrayal of trust between two people as can be imagined',[57] went to 'the heart of marriage',[58] given that 'single sex unions remain proscribed as fundamentally abhorrent to [the] notion of marriage'.[59] The horror that the perception of proximity to homosexuality within marriage evokes is also apparent in the extensive list of deceptions, including the potentially lethal non-disclosure of HIV/AIDS, in relation to which Ward LJ expressed the view that he 'would be very slow to allow an appeal to public policy striking out a claim for ancillary relief'.[60] The view of the marital union between S-T and J as a 'legal impossibility'[61] appears to be premised on a view of J's body as pre-operative or as still in transition. That is to say, it is the fact that J's body lacked a penis that assumes importance in law's characterisation of his relationship with S-T as a 'single sex union'. This becomes especially clear in the contrast drawn between the post-operative body and J's body as one that 'denied him the fulfilment of his desire'.[62] It is also apparent in the contrast drawn between J's body and that of 'a "full blooded"

---

53 *Ibid*, p 467.
54 *Ibid*, p 433.
55 *Ibid*, p 432. The crime J was found to have committed was the crime of perjury (Perjury Act 1911, s 3).
56 *Ibid*, p 465.
57 *Ibid*, p 441.
58 *Ibid*, p 442.
59 *Ibid*, p 465.
60 *Ibid*, p 466.
61 *Ibid*, p 450.
62 *Ibid*, p 458.

male'.[63] Here the pre-operative female-to-male body, or more specifically the vaginaed male body, is, and can only be, read as 'female' and 'lesbian'. This, highly problematic, legal inscription of homosexuality onto the body of J serves to undermine his sex claims in the marriage context and, indeed, the claims of all transgender people who have not undergone phalloplasty or vaginoplasty. This characterisation of J as lesbian is again apparent in the court's assessment of 'the effect ['perjury' had] on the other party'.[64] Thus the court drew particular attention to the 'fact' that the effect on S-T, who had stated that 'I am not into women',[65] had been 'catastrophic and that she has been traumatised by the experience'.[66]

The willingness of the court to accept that S-T was, for the 17 years of her 'marriage' to J, unaware of his transgender status is, at least in part, an effect of the homophobia of law. That is to say, the court refused to see homosexuality from a perspective internal to the marriage. It is not only S-T who saw 'only what she wanted to see and what she expected', as one medical expert put it.[67] Rather, law too averts its eyes until, consequent on the breakdown of the marriage, S-T, and therefore heterosexuality itself, has reached a safe distance from the horror of a 'single sex union'. In this regard the court's emphasis on 'fraud' and 'deception' not only addresses considerations of desert but also serves the psychological purpose of insulating heterosexual identity within marriage from homosexual contamination. Moreover, the court not only denied J heterosexual male status. Rather, in finding J guilty of perjury, of knowingly and wilfully making a false declaration for the purpose of procuring a marriage,[68] the court casts doubt as to the 'authenticity' of any belief in such status that the vaginaed man may harbour. Thus Ward LJ expressed the view 'I cannot accept that in his heart of hearts ... [J] ... did not know that his body did not conform with what he desired for it'.[69] Here the vaginaed male body as harmonious, complete and heterosexual lies beyond the judicial imagination. This view of the pre-operative body as both monstrous and homosexual is, as we will see, one that consistently informs transgender jurisprudence, irrespective of approach. Moreover, and importantly, the 'monstrosity' of the pre-operative body in legal discourse is tied, and crucially so, to a view of this body's sexual practice as homosexual.

The judicial concern to insulate marriage from homosexual incursion is again apparent in the English decision of *W v W*.[70] In this case, the refusal, and the nature of the refusal, of the English judiciary to depart from the (bio)logic of *Corbett* receives particular

---

63   *Ibid*, p 436.

64   *Ibid*, p 479.

65   *Ibid*, p 439.

66   *Ibid*, p 456. Judicial concern over the effect of 'deceit' on the sexual identity of the 'deceived' party is particularly notable in the case of Sean O'Neill (born Sharon Clark), a (bio)logical female who was charged with 11 felony counts of sexual assault, criminal impersonation of the opposite gender and sexual assault on a child due to sexual intercourse with an underage girl (*State of Colorado v Sharon Clark*). Here gender deception is treated as tantamount to rape (Minkowitz, 1995). For further discussion of the Sean O'Neill case, see Califia, 1997, pp 234–37. For an English case very similar on the facts see the case of Jennifer Saunders (*R v Saunders*, unreported, Pink Paper, 196, 12 October 1991; see, also, Smith, 1995).

67   *Ibid*, p 440.

68   *Ibid*, pp 452–54.

69   *Ibid*, p 458.

70   *W v W* (2000) *The Times*, 31 October (Transcript).

illumination. As explained in Chapter 3, *W v W* involved the recognition of the sex claims of a post-operative (male-to-female) intersexed woman for the purposes of marriage. Legal recognition in this case was premised on the fact that chromosomes, gonads and genitalia were not congruent at birth. In view of the inapplicability of the *Corbett* test to the facts, Charles J focused on Mrs W's 'ambiguous' genitalia and chose to privilege the genital factor.[71] While this legal move is consistent with Ormrod J's speculations about situations of sex 'incongruence', it reveals a concern over (bio)logic to be a rhetorical device serving to mask what is really at stake in marriage cases. The fact that Ormrod J privileges the genital factor in determining sex in the event of 'incongruence', and that Charles J builds his judgment around that moment, is to be accounted for by reference to the fact that both cases concerned issues of marriage. The crux of the matter is captured by Ormrod J:

> Having regard to the essentially heterosexual character of the relationship which is called marriage, the criteria must, in my judgment, be biological, for even the most extreme degree of transsexualism in a male ... cannot reproduce a person who is naturally capable of performing the essential role of a woman in marriage.[72]

While phallocentric and performativist assumptions about 'the essential role of a woman in marriage' clearly confront a feminist politics, it is concern over the 'naturalness' of heterosexual capacity that lies at the heart of the passage. In short, Ormrod J and Charles J, who followed Ormrod J's underlying reasoning, seek to ensure that persons to be characterised as female had genitalia at birth that are, in some important sense, 'opposite', and therefore 'complementary', to the male penis. It is this concern that led to considerable scrutiny and speculation about the genital region of April Ashley's and Mrs W's bodies at birth. For Ormrod J, the 'naturalness' of heterosexual intercourse with a man seems to require, at the very least, genitalia that are at birth 'unalterably female or approaching female in character' (Ormrod, 1972, p 86). For Charles J, the mere 'fact' of genital 'ambiguity' at birth, despite the absence of a vagina, appears sufficient.[73] While the two judgments differ by degree, they share a concern to distinguish the 'natural' from the 'unnatural' and to insulate the institution of marriage from the realm of the 'unnatural'. It is especially significant that in both judgments, thinking about 'natural' heterosexual intercourse leads to the invocation of an intersex/transgender dyad. It is curious why this distinction is insisted upon. After all, the heterosexual liaison that Ormrod J and Charles J imagine is only possible on the facts of *Corbett* and *W v W* after sex reassignment surgery. The difference appears to lie in the relationship between sex reassignment surgery and 'nature' as it is constructed in the two judgments. Thus the willingness to characterise Mrs W's post-operative genitalia as 'natural' arises out of viewing her surgery in terms of a process of 'naturalisation', to be contrasted with the process of 'denaturalisation' that culminated in the construction of April Ashley's 'artificial cavity'.[74] This move is possible only through viewing intersexed bodies as nature's 'mistake'. In this regard, recognition of the sex claims of Mrs W proves highly

---

71   *Ibid*, p 17.

72   *Corbett v Corbett* [1970] 2 All ER 33, p 51.

73   *W v W* (2000) *The Times*, 31 October (Transcript), p 17.

74   *Corbett v Corbett* [1970] 2 All ER 33, p 49.

problematic for an intersex politics.[75] It is this view of a 'mistake' in nature at birth that enables Charles J, like Ormrod J before him with regard to the SY decision, to differentiate forms of 'unnaturalness' and to recast them along temporal lines. In other words, it is the 'fact' that Mrs W's genitalia were 'ambiguous' at birth that rendered possible the positioning of her vagina within the limits of the 'unnatural' that the law can accommodate.

However, the trope of the '(un)natural' in the judgment of Charles J cannot be reduced to the signification of 'error' and its correction through sex reassignment surgery. Rather, the fact that the 'unnatural' is differentiated by degree, and that not every degree of 'unnaturalness' can be rescued from that realm through surgical intervention, directs our attention to something else, something more, namely, judicial anxiety over proximity to the homosexual body. Moreover, it is precisely in order to insulate intersexed bodies from homosexuality that an intersex/transgender dyad is instantiated. Indeed, Charles J, like Ormrod J before him, went to considerable length to draw this distinction. Here nature, albeit in 'error', is to be contrasted with the artifice of transgender, and the contrast serves to conflate transgender with homosexuality. However, the very repetition of the distinction reveals its vulnerability (Butler, 1993, p 10), as does Charles J's concern, like Ormrod J's before him, over the 'dangers in analysing too meticulously or theoretically the essential ingredients of normal sexual intercourse'.[76] Indeed, the coupling of intersex with heterosexuality itself produces a degree of judicial anxiety over proximity to the homosexual body. Thus in commenting on a relationship Mrs W had in the mid- to late-1960s with a man from Manchester, Charles J expressed the view that it was 'at least in part of a homosexual nature'.[77] While the reason for this characterisation is not rendered explicit, it appears to be based on either Mrs W's evidence of, or judicial assumptions as to, penile penetration of her anus. This interpretation is supported by passages from Ormrod J's judgment, which Charles J chose to cite, concerning the 'homosexual' pre-operative sexual practices of April Ashley.[78]

The words 'at least in part of a homosexual nature' are revealing in another regard, one that ultimately enables Charles J to hold the transgender/intersex dyad in place. That is to say, pre-operative anal intercourse, or the possibility of its enactment, is characterised as bearing a different relation to intersex and transgender. It is to this point that the judgment of Charles J ultimately leads. The point is captured in Charles J's reiterated statement that Mrs W 'would never have been able to have sexual intercourse as either a man or a woman without surgical intervention'.[79] It is this 'inability' existing in nature, a factor that of itself serves to sanitise the intersexed body, which assumes significance despite pre-operative sexual practice 'in part of a homosexual nature'. In contrast to post-operative transgender people, whose surgery represents a move against nature, sex reassignment surgery in the case of an intersexed person is depicted as a necessary step in the 'naturalisation' and 'heterosexualisation' of the body. This characterisation of surgery as necessary, as a prerequisite to 'natural' heterosexual intercourse, leads to a view of

---

75 For a discussion of an emerging intersex politics see, eg, Triea, 1994; McClintock, 1997; Chase, 1998.

76 *W v W* (2000) *The Times*, 31 October (Transcript), p 18.

77 *Ibid*, p 2.

78 *Ibid*, p 8.

79 *Ibid*, p 18.

intersex as deserving. In contrast, transgender desire, including desire for sex reassignment surgery, much like homosexual desire with which it is so readily conflated, is scripted as wilful rather than given in nature.

While this analysis of the intersex/law nexus appears to break down in relation to the anomalous and much criticised decision of Bell J in *Re the Marriage of C v D (formerly called C)* (Bailey-Harris, 1979, p 660; Finlay, 1996, p 516),[80] that decision, one considered in Chapter 3, is perhaps also explicable, at least in part, in terms of the homophobia of law. That is to say, the different outcomes in *Re the Marriage of C v D (formerly called C)* and *W v W* might be comprehended through reference to judicial findings in *Re the Marriage of C v D (formerly called C)* that Mr C lacked the capacity for heterosexual intercourse,[81] despite undergoing 'four surgical operations at the age of twenty-two years to correct his external sex organs',[82] and, perhaps more significantly, that he had not disclosed his intersexed status to his wife prior to the marriage.[83] As we saw in *S-T (formerly J) v J*, and will see in other decisions to be considered in this chapter and in Chapter 6, non-disclosure of prior status has served to generate considerable anxiety over perceived proximity to the homosexual body, anxiety which calls into question law's psychological commitment to the re-sexing of bodies.

The concern to insulate marriage against homosexual incursion is also apparent in the attitude of the European Court of Human Rights hearing appeals from the UK regarding alleged violations of Art 12 of the European Convention on Human Rights, which provides that: '... men and women of marriageable age have the right to marry and to found a family, according to the national laws governing the exercise of this right.' Refusal to recognise transgender sex claims for the purposes of Art 12 has been especially noticeable within the transgender jurisprudence of the European Court. Thus in *Rees v UK*[84] and *Cossey v UK*[85] Mark Rees and Caroline Cossey challenged the adoption in English law of exclusively (bio)logical criteria for determining a person's sex for marriage purposes, contending that Art 12 was silent as to the criteria to be applied.[86] This contention, while finding support from Martens J who, in his dissenting judgment in *Cossey*, rejected the idea that sex in the context of marriage could only mean 'the biological constitution of an individual which is fixed at birth',[87] was rejected emphatically by the European Court. The Court in both *Rees* and *Cossey* insisted, despite the fact that 'the law can give an autonomous meaning to the concept of "sex", as it does to concepts like "person", "family", "home" [and] "property"',[88] that the 'right to marry' referred to traditional marriage between persons of the opposite (bio)logical sex.[89] In

---

80 *Re the Marriage of C v D (falsely called C)* [1979] 35 FLR 340.

81 *Ibid*, p 342.

82 *Ibid*. This problematisation of heterosexual capacity in the case of the (female-to-male) intersexed man serves to redraw attention to law's view of the penis as a more complex anatomical organ than the vagina and therefore to a gender bias in the differential treatment of male-to-female and female-to-male bodies.

83 *Ibid*, p 344.

84 *Rees v UK* (1986) 9 EHRR 56.

85 *Cossey v UK* (1991) 13 EHRR 622.

86 *Ibid*, p 642.

87 *Ibid*, p 657.

88 *Sheffield v Horsham v UK* (1998) 27 EHRR 163, p 210, *per* Van Dijk J.

89 *Cossey v UK* (1991) 13 EHRR 622, pp 642–43; *Rees v UK* (1986) 9 EHRR 56, p 68.

Rees the Court found that this followed 'from the wording of the Article which makes it clear that Art 12 is mainly concerned to protect marriage as the basis of the family'.[90] This interpretation, which assumes procreation to follow inevitably from the fact of marriage, and therefore effectively converts a 'right to found a family' into a requirement of citizenship, is surely disingenuous, especially in view of the fact that procreation is irrelevant to the law of marriage under English law. As Martens J pointed out in *Cossey*: '... it cannot be assumed that the stated purpose of the right to marry (to protect marriage as the basis of the family) can serve as a basis for its delimitation.'[91] In *Cossey* the European Court sought to justify exclusion of transgender people from the sanctity of marriage in the following terms:

> ... attachment to the traditional concept of marriage provides sufficient reason for the continued adoption of biological criteria for determining a person's sex for the purposes of marriage.[92]

This passage, which has been recited in subsequent decisions of the European Court dismissing allegations of violation of Art 12,[93] is revealing. That is to say, it becomes clear that the exclusion of Caroline Cossey from the category 'woman' for marriage purposes is not an effect of an overriding (bio)logical imperative. Rather, 'biological criteria' are endorsed because they have the effect of bolstering 'the traditional concept of marriage'. In view of the fact that biology is not, of itself, determinative of the issue and that procreation is irrelevant to the validity of marriage, the only way to make sense of the words 'attachment to the traditional concept of marriage' is to interpret them to require the capacity for 'natural' heterosexual intercourse. In this regard, the sexual practices of transgender people are once again conflated with homosexual practice. In other words, homophobic anxiety is central to the European Court's determination of transgender sex claims for marriage purposes. This is perhaps rendered most explicit in dissenting judgments in *B v France*[94] where the European Court's recognition of a violation of Art 8 served to intensify anxiety because it 'could lead to consequences which ... go far beyond the requirements of Art 8'.[95] The particular consequence that most concerned the dissenting judges was the possibility that '[a]fter rectification of civil status, a transsexual will be able to marry a person of his true sex'.[96] Indeed, Valticos J, 'seeing as a

---

90 *Ibid.*

91 *Cossey v UK* (1991) 13 EHRR 622, p 656.

92 *Ibid*, pp 642–43.

93 See, eg, *Sheffield and Horsham v UK* (1998) 27 EHRR 163, p 181.

94 *B v France* (1993) 16 EHRR 1.

95 *Ibid*, p 36, *per* Pinheiro Farinha J. Indeed, but for concern over the possibility of this consequence Pinheiro Farinha J would have found in favour of violation of Art 8. See, also, Pettiti J, p 38, 41; Valticos J, p 43; and Walsh J, p 51.

96 *Ibid*, p 38, *per* Pettiti J. While Martens J in *Cossey* took the view that recognition of violation of Art 8 required that 'the new sexual identity acquired by post-operative transsexuals should be fully and in all respects recognised by the law' (*Cossey v UK* (1991) 13 EHRR 622, pp 654–55) the concern of the dissenting judges in *B v France* is that this will be the practical effect. Moreover, the view that a finding of violation of Art 8 necessarily leads to a finding of violation of Art 12 lacks wide support among the European Court judges. Indeed, Loucaides J has stressed that '"private life" and "marriage" are two different concepts, the scope and protection of which are governed by different factors and considerations. The right to respect for private life does not automatically coincide with the right to marry' (*Sheffield and Horsham v UK* (1998) 27 EHRR 163, p 186). This view maps the analysis of Ellis J referred to earlier in the chapter (*Attorney-General v Otahuhu Family Court* [1995] 1 NZLR 603, p 616).

consequence half-feminised men claiming the right to marry normally constituted men', asked 'where would the line be drawn?'[97] This line or boundary that the dissenting judges sought to clarify is, of course, one that places distance between heterosexual and homosexual desire. Anxiety over perception of proximity to the homosexual body finds expression in another regard. Thus Walsh J stated that '[i]t could be very unfortunate if the law permitted a situation in which a person wishing to marry a person of the other biological sex could not, when a doubt arises, be satisfied as to the true sex of the other party save by the admission of the other party'[98] and for this reason insisted that 'any alleged violation of Art 8 in this sphere must be examined in the context of not totally concealing or falsifying a record of historical fact'.[99] This imagined scenario of 'fraud' or non-disclosure finds further expression in *Sheffield and Horsham v UK*, the most recent transgender case to come before the European Court.[100] Thus Loucaides J insisted that in relation to the right to marry:

> ... the biologically based definition of ... sexual identity may have to be maintained. This is not only because it is in accordance with the concept of marriage in the context of Art 12 of the Convention but also in order to protect the legitimate expectations of the other party to the marriage to know the gender status of his partner on the basis of biological criteria. This status is interwoven with the sexual life of the couple and their capacity to have children which are significant elements in a relationship of marriage.[101]

While Loucaides J links this concern over non-disclosure of transgender status to the absence of procreative capacity it is clear, as explained earlier, that such capacity is irrelevant to the law of marriage. Moreover, and while 'the legitimate expectations of the other party' might encompass procreative capacity, non-disclosure of infertility does not serve to vitiate a marriage contract. By the same token, there is nothing in the reference to 'the sexual life of the couple', including that phrase's possible allusion to an 'incapacity' to consummate a marriage, which precludes a valid marriage from coming into existence. It is, however, precisely this concern over 'the sexual life of the couple' that contains the source of judicial anxiety, namely, male 'horror' at the prospect of engaging unwittingly in 'unnatural' (homo)sexual intercourse.

Legal anxiety over perceived proximity to the homosexual body is also apparent in the transgender jurisprudence of a number of North American jurisdictions. In *Anonymous v Anonymous*[102] the New York Supreme Court held a marriage between a pre-operative (male-to-female) transgender woman and a non-commissioned male officer in the United States army to be a nullity because it found the former not to be 'female at the time of the marriage ceremony'.[103] However, the court did not confine its finding to the fact of pre-operative status at the time of the marriage. Rather, Buschmann J, in speculating that '[i]t may be that since that time the defendant's sex has been changed to female by operative procedures',[104] expressed the view:

---

97 *Ibid*, p 43.
98 *Ibid*, p 51.
99 *Ibid*.
100 *Sheffield v Horsham v UK* (1998) 27 EHRR 163.
101 *Ibid*, p 187, *per* Loucaides J partially dissenting.
102 *Anonymous v Anonymous* 325 NYS 2d 499 (1971).
103 *Ibid*.
104 *Ibid*, p 500.

> ... it would appear from the medical articles and other information supplied by counsel, that mere removal of the male organs would not, in and of itself, change a person into a true female.[105]

While this passage might be interpreted as requiring surgery over and beyond the 'mere' removal of male organs, it is contended that Buschmann J's determination of sex for the purposes of marriage tends toward the (bio)logical and temporal specificity of *Corbett*. This is evident from the following contentious passage of his judgment:

> The mere fact that the law provides that physical incapacity for sexual relationship shall be ground for annulling a marriage is of itself sufficient indication of the public policy that such relationship shall exist with the result and for the purpose of begetting offspring.[106]

However, a reading of the decision as grounded in (bio)logic needs to be tempered by judicial horror generated around the transgender body. This is particularly noticeable in relation to non-disclosure of transgender status prior to the marriage ceremony. Thus we learn that on the night of the wedding the plaintiff soldier 'awoke at 2 o'clock in the morning, reached for the defendant and upon touching the defendant, discovered that the defendant had male sexual organs' at the sight of which '[h]e immediately left the bed' and 'got drunk some more'.[107] This scene, which was vividly portrayed in Neil Jordan's film *The Crying Game*,[108] produces legal anxiety due to an imagined proximity to the homosexual body. In this case, as in others, it is 'cultural imagery' as much as, if not more than, deduction or policy that influences 'judicial rule choice' (Kennedy, 1997, p 405).

Three years later in the case of *B v B*[109] the New York Supreme Court was again called on to consider the sex claims of a transgender person. Here the court held Mark B, a pre-operative (female-to-male) transgender man, to be female for the purposes of marriage. Accordingly, his marriage to a (bio)logical woman was declared to be invalid. This case is significant in a number of respects. While recognising the possibility that Mark B 'may function as a male in other situations and in other relationships' the court insisted that he 'cannot function as a husband by assuming male duties and obligations inherent in the marriage relationship'.[110] The contemplation of a different outcome with regard to 'other situations and in other relationships' links the case to *Corbett* and to many decisions within reform jurisprudence, thereby de-emphasising discontinuity. As for Mark B's 'inability' to function as a husband, Heller J explained:

> [Mark B] does not have male sexual organs, does not possess a normal penis, and in fact does not have a penis. Apparently, hormone treatments and surgery have not succeeded in supplying the necessary apparatus to enable [Mark B] to function as a man for the purposes of procreation. In the same way surgery has not reached the point that can provide a man

---

105 *Ibid.*

106 *Ibid.*

107 *Ibid*, p 499.

108 The Crying Game (1992) Roadshow Entertainment Pty Ltd. For an analysis and critique of the film see, eg, Morkham, 1995.

109 *B v B* 355 NYS 2d 712 (1974).

110 *Ibid*, p 717.

with something resembling a normal female sexual organ, transplanting ovaries or a womb. Those are still beyond reach.[111]

As made clear earlier, procreative capacity has never been a requirement for lawful marriage. Rather, as in *Anonymous v Anonymous* and *Corbett*, Heller J deploys procreative capacity in order to ground judgment in (bio)logical sex. However, the passage also belies a concern over sexual functioning. Thus Mark B is viewed as physically incapable of heterosexual intercourse and therefore of consummating the marriage. It might be thought that judicial fixation on Mark B's sexual '(in)capacity' lends itself to the importance of a pre-/post-operative distinction in the judgment. Certainly, Heller J declared that 'attempted sex reassignment by mastectomy, hysterectomy, and androgenous hormonal therapy' had not had the effect of enabling Mark B 'to perform male functions in a marriage'.[112] However, Heller J's judgment makes clear that this is not due simply to the fact that Mark B lacked a penis. Rather, the reference to the lack of a 'normal penis' suggests that had Mark B undergone phalloplastic surgery his sex claims for marriage purposes would nevertheless have been denied as such surgery would not have produced a capacity for 'normal' heterosexual intercourse. It is at this moment in the judgment, perhaps, that the homophobia of law becomes most apparent. That is to say, it is not so much a concern over the functionality of Mark B's penis that most alarms the court. Rather, it is the 'unnatural' use of, and in the context of legal imagination of the post-operative body use of 'unnatural', sexual organs that produces legal anxiety. That is to say, vaginal penetration occasioned by a surgically constructed penis is viewed as constituting 'unnatural' use of female bodies. Moreover, judicial anxiety is heightened by the fact of Mark B's non-disclosure of his transgender status to his wife.[113] While the depiction of Mark B as fraudulent[114] is an effect of law's imposition of femaleness on his body, non-disclosure with regard to the past serves, once again, to foreground anxiety over inadvertent proximity to the homosexual body.

More recently, in the case of *Ladrach*,[115] an Ohio court held Elaine Ladrach to be male, thereby denying her application for a marriage license. In characterising Elaine as male, Clunk J, who could not bring himself to use female pronouns, rejected the 'very liberal posture'[116] adopted in *MT v JT*, preferring the (bio)logic of *Corbett*. However, it would seem that it is the effect produced by instantiating (bio)logic, rather than a concern for scientific verification, that guides Clunk J's judgment. The effect produced is to insulate marriage from the realm of the 'unnatural', and thereby from homosexual incursion. Thus the following passage is the only portion of Ormrod J's judgment that Clunk J chose to cite:

> Having regard to the essentially heterosexual character of the relationship which is called marriage, the criteria must, in my judgment be biological, for even the most extreme degree of transsexualism in a male or the most severe hormonal imbalance which can exist in a

---

111 *Ibid.*
112 *Ibid.*
113 *Ibid*, p 713.
114 *Ibid.*
115 *Re Ladrach* 32 Ohio Misc 2d 6 (1987).
116 *Ibid*, p 9.

person with male chromosomes, male gonads and male genitalia, cannot reproduce a person who is *naturally* capable of performing the essential role of a woman in marriage.[117]

It is significant that the court, having constituted Elaine Ladrach as 'incapable' of consummating a marriage on account of the 'unnatural' state of her genitalia, considered that 'incapacity' to be fatal to her application. After all, this was not a case in which a husband was seeking to have a marriage annulled, a scenario in which 'incapacity' to consummate a marriage might assume legal significance. Of course, her application is rightly denied under Ohio law if she is considered to be male. The point here is that legal construction of Elaine Ladrach as male arises due to the fact that the court characterises her as lacking a capacity that is irrelevant to the formation of a valid marriage. In other words, in the context of perceived proximity to the homosexual body the distinction between void and voidable marriages, a distinction that has been in place since the time of the Reformation (Cretney and Masson, 1997, p 63), breaks down, or at least 'incapacity' to consummate a marriage is redistributed across that divide.

With the exception of two recent decisions which have recognised sex claims for the purposes of marriage,[118] and which will therefore be considered in Chapter 6, the transgender/marriage relation has been considered on only one occasion since *Ladrach*. In *Littleton v Prange*[119] the Texas Supreme Court had to consider the sex claims of Christie Littleton, a post-operative (male-to-female) transgender woman who had filed a medical malpractice suit under the Texas Wrongful Death and Survival Statute in her capacity as the surviving spouse of Jonathon Littleton, a (bio)logical man with whom she had been through a ceremony of marriage seven years earlier. This claim depended for its success on Christie being considered a woman, as the word 'spouse' does not extend to same-sex marriages under the Act. The case is remarkable in that the majority of the court not only considered Christie to be male but did so in relation to an application for summary judgment against her and in spite of recognition that '[i]n determining whether a material fact issue exists to preclude summary judgment, evidence favoring the nonmovant is taken as true, and all reasonable inferences are indulged in favor of the nonmovant'.[120] The basis for granting summary judgment, as Angelini J explained, rested on the claim that the case involved 'no disputed fact issues for a jury to decide'.[121] Rather, the determination of Christie's sex was viewed as being purely a question of law. As a matter of law the majority contended that 'sex is accurately determined at birth'.[122] Yet, Texas lacks any law that settles the question of what it means to be a man or woman. As Lopez J states in her persuasive dissenting judgment:

> The absence of controlling law precludes a judgment as a matter of law in this case. Notably, neither federal nor state law defines how a person's gender is to be determined. Our state legislature has not determined the guidelines that should govern the recognition of marriages involving transsexuals. Particularly material to this case, the legislature has not

---

117 *Ibid*, p 10 (my emphasis).

118 See *Vecchione v Vecchione* No 95D003769 (Orange County, Calif filed 23 April 1996); *Re the Estate of Marshall G Gardiner* Kan App LEXIS 376 (2001).

119 *Littleton v Prange* [1999] 288th Judicial District Court, Bexar County, Texas (www.4thcoa. courts.state.tx.us/opinions/9900010.htm).

120 *Ibid*, p 5, *per* Hardberger CJ.

121 *Ibid*, p 1, *per* Angelini J.

122 *Ibid*, p 1, *per* Lopez J.

addressed whether a transsexual is to be considered a surviving spouse under the Wrongful Death and Survival Statutes. In an ordinary case, the absence of such law would prevent this court from concluding that the movant was entitled to judgment as a matter of law. In the instant case, however, the majority relies on the absence of statutory law to conclude that this case presents a pure question of law that must be decided by this court rather than to allow the case to proceed to trial; that is, whether Christie is male or female.[123]

This passage serves to redraw our attention to the law/fact distinction in transgender jurisprudence and its potential through rearticulation to disrupt dominant understandings of sex, a theme explored in Chapter 4. With regard to the issue of Christie's sex, she had earlier applied successfully to have her name and gender amended on her birth certificate. While this fact redraws our attention to the point made by Ellis J in *Attorney-General v Otahuhu Family Court* that allowing birth certificate change does not necessarily involve legal recognition for marriage purposes,[124] it is curious that evidence that Christie was female, on which a Texas court relied with regard to her birth certificate application, did not prove satisfactory enough even to raise a genuine question of material fact on a motion for summary judgment. The ease with which restrictive procedural rules surrounding summary judgment are circumvented by the court in the context of the transgender/marriage relation is revealing. It is contended that it is, at least in part, to be accounted for by judicial anxiety over the prospect of homosexual marriage, a prospect, that Hardberger CJ insisted, produces 'wide spread'[125] opposition and 'public antipathy'.[126] This anxiety rests upon a conflation of transgender and homosexuality, a conflation that becomes patent in his judgment. Thus Hardberger CJ's statement that Christie was not 'a homosexual in the traditional sense',[127] while perhaps drawing some distinction between transgender and homosexuality, makes clear that her body bears some relation to homosexuality in the judicial mind. Moreover, his anxiety over perceived proximity of the transgender body to homosexuality is evident in the contrast drawn between 'the more pleasant mysteries'[128] of life attendant to heterosexual discovery, on the one hand, and the 'unpleasant discovery' made by the plaintiff on his wedding night in *Anonymous v Anonymous* on the other.[129] The significance of this kind of cultural imagery to judicial rule choice, which has already been noted (Kennedy, 1997), is perhaps 'even more pronounced when judges rely on imagery from prior opinions' (Keller, 1999, p 337) as it is through citation that this imagery assumes textual authority in law (Butler, 1993, p 225).

A concern to insulate the institution of marriage from homosexual incursion has also been apparent in the transgender jurisprudence of a number of Canadian jurisdictions. The transgender/marriage relation was first tested in Canada in the case of *M v M (A)*.[130]

---

123 *Ibid*.

124 *Attorney-General v Otahuhu Family Court* [1995] 1 NZLR 603, p 616. This is a significant point because many common law jurisdictions allow change of sex on birth certificates once reassignment surgery has been undertaken.

125 *Littleton v Prange* [1999] 288th Judicial District Court, Bexar County, Texas (www.4thcoa. courts.state.tx.us/opinions/9900010.htm), p 2, *per* Hardberger CJ.

126 *Ibid*, p 3.

127 *Ibid*, p 6.

128 *Ibid*, p 1.

129 *Ibid*, p 4.

130 *M v M (A)* [1984] 42 RFL 2d 55.

Here the Prince Edward Island Supreme Court was required to consider the validity of a marriage between a (bio)logically male husband and a (bio)logically female wife who subsequently adopted a transgender identity and indicated a desire for surgery. In deciding the case McQuaid J purported to follow the analysis of Ormrod J in *Corbett*:

> [T]he law of England, with which in this respect I understand the law of Canada conforms, stipulates that the capacity for natural heterosexual intercourse is an essential element and, if there exists an incapacity with respect to the physical capability to engage in that essential element, then the marriage is void or voidable.[131]

However, while assessment of April Ashley as lacking the capacity for 'natural' heterosexual intercourse flowed from Ormrod J's deployment of particular (bio)logical factors in the determination of her sex, this legal move was not possible in relation to Mrs M, whose (bio)logical sex was unequivocally female. Rather, McQuaid J located her 'incapacity' elsewhere. While recognising that 'there was no *apparent* incapacity as respects physical capability',[132] McQuaid J contended that there exist:

> ... psychological factors, inherent in the [transsexual] personality, which preclude or otherwise inhibit the actual exercise of such physical capacity. These psychological factors may be initially patent, in which case there is simply no capacity to exercise the function, or they may be latent or suppressed, in which case the capacity to exercise the function does exist, and may indeed be exercised, but the exercise thereof simply makes patent what was earlier latent and the act of heterosexual intercourse thereby becomes abhorrent to the point where it becomes, in effect, a continuing incapacity. The incapacitating condition was present in the marriage from the outset; it was merely triggered into transition from the state of latent potentiality into the state of patent actuality by the circumstance of the intimacy arising out of the married relationship, which, being heterosexual in nature, was incompatible with the inherent nature of the respondent.[133]

The legal reasoning adopted here elevates Mrs M's 'latent transsexualism' into a physical incapacity. It is somewhat remarkable that her body should be scripted as a locus of 'continuing incapacity', given that for the greater part of a six year period she 'carried on what appeared to the [husband] to be a normal sexual relationship'.[134] Remarkably, and as noted by Johnson, the very act that ought to validate the marriage in the context of these nullity proceedings rendered it voidable due to the 'latent tendencies' of Mrs M (1994, p 167). This strange legal reasoning would seem to be explicable only in terms of judicial anxiety over a perception that Mrs M's body is a locus of/for homosexual practice. This concern is apparent in McQuaid J's contention that heterosexuality is 'incompatible with the inherent nature of [Mrs M]'.[135] While much judicial analysis around the transgender/marriage relation appears to be concerned to insulate marriage from the threat of homosexuality from without, the legal reasoning adopted by McQuaid J suggests, perhaps, a deeper anxiety that 'homosexuality' may already be located within the institution of marriage and practiced by parties of the opposite (bio)logical sex.

---

131 *Ibid*, p 59.
132 *Ibid*.
133 *Ibid*.
134 *Ibid*, p 57.
135 *Ibid*, p 59.

Interestingly, this much criticised judgment (Johnson, 1994 p 167)[136] has the effect of destabilising marriage through undermining dominant legal understandings of heterosexuality. That is to say, law proves unable to rely upon biologically male penile penetration of a biologically female vagina as the sure ground of heterosexuality.

Since the decision of *M v M (A)* three further Canadian decisions throw light on the transgender/marriage relation. In *B v A*[137] the Supreme Court of Ontario had to determine whether a pre-operative (female-to-male) transgender man, who had been in a 20 year relationship with a (bio)logical woman and who had undergone a hysterectomy and a double mastectomy, was a 'spouse' for the purposes of the Family Law Act[138] and therefore entitled to financial support. Section 29 of the Act defines 'spouse' to include 'either of a man and woman who are not married to each other and have cohabited ... continuously for a period of not less than three years'. Section 1(1) defines 'cohabit' to mean 'to live together in a conjugal relationship'. Accordingly, B's claim for financial support depended on a judicial willingness to view him as a man and to characterise his relationship with A as 'conjugal' in kind. In refusing to consider B a male person, Master Cork focused on the fact that B had not undertaken phalloplastic surgery. However, had the court considered the vaginaed male body to be male in law it is clear from Master Cork's judgment that B's claim would have been dismissed as his relationship with A was viewed as other than 'conjugal' in kind. It is significant that 'radical and irreversible [phalloplastic] intervention'[139] is presented as a necessary condition for a favourable finding in either of these respects. While the importance of phalloplastic surgery is informed by the Vital Statistics Act,[140] which enables persons upon whom 'transsexual surgery' has been performed to change the designation of sex on their birth certificate,[141] that legislation does not require 'irreversibility'. For Master Cork, phalloplasty appears to assuage anxiety about the otherwise 'impermanence' of change.[142] It assists in overcoming his evident concern that B, having only undertaken 'transitory changes',[143] might 'revert back' to female at some future time.[144] This fear of mutability in the context of the transgender/marriage relation is again inextricably tied up with the homophobia

---

136 In *R v Harris and McGuiness* (1989) 17 NSWLR 158 Mathews J expressed 'grave reservations as to the correctness of this decision' (p 178) while in *Attorney-General v Otahuhu Family Court* [1995] 1 NZLR 603 Ellis J appears to concur with counsel's submission that 'the decision in *M v M* is illogical and difficult to rationalise on any reasonable basis' (p 18).

137 *B v A* [1990] 29 RFL 3d 262.

138 Family Law Act, SO 1986, c 4.

139 *B v A* [1990] 29 RFL 3d 262, p 266.

140 Vital Statistics Act, RSO 1980, c 524.

141 *Ibid*, s 32(2)(a)(1). It is interesting to note that B had obtained medical certificates attesting to the fact he had undergone 'transsexual surgery' under the Vital Statistics Act 1980. In this regard members of the medical profession had taken a more liberal interpretation of the relevant provisions than Master Cork. While the latter considered these medical views of the legislation to be 'patently erroneous' (*B v A* [1990] 29 RFL 3d 262, p 267) the discrepancy suggests perhaps a contrast between a medical concern for future well-being and a legal concern to ensure that binary sex remains rooted in genitocentrism.

142 In fact phalloplasty is no guarantee against 'reversibility'. Thus a female-to-male transgender person might seek the surgical removal of an artificially constructed penis and the reopening of his vagina (Walters and Ross, 1986, p 113).

143 *B v A* [1990] 29 RFL 3d 262, p 266.

144 *Ibid*, p 263.

of law. An explicit concern over proximity of homosexuality to marriage, as well as the conflation of transgender and homosexual bodies, is apparent in Master Cork's treatment of the suggestion that 'transsexual surgery' for the purposes of the Vital Statistics Act might not require phalloplasty:

> I believe there to be some form of official or unofficial prohibition against homosexual marriages, or marriages between parties of the same gender. In the present case such could be achieved, if after hysterectomy or mastectomy, or perhaps only one of such, the one female partner to the proposed marriage changes the sexual designation under the Vital Statistics Act, and then applies with the other female partner, as male and female, for a marriage licence, which would have to be issued. Surely, this is well beyond the legislative intent of this amendment in the Vital Statistics Act.[145]

Moreover, while phalloplastic surgery is presented as a necessary condition for creating the basis for 'cohabitation' under s 29 of the Family Law Act it is far from clear that it represents a sufficient condition. That is to say, in view of functional difficulties associated with phalloplastic surgical techniques (Walters and Ross, 1986, p 113; Steiner, 1985, p 338) establishing that a relationship is 'conjugal' in kind may prove difficult if not impossible for female-to-male transgender people (Majury, 1990, p 261).

In *C(L) v C(C)* an Ontario court had again to consider the sex status of the female-to-male transgender body.[146] On this occasion the question related to the validity of a four year marriage between a pre-operative (female-to-male) transgender man and a (bio)logical woman. As in *B v A* the transgender respondent had undergone a hysterectomy and double mastectomy. The court held the respondent to be female and therefore the marriage to be void from the beginning, as Ontario law does not permit marriage between members of the same sex. As in *B v A* it was the absence of a penis that proved crucial in the legal construction of the respondent as female. However, while Master Cork recognised the possibility of a sexually functioning female-to-male post-operative body for the purposes of cohabitation, it is far from clear that Jenkins J extends that analysis to the formal institution of marriage. Indeed, Jenkins J, in contrast to Master Cork, placed particular reliance on Ormrod J's emphasis that 'marriage ... is the institution ... in which the capacity for natural heterosexual intercourse is an essential element'.[147] Moreover, reliance on this aspect of Ormrod J's judgment is again apparent in the later decision of the Federal Court of Canada in *Canada v Owen*,[148] a decision considered in Chapter 3. That the 'natural' is invoked in this way suggests that judicial recognition of sex claims depends on more than overcoming difficulties associated with phalloplastic surgery. Rather, as in previous decisions considered, it would seem that the homophobia of law serves to set a 'limit' around marriage to the legal incorporation of transgender people within the existing gender order.

---

145 *Ibid*, p 267.
146 *C(L) v C(C)* [1992] 10 OR 3d 254.
147 *Ibid*, p 256.
148 *Canada v Owen* (1993) 110 DLR (4th) 339.

5.3 INSULATING MARRIAGE IN MOMENTS OF REFORM

So far in this chapter we have considered a number of common law cases that have rejected the sex claims of transgender people for the purposes of marriage. This series of decisions, commencing with *Corbett*, has exhibited a judicial concern to insulate marriage from 'unnatural' homosexual incursion. While the legal reasoning in the cases considered is complex, and in *M v M (A)* bizarre, the decisions have tended, either implicitly or explicitly, to deploy (bio)logic in order to assuage this anxiety. Specifically, what these decisions have in common, despite their differences, is the 'denaturalisation' of transgender genitalia in the construction of heterosexual intercourse within marriage. This effect, which is inextricably connected to the homophobia of law, is not, however, confined to those decisions dealing with marriage. Of more significance, perhaps, is the fact that this effect is apparent in non-marriage decisions within reform jurisprudence.

In particular, Australian courts that have recognised transgender sex claims for purposes other than marriage have been especially careful to locate marriage outside the ambit of their decisions. In this regard, these decisions, ones we examined in a different context in Chapter 4, prove to be particularly instructive. In *R v Harris and McGuiness*[149] the Supreme Court of New South Wales held Lee Harris, a post-operative (male-to-female) transgender woman, to be female for the purposes of criminal law. In doing so, the court adopted the test of *psychological and anatomical harmony* which had been articulated and developed in the United States decisions of *Re Anonymous* and *MT v JT*.[150] Moreover, and in step with these decisions, the court made quite explicit the fact that *psychological and anatomical harmony* in the male-to-female transgender body required the construction of a vagina capable of heterosexual intercourse. However, and despite the particularity of this legal (re)construction of sex, the court insisted on drawing a clear distinction between the criminal law and marriage:

> No question is raised in these appeals as to the sex of marriage partners. Marriage involves special considerations and it is obvious that the determination of these appeals will have no direct application to the law of marriage.[151]

The insulation of the institution of marriage from the decision is particularly curious when one considers that the test of *psychological and anatomical harmony*, upon which the court relied, had received its most sustained endorsement in a United States decision in which the sole issue was marriage.[152] Further, it is somewhat ironic that a legal test for determining sex which has been predicated upon the capacity for heterosexual intercourse should be dispensed with in the context of marriage, an area where that capacity has, and in contrast to the facts of *R v Harris and McGuiness*, some historical relevance.[153] In effect the court invalidate transgender capacity for heterosexual intercourse for the purposes of marriage even though this capacity has been both surgically and discursively produced and has been constructed as an essential element in

---

149 *R v Harris and McGuiness* (1989) 17 NSWLR 158.

150 *Re Anonymous* 293 NYS 2d 834 (1968); *MT v JT* 355 A 2d 204 (1976).

151 *R v Harris and McGuiness* (1989) 17 NSWLR 158, p 189.

152 *MT v JT* 355 A 2d 204 (1976).

153 The capacity to consummate a marriage is no longer relevant to nullity proceedings in Australia (Family Law Act 1975 (Cth), ss 48, 51).

the legal determination of sex. While the 'special considerations' involved in marriage remain undeclared, it is difficult to imagine considerations other than ones grounded in (bio)logic that the court might have had in mind. In other words, it would seem that in seeking to understand why the court should wish to deny, in the marriage context, a heterosexual capacity legally sanctioned and insisted upon in other areas of social life we are led, once again, to the distinction Ormrod J drew in *Corbett* between the 'natural' and the 'unnatural'. While the majority of the court emphasise the 'functionality' of Lee Harris' surgically constructed vagina, and while Mathews J purported to distance herself from a view of such change 'as being artificial and unnatural',[154] it would seem that for the purposes of marriage the court did not want to get too close to this genital site. Rather, it is, perhaps, the dissenting judgment of Carruthers J that best captures the judicial attitude toward the transgender/marriage relation, one which serves, once again, to position the transgender body in relation to homosexuality:

> [I]t cannot be said the 'sexual' intercourse is ordinary and complete intercourse, as understood commonly, or *vera copula* of the natural sort of coitus. This must mean that the 'sexual' intercourse is that of the transsexual kind not intercourse between sexes ... It would seem that 'marriage' is not provided for between persons of the same sex although 'unions' might occur and transsexual intercourse would seem of this kind.[155]

This judicial concern over the 'naturalness' of heterosexual intercourse within marriage is again apparent in Brennan's lone judgment in *Secretary, Department of Social Security v HH*.[156] While agreeing with O'Connor J and Muller on the question of HH's sex for the legal purposes of an age pension under the Social Security Act 1947 (Cth), Brennan made it quite explicit that she would have found HH to be a male person for the purposes of the Act generally despite sex reassignment surgery.[157] In drawing upon Ormrod J's analysis that legal relations can be classified into those in which the sex of the individuals concerned is irrelevant, relevant or an essential determinant of the nature of the relationship, Brennan took the view that in relation to other provisions of the Social Security Act (bio)logical sex might be viewed as a relevant, and perhaps a cardinal, factor in determining the nature of relationships.

In particular, Brennan singled out entitlement to a wife's pension as an example of legal subject matter where the sex of an individual would be a cardinal factor or an essential determinant serving to disentitle a transgender claimant.[158] It is not at all clear why this should be so. The word 'wife' is defined in s 3(1) of the Social Security Act to mean 'a female married person' and the expression 'married person' is defined to include a *de facto* spouse. Therefore, Brennan clearly envisaged the sex of an individual as being a cardinal factor in assessing entitlement to a wife's pension irrespective of whether the wife is formally married or a *de facto* spouse. This view would seem to be premised upon the assumption of heterosexual intercourse between spouses. However, this would not appear to be a sufficient condition for excluding HH from entitlement to a wife's pension as she had undergone sex reassignment surgery, thereby acquiring female genitalia and

---

154 *R v Harris and McGuiness* (1989) 17 NWLR 158, p 192.
155 *Ibid*, p 168.
156 *Secretary, Department of Social Security v HH* [1991] 13 AAR 314.
157 *Ibid*, p 325.
158 *Ibid*, p 324.

the capacity for heterosexual intercourse. Rather, the assertion that HH would not be entitled to a wife's pension is, and can only be, based upon the view that heterosexual intercourse where one of the parties is transgender is not of the 'natural' kind. The reluctance of Brennan to even imagine extending legal recognition to encapsulate entitlement to a wife's pension serves to illustrate the rigidity of the relationship between legal discourse and the institution of 'natural' heterosexual intercourse, which is marriage (legal or *de facto*).

A view of marriage as reform's 'limit' is again apparent in the Federal Court of Australia's decision in *Secretary, Department of Social Security v SRA*.[159] On the facts, and as we saw in Chapter 4, the court held that a pre-operative (male-to-female) transgender woman was not a woman as a matter of law, thereby overturning a decision of the Administrative Appeals Tribunal which had sought to institute a new test for determining legal sex which dispensed with anatomical considerations.[160] The court went on, however, to approve of *R v Harris and McGuiness*, making it clear that a person who was both anatomically and psychologically female, and therefore 'harmonious', would be covered by the social security provisions. The view of the Federal Court that post-operative (male-to-female) transgender women would be treated as female for the purposes of entitlement to a wife's pension might be viewed as a thaw in the rigidity of the relationship between legal discourse and the institution of marriage. However, and even while stressing the need for legal consistency, the Federal Court echoed the concern of the court in *R v Harris and McGuiness*:

> ... questions relating to transsexualism arise in a variety of contexts and different answers may be required. For example the law relating to marriage may require different tests ... the law of marriage may involve special considerations with many factors to be considered by the court and carefully weighed.[161]

As in *R v Harris and McGuiness* care is taken in order to insulate the institution of marriage from the effects of the decision. Once again, the 'truth' of sex, a 'truth' which is (bio)logically and temporally specific, proves to be more durable than judicial articulation of a test of *psychological and anatomical harmony* might suggest. Crucially, not only does the spectre of *Corbett* lurk in the background of Australian reform jurisprudence, but in the marriage context emerges as the 'truth' of sex against which the test of *psychological and anatomical harmony* unravels as a therapeutic concession to 'gender dysphoric' subjects. That is to say, the 'truth' of sex always threatens to impose itself, through a display of repressive legal power, whenever sex actually matters. That is, whenever the judiciary perceive marriage, the institution of the family and of 'natural' heterosexuality, as in danger of being devalued or compromised. It is this desire to privilege, and preserve a space for, a 'natural' form of heterosexuality within marriage that holds in check law's desire to incorporate ('normalise') post-operative transgender people within the existing gender order. In view of the partial nature of the legal recognition granted Lee Harris, HH and SRA its significance and value become questionable. While they were found to have bodies that mattered (Butler, 1993) for the purposes of criminal and social security laws,

---

159 *Secretary, Department of Social Security v SRA* [1993] 118 ALR 467.
160 *Secretary, Department of Social Security v SRA* [1992] 28 ALD 361.
161 *Secretary, Department of Social Security v SRA* [1993] 118 ALR 467, p 495, *per* Lockhart J.

those same bodies were found not to matter for marriage purposes. Rather, at the very moment the male-to-female transgender body is discursively produced as coherently female that 'coherence' would seem to unravel. In the marriage context her body emerges in juxtaposition to the 'real', 'authentic', 'natural' body of genetic woman, a poor copy of whom she can be at best. Thus, the relation of the post-operative transgender person to law, in these reform decisions, proves to be that of both 'insider' and 'outsider'.

5.4 CONCLUSION

This chapter has developed the theme of continuity, established in earlier chapters, through consideration of the relationship between transgender marriage jurisprudence and the homophobia of law. While the homophobia of law is a feature of transgender jurisprudence more generally, it is within marriage contexts that its centrality to an adequate understanding of transgender jurisprudence is rendered most transparent. Indeed, law's anxiety over perceived proximity of transgender to the homosexual body at the site of marriage would appear to effect a 'limit' in many common law jurisdictions to the incorporation ('normalisation') of transgender people within the existing gender order. That is to say, legal desire to reproduce gender in the face of transgender trouble is held in check by a desire to privilege, and preserve a space for, 'natural' heterosexual intercourse within marriage. It is this latter desire which helps explain increased judicial scrutiny of transgender bodies and, of course, legal denial of sex claims. In this regard, judicial defence of marriage proves, somewhat ironically, to hinder the reformist project of heterosexualising 'ambiguous' bodies.

In foregrounding the homophobia of law the chapter calls into question a view of the relation between *Corbett* and reform jurisprudence as discontinuous or as linked only by legal desire to reproduce the gender order. For homophobia proves to be continuous, linking together ostensibly disparate decisions be that through inquiry into pre-operative sexual practice, post-operative heterosexual capacity, transgender desire, gender performance, non-disclosure of transgender status and/or a judicial concern over bodily aesthetics. Indeed, it is precisely homophobic anxiety that accounts for resort to (bio)logic both in *Corbett* and those, including some reform, decisions decided in its wake. That is to say, it is the homophobia of law that helps account for the differential legal treatment of transgender people across legal subject matters. In other words, not only does the chapter reveal marriage law to be a site for glimpsing the 'truth' of sex which is, of course, (bio)logically and temporally specific. It also highlights how this understanding of sex is itself produced through homophobic anxiety. For it is heterosexuality and its 'priority' that ultimately appear to be at stake in transgender jurisprudence, thereby pointing to a need to place the transgender/law relation more firmly on gay and lesbian, as well as feminist, political agendas.

In the following chapter we will consider case law that has recognised transgender sex claims for marriage purposes. We will see, however, that while homophobia does not preclude legal recognition in these decisions it continues to structure the reform moment, thereby linking this body of reform jurisprudence to *Corbett*. That is to say, while law 'uncouples' the post-operative transgender body from homosexuality, and therefore 'unnatural' sexuality, it continues to project its homophobia onto the pre-operative body.

In this regard we will see that the figure of the homosexual haunts transgender jurisprudence as a body. Moreover, we will see that even within this body of law (bio)logic is not expunged. Rather, the question of the 'truth' of sex will be seen to be postponed, displaced on to other legal terrain, namely competitive sport, which much like marriage in the decisions considered in this chapter, functions to 'naturalise' sexed difference (Cole and Birrell, 1990, p 18). Thus we will see that the reformist goal of incorporating transgender people within the existing gender order is not necessarily achieved through a rethinking of the transgender/marriage relation.

CHAPTER 6

BEYOND THE MARITAL 'LIMIT'

Naturally we would not wish to permit homosexual or lesbian marriages; but no such objection can apply to a marriage between a man and a person who is or has become essentially female and can perform the female sexual role (Samuels, 1984, p 165).

In this chapter we will pursue the theme of the homophobia of law through a consideration of case law that has recognised transgender sex claims for marriage purposes. While these cases perhaps represent an attempt to overcome the legal tension between the desire to reproduce the gender order and the desire to preserve a space for 'natural' heterosexual intercourse within marriage, we will see that the reform moment continues to be structured by legal anxiety over the homosexual body. In the first place a certain ambivalence about the coupling of transgender and heterosexuality is evident in the marriage context. Of more significance, perhaps, is the fact that the positioning of post-operative transgender people within the sanctity of marriage relies on homophobia as its foundation. That is to say, inclusion of post-operative bodies within the realm of marriage proves possible only because of the 'renaturalising' efforts law expends around those bodies. In particular, this legal work requires that the 'naturalness' of included bodies be mirrored. It is the pre-operative body, a body that law conflates utterly with homosexuality, which is employed to this end. That is to say, law continues to project its homophobia onto the pre-operative body. Accordingly, homosexuality continues to be coded as 'unnatural' and distanced from the institution of marriage. Further, homophobia is evident in another regard. Thus we will see anxiety expressed over the possibility of 'gay' and 'lesbian' transgender people already being located within marriage. In this regard, it is clear that transgender marriage jurisprudence seeks to resist homosexuality from both inside and out. Indeed, legal anxiety over 'gay' and 'lesbian' transgender desire/practice represents perhaps a completion of a circuit of homophobia in law.

6.1 '(RE)NATURALISING' TRANSGENDER BODIES

A judicial rethinking of the transgender/marriage relation can be traced to *MT v JT*,[1] a decision we encountered in Chapter 4. In this case the Superior Court of New Jersey had to consider the validity of a two year marriage between a (bio)logical man and a post-operative (male-to-female) transgender woman. The court rejected the *Corbett* analysis, preferring instead to articulate a test of *psychological and anatomical harmony*. Accordingly, MT was considered to be female for the purposes of marriage. The court distinguished the earlier New York decisions of *Anonymous v Anonymous* and *B v B*,[2] where transgender sex claims had been denied for marriage purposes, on the basis that the transgender persons in those cases were pre-operative and were therefore incapable of heterosexual intercourse. In other words, and as we saw in Chapter 4, the court placed particular

---

1   *MT v JT* 355 A 2d 204 (1976).
2   *Anonymous v Anonymous* 325 NYS 2d 499 (1971); *B v B* 355 NYS 2d 712 (1974).

emphasis on MT's post-operative vaginal capacity. However, in probing the topography of MT's vagina the court proved interested in more than the fact that she had 'a vagina and labia which were adequate for sexual intercourse and could function as any female vagina, that is, for traditional penile/vaginal intercourse'.[3] That is to say, judicial concern extended beyond the 'mere' fact of post-operative functionality and the phallocentric and performativist assumptions contained therein. In particular, the court evinced a clear concern over the aesthetics of MT's vagina. Thus the court placed emphasis on medical evidence suggesting that MT's vagina had been 'lined initially by the skin of [her] penis', that it would, in all likelihood, later take on 'the characteristics of normal vaginal mucosa', and that though at 'a somewhat different angle, was not really different from a natural vagina in size, capacity and the feeling of the walls around it'.[4]

Here the court seeks reassurance not merely that MT's vagina can function as a site of heterosexual male pleasure (Collier, 1995, p 157), but that it can be viewed as a 'natural' site for such pleasure. In other words, the mapping of MT's genital region belies a concern to 'naturalise' her vagina and thereby the practice of heterosexual intercourse. In emphasising textural, spatial and sensual similarities between MT's vagina and that of a biological woman, the court rearticulates the relation between the transgender body and the 'natural' established in *Corbett* as a prelude to bringing that body within the sanctity of marriage. However, even, and perhaps especially, at the moment of 'naturalising' MT's vagina for marriage purposes, the court, in a passage that suggests judicial anxiety over the coupling of transgender and heterosexuality, was careful to insulate the institution of marriage from 'unnatural' homosexual practices:

> The historic assumption in the application of common law and statutory strictures relating to marriages is that only persons who can become 'man and wife' have the capacity to enter marriage ... The pertinent statutes relating to marriages and married persons do not contain any explicit references to a requirement that marriage must be between a man and a woman ... Nevertheless ... [it] is so strongly and firmly implied from a full reading of the statutes that a different legislative intent, one which would sanction a marriage between persons of the same sex, cannot be fathomed.[5]

Legal anxiety over the coupling of transgender and heterosexuality is perhaps also apparent in the court's rhetorical question '[a]re we to look upon [the post-operative] person as an exhibit in a circus side show?'[6] This question, which certainly suggests a view of the pre-operative body as monstrous, suggests also some discomfort over the heterosexualisation of MT's body. This anxiety is certainly evident in the court's assertion that JT's obligation to support his wife was conditional on the absence of 'fraud'.[7] In view of the finding that MT, on account of her sex reassignment surgery and acquisition of the capacity for heterosexual intercourse, was female as a matter of law, it is revealing that the issue of 'fraud' surfaces. Clearly, there can be no 'fraud' regarding MT's capacity to consummate the marriage, given subsequent heterosexual practice and judicial sanctification of her post-operative vagina. In any event, had incapacity been deduced

---

3   *MT v JT* 355 A 2d 204 (1976), p 206.
4   *Ibid.*
5   *Ibid*, p 208.
6   *Ibid*, p 207.
7   *Ibid*, p 204.

from the fact of transgender status, prior knowledge or subsequent ratification of incapacity, both of which were apparent on the facts, operate as a bar to nullity proceedings under New Jersey law.[8] Rather, anxiety over the possibility of non-disclosure of transgender history prior to marriage serves to emphasise the importance, and perhaps the primacy, of the past. That non-disclosure is viewed, in some unspecified way, as problematising a marriage contract is an effect of judicial anxiety over inadvertent contact with the homosexual body. In this regard, there appears to be a certain inauthenticity about the re-sexing of MT's body. That is to say, the homophobia of law serves to cast a shadow over a reform moment organised around the present.

Despite a degree of judicial ambivalence about the coupling of transgender and heterosexuality, it is clear from *MT v JT*, and other decisions to be considered, that the attempt to distinguish transgender from homosexuality is most marked in reform jurisprudence around marriage. That is to say, while the homosexual body always, at least implicitly, constitutes an important part of the 'outside' necessary to the process of legal subject formation within transgender reform jurisprudence, this legal positioning receives particular emphasis around marriage. Accordingly, transgender marriage jurisprudence serves to exemplify a tension, constituted in law, between transgender and gay and lesbian interests. That is to say, transgender law reform, particularly around marriage, becomes the occasion for the repetition of the 'logic', indeed, the 'inevitability' of exclusion of gay men and lesbians from the institution of marriage. Indeed, this understanding of the transgender/homosexual relation has received endorsement within reformist legal scholarship (see, for example, Samuels, 1984, p 165).

While *MT v JT* might be viewed as 'deheterosexualising marriage' in the sense that it uncouples heterosexuality from (bio)logic and therefore procreation (Coombes, 1998, p 254), it remains clear that heterosexual capacity is not only desirable but essential to the reform moment. In *MT v JT* it is precisely this capacity that enables MT's body to be uncoupled from homosexuality and precisely this uncoupling that enables heterosexual capacity to be thought. It has been suggested that because *MT v JT* 'views the core meaning of the marital relationship as intercourse and intimacy', the decision points to the potential to overcome the splitting of gay and lesbian and heterosexual transgender interests (Coombes, 1998, p 254). While Coombes recognises that such potential rests on a view of 'intimacy and intercourse' as not being exhausted by 'penile-vaginal forms of erotic intimacy' (1998, p 254) it is precisely this form of 'erotic intimacy' that is insisted upon in *MT v JT*. In any event, it should not be assumed that legal developments de-emphasising or dispensing with heterosexual capacity would necessarily produce this effect. Indeed, we will see that reform jurisprudence around marriage in New Zealand suggests caution in this regard.

Since *MT v JT* the United States has produced two further decisions recognising transgender sex claims for the purposes of marriage. In *Vecchione v Vecchione*[9] a Californian court held a (female-to-male) transgender man who had undergone phalloplastic surgery, and therefore had male genitalia, to be male for the purposes of marriage. In doing so the court placed particular reliance on a Californian statute

---

8   See STAT ANN 1987 (NJ), S 2A:34-1(c).

9   *Vecchione v Vecchione* No 95D003769 (Orange County, Calif filed 23 April 1996).

recognising the validity of post-operative sex and allowing for change on the birth certificate.[10] Interestingly, evidence was presented in the case to suggest that Mr Vecchione's surgically reconstructed penis did not function properly for sexual purposes, and specifically, that 'it was continually flaccid'.[11] While the court's judgment did not address directly these contentions, legal recognition in these circumstances might be viewed, at least implicitly, as de-emphasising the relevance of penile-vaginal intercourse in the legal determination of sex. However, while the decision is unclear on this point, and while de-emphasis of sexual function offers to disrupt further the gender order, it should not be thought that this legal move necessarily inhibits to any great degree the deployment of the transgender body in the service of the homophobia of law. Indeed, as we will see in the New Zealand context, it is precisely this legal development that serves to foreground the homophobia of law in legal analysis.

In the most recent United States case to address the transgender/marriage relation, the Kansas Court of Appeals in *Re the Estate of Marshall G Gardiner*[12] had to consider an appeal by a post-operative (male-to-female) transgender woman against a summary judgment finding that she was not entitled to a spousal share under the laws of intestate succession because she was male at birth. The appeal court found that a determination as to legal sex should have been made at the date of marriage, not birth, and remanded the case for a full hearing.[13] While not deciding the question itself, the court made clear its view. First, in rejecting the birth moment as decisive the court rejected the *Corbett*-style reasoning in *Littleton v Prange* as 'rigid and simplistic'.[14] Further, the court specifically endorsed the test of *psychological and anatomical harmony*, looking 'with favor on the reasoning and the language of *MT v JT*'.[15] Moreover, the emphasis placed on this decision included specific reference to portions of the judgment requiring post-operative heterosexual capacity. The importance of heterosexual capacity to a legal understanding of sex is underscored in the judgment in a number of respects. Thus the court drew attention to medical evidence stating that the appellant had a 'fully functional vagina', a site at which the deceased had allegedly experienced orgasm, and to the fact that there was no evidence suggesting that the parties to the marriage 'were not compatible'.[16] Accordingly, and despite uncertainty on this point in *Vecchione*, there is no question in *Gardiner* of moving beyond a legal understanding of sex that is premised on the capacity for penile-vaginal intercourse.

As we saw in Chapter 4, the transgender/marriage relation has also been rearticulated in New Zealand. In *M v M*[17] Aubin J upheld the validity of a 12-and-a-half year marriage between a post-operative (male-to-female) transgender woman and a (bio)logical male. As in *MT v JT* the homophobia of law finds judicial expression. First,

---

10   See Health & Safety Code (Cal) 103425.

11   *Vecchione v Vecchione* No 95D003769 (Orange County, Calif filed 23 April 1996), Declaration of Petitioner in Support of Motion for Summary Judgment, pp 2–3.

12   *Re the Estate of Marshall G Gardiner*, Kan App LEXIS 376 (2001) (www.lexis.com/research/retr...5=9f2f32b7986dffc92d 11de28ce55d46b).

13   *Ibid*, p 18.

14   *Ibid*.

15   *Ibid*.

16   *Ibid*, p 4.

17   *M v M* [1991] NZFLR 337.

and in an analogy that parallels the reference to a 'circus side show' in *MT v JT*, Aubin J asks rhetorically whether the surgery undertaken by M amounted to 'no more than some ultimately futile attempt to change her from an anguished Mr Hyde into a well adjusted Mrs Jekyll, producing a kind of hermaphroditic mutant unable to enter into a valid marriage with a man, or indeed with a woman'.[18] This passage is revealing irrespective of, and perhaps despite, the fact that Aubin J did not view M's sex reassignment surgery as futile. The literary reference to *Jekyll and Hyde* (Stevenson, 1986) invokes the notion of the monstrous body. Moreover, it is clear from the reference to 'an anguished Mr Hyde' that it is the pre-operative body that Aubin J views as monstrous. This invocation of the figure of the monster is interesting for reasons other than the fact that it serves to redraw our attention to the relationship between cultural imagery and judicial rule choice (Kennedy, 1997, p 405).

While there is some debate about the etymology of the term 'monster' it would appear to come from *monere*, to warn, or *monstrare*, to show forth or demonstrate (Epstein, 1995, p 91). Both these words, then, and importantly, refer to signs as well as defective births or malformations.[19] It is contended that one sign that the pre-operative body emits before the legal gaze is the sign of homosexuality. In particular, the male-to-female pre-operative body is imagined as the locus of sodomy. Thus it is not merely that the coupling of the words 'hermaphrodite' and 'mutant' represent a heightened moment of insensitivity toward transgender and intersexed persons, or that resort to the figure of the 'hermaphroditic mutant' serves to remind us that law cannot, and will not, think sex in any other than binary, oppositional and genitocentric terms, that calls for attention. Rather, the invocation of the monstrous serves to issue forth the spectre of homosexuality. Importantly, it is the homosexualisation of the pre-operative body that serves as prelude to the moment of departure from *Corbett*. That is to say, the depiction of the pre-operative body as monstrous/homosexual serves to reduce anxiety with regard to the re-sexing of M's harmonious/heterosexual body which the court subsequently sanctions.

In another vein, and in developing the theme of homophobia, Aubin J notes that 'Mr M was fully aware of his partner's background and accepting of her in a heterosexual relationship'.[20] This statement serves once again to illustrate judicial anxiety over the possibility of non-disclosure. Indeed, the literary reference to the story of *Jekyll and Hyde* might be viewed as indicative of this anxiety. That is to say, it is perhaps significant that Aubin J selects this novel. While the choice of *Jekyll and Hyde* avoids a view of monstrosity as 'fixed' in contrast to other examples within the horror genre, such as Mary Shelley's *Frankenstein* (1993), and while this, no doubt, informs its selection, it is precisely the fact of mutability that concerns the court. In the first place, and while Aubin J describes sex reassignment surgery as transforming 'anguish' into 'adjustment' and therefore as a movement away from monstrosity, the story of *Jekyll and Hyde* captures movement in the opposite direction. That is to say, it moves toward the diabolical Mr Hyde. In this regard Aubin J's choice of horror story suggests, perhaps, uncertainty and discomfort as to the

---

18 *Ibid*, p 347. This was precisely the view taken of a (female-to-male) intersexed man by Bell J in *Re the Marriage of C and D (falsely called C)* [1979] 35 FLR 340. This case has been heavily criticised (see, eg, Bailey-Harris, 1979; Finlay, 1980).

19 In considering the history of the treatment of intersexed people Julia Epstein has suggested that their bodies were taken to signify divine wrath (1995, p 91).

20 *M v M* [1991] NZFLR 337, p 348.

effects of surgery. Further, while Aubin J portrays surgical intervention as leading to 'a well adjusted Mrs Jekyll' the story itself exceeds a once-only movement. It is perhaps this aspect of *Jekyll and Hyde* that is most revealing. For it is precisely in the back and forth movement between Dr Jekyll and Mr Hyde that anxiety is generated around the possibility of inadvertent communion with the monster/homosexual.

As in previous decisions, the concern over non-disclosure is curious. It is not clear why transgender persons should be required to 'out' themselves, to confess to the 'truth' about their pre-surgical bodies or, indeed, why 'truth' should bear this particular temporal relation to transgender bodies. Indeed, anxiety over 'fraud' is especially revealing in the New Zealand context, given that there is no legal basis, at least in the case of post-operative persons, for characterising non-disclosure of transgender status as fraudulent and therefore as a basis for the vitiation of consent.[21] For a potential marriage partner can:

> ... lie about his or her fertility, state of health, social position, financial circumstances, or whether he or she has HIV. The only remedy under New Zealand law once such a deception is discovered is to live apart and obtain a dissolution of the marriage after living apart for two years or more. If the marriage of a post-operative transsexual were to be recognised as legally valid, then his or her marriage partner would have the same remedy available.[22]

Indeed, in my view, the contention that non-disclosure of transgender pasts 'raises legitimate ethical concerns' in marriage contexts (Coombes, 1998, p 262) is also problematic for it serves, through reinscription of the past as 'truth', to impose 'the ideal of Being on the fact of becoming' (Booth, 1985, p 132). It would appear, despite judicial emphasis on present *psychological and anatomical harmony*, that an important, perhaps *the* important, 'truth' about transgender bodies resides in the past. In this regard, the 'retreat' from *Corbett* evident within reform jurisprudence is rendered somewhat inauthentic. It is contended that judicial preoccupation with the revelation of pre-surgical autobiography, particularly within the marriage context, is, in large measure, explicable in terms of fear of coming into contact with the homosexual body. It would seem, then, that while law inscribes heterosexuality onto the post-surgical transgender body, as a means of regulating that body and incorporating it within the gender order, this practice of legal inscription is one in relation to which there remains judicial ambivalence. After all, the body perfected by surgery will carry the mark of that 'perfection', the scars, which demand and produce the integrity of the new body as they also negate it (Ahmed, 1998).

6.2 FROM FUNCTION TO AESTHETICS

The decision of *M v M* prompted an application by the Attorney-General, on behalf of the Registrar of Marriages, for 'a declaration as to whether two persons of the same genetic sex may by the law of New Zealand enter into a valid marriage'.[23] In that case, *Attorney-*

---

21 *Attorney-General v Otahuhu Family Court* [1995] 1 NZLR 603, pp 613–14.

22 *Ibid*, p 613.

23 *Ibid*, p 603.

General v Otahuhu Family Court, the High Court purported to follow the analyses in *MT v JT, R v Harris and McGuiness* and *M v M,* insisting that legal recognition of sex claims for marriage purposes was dependent on sex reassignment surgery. The court made it clear that bodily change brought about through hormone administration or other medical means was insufficient in this regard.[24] Thus, like other common law decisions, the pre- or non-surgical transgender body is constructed as necessary 'outside' to a re-sexed transgender body that is given a presence within law. However, it would be misleading to suggest that the decision in *Otahuhu* followed, in any simple way, previous decisions articulating the test of *psychological and anatomical harmony.* While *Otahuhu* shares much with prior transgender jurisprudence recognising sex claims, there is a striking difference. That is to say, prior to *Otahuhu* the judiciary had exhibited a clear tendency to insist that legal recognition was dependent on not merely sex reassignment surgery, but also post-operative capacity for heterosexual intercourse. In *Otahuhu,* however, while Ellis J stated 'that in order to be capable of marriage two persons must present themselves as having what appear to be the genitals of a man and a woman',[25] he insisted that they did not 'have to prove that each can function sexually'[26] for 'there are many forms of sexual expression possible without penetrative sexual intercourse'.[27] In this regard, *Otahuhu* renders explicit what might be thought to be implicit in *Vecchione.*

Accordingly, the decision points to a need to reassess the underpinnings of transgender jurisprudence. While law's continued insistence on articulating a 'wrong body' story points to a legal desire to reproduce the gender order, it would seem that emphasis within critical legal scholarship (see, for example, Collier, 1995, pp 125, 149; Storrow, 1997, p 291; Robertson, 1998, p 1400; Robson, 1998, p 145) on the production of heterosexual capacity to that end is, perhaps, overstated. While Robson is right in stating that a continued requirement of sex reassignment surgery typically has the effect of producing heterosexual capacity (1998, p 145),[28] and while this fact is clearly not lost on the court, it is clear that the decision cannot be reduced to an assumption about the expected use of that capacity. In short, and while Robson attempts to collapse the distinction, the uncoupling of sex reassignment surgery from the capacity for heterosexual intercourse in *Otahuhu* represents an architectural shift within transgender jurisprudence from functionality to aesthetics. To collapse this distinction is to miss the insight that it offers as to the purpose of sex reassignment surgery as legally comprehended. While an aesthetic concern over bodies is a consistent theme of transgender jurisprudence it is usually masked, at least partially, by a preoccupation with heterosexual capacity. In the judgment of Ellis J, however, law's anxiety over bodily aesthetics is foregrounded. Irrespective of sexual functioning, and guided by an obvious genitocentrism, Ellis J seeks, and finds, reassurance in the fact that the male-to-female post-operative body 'can never appear unclothed as a male'[29] and that the female-to-male

---

24 *Ibid,* pp 614–15.

25 *Ibid,* p 612.

26 *Ibid.*

27 *Ibid,* p 615.

28 In his judgment Ellis J stated that '[a] capacity for vaginal sexual intercourse may be seen as important. The evidence before the Court is that reconstructive surgery has for a long time been able to construct a vagina-like cavity which is lubricated and of adequate size to accommodate a penis' (p 612).

29 *Ibid,* p 607.

post-operative body 'can no longer appear unclothed as a woman'.[30] Absent a concern over sexual functioning, law's view of phallic female and vaginaed male bodies as 'monstrous' becomes all the more evident, as does the homosexual sign they emit in the legal imaginary. These 'monstrous' bodies are required to undergo 'a risky surgical procedure',[31] not in order that they might penetrate/be penetrated, or at least the decision in *Otahuhu* is not directed primarily to that end. Rather, surgery appears to be necessary precisely in order that transgender bodies accord with law's aesthetic sensibility and thereby reduce homophobic anxiety.

Thus while *Otahuhu* might be viewed as a departure from, or even as an anomaly in relation to, prior reform jurisprudence, and while its anomalous features might be explained in terms of the irrelevance of consummation to the law of nullity in New Zealand,[32] it might more usefully be viewed as teasing out law's more fundamental concern. In other words, and while a space for 'natural' heterosexual intercourse is preserved in *Otahuhu*, the decision is directed less toward heterosexual obligation than to the prohibition of 'unnatural' (homo)sexual practices which 'non-complementary' bodies suggest. That is to say, law's re-sexing practices are perhaps premised on the absence rather than the presence of particular forms of sexual practice. Accordingly, while the legal reasoning in *Otahuhu* might be redeployed in the service of sexual politics, it should be recognised that movement beyond heterosexual capacity bears no necessary relation to the homophobia of law. That is to say, while *Otahuhu* perhaps undermines a view of marriage as being the necessary locus of 'natural' heterosexual intercourse, the decision is nevertheless founded on the hetero/homo dyad. For while sexual intercourse may not take place post-operatively, it is its characterisation as heterosexual if it does which proves crucial. Indeed, the potential that *Otahuhu* might be thought to offer for problematising the 'inevitability' of equating marriage with heterosexuality was negated the following year by the New Zealand High Court in *Quilter v Attorney-General*.[33] In this case, three lesbian couples 'sought a declaration that, being same-sex couples, they were nonetheless lawfully entitled to obtain a marriage licence and marry pursuant to the provisions of the Marriage Act 1955'.[34] In emphatically rejecting this claim Kerr J, referring to the judgment of Ellis J in Otahuhu, recognised 'that a valid marriage in New Zealand today did not require the capacity to procreate or achieve penetrative sexual intercourse'.[35] However, and like Ellis J, he insisted that 'for marriage to take place there must be parties who visually at least are male and female'.[36]

The bodily aesthetics of law, and the homophobia that undergrids it, are apparent elsewhere in the judgment of Ellis J. Thus while emphasising that 'the declaration sought is to resolve the capacity to marry and is not intended to resolve questions that arise in

---

30 *Ibid*, p 615. While many, if not most, female-to-male transgender persons do not undergo phalloplasty, de-emphasis of sexual 'functionality' might be viewed as improving the legal situation of those who do. In this regard an effect of the decision in *Otahuhu* is to reduce, at least in some measure, the gender bias that exists within transgender jurisprudence.

31 *Ibid*, p 614.

32 Family Proceedings Act 1980.

33 *Quilter v Attorney-General* [1996] NZFLR 481.

34 *Ibid*.

35 *Ibid*, p 484.

36 *Ibid*, p 486.

other branches of the law such as criminal law, and the law of succession',[37] he departed from previous transgender jurisprudence expressing the opinion that:

> It may be that for other legal purposes, a transsexual who has not had reconstructive surgery or only minimal surgical intervention (such as removal of the testes) could be classified in his or her chosen sex for certain purposes such as employment law, criminal law and the law of inheritance.[38]

In other words, Ellis J, at the very least, held out the possibility that a superior court might dispense with the requirement of anatomical (genital) change. However, while this aspect of the judgment is, perhaps, to be welcomed, the potential for differential treatment of transgender bodies across legal subject matters serves to redraw attention to the bodily aesthetics of law. That is to say, why is it that law can entertain the possibility of creating a legal space in the areas of employment, crime and inheritance for the 'monstrous' body of marriage law? Or to put it another way, why is it that law's aesthetic sensibility cannot be compromised in the marriage context? Such questions might be responded to in a number of ways. One possible explanation might invoke a visibility/invisibility distinction. That is to say, the genital region of the body, which law seeks to police, while visible to parties to a marriage, is not visible in the other contexts referred to by Ellis J. While such an argument may have some explanatory power it appears dubious in the criminal law context where a number of sexual offences would locate the genitalia of non- or pre-surgical transgender persons on the visibility side of the distinction. In any event, to focus on the visibility of the pre-surgical body is to locate 'monstrosity' on corporeal surfaces rather than in any sign that the body may emit.

It is contended that a more convincing explanation for differential treatment of transgender people in the marriage context lies in the sexual significance genitals have in/for marriage law. In other words, and as we have already seen, legal anxiety over perceived proximity to the homosexual body surfaces whenever parties whose genitals are not dissimilar, and therefore not 'complementary', assert heterosexual identity and desire. In sex reassignment surgery law finds at least some assurance that marriage, the institution of heterosexuality, will be insulated from the spectre of the homosexual body. In this sense, law produces heterosexuality not only as identity or sexual practice, but as an effect of the present, and of course 'oppositional', anatomical form of the parties to desire. The concern over proximity of the homosexual body to marriage finds expression in other portions of the judgment. Thus in a passage that evinces a concern that law should not hinder the 'heterosexualisation' of transgender bodies effected by sex reassignment surgery, Ellis J expressed the view:

> If the law insists that genetic sex is the pre-determinant for entry into a valid marriage, then a male-to-female transsexual can contract a valid marriage with a woman. To all outward appearances, such 'marriages' would be homosexual marriages. The marriage could not be consummated.[39]

In this regard, legal recognition emerges as a strategy to insulate marriage from potential contamination by 'homosexuality'. Indeed, homophobic anxiety appears to be heightened

---

37 *Attorney-General v Otahuhu Family Court* [1995] 1 NZLR 603, p 607.

38 *Ibid*, p 615.

39 *Ibid*, p 629.

by the 'fact' that on this legal reading 'homosexuality' may already lie within marriage. In this regard marriage as the locus and 'guarantor' of 'natural' heterosexual intercourse is subverted from the inside, a concern that perhaps accounts for the rather bizarre legal reasoning of McQuaid J in the Canadian decision of *M v M (A)*.[40] Anxiety over the prospect of 'homosexual marriages' is also evident in the fact that Ellis J problematises the word 'marriages' even though such marriages are quite clearly lawful. Moreover, the homophobia of the judgment is further evidenced by his assertion that such a marriage 'could not be consummated'. It is curious why reference to consummation should be made, given its obvious irrelevance to the law of marriage in New Zealand, a point rendered abundantly clear by Ellis J in other portions of his judgment.[41] Rather, it would seem that the idea of consummation is deployed against what Ellis J sees as gay and lesbian transgender people in order to 'denaturalise' their bodies and desires. The concern over proximity to the homosexual body manifests itself in yet another regard:

> From a practical point of view, sex change procedures are unlikely to be undertaken by legitimate medical personnel in New Zealand without the individual having first obtained a dissolution of his or her marriage in the original sex. There is always the possibility that a person could undergo such procedures with less ethical professionals.[42]

This passage of the judgment is revealing. While it is true that psychiatrists are reluctant to refer married persons for sex reassignment procedures and surgeons reluctant to perform those procedures on married persons (see, for example, Hastings, 1969, pp 243, 248–51; Smith, 1971, p 973; Morris, 1974; David, 1975, p 316; King, 1993, p 83; Bolin, 1996, p 454),[43] that attitude is premised on a view of homosexual desire, a desire which medicine, not unproblematically, inscribes onto married persons, as inconsistent with transgender. It is significant that Ellis J finds it necessary to delegitimise, and to characterise as unethical, medical practitioners who might be capable of imagining non-heterosexual transgender identities and desires. While the possibility of post-operative transgender persons marrying their gay or lesbian partners, or remaining in marriage relationships after sex reassignment surgery, has drawn concern from some legal scholars (see, for example, David, 1975, p 320; Dewar, 1985, p 64) others have pinpointed this possibility, which is increasingly being actualised (Flynn, 2001, pp 418–19), as offering potential for disrupting the heterosexual matrix (Coombes, 1998, p 263; Flynn, 2001, pp 418–19). Indeed, this possibility may prove particularly useful in the service of broader reform around marriage, being both legally permissible and one that offers to challenge that institution from within, that is to say, by means of implosion.

---

40 *M v M (A)* [1984] 42 RFL 2d 55.

41 *Ibid*, p 612.

42 *Ibid*, p 619.

43 Thus, the famous transsexual Jan Morris went to Casablanca for her surgery in 1972 after she was told she must divorce her wife in order to receive surgery in the UK (Morris, 1974). More recently, Kristina Sheffield stated that she was informed by her consultant psychiatrist and her surgeon that she was required to obtain a divorce as a pre-condition to surgery being carried out (see *Sheffield and Horsham v UK* (1998) 27 EHRR 163).

6.3 THE RETURN OF (BIO)LOGIC

The analysis so far has characterised marriage cases that have 'departed' from *Corbett* in terms of a rearticulation of the relation between the post-operative transgender body and the 'natural'. That is to say, Ormrod J's view of the post-operative transgender body as 'unnatural' and his equation of transgender sexual practice with homosexuality has given way, though not without equivocation, to legal attempts to 'naturalise' and thereby 'heterosexualise' that body. Moreover, it is precisely this repositioning across the hetero/homo divide that ensures the reform moment becomes the occasion for the continuance of law's homophobic work. However, this focus on the homophobia of law should not blind us to another aspect of reform jurisprudence in the marriage context. Specifically, it should not be thought that legal recognition for marriage purposes, which might be thought of as a sort of litmus test for recognition, necessarily involves an abandonment of (bio)logic within reform jurisprudence. Nor should it be thought that resort to (bio)logic is necessarily underscored by the homophobia of law. Thus in *MT v JT* the court, like Ormrod J in *Corbett*, confined the scope of its decision to the issue of marriage. In relation to other legal subject matters the court envisaged that other tests 'in addition to genitalia'[44] might apply. One example given, where a different legal analysis might be called for, was that of 'participation in certain regulated sports activities'.[45] This exception was given shape by Mathews J in *R v Harris and McGuiness*:

> The area of sport may well involve special problems in relation to transsexuals. For in many sports, including tennis [a reference to the decision of *Richards v USTA*], men and women compete on different levels from each other. This is at least partially because of biological features, such as strength, which may not be directly related to one's genital features or hormonal balance and which might therefore persist even after successful reassignment surgery.[46]

This theme is pursued more recently, and more decidedly, by Ellis J in *Otahuhu*. Thus having suggested that pre-operative status might suffice for legal recognition for certain legal purposes, Ellis J went on to state that there may be 'situations where reconstructive surgery has been completed but where nevertheless recognition of the change of sex may not be appropriate. An example might be the possibility of a male-to-female transsexual who wished to enter competitive sports as a female'.[47] Lest it be thought that Ellis J was undecided on this point, his subsequent claim that 'the decision in *Richards* is wrong, in that in this kind of circumstance, a male-to-female transsexual may have a competitive advantage over other females'[48] reveals otherwise. In explaining his reasoning he emphasised that the issue of competitive sport is:

> ... very different, from a social policy point of view, from the issue of marriage. The professional tennis player who is a male-to-female transsexual is in a position potentially to disadvantage all other women professional tennis players by depriving them of potential

---

44 *MT v JT* 355 A 2d 204 (1976), p 209.
45 *Ibid.*
46 *R v Harris and McGuiness* (1989) 17 NSWLR 158, p 188.
47 *Attorney-General v Otahuhu Family Court* [1995] 1 NZLR 603, p 617.
48 *Ibid.*

earnings and prize money. Marriage is a private contract between two individuals without the potential for disadvantaging other persons not party to that contract.[49]

The treatment of women's sport as a special case is based on a view of transgender inclusion as being unfair, or potentially unfair, to women athletes, especially in the context of professional sport. While considerable opposition exists among many women's sporting groups to transgender inclusion (Cole and Birrell, 1990, pp 5–6),[50] resort to (bio)logic proves problematic in a number of respects. First, the division of sport along sexed lines contains a certain arbitrariness. Differences in factors such as heart size, lung capacity, muscle mass and body fat often traverse, rather than parallel, the division of sex (D'Andrade, 1966, p 175; Nicholson, 1984, p 6). The precise configuration of these attributes in any particular individual is perhaps more a matter of genetics than sex. Indeed, while Ellis J considered the *Richards* decision to have been wrongly decided, Ascione J concluded on the basis of medical evidence presented that Renee Richards had 'no unfair advantage when competing against other women' as '[h]er muscle development, weight, height and physique fit within the female norm'.[51] If there were a genuine concern to institute a level playing field in the arena of sport it would be necessary to take into account (bio)logical and other differences, such as differences of opportunity, among men and women as well as between them and to consider the pertinence of these various differences to a multiplicity of sports (Sharpe, 1997c, p 40). In short, the social organisation of sport along sexed lines is less an effect of biology than of cultural and historical factors (Oglesby, 1978; Willis, 1982). While those factors produce a present reality, to which the courts respond 'pragmatically', the sign-posting of sport as a realm beyond which legal (re)construction of sex terminates functions to 'naturalise' sexed difference.

Irrespective of 'fairness', and precisely through the rhetoric of 'fairness', (bio)logical sexed differences assume importance in locating (male-to-female) transgender women outside the category 'female' for the purposes of sport. Thus judicial concern over (bio)logic is not abandoned within reform jurisprudence around marriage. Rather, it is displaced from the marriage context to the terrain of competitive sport. While in other decisions recognising transgender sex claims, marriage serves as a 'limit' to recognition, in *MT v JT* and *Attorney-General v Otahuhu Family Court* sport provides that 'limit'. In this regard, even these 'progressive' marriage decisions remain tied to *Corbett*. That is to say,

---

49 *Ibid*.

50 Indeed, the political lobbying of women's sport groups, such as the Women in Sport Foundation, has been a significant factor in the exemption of sport from the effects of extension of anti-discrimination law protection to transgender people in a number of Australian jurisdictions. Moreover, this opposition has been based on the 'unfair physical advantage' transgender people are purported to have on account of 'their pre-existing superior anatomical and physiological characteristics' (see the Hon Dr BPV Pezzutti, Debates of the Legislative Council (NSW), 4 June 1996, p 2390). For examples of legislative exemptions see Anti-Discrimination Act (NSW) 1977, Pt 3A, s 38P(1) introduced by the Transgender (Anti-Discrimination and Other Acts Amendment) Act (NSW) 1996, Sched 1, s 4; Victorian Equal Opportunity Act 1995 (Vic), s 66(1) as amended by Equal Opportunity (Gender Identity and Sexual Orientation) Act 2000 (Vic), s 7; Equal Opportunity Act 1984 (WA), Pt IIAA, s 35AP(2)(b) introduced by the Gender Reassignment Act 2000 (WA), Sched 2, s 5. Interestingly, the West Australian provision limits exclusion to transgender persons who 'would have a significant performance advantage as a result of his or her medical history'. While it remains to be tested the provision appears to address the specificity of physical advantage in individual cases. Accordingly, litigation on the point in Western Australia perhaps offers the potential to interrogate and problematise the practice of sexing bodies around, and through, sport.

51 *Richards v United States Tennis Association* 400 NYS 2d 267 (1977), p 271.

sport, like marriage in other decisions, reveals the subtext of reformism to be (bio)logically and temporally specific. In this sense, despite and through reform, the re-sexing of bodies is postponed in law. In other words, law continues to identify sexed space into which the transgender body cannot '(tres)pass'.

Further, this view of sport as 'limit' to the re-sexing practices of law challenges feminist politics through reproducing a culturally dominant view of the female body as physically 'inferior'. It should not be thought, however, that such representations would necessarily be countered by sexing male-to-female transgender bodies as female for the purposes of sport. Thus particular attention has been drawn by various media (Cole and Birrell, 1990), parliamentarians[52] and members of the judiciary, favouring law's re-sexing practices, to the fact that Renee Richards was defeated by Virginia Wade in the first round at Wimbledon in 1977. For example, in his Opinion in *P v S and Cornwall County Council*, Advocate-General Tesauro, commenting on the *Richards* decision, felt it necessary, and in order 'to complete the picture', to state 'I would observe that Richards was beaten in the first round by Wade 6–1, 6–4'.[53] This reference to a less than perfect sporting performance, much like opposition to transgender inclusion within women's sport, serves to structure an understanding of 'woman' around defeat. That is to say, while opposition is premised on fear of defeat, for others it is the fact of a transgender person's defeat that assists in the legal comprehension of her body as female.

6.4 CONCLUSION

In Chapter 5 the theme of the homophobia of law was introduced in order to question further an understanding of transgender jurisprudence as premised on an opposition between (bio)logic and reform. In this chapter this layering exercise has been pursued in the context of case law that has recognised transgender sex claims for marriage purposes. While these decisions perhaps represent an attempt to overcome the legal tension between the desire to reproduce the gender order and the desire to preserve a space for 'natural' heterosexual intercourse within marriage, the chapter demonstrates that the reform moment continues to be structured by legal anxiety over the homosexual body. Indeed, homophobia proves to be essential to 'resolution' of this legal dilemma. That is to say, inclusion of post-operative transgender bodies within the realm of marriage proves possible only because of the 'renaturalising' efforts law expends around those bodies. In particular, this legal work requires that the 'naturalness' of included bodies be mirrored. It is the pre-operative body, a body that law conflates utterly with homosexuality, which is employed to this end. That is to say, law continues to project its homophobia onto the pre-operative body. Accordingly, homosexuality continues to be coded as 'unnatural' and distanced from the institution of marriage. Further, homophobia proves evident in another respect. Thus attention was drawn to anxiety expressed over the possibility of 'gay' and 'lesbian' transgender persons already being located within marriage. In this regard it is clear that transgender marriage jurisprudence seeks to resist homosexuality from both inside and out.

52 See, eg, Dr BPV Pezzutti, Debates of the Legislative Council (NSW), 4 June 1996, p 2390.
53 *P v S and Cornwall County Council* [1996] 2 CMLR 247, p 257.

The homophobia of law is also, and perhaps especially, evident in the architectural shift from function to aesthetics apparent in *Attorney-General v Otahuhu Family Court*. While an aesthetic concern over bodies is a consistent theme of transgender jurisprudence it is usually masked, at least partially, by a preoccupation with heterosexual capacity. In *Otahuhu*, however, law's anxiety over bodily aesthetics is foregrounded. Absent a concern over sexual functioning, law's view of the pre-operative body as 'monstrous' becomes all the more evident, as does the homosexual sign it emits in the legal imaginary. Accordingly, a requirement of sex reassignment surgery would appear to be 'necessary', not so much to guarantee heterosexual penetration, but precisely in order that transgender bodies accord with law's aesthetic sensibility and thereby reduce homophobic anxiety. Indeed, the foregrounding of bodily aesthetics in *Otahuhu* might, at least in some limited sense, be viewed in the context of a more general shift in legal regulation toward the level of appearances, a theme to be explored in Chapter 8 in the context of Australian anti-discrimination legislative frameworks.

Finally, the chapter highlighted that, although the cases considered, and particularly *Otahuhu*, represent the zenith of judicial reform to date, the (bio)logic of law has not been expunged from reform jurisprudence. That is to say, while these decisions uncouple sex from biology for marriage purposes, they do not necessarily do so for all purposes. In particular, rather than abandoning (bio)logical 'truths', a number of decisions considered displace those 'truths' on to the terrain of competitive sport. In this way sport, rather than marriage, functions to 'naturalise' sexed difference. As with the homophobic aspects of reform, this resilience of (bio)logic in the face of transgender bodies serves to remind us that a view of reform as a movement 'beyond' *Corbett* needs to be treated with circumspection. In the following chapters our attention shifts from sex designation to discrimination. We shall see, however, that many of the themes considered in the chapters so far, including the theme of homophobia, persist.

PART III

SEX: FROM DESIGNATION TO DISCRIMINATION

CHAPTER 7

THE 'LIMITS' OF ANTI-DISCRIMINATION LAW SEX

It has been suggested that there is some middle ground between the sexes, a 'no-man's land' for those individuals who are neither truly 'male' nor truly 'female'. Yet the standard is much too fixed for such far-out theories.[1]

In this and the remaining chapters our attention turns from designation to discrimination in thinking about the transgender/law relation. In this chapter we will consider the relationship between transgender and the anti-discrimination law category of sex. In making this distinction my intention is to acknowledge that in contrast to designating persons male or female, that is to say, re-sexing bodies in binary terms, a concern that has provided the focus of earlier chapters, the potential for legal interpretations that move beyond this particular understanding of sex is especially apparent in discrimination law contexts. However, we will see that common law approaches to transgender sex discrimination claims have typically had the effect of limiting the meaning of sex to an understanding premised on the male/female dyad. That is to say, common law courts have tended, if not to collapse transgender into the male/female dyad, then to position transgender in such a way as to reproduce this dyad. In this regard, the chapter will, like earlier chapters, highlight an important link between judicial approaches premised on (bio)logic and more contemporary reform jurisprudence.

Legal resistance to thinking of sex beyond the male/female dyad is apparent in the judicial view that 'the standard is much too fixed for such far-out theories'.[2] While that attitude typifies judicial approaches to legal questions concerned with birth certificates, as accurate records of historical 'fact', and even more so with regard to marriage, an institution premised on opposite-sex relations, it is particularly unconvincing to insist on such a view with regard to the interpretation of the term 'sex' in anti-discrimination law contexts. For sex discrimination involves complex dynamics in which sex, gender and/or sexuality frequently interrelate in a variety of ways. Moreover, (bio)logical and/or anatomical approaches typically fail to capture discriminator motivation for '[o]nly in very rare cases can sex discrimination be reduced to a question of body parts' (Franke, 1995, p 36). Accordingly, the refusal to think sex other than in terms of the male/female dyad is harder to sustain in discrimination law contexts. In this regard, judicial approaches to the relation between transgender and sex discrimination serve, perhaps, to dramatise judicial anxiety over that which lies outside of, or beyond, the male/female dyad. In particular, it will be contended that resistance to expanding the concept of sex is inextricably tied to the homophobia of law and the long-standing conflation of transgender and homosexuality in medico-legal discourse.

While the chapter will focus on sex as a protected anti-discrimination law category, it should be recognised that both disability and sexual orientation as protected categories

---

1   *Re Anonymous* 293 NYS 2d 834 (1968), p 837, *per* Pecora J.
2   *Ibid.* See, also, eg, *MT v JT* 355 A 2d 204 (1976), p 210; *R v Harris and McGuiness* (1989) 17 NSWLR 158, pp 170, 194; *M v M* [1991] NZFLR 337, p 347.

have also been relied on for the purposes of transgender law reform.[3] Moreover, more recently, the instantiation of transgender as a protected category has occurred through legislation in some common law jurisdictions. This has been particularly notable at the municipal level in the United States[4] and at the State level in Australia.[5] In the following chapter we will consider this development in the context of Australian anti-discrimination legislative frameworks, where a critique will be offered as to the interrelationship of the protected categories of transgender, sexuality and sex. The present focus on discrimination on the basis of sex reflects the fact that in the main transgender discrimination claims have been brought under this protected category. While this fact is clearly connected to the protection of sex at earlier historical moments than the other categories referred to, and in some jurisdictions the lack of an alternative base for a claim, it may be that the category sex offers the most valuable means of reform (Franke, 1999, p 381).

Certainly, the grounding of claims in disability has obvious potential for negative discursive fallout for transgender people, given that of necessity such a strategy relies on a view of transgender people as psychiatrically disordered. Moreover, this strategy, placing reliance, as it does, on the inclusion of transgender people within the Diagnostic and Statistical Manual of Mental Disorders (DSM IV) (APA, 1995), not only problematises rationality and autonomy but serves potentially to exclude transgender people who fall outside particular psychiatric classifications.[6] While sexual orientation as a protected category does not present these particular difficulties, it does tend to consolidate the cultural conflation between transgender and homosexuality which has served to undermine transgender claims more generally. Further, reform that is channeled through categories other than sex enables law to distribute marginal groups around sex while maintaining intact a traditional and (bio)logical understanding of sex.

---

3   Reliance on disability as a protected category has generally proved unsuccessful (see, eg, *Somers v Iowa Civil Rights Commission* 337 NW 2d 470 (1983); *Dobre v National Railroad Passen Corporation (AMTRAK)* 850 F Supp 284 (1993); *Holt v Northwest Pennsylvania Training* 694 A 2d 1134 (1997) (cf *Doe v Boeing* 846 P 2d 531 (1993)) as has the less frequently relied on category of sexual orientation (see *Underwood v Archer Management Services* 857 F Supp 96 (1994)). Indeed, in relation to disability, and clearly conflating gender and sexuality, the Americans With Disabilities Act 1991 specifically excludes 'transvestism, transsexualism, paedophilia, exhibitionism, voyeurism, gender identity disorders not resulting from physical impairments, or other sexual behavior disorders' (42 USC 12211 (b)(1) (Supp III 1991)). For a discussion of the legislation see Hiegel, 1994.

4   This has occurred under the rubric of 'gender identity' or 'gender variance' in San Francisco, CA (1994); Iowa City, IA (1995); Benton County, OR (1997); Olympia, WA (1997); New Orleans, LA (1998); West Hollywood, CA (1998); Ann Arbor, MI (1999); Jefferson County, KY (1999); Lexington-Fayette Urban County Government, KY (1999); Louisville, KY (1999) Seattle, WA (1999) Tucson, AZ (1999); Vermont, Hate Crimes Law (1999); Atlanta, GA (2000); Boulder, CO (2000); Ithaca, NY (2000); Madison, WIS (2000); Portland, OR (2000). Other American municipalities have included transgender people within definitions of 'sexual orientation'/'affectional preference' (indeed, this has occurred at the State level in Minnesota) or 'sex' (see Currah and Minter, 2000a, pp 45–50; 2000b, pp 59–65).

5   The jurisdictions of New South Wales, the Australian Capital Territory, Western Australia and Victoria include 'transgender', 'transsexuality', 'gender reassigned persons' and 'gender identity' respectively as independent protected categories within their legislative frameworks (Anti-Discrimination Act 1997 (NSW), Pt 3A, s 38A; Discrimination Act 1991 (ACT), s 7(1)(c); Equal Opportunity Act 1984 (WA), s 35AB; Equal Opportunity Act 1995 (Vic), s 6(ac)) while South Australia and the Northern Territory include 'transsexuality' under the head of 'sexuality' (Equal Opportunity Act 1984 (SA), s 29(3)(c); Anti-Discrimination Act 1992 (NT), s 19).

6   It should not be thought however that proceeding under the protected category of sex necessarily avoids such pitfalls. Indeed, inclusion of transgender persons typically involves the reproduction of medical views that depict transgender as disordered.

In considering case law in this area, the chapter will divide or typologise decisions according to the meaning that the term 'sex' is given. First, a view of sex as (bio)logical sex will be considered. This view, which we considered in Chapter 3, has prevailed in anti-discrimination law transgender jurisprudence until relatively recently and has been particularly notable in the United States context. Secondly, a view of sex as anatomy will be explored. This view, while receiving prior support in dissenting judgments and overturned decisions in the United States, has received its most emphatic endorsement from the European Court of Justice. The type of analysis adopted within this approach maps reform jurisprudence considered in earlier chapters. Finally, the chapter will consider United States Federal Court decisions that represent a shift toward a view of sex as gender. It will be contended that this latter approach is to be preferred not merely because it abandons anatomical considerations but because it de-emphasises the importance of ontology, thereby reducing the possibility of legal circumscription of transgender and therefore the exclusion of some transgender people from the protection of anti-discrimination law. Moreover, this approach, unlike transgender jurisprudence more generally, has the additional advantage of not driving a wedge between transgender and gay and lesbian communities. Rather, it points to greater possibilities for coalition building around the concept of sex.

7.1 SEX AS BIOLOGY

The United States provides both the first common law transgender discrimination case relying on sex as a protected category[7] and the most substantial body of case law in this area. These cases have involved claims under Title VII of the Civil Rights Act 1964, sometimes coupled with constitutional arguments under the Equal Protection clause, and, to a lesser extent, claims under equivalent State legislation. In *Voyles v Ralph K Davies Medical Center* the District Court of California, in considering the meaning of sex under Title VII and guided by an interpretation of its legislative history, took the view that sex discrimination was not intended to 'embrace "transsexual" discrimination, or any permutation or combination thereof'.[8] In excluding transgender from the ambit of sex the court constructed the phrase 'sex discrimination' relationally between opposite sexes grounded in (bio)logic. The effect of the court's reasoning is, as noted by Pearlman (1995, p 862), to position transgender outside of sex irrespective of whether a litigant characterises her/his status as inside or outside the male/female dyad. That is to say, male-to-female transgender claims of discrimination on the basis of femaleness are overlayed with transgender status as the basis for the discrimination while claims of discrimination on transgender grounds simply fall outside sex, constructed as it is around a (bio)logical understanding of maleness/femaleness. The point is exemplified in *Sommers v Budget Marketing*[9] where the United States Appeals Court 8th Circuit viewed Audra Sommers' claim that she had been discriminated against 'because of her status as a

---

7   *Voyles v Ralph K Davies Medical Center* 403 F Supp 456 (1975).
8   *Ibid*, p 457.
9   *Sommers v Budget Marketing* 667 F 2d 748 (1982).

female, that is, a female with the anatomical body of a male' to be a 'manipulation of semantics'.[10]

This analysis has been replicated in numerous common law decisions that have followed in the wake of *Voyles* both at the Federal[11] and State[12] levels as well as outside the United States.[13] In *Holloway v Arthur Anderson* the United States Court of Appeals 9th Circuit took the view that 'Title VII does not prohibit the discharge of an employee for initiating the process of sex transformation',[14] claiming that 'Congress had only the traditional notions of "sex" in mind'.[15] In *Ulane v Eastern Airlines* the United States Court of Appeals 7th Circuit insisted that Title VII referred to 'a traditional concept of sex'[16] while in *Dobre v National Railroad Passen Corporation (AMTRAK)* the District Court of Pennsylvania defined the term to refer to 'an individual's distinguishing biological or anatomical characteristics'.[17] While it might be sought to distinguish between 'biology' and 'anatomy' here it is clear from a wider reading of the above, and other, decisions that the terms are used interchangeably (Franke, 1995, p 35). The approach to the legal determination of the concept of sex undertaken in these cases is one grounded in (bio)logic. It is one ultimately that maps the approach taken in *Corbett*.[18]

In concluding in this fashion, the *Voyles, Holloway, Ulane* and a succession of other courts have sought to ground their decisions in deference to the intention of Congress. In this regard, the decisions have tended to be prefaced by an inquiry into the legislative history regarding the entry of sex into Title VII. This 'history' receives particular attention in *Holloway* where the court noted that 'the major concern of Congress at the time the [Civil Rights] Act was promulgated was race discrimination. Sex as a basis of discrimination was added as a floor amendment one day before the House approved Title VII, without prior hearing or debate'.[19] It was this 'total lack of legislative history supporting the sex amendment'[20] that led both the *Holloway* and *Ulane* courts to conclude that Congress had in mind only 'the traditional concept of sex'.[21] However, it was not merely the fact that silence was equated with normative understandings of sex that

---

10   *Ibid*, p 749.

11   See, eg, *Holloway v Arthur Anderson* 566 F 2d 659 (1977); *Powell v Reads Inc* 436 F Supp 369 (1977); *Sommers v Budget Marketing* 337 NW 2d 470 (1982); *Ulane v Eastern Airlines* 742 F 2d 1081 (1984); *Wood v CG Studios* 660 F Supp 176 (1987); *Doe v Boeing* 846 P 2d 531 (1993); *Dobre v National Passenger Corporation* 850 F Supp 284 (1993); *Underwood v Archer Management Services* 857 F Supp 96 (1994); *James v Ranch Mart Hardware* 881 F Supp 478 (1995); *Brown v Zavaras* 63 F 3d 967 (1995).

12   See, eg, *Kirkpatrick v Seligman* 636 F 2d 1047 (1981); *Dobre v National Passenger Corporation* 850 F Supp 284 (1993); *Underwood v Archer Management Services* 857 F Supp 96 (1994); *Conway v City of Hartford* Conn Super LEXIS 282 (1997).

13   See, eg, *EA White v British Sugar Corporation* [1977] IRLR 121; *Menzies v Waycott and Astrovac (Australia) Pty Ltd* [2001] Victorian Civil and Administrative Tribunal (www.ecruiting.com.au/express/transgend150301.htm).

14   *Holloway v Arthur Anderson* 566 F 2d 659 (1977), p 659.

15   *Ibid*, p 662.

16   *Ulane v Eastern Airlines* 742 F 2d 1081 (1984), p 1085.

17   *Dobre v National Passenger Corporation* 850 F Supp 284 (1993), p 285.

18   *Corbett v Corbett* [1970] 2 All ER 33.

19   *Holloway v Arthur Anderson* 566 F 2d 659 (1977), p 662. Indeed, the introduction of the 'sex' amendment was a failed attempt to defeat the adoption of the Civil Rights Act 1964.

20   *Ulane v Eastern Airlines* 742 F 2d 1081 (1984), p 1085.

21   *Ibid*.

influenced these and other courts. A significant factor in the conclusion that transgender fell outside the term 'sex' was a judicial reading of subsequent and unsuccessful gay and lesbian law reform (Katz, 1982, p 269). That is to say, successive courts have inferred an intention on the part of Congress to exclude transgender from successful legislative resistance to attempts 'to amend Title VII to prohibit discrimination based upon "affectational or sexual orientation"'.[22] The point is put explicitly by the *Ulane* court: '... [w]hile the proposed amendments were directed toward homosexuals their rejection strongly indicates that the phrase in the Civil Rights Act prohibiting discrimination on the basis of sex should be given a narrow, traditional interpretation, which would also exclude transsexuals.'[23] Indeed, the view that sex excludes transgender has been considered to be supported by the fact that Congress has continued to reject gay and lesbian law reform 'even after courts have specifically held that Title VII does not protect transsexuals from discrimination'.[24]

The persistent references to the fate of gay and lesbian law reform in determining the relation between Title VII sex and transgender is particularly revealing, as is the linkage of 'transsexuals, homosexuals or bisexuals'[25] in constructing the 'outside' of the category sex. That is to say, the conflation of (trans)gender with (homo)sexuality proves to be significant in accounting for judicial insistence on the mutual exclusivity of sex and transgender. However, while transgender and homosexuality are woven together as legal outside, courts that have insisted on a view of sex as biology have, as Keller has noted, tended to distinguish between them (1999, p 376). Indeed, Keller suggests that '[i]t is odd that these courts work so hard at this distinction, because nothing in these cases seems to hinge on it' (1999, p 376). It is precisely the fact that this is true in an instrumental sense that points to the excessive work undertaken within transgender jurisprudence in the furtherance of much wider regulatory strategies around bodies. That is to say, the very fact of contemplation of the transgender/sex relation becomes a series of moments for repetition of the 'unthinkability' of homosexuality as anything other than legal 'outside'. In this regard, and as in previous chapters, the homophobia of law proves important, if not central, to an understanding of the transgender/law relation. Moreover, we will see that this theme persists within anti-discrimination law reform jurisprudence. Indeed, in many respects homophobia is rendered more explicit here, given that reform, as noted in earlier chapters, is premised on an uncoupling of (trans)gender from (homo)sexuality.

It should be stressed, however, that while United States courts have tended to interpret Title VII sex through the lens of biology, from the standpoint of 'the natural attitude' (Keller, 1999, pp 343–44), that approach has simultaneously been undermined from within in an important respect. That is to say, courts have interpreted Title VII sex to capture discrimination where the perpetrator believes the victim to be of the opposite (bio)logical sex. Thus in *Ulane* the court contended that '[i]f Eastern [Airlines] considered Ulane to be female and had discriminated against her because she was female ... then the argument might be made that Title VII applied'.[26] This point was clarified in *Dobre* where

---

22 *Ibid.*

23 *Ibid*, pp 1085–86.

24 *Ibid*, p 1086.

25 *Voyles v Ralph K Davies Medical Center* 403 F Supp 456 (1975), p 457.

26 *Ulane v Eastern Airlines* 742 F 2d 1081 (1984), p 1087.

the court stated that 'if AMTRAK considered [Andria] Dobre to be female and discriminated against her on that basis (that is, treated her less favorably than male employees), then Dobre would be able to maintain a Title VII action as a female'.[27] In this respect, anti-discrimination law protection proves to be less an effect of biology or indeed of identity, but rather of transgender performance and discriminating gaze, a theme to be explored in the following chapter. Suffice it to say, for present purposes, that the deeming of persons to be male or female whenever they appear to be so before the discriminating gaze has the regulatory effect of inciting the practice of '(tres)passing' as male or female.

That this is so brings into question judicial insistence on a (bio)logical approach to the question of sex in the first place. If it is not merely the protection of (bio)logical men and women that grounds Title VII but all persons appearing to be (bio)logical men and women then it is not at first apparent why interpretations of Title VII sex should have recourse to biology. The apparent disjunction is, perhaps, to be accounted for by the fact that courts have sought to constrain interpretation of the category sex while simultaneously enabling it to reach those perpetrators whose acts of discrimination are triggered by presumptions as to (bio)logical sex. In this way the (bio)logical approach of the courts to Title VII sex coincides with its underlying purpose, but in a tightly circumscribed manner. Beyond the possibility of legal protection through being 'misread', judicial insistence on sex as biology leaves the (male-to-female) transgender woman only her female-to-male counterpart as a comparator for the purposes of evaluating a sex discrimination claim. Apart from the practical difficulties of locating such a comparator, this strategy would almost inevitably collapse in the face of an 'equal misery' analysis.

7.2 SEX AS ANATOMY

In approaching reform jurisprudence in this area it is necessary to return to *Holloway*. For in addition to being a landmark decision against reform, the dissenting judgment of Goodwin J problematises a (bio)logical understanding of Title VII sex. This judgment is significant and revealing in a number of respects. First, and as noted by Wein and Remmers (1979, pp 1099–100), Goodwin J pointed out that the case was not one concerning 'sexual preference',[28] thereby distinguishing sexuality from gender and insulating Title VII from homosexuality. Then in a series of statements that represent a significant departure from the majority judgment he stated that he 'would not limit the right to claim discrimination to those who were born into the victim class',[29] for Ramona Holloway was 'a person completing surgically that part of nature's handiwork which apparently was left incomplete somewhere along the line'.[30] While this latter statement appears to indicate a possible (bio)logical basis for transgender, this theme is not discussed in the judgment. Rather, Goodwin J places emphasis on the fact, or imminence, of sex reassignment surgery and the implications of this fact for any assessment of sex. Thus he expressed the view that '[a]ssuming that this plaintiff has now undergone her

---

27   *Dobre v National Passenger Corporation* 850 F Supp 284 (1993), p 287.
28   *Holloway v Arthur Anderson* 566 F 2d 659 (1977), p 664.
29   *Ibid.*
30   *Ibid.*

planned surgery, she is, presumably female, at least for most social purposes'.[31] In other words, to discriminate against a post-operative (male-to-female) transgender woman is to discriminate against her because she is, or has become, female and therefore clearly violates Title VII.

However, Ramona Holloway's employment had been terminated prior to undertaking genital surgery. She had been dismissed for 'initiating the process of sex transformation'.[32] Accordingly, inclusion of Ramona's body within the ambit of sex required that the pre-/post-operative distinction be addressed. As Goodwin J put it: '... [t]he only issue before us is whether a transsexual whose condition has not yet become stationary can state a claim under the statute if discharged because of her undertaking to change her sex.'[33] In resolving this issue he stated:

> Had the employer waited and discharged the plaintiff as a post-surgical female because she had changed her sex, I suggest that the discharge would have to be classified as one based upon sex. I fail to see any valid Title VII purpose to be served by holding that a discharge while an employee is in surgery, or a few days before surgery, is not as much a discharge by reason of sex as a discharge a few days after surgery. The result is the same, whenever the employer sends the discharge notice ... It seems to me irrelevant under Title VII whether the plaintiff was born female or was born ambiguous and chose to become female. The relevant fact is that she was, on the day she was fired, a purported female.[34]

While expansion of the category sex, and refusal to insist on a strict application of a pre-/post-operative dyad, serve to disrupt traditional and (bio)logical understandings of sex, this passage presents difficulties. First, it is clear that the temporal relation between the moment of dismissal and surgery assumes importance. That is to say, while absence of surgery does not prove fatal on Goodwin J's analysis, inclusion of transgender within the category sex is premised on the inevitability, indeed the imminence, of surgical intervention. In this way, the expansion of sex to encompass transgender occurs through collapsing the distinction between transgender and the male/female dyad. It is Goodwin J's view that Ramona Holloway has ceased to be, or will soon cease to be, transgender and has become, or will soon become, female that brings her within the category sex. In other words, while Goodwin J uncouples the male/female dyad from (bio)logic and the birth moment he reproduces the majority's view that Title VII sex is confined to maleness and femaleness, that is, to bodies sexed within a binary frame. In this way the possibility of protecting persons who are perceived as defying rather than reproducing the sex/gender system is held at bay.

In the later case of *Ulane* the trial judge, Grady J, found in favour of Karen Ulane, a post-operative (male-to-female) transgender woman and airline pilot, in relation to her Title VII suit.[35] While this decision was, as already mentioned, emphatically rejected on appeal to the United States Appeals Court 7th Circuit it is significant in a number of respects. First, Grady J, like Goodwin J in Holloway, distinguished transgender from

---

31 *Ibid.*
32 *Ibid*, p 659.
33 *Ibid*, p 664.
34 *Ibid.*
35 *Ulane v Eastern Airlines* 581 F Supp 821 (1983).

homosexuality and indeed transvestism. Thus in locating Karen Ulane within the category sex Grady J made it clear that he had 'no problem with the idea that [Title VII] was not intended and cannot reasonably be argued to have been intended to cover the matter of sexual preference, the preference of a sexual partner, or the matter of sexual gratification from wearing the clothes of the opposite sex'.[36] On the other hand, he took the view that it was 'an altogether different question as to whether the matter of sexual identity is comprehended by the word "sex"'.[37] The matter of the relationship between homosexuality and Title VII sex having been safely disposed of, Grady J turned more specifically to the relationship between transgender and the category sex. In this regard, and while recognising that there may be some argument in the medical community about the definition of sex, he contended that 'sex is not a cut-and-dried matter of chromosomes'[38] but 'is in part a psychological question', one of 'self-perception', and in part a social matter, a question of how 'society perceive[s] the individual',[39] and that it is reasonable to hold that the statutory word 'sex' applies 'literally … and scientifically to transsexuals'.[40] In adopting this view Grady J was clearly influenced by the fact that Title VII is remedial legislation requiring a liberal construction.[41]

However, what is most significant about Grady J's judgment is that in the final analysis he refuses to collapse transgender into the male/female distinction. Rather, he locates transgender both within and outside that dyad. Thus while initially finding Karen Ulane to have been discriminated against on the basis of her transgender status, and while interpreting Title VII sex to include transgender, Grady J later amended his findings to hold that Ulane's 'post-operative status is that of a female'[42] and that she has also been discriminated against on this basis. In other words, and as Green has pointed out, Grady J ultimately held that Title VII should apply with equal force irrespective of whether a person is regarded 'as a transsexual or as a female' (1985, p 130). For Green, however, this aspect of Grady J's judgment is the most problematic because 'the court's separation of the two classes in which *Ulane* was ruled protected disserves the fundamental nature of transsexualism' (1985, p 130). He contends that 'the requirement that the transsexual employee alternatively prove discrimination based on status as a woman or a man *and* as a transsexual both creates and enforces an artificial distinction', one that 'undermines the psychiatric significance of the transsexual phenomenon' (Green, 1985, p 130). In other words, Green advocates the collapse of transgender into the male/female dyad so that transgender as a separate entity bearing a relation to sex disappears.

In my view, while an interpretation of sex as gender is to be preferred to an expansive reading of sex to include transgender, it is precisely because Title VII sex is expanded to include transgender without collapsing the latter into the male/female dyad that marks out Grady J's judgment as particularly commendable. In contrast, Green's insistence that the distinction between transgender and male/female is an artificial one serves to erase

---

36 *Ibid*, p 823.
37 *Ibid*.
38 *Ibid*, p 825.
39 *Ibid*, p 823.
40 *Ibid*, p 825.
41 *Ibid*, p 824.
42 *Ibid*, p 839.

transgender identification and to mask discrimination dynamics in transgender contexts. That is to say, and as has become increasingly clear in recent years, not all transgender people conceive of themselves as being of the sex opposite to that designated at birth, nor do sex/gender journeys, surgical or otherwise, necessarily involve 'complete' crossings of that divide (see, for example, Stone, 1991; Denny, 1991, p 6; Boswell, 1991; Feinberg, 1993b; Bornstein, 1994; May-Welby, 1994, p 11; Hooley, 1994; Bruce-Pratt, 1995; Nataf, 1996, p 32; Califia, 1997; Wilchins, 1997; Stryker, 1998, p 149; Cromwell, 1999, p 23). Moreover, irrespective of this point, the fact remains, as the case law so clearly demonstrates, that transgender people are discriminated against typically not because they are male/female but because they are perceived or known to be transgender. Indeed, *Ulane* is itself a case in point, given that Eastern Airlines did not want '[a] *transsexual* in the cockpit'.[43] While endorsement of such a view might be viewed as tantamount to sacrificing male/female self-identification and experience to the discriminating gaze, it is important not to lose sight of the reality of discrimination nor to refrain from attending to the differences that activate it.

Rather, the difficulty with Grady J's judgment lies not in the creation of an 'artificial distinction' between transgender and maleness/femaleness but in the limits of that distinction. That is to say, the construction of transgender that Grady J viewed as protected by Title VII sex is both heavily circumscribed and one that bears a highly proximate relation to the male/female dyad. Indeed, in finding Karen Ulane to be female '[u]pon further reflection'[44] Grady J, in a move uncharacteristic of transgender jurisprudence relating to discrimination, made reference to reform jurisprudence concerned explicitly with the question of sex designation.[45] In this regard, the gulf between Grady J's judgment and Green's analysis should not be overstated. For it is Grady J's claim that the statutory word sex 'literally and scientifically applies to transsexuals' that brings transgender within Title VII sex. In other words, it is the fact of sex reassignment surgery, which Karen Ulane had actually undertaken, or at least a view of such surgery as transgender's logical end, that grounds his interpretation of sex.

The *Ulane* decision is revealing in another respect, one that helps account for Green's insistence that transsexuals are to be comprehended in terms of the male/female dyad and not as something that lies outside or beyond it. At trial the psychiatric experts called for Eastern Airlines contended that Karen Ulane was, and in the view of one expert, 'beyond a shadow of a doubt',[46] a transvestite, not an 'authentic' transsexual. They argued that since surgery is not an appropriate treatment for transvestism, a poor psychiatric outcome would ensue, Karen Ulane would be emotionally unstable and the safety of airline passengers would thereby be compromised. While these concerns are directed toward the future it is clear that characterisation of Karen Ulane as transvestite arises due to an analysis of her past, and in particular her departure from a medically privileged transgender narrative (Stoller, 1968, p 251; 1973; 1975, pp 139–40), one explored in Chapter 2. Thus, diagnosis of transvestism was, as Green notes, 'based on the fact that Ulane had been married as a male and had functioned in a traditionally masculine social

---

43 *Ulane v Eastern Airlines* 742 F 2d 1081 (1984), p 1087.
44 *Ulane v Eastern Airlines* 581 F Supp 821 (1983), p 839.
45 *Ibid*. Reference was made to *Re Anonymous* 293 NYS 2d 834 (1968) and *MT v JT* 355 A 2d 204 (1976).
46 *Ibid*, p 824, testimony of Dr Wise.

role, both in the military and as an airline pilot. The contention was that the capacity to function in this manner precluded the degree of feminine identification necessary for the diagnosis of transsexualism' (1985, p 129, fn 12). Thus in contesting the claim of discrimination on the grounds of both transgender and femaleness, counsel for Eastern Airlines de-emphasised post-surgical reality in favour of prior moments of 'truth'. In short, and despite post-surgical reality, the *discovery story of transsexuality* (King, 1993, pp 45, 63) is deployed against Karen Ulane.

The strategy of coding Ulane as a transvestite serves to problematise the very gender identity upon which her claims of female and/or transgender status rest. Moreover, because medico-legal discourse tends to view transvestism as erotically charged (APA, 1980; APA, 1995) this legal move serves to conflate gender with 'perverse' sexuality, thereby bringing Ulane's body into proximity to that body viewed as unquestionably falling outside Title VII sex, namely the homosexual. Moreover, while Grady J accepted Karen Ulane to be transsexual his opinion that 'there is nothing flamboyant, nothing freakish, about the plaintiff' reveals more than a concern over post-operative prognosis. The word 'freakish' invokes the notion of the 'monstrous' body. As explained in Chapter 6, judicial anxiety over the monstrosity of bodies suggests more than visual horror. It also, and importantly, points to signs that bodies emit (Epstein, 1995, p 91). It is contended that one sign that the 'flamboyant' and 'freakish' transgender body emits before the legal gaze is the sign of homosexuality. It is precisely such conflations that incite a law reform strategy premised on the logic of male/female identity. As for Green, while problematising the psychiatric reading of Karen Ulane as transvestite, he does nothing to contest the view of Eastern Airlines' medical experts and Grady J that transvestites fall outside Title VII sex. Rather, his insistence that transsexuality is to be understood in terms of the male/female dyad serves to restrict the meaning of Title VII sex so that a range of transgender people, including self-identified transvestites, lie beyond the category.

In contrast to Title VII, interpretations of sex at the US State and City levels have proved more receptive to a view of anti-discrimination law sex as anatomy. The first decision to adopt this view is *Richards v United States Tennis Association*,[47] a decision considered in Chapter 4. Here Asicone J concluded 'according to the overwhelming medical evidence',[48] a reference to sex reassignment surgery, that Renee Richards, a (male-to-female) transgender woman, 'is now female'[49] and therefore an attempt to exclude her from competing in the US Tennis Open by introducing a chromosomal test for eligibility constituted 'grossly unfair, discriminatory and inequitable' treatment that was 'violative of her rights under the Human Rights Law of this State'.[50] In this decision, which involved issues of sport rather than workplace discrimination more typical of the case law, the line between discrimination and designation is particularly blurred. That is to say, Richards is not only found to have been discriminated against on the basis of sex. Rather, for the purposes of anti-discrimination law at least, she is found to be unequivocally female. Indeed, given the case involved an attempt to exclude Richards from sporting activity exclusive to women such a conclusion was essential to a finding

---

47 *Richards v United States Tennis Association* 400 NYS 2d 267 (1977).

48 *Ibid*, p 272.

49 *Ibid*.

50 *Ibid*. See Human Rights Law Exec (NY), ss 290 and 297, subd 9.

that her rights had been violated. In accounting for this decision, and the fact that it would be a further two decades before there would be further anti-discrimination law movement on this issue at the State level, it is important to emphasise two factors. First, the facts of the case served perhaps to intensify a concern over human rights. That is to say, and as Asicone J noted, the effect as well as the design of the USTA's decision to institute a chromosomal test was specifically to target Richards.[51] Secondly, the *Richards* decision precedes key and contrary Title VII jurisprudence.[52]

More recently, and in the context of workplace discrimination, New York Courts have departed from the long line of authority exemplified by *Holloway* and *Ulane*. While such cases have not required the re-sexing of bodies for their success, we will see, much like the judgments of Goodwin J and Grady J in the federal context, that this has been substantially the effect. In *Maffei v Kolaeton Industry*[53] the Supreme Court of New York County held that an employer who harasses an employee because the person, as a result of surgery and hormone treatments, is now a different sex violated the New York City Administrative Code on the basis of sex. The importance of this decision, however, needs to be qualified. First, it did not involve a determination regarding Title VII, or even New York State law but rather is confined to a city ordinance. Secondly, that ordinance, while originally referring to sex, was subsequently changed to gender, thereby creating greater space for transgender inclusion.[54] Further, a distinction might also be made between scenarios of dismissal which have tended to characterise the line of Federal Court authority and harassment in the workplace, albeit that the two are not incompatible. That is to say, it is one thing to create a legal space for employers to decide who they employ and quite another to allow an employee to be subjected to a hostile working environment.

More importantly, the judgment of Lehner J proves problematic in a number of respects. That is to say, while viewing federal analyses to be 'unduly restrictive'[55] and insisting that 'anti-discrimination statutes are remedial and thus to be interpreted liberally',[56] he nevertheless confined his judgment in important ways. One difficulty again lies in the relevance of surgical intervention to inclusion within the category of sex. While Lehner J found the record to be 'unclear as to what physical changes have taken place, and to what extent the plaintiff has completed his metamorphosis from a female to a male',[57] he nevertheless framed his decision in such a way that it is difficult to disentangle the fact of surgery from the expansion of sex as an anti-discrimination law category. Moreover, and irrespective of this point, the decision confines the concept of sex to the male/female dyad. In particular Lehner J contended that Daniel Maffei '[b]eing a transsexual male ... may be considered part of a subgroup of men. There is no reason to permit discrimination against that subgroup'.[58] This conclusion appears to follow from

---

51 *Ibid.*

52 While State courts interpreting State legislation are not bound by federal jurisprudence they have until quite recently tended to apply analyses of Title VII sex (see above, note 12).

53 *Maffei v Kolaeton Industry Inc* 626 NYS 2d 391 (1995).

54 Moreover, the court noted that the court in *Dobre v National Railroad Passenger Corporation* 850 F Supp 284 (1993) 'which determined that transsexuals are not covered by the word "sex" in Title VII, observed that the result would be different if instead the term "gender" had been used' (p 395).

55 *Maffei v Kolaeton Industry Inc* 626 NYS 2d 391 (1995), p 394.

56 *Ibid*, p 396.

57 *Ibid*, p 391.

58 *Ibid*, p 396.

Lehner J's observation that 'society only recognizes two sexes',[59] an observation that serves to highlight the rigidity of judicial thinking around the concept of sex even within anti-discrimination law contexts. Indeed, while a view of Maffei as falling within a subgroup of men is confined to an analysis of the meaning of the term 'sex' for the purposes of anti-discrimination law it is again apparent that sex discrimination collapses into sex designation, thereby linking transgender jurisprudence in this area to the case law considered in earlier chapters. Moreover, it is also significant that this subgroup of men Lehner J identifies is marked out as heterosexual. Thus in addition to insisting that 'there is a clear distinction between homosexuals and transsexuals'[60] Lehner J contended that 'transsexual's erotic attractions are generally with persons of their own anatomical sex'.[61] In this way his judgment serves to marginalise non-heterosexual transgender desires and practices and ensures that the reproduction of the male/female dyad continues to bear a heterosexual relation.

The analysis adopted in Maffei was followed a year later by the United States District Court for the Southern District of New York in *Rentos v Oce-Office Systems*[62] where Preska J endorsed Lehner's view that:

> The creation of a hostile working environment as a result of derogatory comments relating to the fact that as a result of an operation an employee changed his or her sexual status, creates discrimination based on 'sex' ... Thus an employer who harasses an employee because the person, as a result of surgery and hormone treatments, is now of a different sex has violated our City provision against discrimination based on sex.[63]

Moreover, Preska J took the view that the same analysis would apply to New York State law, a conclusion she found to be implicit in Lehner J's judgment, alluding as it does 'to the more expansive application of State law compared with Title VII, as well as its citation to the *Richards* case'.[64] The reference to *Richards*, in both *Maffei* and *Rentos*, serves to foreground further the anatomical foundation upon which sex is reconstituted in these decisions.

While United States Federal Courts have been resistant to a view of sex as anatomy, as distinct from biology, the analyses of the New York courts have received support outside the United States. In *P v S and Cornwall County Council* the European Court of Justice decided that the scope of the European Equal Treatment Directive[65] 'cannot be confined simply to discrimination based on the fact that a person is of one or other sex'.[66] While failing to adopt the more purposive and flexible interpretation of sex as gender articulated in the Opinion of Advocate-General Tesauro (Stychin, 1997, p 222; Beger, 2000, p 260; Whittle, 2000, p 34)[67] the Court took the view that the Directive applies to discrimination arising from gender reassignment for:

---

59   *Ibid.*
60   *Ibid*, p 395.
61   *Ibid*, p 393.
62   *Rentos v Oce-Office Systems* US Dist LEXIS 19060 (1996).
63   *Ibid*, p 7.
64   *Ibid.*
65   EEC Directive 76/207 of 9 February 1976.
66   *P v S and Cornwall County Council* [1996] 2 CMLR 247, p 263.
67   *Ibid*, pp 256, 258.

Such discrimination is based, essentially if not exclusively, on the sex of the person concerned. Where a person is dismissed on the ground that he or she intends to undergo, or has undergone, gender reassignment, he or she is treated unfavourably by comparison with persons of the sex to which he or she was deemed to belong before undergoing gender reassignment.[68]

Here the Court, having dismissed the United Kingdom's attempt to characterise the matter as one of 'equal misery',[69] introduce a male comparator, albeit P's former self (Skidmore, 1997, p 108; Wintemute, 1997, p 341). This proves possible due to a view of P as female for anti-discrimination law purposes, or at least as a person whose proximity to femaleness, in an anatomical sense, is such as to blur the distinction between transgender and the male/female dyad.[70] That this is so is evident from the priority accorded to sex reassignment surgery in the decision. In other words, given that the court distinguishes sex (surgery) from gender, and clearly does not inaugurate a third sex,[71] it is a view of P as female (not merely feminine) for the purposes of the European Directive that proves crucial. Thus what might be viewed as gender transgression is protected only through conversion into sexed 'normality'. While 'femaleness' produces a male comparator, it would seem that non-operative transgender people are condemned to 'equal misery' jurisprudence. Moreover, it is this view of sex as anatomy that accounts for the disjunction between *P v S and Cornwall County Council* and the court's subsequent decision in *Grant v South West Train Ltd*.[72] That is to say, in contrast to discrimination motivated by anatomical reconstruction, which the court codes as sex-based, discrimination arising out of the same-sex nature of a relationship is viewed as clearly falling outside the protected category. As the court in *Grant* explained:

> The Court [in P] considered that such discrimination was in fact based, essentially if not exclusively, on the sex of the person concerned. That reasoning, which leads to the conclusion that such discrimination is to be prohibited just as is discrimination based on the fact that a person belongs to a particular sex, is limited to the case of a worker's gender reassignment and does not therefore apply to differences of treatment based on a person's sexual orientation.[73]

More recently, this way of thinking the transgender/sex relation has been adopted in Canada. Thus in *Commission des Droits de la Personne et des Droits de la Jeunesse v Maison des Jeunes and Others*[74] the Human Rights Tribunal of Montreal held that 'a transsexual person who is a victim of discrimination based on his being a transsexual may benefit from provisions against discrimination based on sex [s 10 of the Quebec Charter of

---

68 *Ibid.*

69 *Ibid*, p 262.

70 The case did not establish that transgender persons are entitled to equal rights with those of the sex to which they have been reassigned (see *Bavin v NHS Trust Pensions Agency* [1999] ICR 1192 (EAT), p 1201).

71 The view that transsexuals 'do not constitute a third sex' is also rendered explicit in the Opinion of Advocate-General Tesauro (*P v S and Cornwall County Council* [1996] 2 CMLR 247, p 259).

72 *Grant v South West Train Ltd* [1996] ECR C-249/96 (ECJ).

73 Para 42.

74 *Commission des Droits de la Personne et des Droits de la Jeunesse v Maison des Jeunes and Others* [1998] Quebec Human Rights Tribunal (www2.lexum.canlii.org/qc/cas/ qctdp/1998/1998qctdp236.html).

Human Rights and Freedoms], once his transformations have been completed or, if you like, once his identification is perfectly unified'.[75] This emphasis on a pre-/post-operative dyad that lies at the heart of the sex as anatomy approach is to be accounted for, in some considerable measure, by anxiety that '[i]f such a distinction were not made then there would be some homosexual relationships which would be barely distinguishable from relationships involving transsexuals'.[76] That is to say, sex reassignment surgery, as explained in earlier chapters, serves to assuage judicial anxiety generated by pre-existing cultural conflation of transgender and homosexuality. It might be thought inappropriate to foreground the homophobia of law in the Quebec context, given that s 10 of the Charter of Human Rights and Freedoms includes 'sexual orientation' as a protected category and that s 15(1) of the Canadian Charter of Rights and Freedoms has been interpreted by the Supreme Court of Canada to do the same by reason of analogy (see Stychin, 1995, p 109). However, it is important to emphasise that the protection of gay men and lesbians occurs through the construction of a category outside of sex. In other words, it is precisely because the post-operative transgender body is brought within the protected category of sex that the need to insulate that body from homosexual desire and practice arises. That is to say, sex as anatomy, like sex as biology, requires homosexuality as constitutive outside.

Of course, sex reassignment surgery not only serves to distance transgender from homosexuality. It also assists in the demonstration of the fixed nature of identity, a precondition for compliance with law's categorical imperative within liberal legalism (Bumiller, 1988; Iyer, 1993; Herman, 1994; Morgan, 1996). It is perhaps significant that demonstration of the fixed status of transgender as a precondition of inclusion within the anti-discrimination law category sex proves so much more burdensome than is the case for gay men and lesbians under the protected category of sexual orientation.[77] While legal emphasis on sex reassignment surgery is clearly an effect of the fact that law reduces the category of sex to the male/female dyad and refuses to reimagine that dyad along genital lines, it is perhaps also linked to transgender's lack of solidity as culturally produced. That is to say, a view of sex reassignment surgery as necessary in the demonstration of transgender 'authenticity' perhaps bears a relation to the cultural couplings of (homo)sexuality/depth and (trans)gender/surface, effects, as explained in Chapter 2, traceable through Freud (1905) to von Krafft-Ebing (1965). It has been suggested that the divergence between United States anti-discrimination law federal jurisprudence and the approach taken in Europe is perhaps explicable in terms of the contrast between the human rights-based approach of the latter and the civil rights-based tradition of the former (Beger, 2000, p 265). While this assessment, one that would also account for recent reform jurisprudence in Canada, is perhaps a useful and a historically accurate one, we will see in the following section that it is United States Federal Courts

---

75   *Ibid*, para 113.

76   *Bavin v NHS Trust Pensions Agency* (EAT) [1999] ICR 1192 (EAT), p 1200.

77   Canadian courts have found sexual orientation to be sufficiently immutable to constitute a characteristic analogous to the enumerated grounds of discrimination under s 15(1) of the Canadian Charter of Rights and Freedoms 1982 (see *Veysey v Commissioner of the Correctional Service of Canada* [1989] 44 CRR 364; appeal dismissed, 109 NR 300 (Fed CA).

that have, in recent years, interpreted the concept of sex in the most open-textured manner.

7.3 SEX AS GENDER

A shift toward thinking the anti-discrimination law category of sex as gender is traceable to *Sprogis v United Airlines*[78] (Holt, 1997, p 299) where the United States Court of Appeals 7th Circuit in its discussion of the conduct prohibited by Title VII stated: 'In forbidding employers to discriminate against individuals because of their sex, Congress intended to strike at the entire spectrum of disparate treatment of men and women resulting from sex stereotypes.'[79] This view was endorsed by the Supreme Court in *City of Los Angeles, Department of Water and Power v Manhart*[80] and, more recently, in *Price Waterhouse v Hopkins*.[81] In the latter case, the Supreme Court held that Title VII sex barred not just discrimination based on the fact that Ann Hopkins was a woman, but also discrimination based on the fact she failed 'to act like a woman', that is, to conform to socially constructed gender expectations.[82] While these decisions offer the possibility for opening up Title VII sex to previously excluded groups, a number of critical legal scholars have highlighted their limits with regard to the discrimination claims of gay men and lesbians due to a tendency to reduce the gender aspects of discrimination in such cases to sexual orientation (Case, 1995, pp 57–61; Valdes, 1995, p 18). In other words, there has been a tendency to view sexual orientation as over-determined, a tendency Valdes has referred to as the 'sexual orientation loophole' to claims of sex discrimination (1995, p 18).[83] Thus in *Dillon v Frank*[84] the court rejected a Hopkins-style sex-stereotyping analysis based on Dillon's insistence that he had been discriminated against because he was not deemed macho enough by his male co-workers (Case, 1995, p 59). Specifically, he had been subjected to sustained verbal abuse including the statement that 'Dillon sucks dicks'.[85] The court insisted that:

---

78   *Sprogis v United Airlines* 444 F 2d 1194 (1971).

79   *Ibid*, p 1198.

80   *City of Los Angeles, Department of Water & Power v Manhart* 435 US 702 (1978).

81   *Price Waterhouse v Hopkins* 490 US 228 (1989).

82   The Supreme Court also made clear that gender need not be the sole reason for the discrimination.

83   While the Supreme Court has more recently interpreted 'sexual harassment' to include same-sex sexual harassment (*Oncale v Sundowner Offshore Servs* Inc 523 US 75 (1998)), this does not address the question of whether 'non-abusive' forms of workplace discrimination constitute sex discrimination. Indeed, even in relation to 'sexual harassment' the Supreme Court insisted that 'Title VII does not prohibit all verbal or physical harassment in the workplace' but only 'conduct which a reasonable person in a Plaintiff's position would find severely hostile or abusive' (p 81) and even then, the court made clear, a Title VII claim would collapse in the face of an 'equal misery' argument.

84   *Dillon v Frank* 58 Empl Prac Dec (CCH) §41,332 (1992).

85   *Ibid*, pp 2–3. Irrespective of the court's splitting of gender and sexuality the facts of the case serve to expose the complainant to an 'equal misery' analysis. Indeed, the court noted that Dillon had not advanced evidence that a lesbian would have been accepted in the workplace or that women known to engage in the practice of fellatio would have been treated differently. In other words, even where a court is willing to view discrimination in terms of gender rather than sexuality homophobia and misogyny remain as significant barriers to proving a claim of discrimination on the basis of sex.

> *Price Waterhouse v. Hopkins* does not direct a different result. *Price Waterhouse* was not a hostile environment case. It involved ... [a]n allegation 'that gender played a part in a particular employment decision'. Because of this difference ... we do not read the Court to mean that any treatment that could be based on sexual stereotypes would violate Title VII.[86]

The court sought to narrow further the potential impact of *Price Waterhouse* through emphasising the particularity of its facts. Thus in contrast to Dillon, Hopkins was viewed as having been placed in an 'intolerable and impermissible Catch-22'[87] situation whereby her promotion prospects were linked to aggressiveness, the display of which would render her unacceptable in the workplace. Ironically, this view seems to amount to the claim that if Dillon would simply stop doing whatever it was he was doing then he would not be disadvantaged. What he was doing, of course, was 'failing' to perform masculinity 'successfully'. It is precisely this gender dimension, one that the court strives to erase, which renders *Price Waterhouse* relevant. More recently, and while gender-based arguments under Title VII sex had previously been rejected in transgender contexts, the United States Court of Appeals 9th Circuit took a different view in *Schwenk v Hartford*.[88] In this case the plaintiff, Crystal Schwenk, a (male-to-female) transgender woman, alleged that she had been sexually assaulted by the defendant, a prison guard, while incarcerated. In pursuing a remedy she relied not on Title VII but on the Gender Motivated Violence Act 1994 (GMVA), and the Eighth Amendment of the US Constitution prohibiting 'cruel and unusual punishment'. However, in order to determine the scope of the GMVA, and in particular whether it encapsulated a distinction between sex and gender sufficient to exclude Schwenk from its ambit, as the defendant contended, the court considered Title VII jurisprudence, concluding that both pieces of legislation were to be interpreted in the same way. Specifically, the court rejected the sex as biology approach, insisting that '[t]he initial approach taken in cases such as *Holloway* has been overruled by the logic and language of *Price Waterhouse*'.[89] The court continued:

> What matters, for purposes of this part of the *Price Waterhouse* analysis, is that in the mind of the perpetrator the discrimination is related to the sex of the victim: here, for example, the perpetrator's actions stem from the fact that he believed that the victim [a (male-to-female) transgender woman] was a man who 'failed to act like' one. Thus, under *Price Waterhouse*, 'sex' under Title VII encompasses both sex – that is, the biological differences between men and women – and gender. Discrimination because one fails to act in the way expected of a man or woman is forbidden under Title VII [and the GMVA].[90]

The application of a *Price Waterhouse*-style analysis in *Schwenk* is significant given that all prior federal and State transgender jurisprudence dealing with anti-discrimination law claims of transgender people make no mention of the decision. Rather, this body of law has proceeded implicitly on the basis that a sex as gender approach is inapplicable to transgender people and has therefore positioned transgender claims in relation to either biology or anatomy (Flynn, 2001, p 396). In contrast to the sex as anatomy reform approach, which seeks 'to exclude the transition phase' (Beger, 2000, p 262), the analysis

---

86   *Ibid*, pp 27–28.
87   *Ibid*, p 28.
88   *Schwenk v Hartford* 204 F 3d 1187 (2000).
89   *Ibid*, p 1201.
90   *Ibid*, p 1202.

adopted in Schwenk protects precisely because of the fact of (trans)gender transgression. That is to say, rather than confining the operation of Title VII to re-sexed bodies or subgroups thereof, perpetrator readings of (trans)gender performance as 'failed' serve as a trigger. In this regard, *Schwenk* backgrounds, if not dispenses with, the ontological questions which usually assume such significance in transgender cases. That is to say, the preoccupation with identity so apparent in the sex as biology and sex as anatomy approaches is supplanted by an approach predicated on stereotypical readings of behaviour.

While this approach requires a comparator, on the facts of *Schwenk* a man 'acting like a man', and while perhaps 'all comparison is ultimately comparison to a norm(ality)' (Beger, 2000, p 262), thereby reproducing the norm, reform that proceeds on the basis of a comparison of persons who perform gender 'successfully' with those whose performances are characterised as 'unsuccessful' serves to foreground gender, its frequent and perhaps inevitable failure (Butler, 1991, p 21) and crucially serves to protect individuals precisely because they transgress rather than perform gender according to dominant expectations. Moreover, it should not be thought that the figure of legal comparator serves to reinscribe ontology. That is to say, it should not be thought that the comparator reflects, or indeed bears any necessary relation to, the (bio)logical sex of the victim, as was the case on the facts of Schwenk. Rather, the analysis in *Schwenk* would seem to hold even if the victim were a (bio)logical female, including a (female-to-male) transgender man. That is to say, a (bio)logical female would appear to be covered if discriminated against because she was believed to be a man who 'failed' to act like one.

The sex as gender approach has since received some support from the United States Court of Appeals 1st Circuit. In *Rosa v Park West Bank*,[91] a case involving a bank's refusal to provide a loan application to a (bio)logical man because he was cross-dressed, the court held that if the bank treated 'a woman who dresses like a man differently than a man who dresses like a woman',[92] a scenario it clearly considered plausible, then the bank's actions would constitute discrimination on the basis of sex under the Federal Equal Credit Opportunity Act 1974.[93] In contrast to *Schwenk*, however, the analysis in *Rosa* focuses not merely on whether an employer discriminates against a person because he/she steps outside gender expectations, but requires also that a person of the 'opposite' sex who steps outside such expectations would be treated similarly. In other words, rather than comparing a man who 'failed to act like a man' with a man who performed masculinity 'successfully', the analysis in *Rosa* imagines a woman who 'fails to act like a woman' as a comparator. While this might not present a difficulty given the facts of *Rosa* and the perhaps greater freedom for women to cross-dress in our society, it serves to reintroduce an 'equal misery' argument. In the context of workplace discrimination this might permit an employer who dismissed an employee because she was a (male-to-female) transgender woman to argue that he would have dismissed a (female-to-male) transgender man.

---

91 *Rosa v Park West Bank* 214 F 3d 213 (2000).
92 *Ibid*, pp 215–16.
93 Equal Credit Opportunity Act 1974 (ECOA), 15 USC, ss 1691–1691f.

Indeed, if the analysis in *Rosa*, which, of course, is not directed to Title VII, is applied to the facts of *Price Waterhouse* it would presumably constitute a defence to a sex discrimination claim to show that a man who 'failed to act like a man' would have been treated the same as Ann Hopkins, thereby undermining the importance of the Supreme Court's decision to women in the workplace. Nevertheless, and while the approaches to the concept of sex adopted in *Schwenk* and *Rosa* are perhaps vulnerable to the same judicial treatment with regard to gay men and lesbians noted by Case (1995, pp 57–61) and Valdes (1995, p 18) post-*Price Waterhouse*,[94] a view of sex as gender, particularly as articulated in *Schwenk*, represents an advance over prior approaches to anti-discrimination law concepts of sex in transgender contexts. Moreover, because a view of sex as gender backgrounds questions of identity, focusing instead on gender performance, it constitutes reform at an intersection of discrimination against women, gay men and lesbians and transgender people. In this regard, it might encourage a retreat from identity-based politics in favour of the adoption of shared political strategies.

7.4 CONCLUSION

This chapter has considered judicial constructions of sex for anti-discrimination law purposes. Against a *Corbett*-style view of sex as biology, reform jurisprudence has reconceptualised sex first as actual, imminent and/or inevitable anatomical reconfiguration and, more recently, as gender performance. The first of these reform approaches might be viewed as reproducing the *psychological and anatomical harmony* story considered in Chapter 4, albeit that anti-discrimination law protection does not necessarily depend on sex reassignment surgery preceding discrimination. In this respect, the question of discrimination is effectively converted into one of sex designation. The unwillingness of the judiciary to adopt, until very recently, a more expansive interpretation of anti-discrimination law sex in transgender contexts is indicative of the excessive regulatory work law requires the category of sex to perform. In this regard, and consistent with the analysis adopted in earlier chapters, the re-sexing of bodies has proved to be premised on their prior heterosexualisation. That is to say, the inclusion of transgender within the protected category of sex has consistently required homosexuality as constitutive 'outside'.

The more recent application of the sex as gender approach to transgender represents a significant legal development. It opens up considerably space for the protection of transgender and other people who transgress gender norms. While this approach perhaps inevitably reproduces dominant understandings of femininity/masculinity which provide a point of comparison for a transgressive legal subject, and while a view of sex as

94 That is to say, an approach premised on protecting persons who transgress gender might be viewed as not necessarily applicable to macho gays and lesbian femmes given the tendency noted by Case to reduce transgressive gender practice to sexuality in such cases (1995, p 57). Indeed, in *Rosa v Park West Bank* the court made clear that had Rosa been refused 'the loan application because [the bank employee] thought he was gay, confusing sexual orientation with cross-dressing' then 'he' would have had no recourse under the Federal Equal Credit Opportunity Act 1974 (p 216). However, if persons are discriminated against because they are known or suspected to be gay or lesbian then sexual object choice might, though not unproblematically, be said to constitute 'a failure to act like a man or a woman' thereby bringing discrimination within the sex as gender approach.

anatomy is itself not without disruptive potential, a move toward gender appears to have significant advantages. In addition to protecting a wider range of people who face discrimination the approach represents, in a significant sense, a break with ontology. That is to say, gender performance replaces a concern with transgender 'authenticity' that characterises prior anti-discrimination law reform jurisprudence, as well as jurisprudence considered in earlier chapters dealing explicitly with sex designation. In other words, a view of sex as gender inaugurates a shift from somatic and/or psychological depth to bodily surface. This move not only captures the discrimination dynamic, locating discrimination at the intersection of gender performance and discriminating gaze and thereby better communicating that dynamic. It also represents a challenge to critical legal thinking as to the relationship between law, rights and legal subjectivity. That is to say, a view of rights as dependent on the 'coherent fixed identity' of rights-bearers (Bumiller, 1988; Iyer, 1993; Herman, 1994; Morgan, 1996) is problematised, if not obliterated, by such a development. The following chapter will offer a critique of anti-discrimination law legislative frameworks in the Australian context, where a regulatory shift to surfaces, albeit with a different inflection to United States federal jurisprudence, is particularly discernable at the State level. This will entail consideration of the interrelationship of the protected categories of sex, sexuality and, more recently, transgender as regulatory strategies around bodies. For while this chapter has focused on legal approaches to the anti-discrimination law category sex, a more nuanced understanding of legal regulation of transgender people within this arena requires an appreciation of the interplay between protected categories.

CHAPTER 8

FROM LEGAL ONTOLOGY TO
PERFORMANCE AND GAZE

When you meet a human being, the first distinction you make is 'male' or 'female'? and you are accustomed to make the distinction with unhesitating certainty (Freud, 1964a).

But it seems we are as we appear. What a nonsense we make of our hatreds when we can only recognise them in the most obvious circumstances (Winterson, 1996).

In Chapter 7 we considered judicial interpretations of the anti-discrimination law category sex within a number of common law jurisdictions. Excepting recent United States reform jurisprudence, which has articulated a view of sex as gender, common law approaches to the meaning of anti-discrimination law sex have, in the transgender context, effectively converted, and thereby confined, the concept to a question of designation. In this regard, legal analyses of sex in anti-discrimination law contexts prove continuous with transgender jurisprudence more broadly. That is to say, as with legal questions pertaining, for example, to birth certificates, gendered criminal offences and marriage, considered in earlier chapters, anti-discrimination law reform jurisprudence has sought to reproduce the gender order through reproducing a binary, if reformulated, understanding of sex. To this end, recognition of transgender claims to be male/female for the purposes of marriage, or to be covered by the concept of sex for anti-discrimination law purposes, has proved dependent on the fact, or at least the expectation, of sex reassignment surgery. However, the sexing of transgender bodies has also proved tied to inquiry into transgender 'authenticity'. While sex reassignment surgery has proved crucial in demonstrating 'authenticity' it is clear from the case law, and from the fact of 'demonstration', that the latter is not reducible to the former. In other words, ontological concerns over the coherence and fixity of transgender identity appear central to law and, therefore, reform.

In this chapter, however, it will be contended that the regulation of transgender people within the realm of anti-discrimination law cannot be comprehended adequately through reference to law's positioning of transgender in relation to ontology. Indeed, as we saw in Chapter 7, even a restrictive Title VII jurisprudence contradicts such a view. Thus the court in *Dobre*, for example, made clear that 'if AMTRAK considered [Andria] Dobre [a (male-to-female) transgender woman] to be female and discriminated against her on that basis ... then [she] would be able to maintain a Title VII action as a female'.[1] It is this insight and its regulatory implications that this chapter explores. More particularly, a view of legal regulation as merely interrogative fails to account for the complexity of, and contradictions contained within, a number of Australian and United States anti-discrimination legislative frameworks. The chapter will consider Australian rather than United States developments as, in contrast to the latter which have occurred almost exclusively at the municipal level (Currah and Minter, 2000a, pp 45–50; 2000b, pp 59–65) the former have occurred at the State and Territory levels. Nevertheless, much of the analysis and critique that follows applies to the United States context. In examining the

---

1   *Dobre v National Railroad Passen Corporation (AMTRAK)* 850 F Supp 284 (1993), p 287. See, also, *Ulane v Eastern Airlines* 742 F 2d 1081 (1984), p 1087.

ways in which Australian anti-discrimination legal frameworks serve to regulate transgender people it will emerge that the forms of regulation deployed vary significantly across jurisdictions. In order to appreciate the complex relation of transgender people to practices of discrimination, and to forms of regulation, it is necessary not only to consider the category transgender, which has been added to the list of protected categories within a number of Australian jurisdictions,[2] but to consider also the categories of sex and sexuality. This is not a matter of law's blindness to 'intersectionality' (Crenshaw, 1989, 1995), of the abstraction of legal subjects from embodied particularity, a theme to which the chapter will pay attention, but rather a question of the interplay between these categories within specific regulatory regimes.

Moreover, the regulation of transgender people, and indeed other categories of person protected by Australian anti-discrimination laws, will be seen to occur in ways that call for a re-examination of rights critiques. It has been argued that rights only arise once a fixed group of 'others' is established (Bumiller, 1988; Iyer, 1993; Herman, 1994; Morgan, 1996). That is to say, categories of identity have formed the basis of claims to rights. This has shaped legal development so that new claims to rights are only granted when those claiming them can demonstrate a 'coherent fixed identity', and prove to decision makers that it is unfair to discriminate against them merely because they have that identity (Morgan, 1996, p 128). While I would agree with this account in terms of the emergence of rights, and while it still retains explanatory power both within and outside Australia in terms of both the emergence and invocation of rights,[3] it is my contention that in some Australian jurisdictions the relationship between 'coherent fixed identity' and rights claims has been severed by a shift from an interrogative to a performative mode of regulating bodies.

---

2   While the chapter focuses on the Australian context it should be noted that the legislative creation of transgender as a protected category or its inclusion within existing categories of sex or sexuality has occurred in many United States jurisdictions. However, and in contrast to Australian developments, United States reform has occurred, almost without exception (the State of Minnesota included transgender under the protected head of sexuality in 1993), at the municipal rather than the State level. This has occurred under the rubric of 'gender identity' or 'gender variance' in San Francisco, CA (1994); Iowa City, IA (1995); Benton County, OR (1997); Olympia, WA (1997); New Orleans, LA (1998); West Hollywood, CA (1998); Ann Arbor, MI (1999); Jefferson County, KY (1999); Lexington-Fayette Urban County Government, KY (1999); Louisville, KY (1999); Seattle, WA (1999); Tucson, AZ (1999); Vermont Hate Crimes Law (1999); Atlanta, GA (2000); Boulder, CO (2000); Ithaca, NY (2000); Madison, WIS (2000); Portland, OR (2000); under the rubric of 'sexual orientation' or 'affectional preference' in Minnesota, MN (1975), St Paul, MN (1990), Los Angeles, CA (1992), York, PA (1993), Evanston, Ill (1997), Ypsilanti, MI (1997), Toledo, OH (1998); and under the rubric of 'gender' or sex' in City of Santa Cruz, CA (1992), Harrisburg, PA (1992), Cambridge, MA (1997), Pittsburgh, PA (1997), County of Santa Cruz (1998), Champaign, Ill (2000), Dekalb, Ill (2000), Urbana, Ill (2000) (see Currah and Minter, 2000a, pp 45–50; 2000b, pp 59–65).

3   In the Australian context the regulatory regimes of Western Australia, South Australia and Tasmania confirm the explanatory power of the 'coherent fixed identity' thesis across categories, while the New South Wales legislation does so in relation to the category of 'sex'. The continuing relevance of the 'coherent fixed identity' thesis finds support in United Kingdom legislation (Equal Pay Act 1970; Sex Discrimination Act 1975; Race Relations Act 1976; Sex Discrimination Act 1986) and the Canadian Charter of Rights and Freedoms, Pt 1 of the Constitution Act 1982 though it is not exhausted by these examples. While s 15 of the Canadian Charter extends protection to those basing claims on grounds analogous to the Charter's enumerated grounds, and while this may represent a postmodern turn (Stychin, 1995, Chapter 6), unlike Australian developments, it does not mark a shift from an interrogative to a performative mode of regulation whereby enumerated grounds are disrupted.

In making this argument it will be contended that these laws are to be comprehended not by reference to the 'immutability' of some attribute or characteristic, but rather in the interplay of performance and gaze. Of course, in the anti-discrimination law context 'appearing' is always a necessary pre-condition to the invocation of right, given that to be discriminated against on the basis of membership of an identity category one must first appear to be a member of that category. The important regulatory shift, however, is one which dispenses with the requirement that appearance conform to a pre-given and fixed identity. That is to say, the demonstration of fixed identity is not necessarily a prerequisite to invocation of right. Indeed, it would seem that, in the Australian context, law increasingly is being brought into accord with the reality of the discrimination dynamic whereby what matters is not the nature of identity, but rather what is 'seen', what is presented for 'seeing' and how the latter negotiates the former. Therefore I would contend that in important respects anti-discrimination laws do not serve merely to ossify identity categories, as some rights critics suggest, but rather serve also to disrupt those categories. Categorising serves to heighten 'differences between members and non-members of a category, while suppressing any similarities that some members might share with non-members' (Iyer, 1993, p 183). In the anti-discrimination law context, however, particular Australian regulatory regimes render visible inter-group sameness and intra-group difference(s). That is to say, particular modes of regulation contain the possibility for the disruption of legal categories. Moreover, this tension is an effect of contradictory legal desires. On the one hand, faced with transgender, law desires to fix the categories of sex and, to the extent that it is produced as a legal category, transgender, as a mode of regulation, while on the other hand, law desires to regulate positively (Foucault, 1981a; 1982) beyond those legally constituted categories. That is to say, law seeks to regulate more than the categories it produces. It also seeks to regulate those bodies that constitute the 'beyond' or 'outside' necessary to the formation of legal subjecthood.

A disruptive moment occurs when law, through seeking to regulate that which it refuses to produce as identity, incites border crossings which serve to produce the very subject of law's refusal at the level of appearance, thereby problematising the boundaries of extant legal categories. Thus, it will become apparent that while law refuses to produce the cross-dresser, in any sense other than as constitutive outside to the category transgender, law does produce transgender and female performance in bodies positioned outside the legal categories 'transgender' and 'female'. In this sense, law is implicated in the exercise of more subtle forms of productive power than, for example, the legal recognition of the sex claims of transgender people or the constitution of transgender as a legal category.[4] Thus Australian anti-discrimination laws produce an exploitable tension between ontological inquiry and forms of regulation that confine their gaze to bodily surfaces. In other words, while ontological depth is clearly reproduced within this area of the law it seems to have been supplemented, if not exceeded, by a concern with appearances. Attention will now be turned to an analysis and critique of the categories transgender, sexuality and sex, and the interplay between them which is crucial to

---

4   This mode of deploying power is not confined to the realm of anti-discrimination law. Thus, in the criminal law context, the law of 'impossible' attempts produces a similar effect in relation to transgender bodies and the offence of rape (see Sharpe, 1997d).

identifying and understanding the modes of regulation to which transgender people are subjected.

8.1 DISCRIMINATION ON TRANSGENDER GROUNDS

The legal position of transgender victims of discrimination within Australia varies significantly across jurisdictions. With the exceptions of Queensland and Tasmania all other jurisdictions prohibit in some form discrimination against transgender people, albeit that the lexicon of transgender terminology produced varies. By virtue of the New South Wales transgender legislation,[5] protection is extended to all people discriminated against on 'transgender grounds' irrespective of sex reassignment surgery. The phrase 'transgender person' is defined in s 38A of the new Pt 3A of the Anti-Discrimination Act 1977 (NSW):

> A reference in this Part to a person being transgender or a transgender person is a reference to a person, whether or not the person is a recognised transgender person:
>
> (a) who identifies as a member of the opposite sex by living, or seeking to live, as a member of the opposite sex, or
>
> (b who has identified as a member of the opposite sex by living as a member of the opposite sex ...

By refusing to confine protection against discrimination to 'recognised transgender persons', a phrase which refers to transgender people who have received legal recognition of their change of sex, the legislation clearly extends to pre- or non-surgical transgender people. In a similar vein, more recent Victorian legislation[6] creates the protected category of 'gender identity' which, by virtue of s 4, it defines to mean:

> (a) the identification on a *bona fide* basis by a person of one sex as a member of the other sex (whether or not the person is recognised as such):
>
> (i) by assuming characteristics of the other sex, whether by means of medical intervention, style of dressing or otherwise; or
>
> (ii) by living, or seeking to live, as a member of the other sex.

Using different language again the Australian Capital Territory anti-discrimination legislation prohibits discrimination on the basis of transsexuality.[7] This term is defined broadly and is in many respects similar to the New South Wales and Victorian transgender legislation. Thus the term 'transsexuality' is not confined to persons undergoing surgical procedures but rather extends to precisely those persons covered by the other Acts.[8] Thus in terms of the scope of anti-discrimination protection nothing would appear to hinge upon any distinction between the terms 'transgender' and 'transsexual'. Conversely, the West Australian legislation which prohibits discrimination

---

5   Anti-Discrimination Act 1977 (NSW), New Pt 3A, s 38A introduced by the Transgender (Anti-Discrimination and Other Acts Amendment) Act 1996 (NSW), Sched 1, s 4.
6   Equal Opportunity Act 1995 (Vic), s 6(ac) introduced by the Equal Opportunity (Gender Identity and Sexual Orientation) Act 2000 (Vic), s 5.
7   Discrimination Act 1991 (ACT), s 7(1)(c).
8   *Ibid*, s 4.

against 'gender reassigned persons' defines that phrase to exclude pre- or non-operative bodies.[9] Here sex reassignment surgery and legal recognition of change of sex serve as prerequisites to being brought within a class of persons to whom the law offers protection.

There are a number of important and contrasting points to make regarding the emergence of transgender as a distinct anti-discrimination law category. First, it would seem that, consistent with a number of rights critiques (Bumiller, 1988; Iyer, 1993; Herman, 1994; Morgan, 1996) the emergence of this category and the conferral of rights upon its members proves tied to the demonstration of a 'coherent fixed identity'. Thus in each of the four jurisdictions which create a distinct 'trans' space within an anti-discrimination legislative framework there is an attempt to close off fluidity. That is to say, transgender subjectivities are filtered through a legal lens and this process of filtration, as a strategy of 'normalisation', serves to hierarchicalise, sanitise and exclude (Fuss, 1991; Seidman, 1993). In Western Australia this occurs through the deployment and imposition of medico-scientific 'truth'. Thus the Bill is based on the 'fact' of gender dysphoria and the process 'gender dysphoric' persons go through to receive the benefit of anti-discrimination protection does not take effect until:

... they have satisfied the [Gender Reassignment] board that they have that *disability* and that they are genuinely committed to having a gender other than that with which they were born.[10]

The demonstration of this commitment, and therefore of 'authentic' transgender identity, under the West Australian legislation necessitates surgical intervention. In the New South Wales, Victorian and Australian Capital Territory contexts surgical intervention is de-emphasised.[11] However, despite this difference the New South Wales, Victorian and Australian Capital Territory legislation share with the West Australian legislation a concern to delimit transgender as a legal category. Thus, as the Attorney-General (NSW) makes clear, the definition of the term' transgender' is not intended to cover:

... persons who cross dress or who have adopted the characteristics of the other sex, say for example, a male person who from time to time wears makeup, or high heels, who has not chosen to live as a member of the other sex.[12]

It is clear that while the New South Wales, Victorian and Australian Capital Territory legislation are wider in scope than their West Australian counterpart, there is a shared concern to fix the identity of beneficiaries. Thus the transgender person is marked by permanence of sex/gender transformation and not episodic or transitory alternative gender performance. Indeed, and despite the views of some Victorian parliamentarians to

---

9   Equal Opportunity Act 1984 (WA), New Pt IIAA, s 35AB introduced by the Gender Reassignment Act 2000 (WA), Sched 2, s 4.

10   The Hon Peter Foss, Debates of the Legislative Council (WA), 8 April 1997, p 1132 (my emphasis).

11   In New South Wales this was despite Liberal opposition attempts to create precisely this particular hierarchy of deserving/undeserving transgender persons that subsequently emerged in the form of the West Australian legislation (see the Hon Mr Tink, Debates of the Legislative Assembly (NSW), 22 May 1996, p 1344; the Hon Mr Peacocke, Debates of the Legislative Assembly (NSW), 22 May 1996, p 1347; the Hon Mr Richardson, Debates of the Legislative Assembly (NSW), 22 May 1996, p 1351).

12   The Hon Jeff Shaw (A-G), Debates of the Legislative Council (NSW), 30 May 1996, p 1795.

the contrary,[13] both the New South Wales and Victorian legislation necessarily exclude cross-dressers as a precondition of protection proves to be sexed identification contrary to birth designated sex. An emphasis on 'authentification' of persons claiming to fall within the ambit of the delimited category transgender is especially apparent in the Victorian Act, given the requirement that 'opposite' sex identification be on 'a *bona fide* basis'.[14] Indeed, the Hon Mr Savage who introduced the amendment requiring the *bona fide* requirement expressed the view that 'people who are not committed to changing their sexual identity could, on a whim, cause disruption in their employment, in public toilets or in other public places'.[15] It would seem that cross-dressing, much like class, cannot be accommodated within anti-discrimination law regulatory frameworks because of actual or potential mobility (Thornton, 1990, Chapter 1; Iyer, 1993, p 189; see, also, Hasson, 1989; Jackman, 1993). In other words, the exclusion of the cross-dresser occurs precisely because his/her border crossings are not finite. Due to the fact that law cannot conceive of persons as compelled, and therefore deserving, in inter-category terms the cross-dresser cannot formally be brought within a protected category.

Moreover, in the New South Wales context law reform presents an additional difficulty. For it is only the New South Wales legislation that inaugurates the term 'transgender'. In this regard, the exclusionary practices of law serve to appropriate and reconstitute a community term, one that represents a 'reverse discourse' (Foucault, 1981a, p 101) against the medically imposed terms of 'transsexuality' and 'transvestism', so as to exclude some individuals from its ambit. Of course, it is important to recognise that the actual structure and wording of particular legislation is, at least in part, a consequence of the advocacy of rights activists and relevant communities. This raises questions about responsibility for the infliction of textual violence. Moreover, it may be that law reform produces less in the form of self-inflicted violence and more in the form of violence against others. Indeed, the most acute form of textual violence is, perhaps, that perpetrated against groups without whom assertions of 'coherent fixed identity' by beneficiaries of legislative reform might falter.

However, while the conferral of rights upon transgender people has been based upon the establishment/imposition of 'coherent' transgender identities, this type of 'rights' critique proves inadequate in the context of New South Wales, Victoria and the Australian Capital Territory as the legislative provisions in each of these jurisdictions serve to undermine, in important respects, the very identities which give rise to rights claims. Thus in each of these jurisdictions it constitutes discrimination to discriminate against a person thought to be a transgender person irrespective of whether that person is in fact a transgender person.[16] In this regard, the attempt to exclude cross-dressers from the ambit

---

13 See, eg, the Hon Ms Beattie, Debates of the Legislative Assembly (Vic), 29 August 2000, p 238; the Hon CA Furletti, the Hon Mr Hallam, the Hon AP Olexander, Debates of the Legislative Council (Vic), 6 September 2000, p 263.

14 Equal Opportunity Act 1995 (Vic), s 4 as amended by the Equal Opportunity (Gender Identity and Sexual Orientation) Act 2000 (Vic), s 4.

15 The Hon Mr Savage, Debates of the Legislative Assembly (Vic), 29 August 2000, p 238.

16 Anti-Discrimination Act 1977 (NSW), s 38A; Discrimination Act 1991 (ACT), s 7(2)(c) as amended; Equal Opportunity Act 1995 (Vic), s 7(2)(d). It should be noted that legislation enacted by many United States municipalities contains a deeming provision of this kind (see Currah and Minter, 2000a, pp 45–50; 2000b, pp 59–65).

of anti-discrimination protection inevitably fails, serving instead to highlight inter-group sameness. The structure of this legislation, and the possibility for invocation of right, are then to be comprehended not by reference to the 'immutability' of identity but rather in the interplay of performance and gaze. Further, this central fact remains true irrespective of whether the claimant of right is post-, pre- or non-surgical and extends to people whether labelled or self-identifying as transvestites/cross-dressers. In other words, protection is based upon discrimination on transgender grounds; such discrimination can only occur where the object caught within the discriminating gaze is perceived to be transgender, and this perception is inevitably mediated by transgender performance. Crucially, performance and gaze bear no necessary relation to the range of protected 'trans' categories or their constitutive 'outsides'.

Thus in New South Wales, Victoria and the Australian Capital Territory a hierarchical opposition of transgender/cross-dresser is constituted in law.[17] The former term is privileged, granted a presence in law, while the latter is erased from the legal scene. It is only through the deeming provision that the cross-dresser is able to come within the protection of the law. In other words, anti-discrimination protection is premised upon sameness to, rather than difference from, a legally conceived notion of transgender. Thus the trigger for protection is the concealment of difference. Nevertheless, the deeming provision creates the conditions for the disruption, and radical rearticulation (Butler, 1993) of the privileged term, as it serves to highlight its provisionality and contingency through enabling the demonstration of imitation. In imitating (trans)gender the imitative structure of gender itself is revealed (Butler, 1993, p 137). While the beneficiary of the deeming provision necessarily '(tres)passes' as transgender, upholding a discrimination claim serves to implicate law in this revelatory and disruptive effect.

8.2 DISCRIMINATION ON THE GROUND OF SEXUALITY

While the New South Wales, Victorian, West Australian and Australian Capital Territory legislation treat transgender people as a distinct protected category, albeit that they deploy different lexicons to that effect, the South Australian and Northern Territory legislation include transsexuality under the protected ground of sexuality.[18] Thus discrimination in these jurisdictions on the basis of 'heterosexuality, homosexuality, bisexuality or transsexuality' is prohibited. It is curious that transsexuality is scripted as a sexuality in these two jurisdictions, given that it relates to gender identity rather than sexual preference and that this understanding seems to be acknowledged in the fact that

---

17 'Cross-dressers' have been defined as 'people who don the clothing and other accoutrements of the opposite gender temporarily for whatever purpose'. Conversely, 'transvestites' have been defined as 'people who have a compulsion to dress in the clothes of the alternative gender', and 'transvestism' as a term 'covering behaviours ranging from anyone who cross-dresses to those who have changed their social gender permanently without surgical intervention' (Sex Discrimination Commissioner/ Human Rights and Equal Opportunity Commission, 1996, p 4). I have decided to use the term 'cross-dresser' in preference to the term 'transvestite' for two reasons. First, the term 'cross-dresser' is more a term of self-description than the medically imposed term 'transvestite' and lacks the latter term's pathological overtones. Secondly, the term 'transvestite', as defined in the Discussion Paper, straddles the binary division constituted by the New South Wales, Victorian and Australian Capital Territory legislation.

18 Equal Opportunity Act 1984 (SA), s 29(3)(c); Anti-Discrimination Act 1992 (NT), s 19.

in both jurisdictions provision exists for legal recognition of change of sex.[19] Further, the notion of transsexuality as a sexuality distinct from heterosexuality runs counter to reform jurisprudence which has consistently defined transsexuality by reference to heterosexuality and in opposition to homosexuality, a theme developed in earlier chapters. The South Australian legislation defines transsexuality as 'the condition of being a transsexual' and transsexual as 'a person of the one sex who assumes characteristics of the other sex'.[20] These definitions are not overly helpful. While the South Australian definition of transsexuality can be viewed as de-emphasising surgical procedures it can also be viewed as endorsing a medical model of transsexuality whereby the 'truth' of transsexuality needs to be discovered (King, 1993, pp 45, 63).[21] Conversely, the definition of transsexual appears to depart from ontological considerations requiring only a change in 'characteristics'. However, further equivocality is introduced here as it is unclear whether this term means physical characteristics. If so, only those persons undergoing surgical, or perhaps other medical, procedures would derive any protection under the legislation. Whatever the precise forms of exclusion and hierarchy created by the South Australian legislation it would seem unlikely that coverage extends beyond transgender people who have permanently transformed, or are in the process of transforming, their sex/gender so that it is brought into conformity with dominant understandings.[22] Thus even a permissive reading of the term 'transsexual' is likely to lead to the exclusion of transgender people who engage in episodic or transitory sex/gender practices. It is

---

19 Sexual Reassignment Act 1988 (SA); Births, Deaths and Marriages Registration Amendment Act 1997 (NT).

20 Equal Opportunity Act 1984 (SA), s 4.

21 As we saw in Chapter 1 the 'discovery story of transsexuality' refers to a process of acquiring a condition as a result of as yet unknown psychological or (bio)logical factors and is therefore viewed as independent of self-identification.

22 It appears uncertain how widely the term 'transsexual' will be interpreted. The question has not yet arisen for judicial determination. According to the Chief Legal Officer of the South Australian Equal Opportunity Commission, Mr Michael Ahern, the view of the Commission is that the term is to be interpreted broadly and extends to cross-dressing without any requirement for a permanent change of lifestyle. This view appears to have two sources of support. First, it is articulated in the parliamentary debates surrounding the legislation including a statement from the then Attorney-General (the Hon Mr CJ Sumner, Debates of the Legislative Council (SA), 31 October 1984, p 1645; see, also, the Hon Ms B Wiese, Debates of the Legislative Council (SA), 31 October 1984, p 1645). Secondly, it is suggested that s 29(4) of the legislation, a provision creating an exemption in relation to 'appearance or dress', enables an inference along these lines to be drawn. While such an interpretation is perhaps open, and in my view desirable, I remain unpersuaded as to its correctness. This interpretation treats the term 'transsexual' as an umbrella term for all trans subjectivities. Yet, the term has a relatively stable meaning in medico-legal discourse. Moreover, Australian judges have sought to distinguish the terms 'transsexual' and 'cross-dresser' (see, eg, the judgment of Mathews J in *R v Harris and McGuiness* (1988) 17 NSWLR 158, p 173). In relation to s 29(4) an understanding of the argument requires that the provision be detailed: Where:

(a) a person discriminates against another on the basis of appearance or dress;

(b) that appearance or dress is characteristic of, or an expression of, that other person's sexuality;But

(c) the discrimination is reasonable in all the circumstances; the discrimination will not ... be taken to be discrimination on the ground of sexuality.

The view of the South Australian Equal Opportunity Commission is that this provision enables the inference that 'transsexual' must also include 'cross-dresser' otherwise the provision would be superfluous. Such a view must flow presumably from a particular interpretation of the words 'appearance or dress'. However, the fact that a person discriminates against another on the basis of 'appearance or dress' does not lead to the conclusion that the legislation covers cross-dressers. Rather, it points to the reality of the discrimination dynamic whereby discrimination against transsexuals is an effect of performance and gaze, not genital status.

precisely these forms of transgender practice which prove necessary, as constitutive 'outside', to the very formation of transsexual as a meaningful legal category.

While the Northern Territory legislation fails to define the term transsexuality, it differs in a crucial respect from its South Australian counterpart in that it contains a provision prohibiting discrimination against persons believed to be transsexual.[23] Thus like the New South Wales, Victorian and Australian Capital Territory legislation the structure of the Northern Territory legislation, and the possibility for invocation of right, are to be comprehended not by reference to the 'immutability' of identity, but rather in the interplay of performance and gaze. That is to say, irrespective of whether a person discriminated against is legally considered transsexual, any person appearing to be before the discriminating gaze is protected. As discrimination need not be continuous, the deeming provision not only dispenses with ontology but also with the need even for a performance of a 'permanent' crossing. In other words, while formally excluding the figure of the cross-dresser from legal subjecthood the deeming provision anticipates his/her inevitable return. In the final analysis, and in a manner analogous to the dilemma faced by rape victims, the 'objective' facts regarding the victim are readily trumped by the subjective understanding of the perpetrator (see, for example, Bell, 1991; Duncan, 1995).

The location of transsexuality within the category of sexuality is not only problematic in the sense that it conflates gender identity with sexual preference. It also raises the question of whether transgender people will be protected against discrimination based on sexuality. Of course, this question is not confined to legislation that locates transsexuality within the domain of sexuality. Rather, the question pertains to all those jurisdictions that prohibit, in various styles, discrimination on the grounds of sexual preference.[24] That is to say, the question is pertinent to all jurisdictions except Western Australia and Tasmania. In addressing same-sex desire, these legislative provisions have tended to employ the term 'homosexual' and it therefore becomes of theoretical and practical importance to inquire after the term's elasticity. The potential difficulty lies in the fact that normative understandings which inform these legislative initiatives conceive of homosexuality and homosexual preference as firmly anchored in (bio)logical sex. Indeed, as we saw in Chapter 4, this understanding of homosexuality has been insisted upon in law even, and perhaps especially, at the moment of the uncoupling of heterosexuality from (bio)logic. This is not an argument about the 'gay gene' (Levay, 1991, 1993). Rather, it is simply aimed at pointing out the fact that when medicine and law talk about homosexuality it is both intended and typically does signify something unequivocal about the biological status of the desiring parties.[25] Moreover, it is important to recognise how this way of

---

23 Anti-Discrimination Act 1992 (NT), s 20(2).

24 While South Australia, the Australian Capital Territory and the Northern Territory prohibit discrimination on the basis of 'sexuality' which is defined to include a range of sexualities including homosexuality (Equal Opportunity Act 1984 (SA), s 29(1); Discrimination Act 1991 (ACT), s 7(1)(b); Anti-Discrimination Act 1992 (NT), s 19, New South Wales prohibits discrimination on the basis of 'homosexuality' (Anti-Discrimination Act 1977 (NSW), s 49ZG), Queensland prohibits discrimination on the basis of 'lawful sexual activity' (Anti-Discrimination Act 1991 (Qld), s 7) and Victoria prohibits discrimination on the basis of 'lawful sexual activity' and 'sexual orientation' (Equal Opportunity Act 1995 (Vic), s 6). For a discussion of these provisions see Chapman, 1997 and Morgan, 1996.

25 Curiously, this is less true of 'heterosexuality'. This term has been rendered considerably more fluid through law's accommodation of transgender desire in the context of the legal recognition of sex claims. That is to say, medicine and law have inscribed heterosexuality on to the sexual practices and desires of transgender persons. This has been effected through detaching heterosexuality (contd)

conceiving of homosexuality is bolstered by a gay and lesbian law reform agenda that asserts fixed identity.

In the transgender context, however, non-heterosexual desire becomes either desire for persons of the same psychological sex irrespective of whether this conforms with the (bio)logical sex of those persons or their objects of desire, or it escapes altogether the binary logic of the hetero/homo dyad whereby shades of identification and desire begin to proliferate. In this latter regard, and as we saw in Chapter 2, some transgender people are refusing to identify as heterosexual, lesbian or gay and in a number of cases partners are themselves transgendered (see, for example, Califia, 1997, p 196).[26] Thus it may be that transgender forms of homosexual desire and practice are not formally covered under the protected category of sexuality. It would seem that non-heterosexual transgender desire perhaps marks a 'limit' to law's capacity to imagine the sexual.

However, with the exception of South Australia a space for the protection of transgender (homo)sexualities is opened up in those jurisdictions that prohibit discrimination on the basis of sexual preference. This effect is produced through a provision that prohibits discrimination based on the belief that someone is homosexual.[27] This deeming provision is not only absent in the South Australian legislation, but that legislation's definition of sexuality to include transsexuality perhaps renders it less likely that the same person will be viewed as transsexual and homosexual. Conversely, the juxtaposition of transsexuality to the hetero/homo dyad, rather than its incorporation within that dyad, apparent in both the South Australian and Northern Territory legislation, might perhaps engender arguments around, and for, recognition of transgender non-heterosexualities.

However, while transgender people may be able to rely on a provision that prohibits discrimination based on the belief that someone is homosexual, protection may prove conditional on the invisibility of transgender. That is to say, and putting to one side cultural conflation of transgender and homosexuality whereby transgender 'visibility' may be read as homosexuality, what may be required is a performance that links sexuality to biology. Thus irrespective of the complexities of transgender identification and desire, a (male-to-female) transgender woman who seeks protection against discrimination on the basis of non-heterosexual desire will need to appear as lesbian before the discriminating gaze. What this effectively means is that she must '(tres)pass' as female for, somewhat ironically, the more her performance departs from the feminine the more unlikely it is that her sexuality will be read as lesbian. However, while this mode of legal regulation produces 'lesbian bodies', it serves simultaneously to disrupt the category 'lesbian'. For if

---

25 (contd) from its biological mooring and reinventing it through recourse to psychological sex. Crucially, law does not permit a parallel reconceptualisation of same-sex desire. After all, as we saw in Chapter 3, according to law transgender persons desire surgical assistance 'in order that they may enter into heterosexual relationships' (*Secretary, Department of Social Security v HH* [1991] 13 AAR 314, p 317, *per* O'Connor J and Muller).

26 This strategy opposes the assumption that a transgender person needs to have his or her gender identity bolstered by intimate affirmation from someone whose self-image is consistent with his or her genetic sex.

27 Anti-Discrimination Act 1977 (NSW), s 49ZG(2); Anti-Discrimination Act 1991 (Qld), s 8(c); Discrimination Act 1991 (ACT), s 7(2)(c); Anti-Discrimination Act 1992 (NT), s 20(2)(a); Equal Opportunity Act 1995 (Vic), s 7(2)(d).

a discrimination claim were to be upheld on the ground of sexuality the effect would be to demonstrate the imitative structure of gender and, of course, legally constructed.

In South Australia prohibition of discrimination on the basis of sexuality is subject to a further regulatory strategy. In this State it is not unlawful to discriminate on the basis of 'appearance or dress' that is characteristic of, or an expression of, a person's sexuality if reasonable in all the circumstances.[28] Moreover, because the South Australian legislation locates transsexuality under the head of sexuality the 'dress or appearance' clause permits discrimination on the basis of both transgender status and, assuming it to be a protected category, non-heterosexual transgender desire. The rationale for the escape clause, which serves to normalise bodies around idealised notions of femininity and masculinity, was made clear in the South Australian legislative debates:

> If the employment of ... a homosexual, bisexual or transsexual is driving customers and potential customers away from a small business, it is not fair on the employer that he or she should be penalised for the prejudiced views of customers and potential customers (quoted by Chapman, 1995, p 326).[29]

While an employer must establish that the visibility of a transgender person, or perhaps her sexual orientation in the South Australian context, is sufficiently detrimental to the business in order to render discrimination reasonable, it would seem that transgender people are perhaps especially vulnerable to invocation of a 'dress and appearance' clause. In Victoria this type of regulation is even more pronounced. First, like South Australia, the Victorian legislation contains a 'dress, appearance and behaviour' provision, albeit formally 'generic' in its application.[30] Despite the existence of this provision, however, recent legislation adding 'gender identity' as a protected category enables 'an employer to discriminate against another person on the basis of gender identity' where it is reasonable to do so.[31] It is significant that transgender persons are singled out in this way, given that all other exceptions in the Victorian legislation are, at least formally, of general application. Moreover, assuming a provision allowing discrimination on the basis of 'gender identity' to be more than mere replication of the 'dress, appearance and behaviour' clause, and therefore not superfluous, it seems clear that permission to discriminate against transgender people traverses the act/identity dyad. Moreover, in addition to gender conformity the Victorian legislation requires transgender confession. That is to say, the legislation permits discrimination on the basis of 'gender identity', irrespective of reasonableness, if a transgender person 'does not give the employer adequate notice of ... gender identity'.[32] In effect this requirement to announce oneself, which has no parallel with other protected categories, amounts to a form of institutionalised 'outing'. It not only produces identity but makes 'protection' dependent on rendering visible precisely that, perhaps, most likely to activate discrimination.

---

28 Equal Opportunity Act 1984 (SA), s 29(4).

29 The Hon Mr Lucas, Debates of the Legislative Council (SA), 25 October 1984, p 1507.

30 While the 'dress, appearance and behaviour' clause applies across protected categories it was clearly formulated with gay men and lesbians in mind (see, eg, Forbes, 1995; Chapman, 1997, p 74).

31 Equal Opportunity Act 1995 (Vic), s 27B(1)(b) introduced by the Equal Opportunity (Gender Identity and Sexual Orientation) Act 2000 (Vic), s 6.

32 *Ibid*, s 27B(1)(a).

The anti-discrimination law frameworks considered so far have created a legal space, however contracted by legislative exceptions, for the protection of particular types of transgender person irrespective of whether the protected category has been coded transgender, or some permutation thereof, or the more generic, and in the present context misleading, sexuality. Conversely, the jurisdictions of Queensland and Tasmania refuse to produce transgender as a legal category. Moreover, the failure of these latter jurisdictions to offer protection to any transgender people, as well as the failure of other jurisdictions to offer protection to all visibly transgender people,[33] raises a distinct set of problems. These regulatory regimes, in addition to exposing all, or particular, transgender people to transphobia, serve to conceal, and indeed create a space for, other forms of discrimination, namely sexism, racism and homophobia. This is because, where the object caught in the discriminating gaze is visibly transgender, yet unprotected, the sexist/racist/homophobic discriminator can always, and within these regulatory regimes is incited to, point to transgender status as the motivation for discrimination. To the extent that jurisdictions discourage transgender visibility generally this regulatory strategy becomes especially pronounced in the context of non-white and non-heterosexual transgender people.[34]

8.3 DISCRIMINATION ON THE GROUND OF SEX

The legal position of transgender people is complicated further by the way discrimination on the basis of sex is defined across jurisdictions. While all jurisdictions define sex discrimination as discrimination on the basis of sex, characteristics that appertain generally to persons of that sex, or characteristics generally imputed to persons of that sex,[35] only the jurisdictions of South Australia, New South Wales, the Northern Territory, the Australian Capital Territory and Western Australia provide legal recognition for change of sex.[36] Thus these jurisdictions enable (male-to-female) transgender women who through surgical procedures have been brought into *psychological and anatomical harmony* to sustain a discrimination claim on the basis of their female status. This claim needs to be qualified, however, as the sex change legislation in each of these jurisdictions contains a provision prohibiting recognition of the sex claims of transgender people who are married.[37] The purpose of this provision is rendered explicit by the former South Australian Attorney-General:

---

33   Only the jurisdictions of New South Wales, the Northern Territory and the Australian Capital Territory create a space, through a deeming provision, for the protection of all transgender persons irrespective of whether they fall within the ambit of 'transgender' as legally comprehended. Of course, protection here is premised upon '(tres)passing' as a member of a legally constituted category.

34   It is important to emphasise that, in particular instances, the discriminating gaze may be polyphobic. That is to say, it may be activated not by homosexuality or colour alone, or even in combination, but by the intersection of transgender, homosexuality and/or colour (Crenshaw, 1989, 1995).

35   Anti-Discrimination Act 1977 (NSW), s 24(1A); Equal Opportunity Act 1984 (SA), s 29(2); Equal Opportunity Act 1984 (WA), s 8(1); Discrimination Act 1991 (ACT), s 7(2)(c); Anti-Discrimination Act 1991 (Qld), s 8; Anti-Discrimination Act 1992 (NT), s 20(2); Sex Discrimination Act 1994 (Tas), s 16; Equal Opportunity Act 1995 (Vic), s 7(2).

36   Sexual Reassignment Act 1988 (SA); Transgender (Anti-Discrimination and Other Acts Amendment) Act 1996 (NSW), Sched 2; Births, Deaths and Marriages Registration Amendment Act 1997 (NT); Births, Deaths and Marriages Registration Act 1997 (ACT); Gender Reassignment Act 2000 (WA).

37   Sexual Reassignment Act 1988 (SA), s 10; Transgender (Anti-Discrimination and Other Acts Amendment) Act 1996 (NSW), Sched 2, s 4; Births, Deaths and Marriages Registration Amendment Act 1997 (NT), s 6; Births, Deaths and Marriages Registration Act 1997 (ACT), s 24(1)(c); Gender Reassignment Act 2000 (WA), s 15(3).

> The Bill ... provides that a person undergoing a reassignment procedure or applying for recognition should be unmarried. This will ensure that two persons designated as the same sex are not married.[38]

This particular form of exclusion is explicable in terms of legal desire to insulate the institution of marriage from the threat of homosexuality from within. It is this fear, one considered in Chapters 5 and especially 6, that serves to preclude the possibility of a successful claim of discrimination on the basis of sex. Moreover, this regulatory move serves to reorient the legal test for determining sex in the case of married transgender people so as to effect a reversal of the relation between sex and sexuality so that the latter comes to determine the former. In other words, the legal desire to insulate marriage from homosexuality is so acute that it actually serves to deny female status to (male-to-female) transgender women who remain married to (bio)logical women. Thus Australian sex change legislation that recognises (male-to-female) transgender women as female, though not for the purposes of marriage,[39] refuses to recognise as female married (male-to-female) transgender women. It is clear, therefore, not only that 'marital status' is substituted for *psychological and anatomical harmony* as the legal test for determining sex in the case of married transgender people, but also that legal recognition of transgender sex claims bears a mutually exclusive relation to inclusion within the sanctity of marriage.

Thus the anti-discrimination regulatory regimes of South Australia, West Australia, New South Wales, the Northern Territory and the Australian Capital Territory, which incite post-surgical (male-to-female) transgender women to '(tres)pass' as female, refuse to do so in the case of married transgender women,[40] whose bodies law, not unproblematically, attempts to inscribe as lesbian. Instead, the married transgender woman, despite having been subjected to strategies of sex/gender 'normalisation', is incited to render her transgender status visible. This strategy is curious in that it attempts to locate *psychologically and anatomically harmonious* woman within a more 'incongruous' category, thereby disrupting the genitocentric logic of law. Moreover, legal recognition of

---

38 The Hon Mr CJ Sumner (A-G) Debates of the Legislative Council (SA), 2 December 1987, p 2373.

39 No Australian State or territory can conclusively grant legal recognition to a transgender person for the purposes of marriage because marriage law in Australia is commonwealth law (Marriage Act 1961 (Cth)) which would override any inconsistent state law (Australian Constitution, s 109) (see Otlowski, 1990). This is not to say, despite parliamentary statements to the contrary at the State level (see, eg, the Hon Mr Jeff Shaw (A-G), Debates of the Legislative Assembly (NSW), 5 June 1996, p 2501; the Hon Mr Paul Whelan, Debates of the Legislative Assembly (NSW), 22 May 1996, p 1358), that legal recognition of transgender sex claims for the purposes of marriage is thereby precluded. Rather, in the absence of commonwealth legislative clarification legal recognition must depend upon judicial interpretations of the meaning of the words 'man' and 'woman' in the Marriage Act 1961 (Cth). The only case decided in Australia that is remotely on point is a Queensland decision, considered in Chapters 3 and 5, in which Bell J held a male-to-female intersexed person to be neither male nor female and therefore incapable of marrying anyone (*Re the Marriage of C and D (falsely called C)* [1979] 35 FLR 340). While it seems highly unlikely that this much criticised decision (see, eg, Bailey-Harris, 1979; Finlay, 1980) would be followed, a reading of the subtexts of Australian case law considered in Chapter 5 suggests a (bio)logical understanding of transgender sex claims in relation to marriage.

40 This is not the case in the Northern Territory and the Australian Capital Territory as anti-discrimination legislation in each of these jurisdictions contains a deeming provision with regard to the protected category of sex. Accordingly, within these regulatory regimes post-surgical male-to-female 'married transsexuals' are incited to '(tres)pass' as female (Discrimination Act 1991 (ACT), s 7(2)(c); Anti-Discrimination Act 1992 (NT), s 20(2)).

the sex claims of post-operative transgender people, as well as the refusal to recognise those claims on the basis of marital status, serves to highlight the fluidity and contingency of legal positionings across the male/female dyad. This in turn serves to highlight the difficulties associated with attempting an interpretation of rights in transgender/law contexts.

However, the possibility for married and pre- and non-surgical transgender people bringing successful sex discrimination claims nevertheless exists in Victoria, Queensland, the Northern Territory and the Australian Capital Territory, because the legislation in each of these jurisdictions includes within the ambit of sex discrimination, discrimination in the belief that a person is of a particular sex.[41] Accordingly, in these jurisdictions sex discrimination, rather than being tied to a fixed characteristic, such as chromosomes or anatomy, is structured to accord with the reality of the discrimination dynamic. That is to say, discrimination, and the possibility for invocation of right, are to be comprehended in the interplay of performance and gaze. Thus in these jurisdictions, and in a transphobic society, (male-to-female) transgender women, whatever their anatomical specificities, are subject to a mode of regulation which incites '(tres)passing' as female. This is not to suggest that to perform femaleness is to occupy a position of safety, to thereby avoid discrimination. Rather, it is, given the alarmingly high rates of discrimination against transgender people (Perkins, Griffin and Jakobsen, 1994), to suggest that the practice is likely to lower the incidence of discrimination. As a mode of regulation, incitement to '(tres)pass' as female proves disruptive for, in upholding a sex discrimination claim, law draws attention to the imitative structure of gender. Thus activists might, through repetitive practices of 'imitating' the 'real', seek to disrupt the category of sex and implicate law in precisely this effect. Moreover, Shapiro's claim that the maintenance of gender is occurring through its detachment from sex (1991, p 272) appears to hold in this context, as a successful claim serves to problematise the priority of sex in dominant understandings of sex/gender relations. The imperative to '(tres)pass' as female takes on added significance in the jurisdiction of Queensland, given its failure to produce transgender as a legal category. Moreover, the imperative to '(tres)pass' as female in jurisdictions yet to birth transgender as a protected legal category is perhaps particularly acute for non-heterosexual and non-white transgender persons, as the absence of transgender protection creates a legal space for homophobia and racism with impunity. Accordingly, law is perhaps implicated in rendering invisible figures such as the 'transgender lesbian'.[42]

The reasons for different approaches to sex discrimination across jurisdictions are complex. However, it is apparent that, with the exceptions of the Northern Territory and the Australian Capital Territory, the absence of a provision rendering discrimination in the belief that a person is of a particular sex – sex discrimination – correlates with legal recognition of the sex claims of post-surgical transgender people. This perhaps reflects a

---

41 Anti-Discrimination Act 1991 (Qld), s 8(c); Discrimination Act 1991 (ACT), s 7(2)(c); Anti-Discrimination Act 1992 (NT), s 20(2); Equal Opportunity Act 1995 (Vic), s 7(2)(d).

42 Of course, the 'transgender lesbian' may keep her transgender status invisible not merely out of fear of the homophobic gaze but precisely in order to avoid rendering visible before the discriminating gaze the intersection of transgender and lesbian. That is to say, in particular instances the discriminating gaze might be polyphobic, activated by the fact that transgender and lesbian reside within the one subject or by the intersection of some other combination of denigrated selves (Crenshaw, 1989, 1995). For a discussion of the intersection of gender and sexuality in discrimination contexts, see Chapman and Mason, 1999.

concern to limit protection against sex discrimination to genetic women and post-surgical transgender people who have been granted a certificate recognising their change of sex. This observation seems particularly apposite in the New South Wales context, where equivalent provisions prohibit discrimination in the belief that a person is homosexual or transgender.[43]

8.4 CONCLUSION

The various anti-discrimination regulatory regimes, as they pertain to transgender people, would appear to produce myriad and contradictory effects. While a number of themes emerge, the central tension appears to be between the legal desire to fix categories and the legal desire to regulate positively beyond those categories. Indeed, these legal desires appear incommensurable, the latter always threatening to disrupt the former. A disruptive moment occurs when law, through seeking to regulate that which it refuses to produce as identity, incites border crossings which serve to produce the very subject of law's refusal at the level of appearance, thereby problematising the boundaries of extant legal categories.

However, while an emphasis upon performance serves to destabilise the fixity of categories, and while this may reflect a trend in anti-discrimination law, it is important to stress that the genitocentric logic of law persists within particular regulatory regimes and serves as powerful counterpoise to a performance-oriented mode of regulation. Moreover, the particular and varied relations borne by different regulatory regimes to the categories of transgender and sex are to be comprehended by reference to differences in attempts to resolve these contradictory legal desires.

In Queensland and Tasmania transgender people are completely excluded from anti-discrimination laws. In the remaining jurisdictions, although transgender people are granted a presence within the framework of anti-discrimination law this proves contingent upon a demonstration of the fixed nature of transgender identity. Thus in West Australia it is only post-surgical transgender people who are given a presence within the law. This particular form of circumscription of transgender as a legal category is the effect of a regulatory regime premised on genitocentrism. Conversely, the jurisdictions of New South Wales, Victoria and the Australian Capital Territory, and perhaps South Australia and the Northern Territory, divide transgender people not on the basis of some genitocentric imperative, but rather on the basis of the permanence with which they live as members of the 'opposite' sex. What these regulatory regimes have in common is the fact that the production of transgender, when it is produced as a legal category, functions to exclude alternative transgender subjectivities.

However, while granting transgender people a presence within the law is extremely important, in and of itself, it would appear that legal protection is not necessarily tied to conferral of this status. Thus in New South Wales, Victoria the Northern Territory and the Australian Capital Territory it constitutes discrimination to discriminate against a person in the belief that the person is transgender. Accordingly, in these jurisdictions protection

---

43   Anti-Discrimination Act 1977 (NSW), ss 49ZG(2) and 38A.

against discrimination is an effect of transgender performance, not surgical intervention or permanence of transgender lifestyle. Moreover, this particular manifestation of law's desire to regulate beyond transgender, as a legally constituted category, serves to disrupt that very category. Thus to uphold a discrimination claim on transgender grounds where the claimant falls outside the category transgender as legally constituted serves to destabilise transgender as a legal category. That is to say, the deeming provision creates the conditions for the disruption, and radical rearticulation, of the transgender category as it serves to highlight its provisionality and contingency through enabling the demonstration of the imitative structure of (trans)gender.

The requirement for transgender performance at first appears curious, as it requires (male-to-female) transgender women to engage in female gender performance sufficient to be read as transgender but not so successful as to be read as genetically female. This observation is not confined to those jurisdictions that deem persons to be transgender for anti-discrimination law purposes. Rather, all jurisdictions that offer protection to transgender people require, given the nature of the discrimination dynamic, that they appear as transgender before the discriminating gaze. However, while these forms of regulation appear to incite 'third' gender visibility, this is not necessarily the case. Rather, an adequate understanding of the regulation of transgender people requires an appreciation of the complex relation between the categories sex and transgender.

In South Australia, New South Wales, the Northern Territory, the Australian Capital Territory and Western Australia the categories of sex and transgender have become blurred as post-surgical transgender people have had their sex claims legally recognised. Thus in these jurisdictions a (male-to-female) transgender woman who has succumbed to the genitocentric logic of law becomes legally female, and for anti-discrimination law purposes any distinction between transgender and genetic women disappears. Curiously, the genitocentric logic of law breaks down in the context of married transgender people. Here the fear of homosexual incursion upon the sanctity of marriage serves further to blur the boundary between sex and transgender,[44] as *psychologically and anatomically harmonious* women are incited to render visible their transgender status.

However, irrespective of law's treatment of transgender people who remain married, the relation between the categories of sex and transgender cannot be reduced to a surgical one. This is because the anti-discrimination legislation of Victoria, Queensland, the Northern Territory and the Australian Capital Territory all include within the ambit of sex discrimination, discrimination in the belief that a person is of a particular sex. In these jurisdictions law proves to be concerned primarily with the regulation of appearances. Thus in the context of sex discrimination, law is concerned less with female bodies (whether genetic or legal) and more with female gender performance. The effect of law here is not to render transgender women worse off than genetic women but to render all women who fail to accomplish gender worse off than those who succeed. Thus it is conceivable that the genetic female who fails to accomplish gender may be read as transgender, and thereby exposed to transphobia. Crucially, the deeming provision

---

44 The refusal to recognise as female the male-to-female post-operative transgender person who remains married to a biological woman also serves to blur the boundary between sex and sexuality. Indeed, this regulatory strategy involves a reversal of the relation between these categories whereby the latter comes to determine the former.

creates the conditions for the disruption, and further radical rearticulation, of the category sex through enabling the demonstration of the imitative structure of gender. Accordingly, this regulatory strategy serves to highlight inter-group sameness and intra-group difference(s).

Moreover, it is contended that, in those jurisdictions that have a deeming provision pertaining to sex, the legal relation between the categories transgender and sex is one which serves to transform the former into the latter. That is to say, the imperative to appear not as transgender but as a member of the 'opposite' sex is the dominant one in anti-discrimination law. In this regard, regulation of transgender people within the realm of anti-discrimination law proves continuous with transgender jurisprudence considered in earlier chapters. Law produces this effect through constructing sex to include post-surgical transgender people and by further detaching sex from its biological referent through the mechanism of the deeming provision.

However, an analysis of anti-discrimination law which views the central relation between the categories of transgender and sex as one whereby the former is transformed into the latter must account for the constitution of transgender as a legal category if it is to be seen as something other than superfluous. It is contended that the constitution of this category is to be comprehended in the context of normalising strategies targeting an inability to '(tres)pass' as a member of the opposite sex and, in some jurisdictions, the genitocentrism of law which resists too easy a slide between the categories of transgender and sex.

What the jurisdictions that create transgender as a legal category have in common is a desire to regulate and normalise transgender bodies, thereby reproducing the gender order. However, while strategies of 'normalisation' deployed in the Australian Capital Territory, Victoria and the Northern Territory apply generically to all transgender people unable to '(tres)pass' as members of the opposite sex, the regulatory regimes of New South Wales, South Australia and, to a lesser extent, Western Australia incite all non-surgical transgender people to render their transgender status visible irrespective of an ability to '(tres)pass'. Accordingly, within these particular transgender economies the legal desire to insulate the category of sex from 'erroneous' anatomical incursion has proved paramount. This is particularly noticeable in the New South Wales context, given that that jurisdiction possesses deeming provisions in relation to the categories of homosexuality and transgender. Moreover, it may be that legal incitement to '(tres)pass' as a member of the 'opposite' sex that refuses to traverse the pre-/post-operative divide suggests anxiety over proximity to the homosexual body. Thus it may be, at least in some jurisdictions, that the homophobia of law provides a 'limit' to legal strategies of regulation around appearance as it has in relation to the re-sexing of bodies considered in earlier chapters.

This chapter, while teasing out a number of themes within the anti-discrimination law context, has sought primarily to highlight two contradictory legal desires and the disruptive possibilities contained therein. What has been mapped is a shift from an interrogative toward a performative mode of regulation that has served to blur the boundaries of particular legal categories. While further theoretical work is required in order to address the implications of this trend, and to provide the conceptual apparatus for (re)characterising law's relation to subjects, it would appear that critiques which concern themselves only with the ossifying effects of rights are inadequate to the task. That is to say, the relationship between 'coherent fixed identity' and the enjoyment of rights has, in various Australian contexts, been severed. Rather, invocation of rights becomes possible for persons located outside of the legally constituted categories of transgender, sexuality and sex. While legal protection is an effect of perpetrator 'mis-readings' of bodies rather than a concern for the excess of bodies that lie beyond legally protected categories, this development nevertheless creates a space both for protection and the disruption, through imitation and repetition, of supposedly 'fixed' categories. Moreover, this disruptive potential might be exploited in order to challenge legal understandings of identity and desire across a range of sexual/political terrains.

In Chapter 9 our attention moves from this moment of opportunity to consider recent transgender law reform in Western Australia. In this regard, the chapter situates reform within a specific political context and draws attention to the potential dangers of a legislative approach to transgender rights claims. The selection of Western Australia is informed by the fact that transgender and gay and lesbian law reform coincide in time. This fact, as we will see, serves to foreground the homophobia of law in the context of transgender law reform. In this respect, Chapter 9 will focus on a theme which earlier chapters have shown to be central to understanding transgender jurisprudence and thereby bring back into view the need for, and the legal constraints surrounding, transgender and gay and lesbian political alliance.

IN THE SHADOW OF HOMOSEXUAL ANXIETY:
TRANSGENDER LAW REFORM
IN WESTERN AUSTRALIA

[T]he [Gender Reassignment] Bill should not be treated frivolously or lightly ... essentially the Bill is not about sexuality or sexual preference.[1]

Other members have mentioned, and I would like to reinforce, the fact that [the Gender Reassignment] Bill has nothing to do with sexual preference.[2]

These parliamentary statements and others like them capture the key theme of this chapter, which is that transgender law reform tends to take place in the shadow of homosexual anxiety. The chapter will consider this theme in the context of recent transgender legislation enacted in Western Australia, where the homophobia of law has proved to be particularly transparent, and situate it within a broader law reform context. After three years before the West Australian parliament, the Gender Reassignment Bill finally became law on 23 March 2000.[3] In enacting this legislation Western Australia, like South Australia, New South Wales, the Australian Capital Territory and the Northern Territory before it,[4] conferred, subject to certain medical and administrative conditions,[5] legal recognition on transgender people who have undergone sex reassignment surgery. That is to say, provision now exists in Western Australia for classifying as female a person who was born with male chromosomes, gonads and genitalia, and as male a person who was born with female chromosomes, gonads and genitalia. However, while the West Australian legislation mirrors other jurisdictions that have enacted transgender legislation with regard to legal recognition of sex claims, it is clear that it is far less progressive in the context of discrimination law.

In addition to creating provision for amending birth certificates the Gender Reassignment Act 2000, by virtue of Sched 2, amends the West Australian Equal Opportunity Act 1984, thereby providing coverage to a class of transgender persons. This class, referred to in the legislation as 'gender reassigned persons', mirrors precisely the class of persons whose sex claims may now be recognised. In short, those transgender people who have undertaken sex reassignment surgery are included within a West Australian legislative framework that protects against discrimination. It is the fact that sex reassignment surgery operates as a 'trigger', as the former Attorney-General, Peter Foss,

---

1   The Hon Mr Pendal, Debates of the Legislative Assembly (WA), 24 November 1999, p 3765.
2   The Hon Mrs Holmes, Debates of the Legislative Assembly (WA), 24 November 1999, p 3766.
3   Gender Reassignment Act 2000 (WA).
4   Sexual Reassignment Act 1988 (SA); The Transgender (Anti-Discrimination and Other Acts Amendment) Act 1996 (NSW); Births, Deaths and Marriages Registration Amendment Act 1997 (NT); Births, Deaths and Marriages Registration Act 1997 (ACT).
5   West Australian Act, s 15, makes clear that a recognition certificate will only issue where 'the reassignment procedure was carried out in the State', 'the birth of the person to whom the application relates is registered in the State' or 'the person to whom the application relates is a resident of the State and has been so resident for not less than 12 months' (s 15(1)(a)) and where the Gender Reassignment Board is satisfied that the person 'believes that his or her true gender is the gender to which the person has been reassigned', 'has adopted the lifestyle and has the gender characteristics of a person of the gender to which the person has been reassigned' and 'has received proper counseling in relation to his or her gender identity' (s 15(1)(b)).

put it,[6] for protection against discrimination, that distinguishes the legislation from other jurisdictions.[7] The harnessing of protection against discrimination to sex reassignment surgery is especially troublesome, given the alarming rates of discrimination faced by transgender people[8] and the fact that, on the West Australian government's own figures, less than one-third of people designated 'gender dysphoric' in Western Australia have undertaken surgical procedures.[9]

While this chapter is directed toward an analysis and critique of this deficit in West Australian law reform, it should not be thought that discursive violence toward transgender people or homophobia are absent from the legislative frameworks of other Australian jurisdictions. As we saw in earlier chapters, invocation of a pre-/post-operative dyad is problematic with regard to sex designation as well as discrimination. Accordingly, much of the critique that follows applies to Australian legislation and

---

6   The Hon P Foss, Debates of the Legislative Council (WA), 8 April 1997, p 1133.

7   Prior to the Gender Reassignment Act all Australian jurisdictions enacting legislation so as to include transgender people within anti-discrimination legislative frameworks had done so irrespective of surgical status.

8   See the Hon Mr Sulc, Debates of the Legislative Council (WA), 8 April 1997, p 1130; the Hon Ms Warnock, Debates of the Legislative Assembly (WA), 24 November 1999, p 3764; the Hon Ms McHale, Debates of the Legislative Assembly (WA), 24 November 1999, p 3764. In one Australian study, using a sample of 146 transgender people, 37% reported systematic discrimination (once or more a week) while only 12% reported no discrimination at all (Perkins, Griffin and Jakobsen, 1994, p 58). In the workplace context 45 (30.8%) reported discrimination (Perkins, Griffin and Jakobsen, 1994, p 59). Moreover, the study compared employment levels before and after gender crossings. With the exceptions of sex work and pornography, employment levels were found to have fallen significantly (factory work down from 40 (27.4%) to 11 (7.5%); service industry down from 38 (26%) to 15 (10.3%); sales work down from 47 (32.2%) to 8 (5.5%); skilled trade down from 31 (21.2%) to 10 (6.8%); office work down from 34 (23.3%) to 16 (11%) (p 24). Further, there are high levels of unemployment amongst transgender people (Sydney Gender Centre, 1994, p 21) and unemployed transgender people report alarming levels of discrimination by the Department of Social Security (30 (20.5%)) (Perkins, Griffin and Jakobsen, 1994, p 59). High levels of discrimination against transgender people have also been noted in the United States context (see, eg, Green, 1994; It's Time Illinois, 2000). It should be noted that transgender people are also subjected to high levels of violence including sexual violence (see Perkins, Griffin and Jakobsen, 1994, pp 37–42; Hooley, 1996; Short, 1997; GenderPAC, 1997; Plant, Mason and Thornton, 1999; National Coalition of Anti-Violence Programs, 1998; Sharpe and Moran, forthcoming).

     Moreover, and as noted in Chapter 2, transgender people intent on sex reassignment surgery are required to undergo a lengthy period of assessment while living in the 'opposite' gender role, a so-called 'real life test' (Money and Walker, 1977, p 1292). How it might be asked, and while not wishing to reinscribe sex reassignment surgery as a legal requirement, are pre-operative transgender people to 'successfully undergo this assessment period and raise the necessary funds for the operation if they are suffering discrimination in employment, housing and the provision of goods and services?' (the Hon Ms Warnock, Debates of the Legislative Assembly (WA), 24 November 1999, p 3763).

9   According to statistics referred to repeatedly in the parliamentary debates there are estimated to be approximately 250 persons classified as gender dysphoric in Western Australia (the estimate of 250 has its source in ongoing discussions between government departments and the Gender Council of Australia (WA) Inc (see the Hon Mrs van de Klashorst, Debates of the Legislative Assembly (WA), 2 December 1998, p 4758). Of this group only 80 have undergone sex reassignment surgery (SRS) and therefore stand to benefit from the legislation. During the period 1997 to 1998 no SRS procedures were performed in Western Australia (see the Hon Mr Prince, Debates of the Legislative Assembly (WA), 16 September 1998, p 1533). For some transgender persons the reason for continued pre-operative status is the prohibitive cost of surgery, which has been estimated at approximately $10,000 (see the Hon Ms Warnock, Debates of the Legislative Assembly (WA), 24 November 1999, p 3763). This is significant as it reveals how, unlike other protected categories, inclusion within an anti-discrimination legislative framework is tied to economic wealth, a point not without irony given the social and economic marginalisation consequent on gender crossing (see Perkins, Griffin and Jakobsen, 1994; Sydney Gender Centre, 1994).

judicial decisions that have re-sexed bodies.[10] Moreover, while the pre-/post-operative distinction, insisted upon for the purposes of sex designation, is dispensed with in the context of transgender discrimination in other Australian jurisdictions, the circumscription of transgender nevertheless proves central. That is to say, and as we saw in Chapter 8, Australian anti-discrimination law legislative frameworks dispensing with surgical requirements have nevertheless divided transgender people, employing typically a transgender/cross-dresser distinction. As for the homophobia of transgender law reform in these jurisdictions, it is evident in the conditions of legal recognition of sex claims. That is to say, legal recognition in each of these jurisdictions requires, like Western Australia, that the transgender applicant be post-operative, the pre-operative body being too readily associated with homosexuality and homosexual practice. In a similar vein, each of these jurisdictions requires, again like Western Australia, that the transgender applicant be 'unmarried'.[11] That is to say, a married person who undergoes sex reassignment surgery cannot have her/his sex claims recognised while the marriage subsists.[12] As we saw in Chapter 8 this provision is designed to insulate marriage from what law imagines to be homosexuality.

In the West Australian political context, however, homophobia extends beyond these concerns. That is to say, the legislation invokes a pre-/post-operative dyad in relation not only to sex designation but also anti-discrimination law protection on the ground of transgender. It is contended that the conflation of homosexuality with the pre- or non-operative transgender body in this latter context is to be accounted for, in some considerable measure, in the context of the West Australian political landscape regarding gay and lesbian rights claims. More specifically, it is to be comprehended in relation to legislation introduced at the same time as the Gender Reassignment Bill, namely the Acts Amendment (Sexuality Discrimination) Bill, and its pre-history. This is not to suggest that

---

10 In relation to Australian legislation that has re-sexed bodies, see above, fn 4. In relation to case law, see *R v Harris and McGuiness* [1988] 35 A Crim R 146; *Secretary, Department of Social Security v HH* [1991] 13 AAR 314; *Secretary, Department of Social Security v SRA* [1993] 118 ALR 467.

11 Sexual Reassignment Act 1988 (SA), s 7(10); Transgender (Anti-Discrimination and Other Acts Amendment) Act 1996 (NSW), Sched 2, s 4; Births, Deaths and Marriages Registration Act 1997 (ACT), s 24(1)(c); Births, Deaths and Marriages Registration Amendment Act 1997 (NT), s 6; Gender Reassignment Act 2000 (WA), s 15(3). It should be pointed out that during the West Australian parliamentary debates several members of parliament, including the former Attorney-General, sought to emphasise that the issue of a recognition certificate did not confer a right to marry in the 'new' sex as that question is governed by commonwealth law (see the Hon NF Moore, Debates of the Legislative Council (WA), 13 March 1997, p 292; the Hon Mr Prince, Debates of the Legislative Council (WA), 9 April 1997, p 1361; the Hon Mr Foss, Debates of the Legislative Council (WA), 25 November 1999, p 3823). This point has also been stressed in parliamentary debates in other jurisdictions in the context of legal recognition of transgender sex claims. Further, in the NSW debates there was considerable insistence that 'sex' for the purposes of the Marriage Act 1961 (Cth) was to be equated with chromosomes (see the Hon Mr J Shaw (A-G), Debates of the Legislative Assembly (NSW), 5 June 1996, p 2501; the Hon Mr P Whelan, Debates of the Legislative Assembly (NSW), 22 May 1996, p 1358). While it is true that the point must be determined in accordance with commonwealth law the widespread assumption that under commonwealth law sex means (bio)logical sex remains a moot point. It would be open to the Australian High Court to depart from the view that sex is determined at birth and by reference to chromosomes for the purposes of marriage. This approach has already been adopted by the New Zealand High Court in the cases of *M v M* [1991] NZFLR 337 and *Attorney-General v Otahuhu Family Court* [1995] 1 NZLR 603.

12 The Gender Reassignment Act, and indeed other Australian transgender legislation, renders married transgender persons worse off than at common law as it prohibits legal recognition of sex claims irrespective of legal subject matter. In the case of *R v Harris and McGuiness* (1989) 17 NSWLR 158, there is no suggestion by the Supreme Court of New South Wales that a married (male-to-female) transgender woman would not be treated as female for the purposes of the criminal law.

conflation of transgender and homosexuality is novel. On the contrary, as we saw in Chapter 2, it is apparent in the 19th century sexological trope of inversion (Chauncey, 1982–83; Hekma, 1996; Prosser, 1998) and can in cultural terms be traced back centuries earlier (Trumbach, 1977, 1987; Davenport-Hines, 1990). Rather, the point here is that anxiety over gay and lesbian law reform occasioned by the introduction of the Acts Amendment (Sexuality Discrimination) Bill serves to bring to the fore a pre-existing cultural conflation.

As will become apparent, passage of the Gender Reassignment Act 2000 proved possible only through constituting 'gender reassigned persons' in opposition to an undeserving homosexual 'other'. Accordingly, and as we will see, transgender law reform in Western Australia serves to foreground questions regarding the relationship between transgender and gay and lesbian politics and possibilities of/for coalition. Moreover, while, and because, the legislation represents a political compromise on the part of transgender communities in order to produce some kind of reform, issues of transgender responsibility arise in relation to the effects thereby produced. Indeed, this is especially apparent given that parliamentarians noted that transgender people 'are keen that the distinction [between gay men and lesbians and transgender people] should be made'.[13] The conflation of the pre-operative body with homosexuality is particularly observable in the West Australian parliamentary debates that approach the subject matter through a series of interrelated dyads; pre-/post-operative, act/identity, deserving/undeserving, visibility/invisibility, sexual/non-sexual. Before considering these issues it is first necessary to situate them within a broader legal and political context.

9.1 A LEGAL AND POLITICAL CONTEXT

After much campaigning the West Australian Law Reform (Decriminalisation of Sodomy) Act was passed in 1989.[14] This legislation proved highly controversial within the parliament and was only passed when two parliamentarians, including the former Attorney-General, crossed the floor of the house.[15] They did so, however, only on the basis of two concessions. First, the age of consent for gay men was to be set at 21 rather than 18 as stipulated in the Bill.[16] Secondly, the so-called, and highly criticised, 'Foss preamble' was inserted into the new legislation. The preamble emphasises the 'inappropriateness' of homosexual behaviour ('the Parliament disapproves of sexual relations between persons of the same sex') and seeks to prevent any attempt to present

13 The Hon Ms Warnock, Debates of the Legislative Assembly (WA), 24 November 1999, p 3763. Of course, this strategy of splitting is also one that has featured prominently in gay and lesbian law reform. That is to say, transgender has often been viewed as a political liability, as something likely to derail reform (see, eg, Rubin, 1992; Nataf, 1996; Califia, 1997).

14 For a discussion of the Law Reform (Decriminalisation of Sodomy) Act 1989 in the criminal law context see Morgan, 1990. For a discussion of the relationship between the legislation and the suicide of homosexual youth see Kendall, 1998.

15 The Hon P Foss, Debates of the Legislative Council (WA), 19 November 1997, pp 8133–34. The other Liberal parliamentarian to cross the floor of the house was the Hon M McAleer.

16 *Ibid.* The age of consent for heterosexuals in Western Australia is 16. Through retaining a differential age of consent the legislation served to couple the act of sodomy with gay men. Previously the offence had operated generically within the Criminal Code Act 1913 (WA). This legal move has been explored by L Moran in the English context (see Moran, 1996).

homosexuality in a positive light both generally ('the Parliament disapproves of the promotion or encouragement of homosexual behaviour') and specifically within schools ('the Parliament disapproves of persons with care supervision or authority over young persons urging them to adopt homosexuality as a lifestyle and disapproves of instrumentalities of the State so doing'). The legislation, while obviously a step forward in an instrumental sense, provides a perfect, and somewhat dramatic, illustration of the negative discursive fallout always likely to be attendant to gay and lesbian law reform (Morgan, 1996, p 123).

The introduction of the Gender Reassignment and Acts Amendment (Sexuality Discrimination) Bills into the West Australian parliament in 1997 needs to be understood against this backdrop. The latter Bill sought to lower the age of consent for gay men to 16, extend anti-discrimination protection to cover discrimination based on sexuality and transgender status irrespective of sex reassignment surgery,[17] and remove the preamble to the 1989 legislation. Considerable opposition exists in the parliament to each of these aims, and the former West Australian Liberal government made it clear that it viewed the Bill as irredeemable and that it opposed the Bill 'in every single respect'.[18] The main source of opposition is given voice by the former Attorney-General:

> My concern and the concern of the Government is that we have gone very rapidly from the situation in 1989 when all sorts of assurances were given that this was not the beginning of the end ... I must confess to feeling to some extent slightly duped because the people who persuaded me to vote for the 1989 Bill indicated that all they wanted was to have the stigma and fear of criminal prosecution taken away. In a decade they have gone from that position to wanting to be morally endorsed and supported by removing other people's civil rights in order to support the anti-discrimination. The people with their firmly held religious beliefs were right; we are now being asked not only to give ordinary rights – perfectly deserved rights – to those people, but also to further offend the moral sensibilities of a significant part of our society in order to give this Bill its standing ... There is no basis upon which we can say to our community that this has the same moral rectitude as not discriminating against people on the basis of disability, race or gender.[19]

It is apparent that objections to the Acts Amendment (Sexuality Discrimination) Bill are based in religious morality. While this strategy has been pursued most vigorously in the United States by Christian fundamentalists (Herman, 1997) it is important to recognise how 'mainstream' religion is both implicated in, and deployed to, undermine lesbian and gay equality rights. As the former Attorney-General pointed out:

> ... [p]eople from all parts of the religious spectrum are offended by this. Within the Christian religion, Roman Catholics to fundamentalists are opposed to it. Members of other

---

17   The Hon Ms H Hodgson, Debates of the Legislative Council (WA), 17 September 1997, p 6304.

18   The Hon P Foss, Debates of the Legislative Council (WA), 21 March 2000, p 5212. In relation to discrimination against gay men and lesbians the Liberal government maintained this position despite a report by the West Australian Commission for Equal Opportunity recommending inclusion of 'sexuality' as a protected category having found that 'discrimination on the ground of homosexuality in the areas of employment, education, accommodation, and the provision of goods, services and other facilities is widespread' (Commission for Equal Opportunity, 1994, p 45).

19   *Ibid*, p 5213.

religions, such as Muslims, are opposed to it and feel it is a moral insult to them. We must keep in mind that degree of opposition when we consider this Bill.[20]

That anti-discrimination law protection is presented as 'undeserved' reveals a view of homosexuality, and especially homosexual behaviour as freely chosen. Moreover, it would seem that male homosexual behaviour is always coded as the 'unnatural' act of sodomy, or at least sodomy is scripted as its logical and inevitable end (Moran, 1996, Chapter 2). Thus, and in a passage characterised by considerable anxiety, the Hon Greg Smith insisted that '[m]embers must face the fact that the majority of the population is heterosexual and, just as homosexual people are probably uncomfortable about the thought of a sexual relationship with a member of the opposite sex, so heterosexual people feel the same about sodomising another man, for example, I do not like the thought of it, and do not want to do it'.[21]

The characterisation of homosexual practice as both wilful and 'unnatural' serves not only to denigrate such practice. It also, given law's categorical imperative, serves to distance gay men and lesbians from rights claims. That is to say, an emphasis on choice serves to undermine a claim of coherent fixed group identity so central to the conferral of rights within liberal legalism (Bumiller, 1988; Iyer, 1993; Herman, 1994; Morgan, 1996).[22] It is for this reason that the former Attorney-General, not unproblematically, contrasts homosexuality with the 'fixed' categories of 'disability', 'race' and 'gender'. It is a concern to prevent the 'promotion' of transgressive and 'deliberate' (homo)sexual practices, especially sodomy, and a belief that anti-discrimination law protection will aid promotion that accounts for the fact that sex reassignment surgery serves as a trigger for, and we might say gatekeeper to, protection against discrimination under the Gender Reassignment legislation. That is to say, phallic women and vaginaed men are too readily associated with homosexuality. It is against this backdrop that the specificity of the Gender Reassignment Act is to be comprehended.

9.2 A CRITIQUE OF REFORM LEGISLATION

Protection against discrimination under the Gender Reassignment Act 2000 proves dependent on the issue of a recognition certificate. The issue of a certificate which, of course, requires that sex reassignment surgery has occurred, also requires that the Gender Reassignment Board be satisfied that a transgender applicant:

(i) believes that his or her true gender is the gender to which the person has been reassigned;

---

20 *Ibid*, p 5212.

21 The Hon Mr G Smith, Debates of the Legislative Council (WA), 19 November 1997, p 8150.

22 While the emergence of rights in the anti-discrimination law context appears tied to the demonstration of fixed group identity the enjoyment of such rights is, as we saw in Chapter in 8, not necessarily constrained in this way. That is to say, in a number of jurisdictions (see below, fn 56), though not Western Australia, deeming provisions exist whereby persons falling outside protected groups come within the ambit of the legislation if belief in group membership is the motivation for discrimination. Indeed, the Acts Amendment (Sexuality Discrimination) Bill contained such provisions (see the Hon Ms Hodgson, Debates of the Legislative Council (WA), 17 September 1997, p 6304).

(ii) has adopted the lifestyle and has the gender characteristics of a person of the gender to which the person has been reassigned; and

(iii) has received proper counselling in relation to his or her gender identity.[23]

These conditions, and the discourse generated around them, reveal a number of things. In particular, they serve to differentiate the post-operative transgender body from homosexuality. Thus, and in contrast to, the 'mere' assertion of identity by gay men and lesbians, transgender 'authenticity' must be diagnosed. This occurs through the deployment and imposition of medico-scientific 'truth'. Thus the Act is based on the 'fact' of gender dysphoria, the most contemporary of medical knowledges that have sought to account for transgender desire (Fisk, 1973; Laub and Gandy, 1973).[24] As the former Attorney-General explained:

> The scheme of this Bill is to have a trigger point which is the issuing of the certificate. The Bill is based on the fact that the people are gender dysphoric – not merely that they have dressed in clothes that are inappropriate for their initial gender, but that they are committed to the fact and feel that they are of another gender. The process they go through to receive the benefit of this antidiscrimination provision does not take effect until they have satisfied the [Gender Reassignment] board that they have that *disability* and that they are genuinely committed to having a gender other than that with which they were born. There will be no process for addressing discrimination against people prior to receiving their gender reassignment certificate. The purpose of the certificate is to trigger all that happens in the legislation.[25]

The fact that the former Attorney-General distinguishes a genuine commitment 'to having a gender other than that with which they were born' from the 'disability' of gender dysphoria suggests that undergoing sex reassignment surgery and an ability to 'pass' are insufficient for the purposes of legal recognition. Rather, it is clear that conferral of a recognition certificate is additionally an effect of demonstration before the Gender Reassignment Board of transgender 'authenticity', which requires ideally an autobiographical account of a particular and privileged form of transgender narrativisation.[26] In addition to the instantiation of a pre-/post-operative dyad and the intrusive requirement that the undertaking of sex reassignment surgery be substantiated by the Gender Reassignment Board, this aspect of the legislation has provoked opposition within West Australian transgender communities.[27]

---

23 Gender Reassignment Act 2000 (WA), s 15(1)(b). Section 3 of the Act defines 'gender characteristics' to mean 'the physical characteristics by virtue of which a person is identified as male or female' and therefore refers to sex reassignment surgery.

24 For a sociological analysis of the concept of 'gender dysphoria' as well as preceding medical models, see (King, 1993).

25 The Hon P Foss, Debates of the Legislative Council (WA), 8 April 1997, pp 1132–33.

26 The medical script to which transgender persons seeking SRS are expected to conform includes ideally hatred of genitalia, heterosexual desire, absence of pre-operative sexual activity, early onset of gender identity and stereotypical assumptions about present and past gender performance (for a discussion of these themes see, eg, Califia, 1997; Cromwell, 1999; Nataf, 1996).

27 See the Hon Ms Warnock, Debates of the Legislative Assembly (WA), 24 November 1999, p 3763; the Hon G Watson, Debates of the Legislative Council (WA), 15 March 2000, p 4995; the Hon H Hodgson, Debates of the Legislative Council (WA), 16 March 2000, p 5097. Indeed, the Hon Ms Hodgson informed the Legislative Council that it had been put to her by members of the transgender community that 'some people will choose not to go through the process of obtaining the appropriate certification simply because they feel the processes to be followed are too intrusive' (p 5097).

Moreover, the characterisation of an 'authentic' transgender state as a 'disability' illustrates how desire is reinscribed as need and how the pathologisation of the transgender body is the price to be paid for legal protection. An emphasis on transgender as 'disorder' was a consistent feature of the parliamentary debates. For example, the Hon Muriel Patterson spoke 'compassionately' of transgender people as 'afflicted'[28] souls, while the Hon Mrs Holmes described the transgender body as an 'accident of nature'[29] and as 'nature's misprint'.[30] Indeed, and without contestation, the Hon Ms Patterson insisted that gender dysphoria is a congenital condition, adding that '[n]ot one person in this House would not support a Bill to give quality of life to any child suffering from blindness, deafness, deformed limbs or any other congenital distortion or malformation'.[31] This view presents difficulties, other than the fact that some physically challenged persons might not thank Ms Patterson for this particular characterisation. In the case of transgender persons, there is no distortion or malformation of the body.[32] On the contrary, the body is perfectly formed. Rather, for some transgender people the body does not conform with their sense of gender identity. It is the characterisation of this dilemma that is of most significance. The claim by the Hon Ms Patterson that gender dysphoria is to be traced to a congenital condition is both scientifically suspect and politically dangerous.

First, this argument, while not articulated clearly in the parliamentary debates, is based on the claimed influence of hormones on transgender bodies during pregnancy. As explained in Chapter 2, a number of contemporary scientific studies conducted *post mortem* on the bodies of (male-to-female) transgender women have suggested that they possess a female brain structure (Gooren *et al*, 1995; Kruijver, 2000). This view is a controversial one within medicine (Breedlove, 1995). Moreover, it was rejected by Ormrod J in the classic English decision of *Corbett v Corbett* in 1970[33] and more recently, and on several occasions, by the European Court of Human Rights.[34]

The attempt to ground transgender legitimacy, and rights claims, in (bio)logic is perhaps understandable given the power of medical science, the fact that a congenital argument serves to counter a view of legal recognition as inconsistent with the aim of maintaining accurate historical records[35] and the degree of anxiety surrounding the pre-operative body in the West Australian political context. Indeed, it is no doubt significant that (bio)logical arguments have featured less in parliamentary debates surrounding the

---

28   The Hon M Patterson, Debates of the Legislative Council (WA), 26 March 1997, p 945.

29   The Hon Mrs Holmes, Debates of the Legislative Assembly (WA), 24 November 1999, p 3766.

30   *Ibid*, p 3767.

31   *Ibid*, p 3766.

32   This view of bodies as malformed is also problematic in the context of intersexed persons (see, eg, Triea, 1994; McClintock, 1997; Chase, 1998). The fact that particular configurations of chromosomes, gonads and genitalia do not correspond to medico-legal binary divisions of sex does not suggest distortion, malformation or disharmony. Rather, it brings into question the rigidity of hegemonic understandings of sex.

33   *Corbett v Corbett* [1970] 2 All ER 33.

34   See *Rees v UK* (1986) 9 EHRR 56; *Cossey v UK* (1991) 13 EHRR 622; *X, Y and Z v UK* (1997) EHRR 143; *Sheffield and Horsham v UK* (1998) 27 EHRR 163.

35   This concern, which is often voiced in both legislative and judicial transgender law reform contexts, finds expression in the parliamentary debates over the Gender Reassignment Bill (see the Hon Mr Pendal, Debates of the Legislative Assembly (WA), 24 November 1999, p 3765).

more comprehensive reforms of other Australian jurisdictions. Moreover, biology has been paid scant attention within Australian transgender jurisprudence. Its deployment by reformers tends to occur where there is opposition to, or anxiety about, proposed change. This perhaps accounts for the consistent references to biology in the English context, a jurisdiction that has so far failed to initiate any reform either at the judicial[36] or legislative[37] levels. In any event, and as noted in Chapter 3, resort to (bio)logic proves problematic irrespective, and precisely because, of claims of scientific validity. This strategy in the aid of law reform is not a new one. In the modern context it is perhaps traceable to the sexological writings of Ulrichs in the 1860s (Ulrichs, 1898, 1994; Kennedy, 1981, 1988). As we saw in Chapter 2, Ulrichs argued for a congenital, as distinct from a hereditary, base for Uranian desire in order to make a case for natural variation in human sexuality (Ulrichs, 1994, p 36).[38] The dangers of this move are evident in the writings of many of Ulrich's sexological successors, particularly Krafft-Ebing, who converted Ulrich's view of Uranian desire into a pathology inhering within the body (von Krafft-Ebing, 1877). Not only are marginalised groups always vulnerable to reinscription of difference as 'excess', 'deficiency' or 'imbalance' (Sedgwick, 1990, p 43) whenever claims are tied to (bio)logic, but interestingly this is the precise effect produced in the West Australian parliamentary debates by the champions of reform. Moreover, it is this shift from natural difference to pathological bodies that serves to strip transgender people of agency. That is to say, it leads to a situation where conferral of rights is tied to pity, not respect. Ironically, conferral of legal rights is premised not on the demonstration of the qualities of the liberal legal subject – rationality, autonomy, free will – but rather proves possible only in their absence.

It is curious that the congenital argument did not prove more controversial in the parliamentary debates, given that it serves to problematise the pre-/post-operative dyad. That is to say, if the congenital argument is accepted it may support a view that hormonal sex at birth, rather than the fact of sex reassignment surgery, should operate as the trigger for legal recognition. By the same token, this may entail denial of legal recognition to some transgender people who have undertaken sex reassignment surgery. However, irrespective of (bio)logical 'truth' and the conclusions to be drawn from it, the emphasis on a (bio)logical basis for rights claims ought to be resisted. For the effect of instantiating (bio)logic as the measure of transgender claims is to reify the birth moment and is of necessity to exclude even as, and precisely when, rights are conferred. That is to say, the

---

36 See *Corbett v Corbett* [1970] 2 All ER 33; *Dec CP* 6/76 National Insurance Commissioner Decisions; *EA White v British Sugar Corporation* [1977] IRLR 121; *Social Security Decision Nos R(P)1 and R(P)2* [1980] National Insurance Commissioner Decisions; *R v Tan* [1983] QB 1053; *Peterson v Peterson* (1985) *The Times*, 12 July; *Franklin v Franklin* (1990) *The Scotsman*, 9 November; *Collins v Wilkin Chapman* [1994] EAT/945/93 (Transcript); *S-T (formerly J) v J* [1998] 1 All ER 431; *W v W* (2000) *The Times*, 31 October (Transcript); *Bellinger v Bellinger* (2000) *The Times*, 22 November.

37 See the parliamentary debates surrounding the failed Gender Identity (Registration and Civil Status) Bill (UK). Eg, see the Hon A Carlile, Debates of the House of Commons, 2 February 1996, pp 1282–86.

38 In opposition to Foucault's view that inversion marked homosexuality's origins as a 'species' (Foucault, 1981a, p 43), a view well rehearsed in much gay and lesbian historiography, it seems more convincing as Prosser contends that Ulrichs' figure of the Uranian effectively commenced 'the mapping of transgender as an identity in the West' for he sought to describe not homosexuality but a broad transgender condition of which same-sex desire was but one symptom, and not vice versa (Prosser, 1998, p 143).

strategy serves to undermine and marginalise further those transgender people unable to demonstrate a hormonal basis for their claims. On this account, a lack of compulsion renders such people undeserving. This compulsion/choice dyad is not, of course, one confined to transgender issues. In the parallel debates over the Acts Amendment (Sexuality Discrimination) Bill it features prominently. Thus several MPs contended that homosexuality is genetically based.[39] Indeed, the Hon Helen Hodgson tabled a letter from 24 noted clinical psychologists, a passage of which stated: 'It is very difficult for heterosexual people to understand the lack of choice that homosexuals have about their sexual orientation. There may be some choice (as we all have) about the way people live their lives, but sexuality is an innate part of our humanness.'[40] Conversely, many MPs insisted that homosexuality is behaviourally based, the Hon Greg Smith insisting 'it is not a benign factor such as race, colour and sex'.[41] Moreover, resort is again made to science. Thus the former Attorney-General claimed that 'homosexuality is learnt and is not a genetic behaviour. I accept that as the appropriate scientific knowledge'.[42] However, in a rare moment of clarity one MP revealed this type of argument to be:

> ... one of the great red herrings that has been brought into this debate. I do not think it matters in this debate tonight whether it is a genetic or a behavioural issue. The issue is: Regardless of why people are that way, should they be discriminated against because of that? That is the fundamental question. The question is not how people came to be at that point, but whether by being at that point they are treated differently and unfairly by others in society. When people start talking about why people are homosexual and whether it is a behavioural issue, it is nonsense; it is irrelevant to the debate tonight.[43]

It is, of course, also nonsense in relation to transgender people. However, in relation to the debates over the Gender Reassignment Bill it occurred to no one to make this point. Moreover, in the transgender context a view of transgender lifestyles as chosen was lacking, and in the case of people undergoing sex reassignment surgery completely absent. This is, no doubt, due to a combination of factors, including societal failure to understand transgender desires, especially the desire to remove 'healthy' genital organs, the relative powerlessness of transgender compared, for example, to gay and lesbian, communities, and the power over, and the dependence of, many transgender people enjoyed by the medical profession. Indeed, the fact that homosexuality officially ceased to be considered a mental illness by the American Psychiatric Association (APA) in 1973 (Lewes, 1988, p 201), while transgender people continue to feature in the Diagnostic and Statistics Manual of Mental Disorders currently under the head of 'Gender Identity Disorders' (APA, 1995, pp 546–52), might be viewed, in important ways, as an effect of such power relations.

The strategy of differentiating the post-operative transgender body from homosexuality also draws on assertions around demography. That is to say, the issue of

---

39 See, eg, the Hon JA Scott, Debates of the Legislative Council (WA), 19 November 1997, p 8155; the Hon Ms Hodgson, Debates of the Legislative Council (WA), 19 November 1997, p 8161.

40 *Ibid.*

41 The Hon G Smith, Debates of the Legislative Assembly (WA), 19 November 1997, p 8149.

42 This statement was attributed to the Hon P Foss by the Hon JA Cowdell, Debates of the Legislative Council (WA), 19 November 1997, p 8149. See, also, the Hon G Smith, Debates of the Legislative Council (WA), 19 November 1997, p 8149.

43 The Hon K Travers, Debates of the Legislative Council (WA), 19 November 1997, p 8157.

size featured significantly in the parliamentary debates. The presumed 'small' size of the so-called 'gender dysphoric' group was emphasised countless times.[44] This characterisation of the transgender population as 'small' is problematic in a number of respects. First, it proves to be an effect of coupling transgender with the desire for sex reassignment surgery, whereas many transgender people have no desire for sex reassignment surgery or, for that matter, other, often risky, medical procedures (see, for example, Stone, 1991; Feinberg, 1993b; Hooley, 1994; Hale, 1995, p 26; Califia, 1997; Cromwell, 1999, p 23). Moreover, it conceals the fact that some transgender people have been denied access to sex reassignment surgery because their autobiography fails to conform to a medical script that, amongst other things, presumes heterosexual desire.[45] Nevertheless, an insistence on 'smallness' proved significant in that it appeared to reduce anxiety about the perceived effects of reform. A small group, perhaps, especially a 'disordered', highly marginalised and post-operative one, offers little threat to the heterosexual matrix and is therefore more readily contained. This can be contrasted with the issue of community size in the context of the parallel debates over the Acts Amendment (Sexuality Discrimination) Bill. While there was disagreement over the number of gay men and lesbians in society, a widely held view estimated the population to be approximately 10%.[46] This figure is unlikely to assuage homophobic anxiety. The contrast between transgender and homosexuality is also apparent in terms of visibility. In addition to being characterised as a 'small' group, transgender people are thought of as being programmed to disappear into society post-surgically (Kessler and McKenna, 1978). This reassuring and teological view of transgender can be juxtaposed with a view of gay men and lesbians as highly visible. This view is put by the former Attorney-General:

> The thing people find offensive are people who are 'in your face' about their sexuality. I do not go around saying I am a heterosexual. It happens to be the case; I accept that as being me. People who are homosexual can accept themselves as being homosexual. It is not a matter of having to tell everybody about it; it is a matter of their accepting that is what they are.[47]

A view of post-operative transgender people as more deserving than gay men and lesbians for the purposes of inclusion within the ambit of the West Australian Equal Opportunity Act 1984 is further cemented, and crucially so, through discourse around sex. That is to say, members of parliament sought repeatedly to distance transgender from issues of (homo)sex. That some parliamentarians sought to draw this distinction is due not simply to an attempt to distinguish gender identity from sexual desire, but rather to insulate transgender from the weight of negative representations of, particularly gay male, homosexual practice. It is to disassociate transgender from characterisations of gay men as predatory, seductive, addicted and contagious, characterisations that circulate in

---

44 See above, fn 9.

45 See above, fn 26.

46 Eg, see the Hon Ms Hodgson, Debates of the Legislative Council (WA), 17 September 1997, p 6302; the Hon G Watson, Debates of the Legislative Council (WA), 19 November 1997, p 8124; the Hon J Halden, Debates of the Legislative Council (WA), 19 November 1997, pp 8144, 8146. Cf the Hon G Smith who cited overseas studies indicating figures of between 0.9–1.4% (for gay men) and 0.4–0.9% (for lesbians), Debates of the Legislative Council (WA), 19 November 1997, p 8152.

47 The Hon P Foss, Debates of the Legislative Council (WA), 19 November 1997, p 8139.

the legislative debates surrounding the Acts Amendment (Sexuality Discrimination) Bill, and, of course, in society more generally (see, for example, Douglas, 1966; Watney, 1989; Edelman, 1989, pp 309–10; Jones, 1992; Stychin, 1995, Chapter 7). That is to say, it is views such as '[i]t is no secret that many people are voracious homosexuals and spend their time looking for young people who are vulnerable'[48] and that it is perfectly proper to consider same-sex practice to be 'immoral, improper or even disgusting',[49] that account for this political move.

Thus the Hon Mrs Holmes expressed the view that violence and discrimination against transgender people occurs 'because a person's gender status is changed ... It is not because they have a sexual predisposition towards a particular gender. Other members have mentioned, and I would like to reinforce, the fact that this Bill has nothing to do with sexual preference ... This Bill is not a matter of tolerance or homosexuality versus heterosexuality or bisexuality',[50] adding that the dilemma transgender people face arises 'through no fault of their own'.[51] This statement is of interest in a number of respects. First, the reference to fault in the context of a passage devoted to distinguishing transgender from homosexuality makes clear that homosexual behaviour remains culpable. Secondly, the view that the 'Bill has nothing to do with sexual preference' conceals as much as it reveals. While it is true that the legislation offers no protection on the basis of sexual preference, it does bear a relation to sexuality. Indeed, through recognition of sex claims, the Gender Reassignment Act 2000 necessarily inaugurates sexuality, given that sex reassignment surgery is premised on the heterosexualisation of bodies. Thirdly, the claim that violence and discrimination against transgender people occurs 'because a person's gender status is changed' and not 'because they have a sexual predisposition towards a particular gender' is somewhat problematic. While gender transgression is a significant factor in understanding violence and discrimination against transgender people, and indeed against gay men and lesbians,[52] it may be that it operates as a sign of homosexuality in both cases. In this respect, it is perhaps mistaken to assume that motivation for discrimination can be read off transgender self-identification. Indeed, there is evidence to suggest that homophobia is a significant factor in explaining violence and discrimination against transgender people (Hooley, 1996; Short, 1997; Sharpe and Moran, forthcoming). This is, perhaps, due to the relative invisibility of transgender and the cultural conflation between transgender and homosexuality that continues to persist and which is, in and of itself, a significant factor in erasing transgender. Indeed, it is precisely this cultural conflation that requires the Hon Mrs Holmes to emphasise the distinction.

What is clear, however, is that successful passage of the Gender Reassignment Bill required that this distinction be made, forcibly and repeatedly. Anxiety over proximity to homosexuality is assuaged by the fact of sex reassignment surgery. It becomes possible to

---

48 The Hon P Foss, Debates of the Legislative Council (WA), 21 March 2000, p 5216.

49 The Hon P Foss, Debates of the Legislative Council (WA), 19 November 1997, p 8128.

50 The Hon Mrs Holmes, Debates of the Legislative Assembly (WA), 24 November 1999, p 3766. See, also, the Hon ND Griffiths, Debates of the Legislative Council (WA), 26 March 1997, p 945; the Hon Ms McHale, Debates of the Legislative Assembly (WA), 24 November 1999, p 3764; and the Hon Mr Pendal, Debates of the Legislative Assembly (WA), 24 November 1999, p 3765.

51 *Ibid*, the Hon Mrs Holmes.

52 There is evidence to suggest that perpetrator readings of bodies as gay or lesbian is linked to gender transgression (see, eg, GALOP, 1991; Derbyshire, 1993; Truman, 1994; Moran, 1995; Mason, 1997).

view persons who have sacrificed genital pleasure in terms other than sexual ones, albeit that the surgical rite of passage is viewed implicitly in terms of the heterosexualisation of bodies. In other words, sanitised by surgery the post-operative body is distanced from 'sinful' and 'unnatural' gay male practice. Moreover, submission to the knife brings the body fully within the realm of medicine, where desire is translated into need, thereby undermining the autonomy of transgender people and, importantly, removing responsibility and therefore blame. However, the relationship established between transgender and homosexuality by the Gender Reassignment Act proves unstable. That is to say, the pre-/post-operative dyad instantiated cannot be relied upon to map a boundary that separates transgender from homosexuality. This is especially apparent from s 15(3) of the Act that stipulates that '[a] recognition certificate cannot be issued to a person who is married'.[53] That is to say, a married person who undergoes sex reassignment surgery cannot have her/his sex claims recognised while the marriage subsists. The provision aims, as explained earlier, to ensure that two persons designated the same sex are not married.

While the married exception provision is not peculiar to the Gender Reassignment Act, its impact is of greater significance than is the case with corresponding legislation in other Australian jurisdictions. That this is so arises out of the fact that in Western Australia, unlike other jurisdictions, the issue of a recognition certificate is the trigger for 'all that happens in the legislation'.[54] Accordingly, and in particular, the fact of married status serves to exclude post-operative transgender people from the protection of anti-discrimination law. The rationale for this outcome, which is a departure from prior Australian transgender legislative reform, is to be comprehended in terms of anxiety over homosexuality and the conflation of homosexuality with the married transgender body, and is to be situated specifically within the context of the considerable controversy generated by the Acts Amendment (Sexuality Discrimination) Bill. In other words, to have structured the Gender Reassignment legislation so that sex reassignment surgery and marital status operate as preconditions to legal recognition of sex claims, while being irrelevant to anti-discrimination law protection, as is the case in other Australian jurisdictions, would have rendered the former West Australian Liberal government's opposition to the Acts Amendment (Sexuality Discrimination) Bill more difficult to sustain. This concern is, of course, absent in the other jurisdictions that have brought transgender people within the framework of anti-discrimination legislation because without exception those frameworks extend to gay men and lesbians.[55]

Moreover, the construction of the Gender Reassignment Act serves to contain 'homosexuality' in another regard. In contrast to the anti-discrimination legislative

---

53 Gender Reassignment Act 2000 (WA), s 15(3).

54 The Hon P Foss, Debates of the Legislative Council (WA), 8 April 1997, p 1133.

55 South Australia, the Australian Capital Territory and the Northern Territory prohibit discrimination on the basis of 'sexuality' (Equal Opportunity Act 1984 (SA), s 29(1); Discrimination Act 1991 (ACT), s 7(1)(b); Anti-Discrimination Act 1992 (NT), s 19), New South Wales prohibits discrimination on the basis of 'homosexuality' (Anti-Discrimination Act 1977 (NSW), s 49ZG), Queensland prohibits discrimination on the basis of 'lawful sexual activity' (Anti-Discrimination Act 1991 (Qld), s 7) and Victoria prohibits discrimination on the basis of 'lawful sexual activity' and 'sexual orientation' (Equal Opportunity Act 1995 (Vic), s 6). For a discussion of these provisions, see Morgan, 1996 and Chapman, 1997.

frameworks of other jurisdictions, the West Australian Act contains no deeming provisions. That is to say, in other jurisdictions, as we saw in Chapter 8, a person thought to be transgender or homosexual and who is discriminated against on either basis, even though falling outside the category transgender or homosexual as legally constructed, is protected because perpetrator motivation effectively trumps inclusion within a legally constructed identity category.[56] These provisions recognise explicitly 'misrecognition' on the part of discriminators. While such 'misrecognition' might manifest itself in numerous ways an instance of it, obvious in cultural terms, and given the centrality of the pre-/post-operative dyad in the structure of the Gender Reassignment Act, revolves around homosexual/transgender conflation. In this context the absence of such provisions is perfectly consistent with the former Liberal government's concern to do nothing that might be seen as 'promoting' homosexuality.

9.3 CONCLUSION

This chapter has sought to interrogate the recent West Australian Gender Reassignment Act 2000 and, in particular, its failure to provide anti-discrimination law protection to transgender people as a whole. It has situated this failure, which it contrasted with the more comprehensive reforms of other Australian jurisdictions, in the context of major political opposition to gay and lesbian law reform. It is in this context that anxiety over non- and pre-operative transgender bodies is intensified. That is to say, in the context of political resistance to the conferral of equal rights on gay men and lesbians, a conflation of phallic female and vaginaed male bodies with homosexuality takes on special significance. In order to assuage this anxiety the legislation requires both diagnosis of transgender 'authenticity' and demonstration of a commitment to adopt the lifestyle of a member of the 'opposite' sex, a demonstration that can only be met, in the final analysis, through sex reassignment surgery. In conforming to these stipulations, transgender becomes uncoupled from homosexuality. In contrast to gay male desire, which is scripted as behavioural and hedonistic, post-operative transgender people emerge as both disabled and sacrificial.

This discursive move, which serves both to denigrate gay men and lesbians and to undermine transgender autonomy, is particularly apparent in the West Australian parliamentary debates. While the Gender Reassignment Act represents an advance in terms of transgender rights, and while it clearly represents a political compromise in order to achieve some degree of reform,[57] the styles of argumentation around

---

56 Anti-Discrimination Act 1977 (NSW), s 49ZG; Discrimination Act 1991 (ACT), s 7; Anti-Discrimination Act 1991 (Qld), s 8(c); Anti-Discrimination Act 1992 (NT), s 19; Equal Opportunity Act 1995 (Vic), s 7(2)(d). These deeming provisions while creating spaces for protection are problematic, of course, because they only do so by default. That is to say, coverage by virtue of a deeming provision occurs despite, and not because of, self-identification. Such provisions, however, do capture the reality of the discrimination dynamic. That is to say, and as we saw in Chapter 8, protection against discrimination proves to be an effect of performance and discriminating gaze rather than the 'fixed' nature of identity categories.

57 Indeed, several parliamentarians spoke of the Gender Reassignment Bill as a first step in the process of reform acknowledging that the West Australian transgender community opposed many aspects of the Bill (see the Hon Ms Warnock, Debates of the Legislative Assembly (WA), 24 November 1999, p 3763; the Hon H Hodgson, Debates of the Legislative Council (WA), 16 March 2000, p 5097; the Hon G Watson, Debates of the Legislative Council (WA), 15 March 2000, p 4995).

transgender issues raise serious concerns for future transgender and gay and lesbian law reform. That is to say, the deployment of tropes of desert, visibility and the sexual in the context of transgender law reform serves to set back the cause of gay and lesbian rights claims. Accordingly, transgender law reform emerges as an important site for future gay and lesbian political struggle. In relation to transgender people, the structure of the legislation and the surrounding parliamentary debates reveal the costs of reform. These costs are to be located in the characterisation of transgender people as 'disordered', whereby their desires are translated into needs, in the coupling of 'authenticity' with sex reassignment surgery, and in the erasure of non- and pre-operative transgender people through their conflation with homosexuality. In recognising the relationship between these effects, and the distancing of post-operative transgender bodies from homosexuality, the chapter points to both the problematic nature of identity-based politics and the, perhaps contradictory, need to embrace a broader coalitional politics for the future. Sadly, however, a more inclusive politics has not eventuated in the aftermath of these events.

9.4 POSTSCRIPT

In February 2001 the West Australian Liberal government, that had expressed, and continues to express, so much hostility toward gay and lesbian law reform, was defeated in a State election. The new Labour government appears to be committed to reform across a range of areas affecting gay men and lesbians. In March 2001 a Ministerial Committee was convened by the Attorney-General, Jim McGinty, to assist in the development of amendments to legislation to end the discrimination encountered by gay men and lesbians in the State. The committee recommended, consistent with the policies endorsed at the 1999 Australian Labour Party Conference, a series of wide ranging legislative amendments the bulk of which have been accepted by the West Australian Labour government, which plans to introduce a package of legislative and policy reforms (West Australian Government Report, 2001).[58] While proposed reform dealing with matters such as access to IVF treatment and adoption will, no doubt, prove more difficult to secure than other committee recommendations, the prospects for translating into law the bulk of the reform package are favourable, given that the Labour Party controls the lower house while the Greens, who also support the general tenor of the proposed reform, hold the balance of power in the upper house.

Interestingly, however, three of the supported recommendations are that the West Australian Equal Opportunity Act be amended so as to prohibit discrimination on the basis of sexual orientation, that the West Australian Criminal Code provide uniform ages of consent to sexual conduct, and that the preamble (the 'Foss' preamble) to the Law Reform (Decriminalisation of Sodomy) Act 1989 be repealed.[59] In other words, in these

---

58   For information regarding which recommendations were supported, deferred for further consideration or rejected see www.ministers.wa.gov.au/mcginty/Features/Ministerial Statement GayLesbianReform.pdf.

59   *Ibid*, p 35. Moreover, Recommendation 3 makes clear that discrimination on the basis of 'sexual orientation' includes 'perceived sexual orientation' and therefore protects persons against homophobia irrespective of their sexual identification.

particular respects, the package of reform serves to resuscitate the Acts Amendment (Sexuality Discrimination) Bill that lapsed with the fall of the Liberal government. Yet, a key aspect of that Bill has been ignored by the West Australian Labour Party and gay and lesbian advocacy groups in the construction of a legislative agenda. While the Acts Amendment (Sexuality Discrimination) Bill sought to prohibit discrimination on the basis of gender identity irrespective of surgical status,[60] as well as on the basis of sexual orientation, thereby extending a concern to transgender people who fall outside the ambit of the Gender Reassignment Act, the package of reform now proposed is silent on this question. In view of the fact that transgender inclusion was a stated aim of the lapsed Bill, and that the Ministerial committee received submissions from transgender groups,[61] though there is no reference to these submissions in the report, it is hard to avoid the conclusion that pre-operative transgender people have been viewed as likely to derail reform, and therefore as expendable, an unfortunate, but by no means new, political strategy (see, for example, Rubin, 1992; Nataf, 1996; Califia, 1997).

In much the same way that passage of the Gender Reassignment Act 2000 was predicated on the uncoupling of the post-operative transgender body from homosexuality, the proposed reform appears to distance a 'normalised' homosexuality from 'transgressive' pre-operative transgender bodies and practices. While it is important to recognise the need for, and the urgency of, gay and lesbian law reform in the West Australian context, as well as the 'normalising' desire of law, it is also essential to consider what the discursive effects of eventual reform might be. The passage of the Gender Reassignment legislation offers itself as a cautionary note in this respect.

---

60 The Hon Ms H Hodgson, Debates of the Legislative Council (WA), 17 September 1997, p 6304. Moreover, the exclusion of transgender people is especially curious given that the policy of the Australian Labour Party in relation to transgender people purports to support anti-discrimination law protection irrespective of sex reassignment surgery (see ND Griffiths, Debates of the Legislative Council (WA), 26 March 1997, p 945).

61 See, eg, International Foundation for Androgynous Studies Submission to the Ministerial Reform Committee (2001), esp Recommendation 2.

CHAPTER 10

CONCLUSION

The study of transgender/law relations within critical legal scholarship represents a fairly recent development. Critical legal thinking around this nascent jurisprudence offers not only to illuminate a particular history and encounter between transgender people and law. It also offers to inform thinking about law more generally and its changing regulatory strategies around bodies. Moreover, it offers to complement the broad and growing field of gender, sexuality and the law through thinking through gender/law and sexuality/law relations from a locale that in many respects represents an intersection of these two axes and sets of concerns. That is to say, thinking about gender, sexuality and the law stands to be enriched through viewing those concerns through a window, as yet still only ajar with critical legal scholarship, which opens onto a particular and contemporary site of legal trouble. With these aims in mind this book has sought to offer, for the first time, a sustained, integrated and comparative critique of transgender/law relations across common law legal cultures and legal subject matters and to situate this jurisprudence in contexts of law's relationship with medicine.

In thinking through the intersection of transgender and law in a variety of legal contexts the book has been concerned to interrogate legal reasoning as a response to transgender's troubling of the categories of sex, gender and heterosexuality. To that end, a number of common law approaches, which the book distributed across a (bio)logic/reform divide, were considered in relation to the legal determination of sex. This consideration of judicial practices of interpretation around the concept of sex was not confined to the question of designation, in the sense of locating bodies within a male/female binary, but rather extended to an analysis of the concept of sex within anti-discrimination law contexts. In thinking through legal constructions of sex the book has sought to move beyond the preoccupations of traditional legal scholarship and reform agendas. That is to say, the book does not represent another 'humanitarian' call for the legal recognition of the sex claims of post-operative transgender people. Rather, it has sought to tease out and foreground the medico-legal modes of regulation and exclusion that reform instantiates and the discursive effects thereby produced. In other words, it has considered the costs of engagements with law both for transgender people and for other groups. In short, the book has viewed transgender jurisprudence principally as a site of cultural production and contestation. For as Moran has pointed out '[e]ngagement with or intervention in the law is primarily not so much an engagement with rules and rationality but more an engagement with the dynamics of representation' (1996, p 199).

Despite differences in approach within and across legal cultures and legal subjects matters the book, in mapping this jurisprudence, has highlighted a series of continuities. In particular, a desire to reproduce the gender order proved to be a central feature of transgender jurisprudence, serving to link the repressive legal moment in the landmark English decision of *Corbett*[1] to a series of productive ones culminating in *Otahuhu*.[2] That is

---

1   *Corbett v Corbett* [1970] 2 All ER 33.
2   *Attorney-General v Otahuhu Family Court* [1995] 1 NZLR 603.

to say, the appeal to (bio)logic, as fidelity to science, in *Corbett* proves to be a rhetorical move masking a genitocentric logic that coincides with the reformist fantasy of *psychological and anatomical harmony*. The reproduction of the gender order across legal approach is also apparent in phallocentric and performativist assumptions law produces around bodies. In particular, the gender order is bolstered by medico-legal constructions of the 'passing' woman, the deployment of the active/passive dichotomy, the privileging of male-to-female capacity for penetrative heterosexual intercourse in legal determinations of sex, and law's differential treatment of male-to-female and female-to-male transgender bodies. Another key point of unity proved to be the homophobia of law that manifested itself primarily through a concern to privilege, and preserve a space for, 'natural' heterosexual intercourse. While an evident tension existing between these two related legal desires is perhaps resolved in some reform decisions around marriage, it is clear that any such 'resolution' does not serve to detach transgender jurisprudence from the homophobia of law which continues to operate as a structuring principle. Indeed, the book has placed particular emphasis on law's conflation of transgender and homosexuality, a conflation that has its modern roots in late 19th century sexological science. This conflation and the anxiety that lies behind it was seen to manifest itself in terms of judicial analysis of pre-operative sexual practice, gender performance, post-operative heterosexual capacity, non-disclosure of transgender status and bodily aesthetics. It is perhaps at the intersection of desire to reproduce the gender order and desire to insulate that order from the mark of homosexuality that legal constructions of sex are to be comprehended. That is to say, it is in the context of these legal desires, and frequently in the tension existing between them, that (non)sense is to be made of transgender jurisprudence.

The 'satiation' of these desires and/or 'resolution' of this tension has, in moments of reform, led to an insistence on sex (genital) reassignment surgery. Indeed, even in those few decisions that ostensibly abandon anatomical considerations, and which have been emphatically overturned on appeal, an insistence that a 'wrong body' story be voiced in the sense of willingness and desire to undertake surgery has proved crucial. This not only proves to be the case in relation to the re-sexing of bodies as male/female for the purposes of birth certificates, criminal law, social security law or marriage. It would also appear in the main to account for the inclusion of transgender people within the protected anti-discrimination law category sex. That is to say, judicial and legislative positioning of transgender bodies within the anti-discrimination law category sex has tended to occur in relation to the actuality, or, at the very least, the imminence, of sex reassignment surgery. In this regard, and despite the possibility of more expansive readings of the category within anti-discrimination law contexts, sex continues to be equated with the male/female dyad. In all of these respects then, and contrary to the view that the maintenance of gender is occurring through its detachment from sex (Shapiro, 1991, p 272), what we are witnessing in transgender jurisprudence is a process whereby one notion or fantasy of sex (Butler, 1993, p 6) is being replaced by another. That is to say, an understanding of gender as edifice to sex as 'foundation' is one replicated through reform.

However, in other crucial respects Shapiro's claim proves accurate. That is to say, and though confined to contexts of anti-discrimination law, there is a clear sense in which law's regulatory practices no longer require sex. We saw this development in Chapter 7 in the context of United States federal jurisprudence that has interpreted Title VII sex to mean gender. Here legal protection flows not from a person's sex, whether grounded in (bio)logic or anatomy, but rather from the fact of gender transgression. That is to say, it is the very 'failure' of gender that grounds rights claims. While the coding of particular forms of gender performance as 'failed' might be viewed as reproducing the gender order through inevitable comparison to 'successful' performance, it is clear from the decision in *Schwenk*[3] that the figure of legal comparator does not serve to reinscribe ontology. Indeed, the comparator does not reflect, or indeed bear any necessary relation to, the sex of the victim. Rather, the analysis in *Schwenk* would appear to apply to a (bio)logically female victim, including a (female-to-male) transgender man. That is to say, a (bio)logical female would appear to be covered if discriminated against because she was believed to be a man who 'failed' to act like one. This legal move, which disrupts legal understandings of sex/gender relations apparent in the case law considered in Chapters 3–6, and which resonate more widely in cultural terms, is present in another regard. In Chapter 7 it was noted that even within the 'sex as biology' approach, which refuses to countenance transgender sex claims, a space for protection is nevertheless created. That is to say, United States Federal Courts espousing a (bio)logical approach to the interpretation of Title VII sex have made clear that the protected category does include discrimination against a (male-to-female) transgender woman thought to be female.

This theme was pursued in Chapter 8 in the Australian context, where a number of anti-discrimination legislative frameworks were seen to produce similar effects through a series of deeming provisions. These developments, which are perhaps to be understood as normalising strategies around gender, strategies which incite (male-to-female) transgender women to perform femininity, and (female-to-male) transgender men to perform masculinity, serve once again to redirect attention away from ontological considerations. Moreover, while, and precisely because, legal protection occurs by means of default, that is, through the appearance of being a member of a category from which one is legally excluded, the effect is to call into question the priority of sex, however it is to be conceptualised. In this regard, recognition of a legal claim serves to disrupt the primacy of sex as well as demonstrating the imitative structure of gender (Butler, 1993, p 137). These shifts within anti-discrimination law from legal ontology to performance and gaze perhaps offer an insight into changing patterns of legal regulation around bodies. In any event, they serve to challenge rights critiques that occupy themselves only with the ossifying effects of rights and point to a need to rethink critically the relationship between law, rights and subjectivity. In terms of political activism, it may be that deeming provisions, which exist across a range of protected categories, might be exploited. That is to say, activists might, through repetitive practices of 'imitating' the 'real', seek to disrupt 'fixed' categories and implicate law in precisely this effect.

Of course, anti-discrimination law developments are not alone in disrupting sex/gender relations or the ontological pretensions of law. As we saw in Chapter 4, the shift from (bio)logic to the legal test of *psychological and anatomical harmony* cannot be reduced to the recuperation of the gender order, as a 'safety valve in the service of dominant ideology' (Epstein, 1995, p 9). Rather, and because transgender 'exceeds and refuses that ideology' (Epstein, 1995, p 9) law's attempt to deploy transgender bodies as a

---

3   *Schwenk v Hartford* 204 F 3d 1187 (2000).

heterosexual prop in the service of the gender order meets with only partial success. Indeed, the test of *psychological and anatomical harmony*, and its endless citation within reform jurisprudence, serves to destabilise gender through uncoupling it from its anchor in (bio)logical sex. That is to say, while law continues to tie gender to a notion of sex as foundation, the shift to anatomy introduces malleability. Crucially, it serves to demonstrate the radically performative nature of anatomical sex, a fact that might be redeployed in other sexual political contexts. Further, possibilities for disrupting dominant understandings of sex are suggested by legal articulation of a test of *psychological, social and cultural harmony*. Moreover, this test, and uncertainty within reform jurisprudence over whether the determination of sex involves a question of law or fact, offer to problematise not only the content of sex, but the place from which decision-making is to proceed. In another regard, reform jurisprudence serves to 'denaturalise' heterosexuality through uncoupling it from its (bio)logical referent. Conversely, a legal view of sex reassignment surgery as an orchestration of one-way sexual traffic has led to legal insistence that homosexuality remain grounded in (bio)logical sex. This differential deployment of psychology and biology across the hetero/homo divide calls into question the priority of heterosexuality while simultaneously 'naturalising' homosexuality. In this strange twist of legal reasoning, it is homosexuality that becomes the very ground of sex, its most concrete materialisation. While this move is problematic, in that it erases non-heterosexual transgender desire, it offers itself as legally produced counter-discourse to a legal view of gay men and lesbians as the embodiment of the 'unnatural'.

However, while transgender jurisprudence proves capable of disrupting precisely that which it seeks to bolster, and across a range of legal subject matters, it would seem that law's disruptive effects are not distributed evenly. Thus while recent legal developments within anti-discrimination law call into question law's commitment to ontology as a strategy of regulating transgender and other bodies, this does not prove to be the case in other areas that are concerned solely with sex designation. For while concerns over transgender 'authenticity' are apparent in anti-discrimination law contexts, they have been especially pronounced in relation to legal determination of male/female status for purposes such as amendment of birth certificates, social security benefits, criminal prosecution and, most notably, marriage. That is to say, while law deploys both sides of the act/identity dyad across legal subject matters as regulatory strategies, the identity side of that distinction would appear to receive more attention in contexts of sex designation. Thus, and in contrast to anti-discrimination law, some reform judgments in these areas, as well as law reform strategies mindful of law's concerns, have pursued inquiry into the possibility of a (bio)logical basis for transgender identity. More consistently, a concern over transgender 'authenticity' has manifested itself in judicial mapping of pre-surgical transgender histories.

This preoccupation with the past is interesting and revealing. In contrast to medicine that, in an era of gender dysphoria, might explain interrogation of the past by reference to a concern for future well-being post-surgically, legal preoccupation with the past cannot be explained through a relationship of correlation between the past and the future. Rather, law's concern to excavate the past can only be accounted for in terms of anxiety about transgender 'authenticity', thereby revealing a preference for the *discovery story of transsexuality* (King, 1993, pp 45, 63). The fact that this knowledge has such cultural purchase in legal discourse, especially around the determination of male/female status, in an era of gender dysphoria, with which it is frequently confused, is to be accounted for by the relationship between this knowledge and legal desire. That is to say, it is understandings of pleasure, identity and desire that lie at the heart of this medical knowledge that inform its use. Specifically, it is the emphasis on the establishment of (trans)gender identity prior to adolescence and on heterosexual desire, in the psychological sense, after that point, that produce this legal practice. For it is the presence of these fragments of transgender histories that serve to assuage legal anxiety over a perception of proximity to the homosexual body. By the same token, their endless repetition within legal discourse serves to consolidate a view of legally accommodated transgender and homosexuality as incommensurable. However, it should not be thought that the constitution of a distinction between the homosexual and post-operative transgender people able to provide appropriate transgender narrativisation proves stable within reform jurisprudence. Thus, for example, in the marriage context non-disclosure of transgender status serves to problematise law's commitment to that distinction.

Indeed, while homophobic anxiety is not absent in anti-discrimination law contexts, as we saw in Chapter 7, and perhaps most vividly in Chapter 9, it tends to be most intense, and most consistently so, around law's re-sexing practices, particularly at the site of marriage. Indeed, as we saw in Chapters 5 and 6, the transgender/marriage relation serves to foreground the homophobia of law more than any other area of transgender jurisprudence, and does so in multiple ways. Accordingly, within transgender jurisprudence it is legal reasoning around marriage that most constrains, and demonstrates the need for, greater links between transgender and gay and lesbian political activism. Interestingly, however, transgender marriage jurisprudence, which operates as the most concrete 'limit' to future dissolution of the pre-/post-operative dyad and which represents the most notable challenge to feminist and gay and lesbian interests, produces, and alludes to, possibilities for challenging this primary institution of heterosexuality over and above those generated by the reform story of *psychological and anatomical harmony*.

Thus, while even the most 'progressive' marriage decisions have insisted on building the moment of reform around the pre-/post-operative dyad, the reasoning of Ellis J in *Otahuhu* serves to undermine a view of marriage as being of a different order than same-sex relationships or relationships involving phallic women and vaginaed men, which, of course, law readily conflates with homosexuality. In the body of reform jurisprudence prior to *Otahuhu* and stemming from *MT v JT*[4] the courts have proved unable to re-sex bodies or even to imagine marital union other than in terms of the production of heterosexual capacity. Indeed, such capacity is viewed implicitly, and sometimes explicitly, as conferring meaning upon the practice of sex reassignment surgery. In contrast to this analysis, however, Ellis J insisted that the parties to a marriage need not 'prove that each can function sexually' noting that 'there are many forms of sexual expression possible without penetrative sexual intercourse'. In this moment we witness a formal shift in legal concern over the body from function to aesthetics. This privileging of law's bodily aesthetics in *Otahuhu* suggests perhaps that sex reassignment surgery functions for law not so much to guarantee penile-vaginal penetration within the martial union than to assuage legal anxiety over the horror of the 'monstrous' body and the

---

4   *MT v JT* 355 A 2d 204 (1976).

homosexual sign it emits in the legal imaginary. That is to say, law seeks not so much to ensure that particular sexual practices occur within marriage but rather seeks to ensure that other sexual practices do not. Accordingly, and for this reason, this moment of more 'radical' reform in *Otahuhu* continues to ensure the splitting of heterosexual transgender from gay and lesbian interests.

Nevertheless, the de-emphasis of sexual capacity within marriage might be exploited by pre- and non-surgical transgender people to contest the logic of a requirement of sex reassignment surgery for the purposes of legal recognition both in relation to marriage and other legal subject matters. Moreover, gay men and lesbians might deploy this development in transgender jurisprudence in legal and political arguments around marriage. That is to say, and despite the insulation of marriage from homosexuality in *Otahuhu*, the decision might be viewed as removing yet another barrier or argument for excluding gay men and lesbians from the institution of marriage. Another strategy for disrupting hegemonic understandings of marriage suggested by the case law, and noted by Coombes (1998, p 263), is to encourage gay and lesbian transgender people, irrespective of surgical status and who have not been granted legal recognition, to marry, as they are permitted to do under existing laws, thereby drawing attention to the diversity of people, bodies and sexual practices already existing within marriage. It is, of course, precisely anxiety over this prospect that led Ellis J to consolidate his view around legal recognition in *Otahuhu*.

However, it is not my aim to tell activists what strategies to use. That is a matter for particular groups making decisions in specific places and at particular times and always in circumstances of constraint. Rather, the book has highlighted gaps, inconsistencies and contradictions produced by legal reasoning that seeks to contain unruly bodies that threaten a particular understanding and constellation of sex, gender and heterosexuality. These gaps offer transgender people and other groups opportunities for resisting and rearticulating legal understandings of their bodies and practices. However, in exploiting legal reasoning within transgender jurisprudence it should not be thought that there is a single point around which resistance might rally. On the contrary, there appear to be multiple points within transgender jurisprudence from which challenge might occur. Nor is there necessarily any common thread to such challenges. Indeed, some forms of rearticulation might contradict others. For example, and as already noted, there is clearly a tension in the possibility of exploiting law's 'naturalisation' of gay and lesbian desire on the one hand and the need to affirm transgender non-heterosexualities on the other. Again strategies developed around a legal shift from a concern with ontology to performance and gaze evident within some anti-discrimination law contexts would clearly be of a different order to a strategy that sought to capitalise on law's production of homosexuality as the most concrete materialisation of sex. Nevertheless, the deployment of contradictory legal arguments might be considered strategically useful, given that transgender jurisprudence is founded on such contradictions, and indeed it is within these very contradictions that opportunities for resistance are constituted. In other words, to counter law's illogic and irrationality with the language of reason is not necessarily the most productive way to proceed, especially at the level of discursive effects. While a great deal more critical legal thinking needs to be done around transgender/law relations, I hope this book has made an important contribution to that project and that it assists activists and theorists alike in contesting legal representations of transgender, and other, bodies, practices and desires as 'unimaginable', 'incoherent' and 'impossible'.

BIBLIOGRAPHY

A

Abraham, K, 'Uber Hysterische Traumzustande' (1910) 2 Jahrbuch fur Psych-anal Forsch, cited by Ellis, H, 'Sexual Inversion', in *Studies in the Psychology of Sex*, 1936, New York: Random House, Vol 2, Part 1, p 16

Ahmed, S, 'Animated Borders: Skin, Colour and Tanning', in Shildrick, M and Price, J (eds), *Vital Signs: Feminist Reconfigurations of the Bio/Logical Body*, 1998, Edinburgh: Edinburgh UP, pp 45–65

American Psychiatric Association (APA), *Diagnostic and Statistics Manual of Mental Disorders*, revised 3rd edn, 1980, Washington, DC: APA

American Psychiatric Association (APA), *Diagnostic and Statistical Manual of Mental Disorders*, 4th edn, 1995, Washington, DC: APA

Andrews, J, 'Transsexual Rights in the United Kingdom' (1991) 16 EL Rev, pp 262–66

Armstrong, CN and Walton, T, 'Transsexual Metamorphoses' (1992) 142 NLJ 96

B

Bailey-Harris, R, 'Recent Cases in Family Law – Decree of Nullity of Marriage of True Hermaphrodite Who Has Undergone Sex-Change Surgery' (1979) 53 ALJ 660

Bailey-Harris, R, 'Sex Change in the Criminal Law and Beyond' (1989) 13 Crim LJ 353

Bates, F, 'When is a Wife ...?' (1993) 7 Australian Journal of Family Law 274–82

Beaumont Society, *A Study of Tranvestism and Allied States in the Family and Society*, 1975, Conference Report: Beaumont Society

Beaumont Society, *Beaumont Society Constitution*, 1983, London: Beaumont Society

de Beauvoir, S, *The Second Sex*, 1953, New York: Bantam

Bell, V, 'Beyond the "Thorny Question": Feminism, Foucault and the Desexualisation of Rape' (1991) 19 International Journal of the Sociology of Law 83–100

Benjamin, H, 'Transvestism and Transsexualism' (1953) 7 International Journal of Sexology 12–14

Benjamin, H, 'Nature and Management of Transsexualism' (1964) 72 Western Journal of Obstetrics and Gynecology 105–11

Benjamin, H, *The Transsexual Phenomenon*, 1966, New York: Julian Press

Beger, N, 'Queer Readings of Europe: Gender Identity, Sexual Orientation and the (Im)Potency of Rights Politics at the European Court of Justice' (2000) 9 Social and Legal Studies: An International Journal 249–70

Billings, DB and Urban, T, 'The Socio-Medical Construction of Transsexuality: An Interpretation and Critique' (1982) 29 Social Problems 266–82

Blanchard, R, 'Research Methods for the Typological Study of Gender Disorders in Males', in Steiner, BW, *Gender Dysphoria: Development, Research, Management*, 1985, New York and London: Plenum, pp 227–57

Blanchard, R, Clemmensen, BA and Steiner, B, 'Heterosexual and Homosexual Gender Dysphoria' (1987) 16 Archives of Sexual Behavior 139–52

Blanchard, R, 'The Classification and Labeling of Nonhomosexual Gender Dysphorias' (1989) 18 Archives of Sexual Behavior 315–34

Blanchard, R, Steiner, B, Clemmensen, LH and Dickey, R, 'Prediction of Regrets in Post-Operative Transsexuals' (1989) 34 Canadian Journal of Psychiatry 43

Bloch, I, *The Sexual Life of Our Time in its Relation to Modern Civilization*, 1908, New York: Allied Book Company

Bloch, I, *Sexual Life in England*, 1965, London: Corgi

Blumer, D, 'Transsexualism, Sexual Dysfunction and Temporal Lobe Disorder', in Green, R and Money, J, *Transsexualism and Sex Reassignment*, 1969, Baltimore: John Hopkins

Bolin, A, *In Search of Eve: Transsexual Rites of Passage*, 1988, South Hadley, MA: Bergin & Garvey

Bolin, A, 'Transcending and Transgendering: Male-to-Female Transsexuals, Dichotomy and Diversity', in Herdt, G (ed), *Third Sex Third Gender: Beyond Sexual Dimorphism in Culture and History*, 1996, New York: Zone Books, pp 447–85

Booth, D, 'Nietzsche on the Subject as Multiplicity' (1985) 18 Man and World: International Philosophical Rev 121–46

Bornstein, K, *Gender Outlaw: On Men, Women and the Rest of Us*, 1994, New York: Routledge

Boswell, H, 'The Transgender Alternative' (1991) 59 TV/TS Tapestry Journal 31–33

Boswell, J, *Christianity, Social Tolerance and Homosexuality*, 1980, Chicago, Illinois: Chicago UP

Bourke, J, 'Transsexualism – The Legal, Psychological and Medical Consequences of Sex Reassignment Surgery' (1994) 6(2) Current Issues in Criminal Justice 275–89

Bray, A, *Homosexuality in Renaissance England*, 1982, London: Gay Men's Press

Breedlove, SM, 'Another Important Organ' (1995) 378 Nature 15–16

Bristow, J, *Sexuality*, 1997, London and New York: Routledge

Bromley, PM, *Family Law*, 6th edn, 1981, London: Butterworths

Bruce-Pratt, M, *S/He*, 1995, Ithaca, New York: Firebrand

Bullough, VL, 'Transsexualism in History' (1975) 4 Arch Sex Behavior 561–71

Bullough, VL, *Sexual Variance in Society and History*, 1976, Chicago, Illinois: Chicago UP

Bullough, VL and Bullough, B, *Crossdressing, Sex and Gender*, 1993, Pennsylvania: University of Pennsylvania Press

Bumiller, K, *The Civil Rights Society: The Social Construction of Victims*, 1988, Baltimore: John Hopkins

Butler, J, 'Imitation and Gender Insubordination', in Fuss, D, *Inside/Out: Lesbian Theories, Gay Theories*, 1991, London: Routledge, pp 13–31

Butler, J, *Bodies That Matter: On the Discursive Limits of 'Sex'*, 1993, New York and London: Routledge

C

Cain, P, 'Stories from the Gender Garden: Transsexuals and Anti-Discrimination Law' (1998) 75 Denver UL Rev 1321–59

Califia, P, *The Politics of Transgenderism*, 1997, San Francisco: Cleis

Case, MAC, 'Disaggregating Gender from Sex and Sexual Orientation: The Effeminate Man in the Law and Feminist Jurisprudence' (1995) 105 Yale LJ 1

Casey, WC, 'Transsexual Lesbians', paper presented at the meeting of the Harry Benjamin International Gender Dysphoria Association, 4–8 March 1981, Lake Tahoe, Nevada

Casper, JL, *Vierteljahrsschrift fur Gerichliche und Offentliche Medizin*, 1852, Berlin: August Hirschwald, Vol 1 (reprinted in Hohmann, JS (ed), *Der Unterdruckte Sexus*, 1977, Berlin: Andreas Achenbach Lollar, pp 239–70)

Cauldwell, D, '*Psychopathia Transsexualis*' (1949) 16 Sexology 274–80

Chapman, A, 'Sexuality and Workplace Oppression' (1995) 20 Melbourne UL Rev 311–49

Chapman, A, 'The Messages of Subordination Contained in Australian Anti-Discrimination Statutes', in Mason, G and Tomsen, S (eds), *Homophobic Violence*, 1997, Sydney: Hawkins, pp 58–76

Chapman, A and Mason, G, 'Women, Sexual Preference and Discrimination Law: A Case Study of the NSW Jurisdiction' (1999) 21 Sydney L Rev 525–66

Charcot, JM and Magnan, V, 'Inversion du Sens Genital' (1882) 3 Archives de Neurologie 53–60

Chase, C, 'Hermaphrodites with Attitude: Mapping the Emergence of Intersex Political Activism' (1998) 4 GLQ: A Journal of Lesbian and Gay Studies 189–211

Chauncey, G, 'From Sexual Inversion to Homosexuality: Medicine and the Changing Conceptualization of Female Deviance' (1982–83) 58/59 Salmagundi 114–46

Clare, D and Tully, B, 'Transhomosexuality or the Dissociation of Sexual Orientation and Sex Object Choice' (1989) 18 Archives of Sexual Behavior 531–36

Cole, CL and Birrell, S, 'Double Fault: Renee Richards and the Construction and Naturalization of Difference' (1990) 7 Sociology of Sport Journal 1–21

Coleman, E and Bockting, W, 'Heterosexual Prior to Sex Reassignment – Homosexual Afterwards: A Case Study of a Female-to-Male Transsexual' (1988) 12 Journal of Psychology and Human Sexuality 69–82

Collier, R, *Masculinity, Law and the Family*, 1995, London: Routledge

Commission for Equal Opportunity (Western Australia), *Discrimination on the Basis of Sexual Orientation*, 1994, Perth, WA: Commission for Equal Opportunity

Coombes, M, 'Queer Matters: Emerging Issues in Sexual Orientation Law: Sexual Dis-Orientation: Transgender People and Same-Sex Marriage' (1998) 8 UCLA Women's LJ 219

Cossey, C, *My Story*, 1992, Winchester, Mass: Faber

Cover, R, 'Violence and the Word' (1986) 95 Yale LJ 1601

Cox, C, *The Enigma of the Age: The Strange Story of the Chevalier d'Eon*, 1966, London: Longmans, Green and Company

Crenshaw, K, 'Demarginalizing the Intersection of Race and Sex' (1989) U Chi Legal F 139

Crenshaw, K, 'Mapping the Margins: Intersectionality, Identity Politics, and Violence Against Women of Color', in Crenshaw, K, Gotanda, N, Peller, G and Thoma, K (eds), *Critical Race Theory: The Key Writings that Formed the Movement*, 1995, New York: New Press, pp 357–83

Cretney, SM and Masson, JM, *Principles of Family Law*, 6th edn, 1997, London: Sweet & Maxwell

Cromwell, J, *Transmen and FTMs: Identities, Bodies, Genders & Sexualities*, 1999, Chicago, Illinois: Chicago UP

Currah, P and Minter, S, *Transgender Equality: A Handbook for Activists and Policymakers*, 2000, New York: National Center for Lesbian Rights and National Lesbian and Gay Task Force (2000a)

Currah, P and Minter, S, 'Unprincipled Exclusions: The Struggle to Achieve Judicial and Legislative Equality for Transgender People' (2000) 7 William and Mary Journal of Women and the Law 37 (2000b)

D

D'Andrade, RG, 'Sex Differences and Cultural Institutions', in Maccoby, EE (ed), *The Development of Sex Differences*, 1966, Stanford: Stanford UP, pp 174–204

David, ES, 'The Law and Transsexualism: A Faltering Response to a Conceptual Dilemma' (1975) 7 Connecticut L Rev 288

Davenport-Hines, R, *Sex, Death and Punishment*, 1990, London: W Collins

Denny, D, *Dealing with Your Feelings*, 1991, Decater, GA: Aegis

Denny, D, 'The Politics of Diagnosis and a Diagnosis of Politics: The University-Affiliated Gender Clinics, and How they Failed to Meet the Needs of Transsexual People' (1992) Chrysalis Quarterly 9

Denny, D, 'In Search of the "True" Transsexual' (1996) 2 The Journal of Transgressive Gender Identities 39–44

Denny, D, *Current Concepts in Transgender Identity*, 1998, New York: Garland

Denny, D, and Roberts, J, 'Results of a Questionnaire on the Standards of Care of the Harry Benjamin International Gender Dysphoria Association', in Bullough, B, Bullough, V and Elias, J (eds), *Gender Blending*, 1997, New York: Prometheus, pp 320–36

Derbyshire, P, *Insufficient Force? The Policing of Homophobic Violence in the London Borough of Islington*, 1993, London: GALOP/Islington Safer Cities Project

Derrida, J, 'La Loi Du Genre/The Law of Genre', Ronell, A (trans) (1980) 7 Glyph 176 (French); 202 (English)

Devor, H, *FTM: Female-to-Male Transsexuals in Society*, 1997, Bloomington and Indianapolis: Indiana UP

Dewar, J, 'Transsexualism and Marriage' (1985) 15 Kingston L Rev 58

Dickens, C, *The Adventures of Oliver Twist*, 1892, London: MacMillan

Dickey, A, *Family Law*, 3rd edn, 1997, Sydney: LBC

Dollimore, J, *Death, Desire and Loss in Western Culture*, 1999, London: Penguin

Douglas, M, *Purity and Danger: An Analysis of Concepts of Pollution and Taboo*, 1966, London: Routledge

Duncan, S, 'Law's Sexual Discipline: Visibility, Violence, and Consent' (1995) 22 Journal of Law and Society 326–52

E

Edelman, L, 'The Plague of Discourse: Politics, Literary Theory, and AIDS' (1989) 88 South Atlantic Quarterly 301

Eichler, M, *The Double Standard: A Feminist Critique of Feminist Social Sciences*, 1980, London: Croom Helm

Ellis, H, 'Sexual-Aesthetic Inversion' (1913) 34 Alienist and Neurologist 156

Ellis, H, 'Sexual Inversion', in Ellis, H, *Studies in the Psychology of Sex*, 1936, New York: Random House, Vol 2, Part 1 (1936a)

Ellis, H, 'Eonism', in Ellis, H, *Studies in the Psychology of Sex*, 1936, New York: Random House, Vol 2, Part 2, pp 1–120 (1936b)

Epstein, J, *Altered Conditions: Disease, Medicine and Storytelling*, 1995, London and New York: Routledge

Epstein, J, and Straub, K, *Body Guards: The Cultural Politics of Gender Ambiguity*, 1991, London: Routledge

F

Feinberg, L, *Transgender Liberation: A Movement Whose Time Has Come*, 1992, New York: World View Forum

Feinberg, L, 'The Life and Times of a Gender Outlaw: An Interview with Leslie Feinberg' (1993) 1 TransSisters: The Journal of Transsexual Feminism 4 (1993a)

Feinberg, L, *Stone Butch Blues*, 1993, Ithaca, New York: Firebrand (1993b)

Feinberg, L, *Transgender Warriors: Making History from Joan of Arc to RuPaul*, 1996, Boston: Beacon

Feinbloom, DH, Fleming, M, Kijewski, V and Schulter, M, 'Lesbian/Feminist Orientation among Male-to-Female Transsexuals' (1976) 2 Journal of Homosexuality 59–71

Fere, C, *L'instinct Sexuel: Evolution et Dissolution*, 1899, Paris: Felix Alcan

Finlay, HA, 'Sexual Identity and the Law of Nullity' (1980) 54 ALJ 115

Finlay, HA, 'Transsexuals, Sex Change Operations and the Chromosome Test: *Corbett v Corbett* (1971) Not followed' (1989) 19 University of Western Australia L Rev 152

Finlay, HA, *Transsexualism in a Modern State: Options for Reform*, 1995, privately printed by the author, from whom copies can be obtained by writing to 122 Nelson Road, Sandy Bay, Tasmania, Australia 7005

Finlay, HA, 'Legal Recognition of Transsexuals in Australia' (1996) 12 Journal of Contemporary Health Law and Policy 503–33

Finlay, HA and Walters, WAW, *Sex Change, Medical and Legal Aspects of Sex Assignment*, 1988, Box Hill: HA Finlay

Fisk, N, 'Gender Dysphoria Syndrome: The How, What and Why of a Disease', in Laub, DR and Gandy, P, *Proceedings of the Second International Symposium on Gender Dysphoria Syndrome*, 1973, Stanford, CA: University Medical Center, pp 7–14

Fisk, N, 'Five Spectacular Results' (1978) 7 Archives of Sexual Behavior 351–69

Fleming, M, MacGowan, B and Costos, D, 'The Dyadic Adjustment of Female-to-Male Transsexuals' (1985) 14 Archives of Sexual Behavior 47–55

Flynn, T, 'Transforming the Debate: Why We Need to Include Transgender Rights in the Struggles for Sex and Sexual Orientation Equality' (2001) 101 Columbia L Rev 392

Forbes, M, 'Law Reforms to Tackle Prejudice' (1995) *Melbourne Age*, 23 April

Forel, AH, *Die Sexuelle Frage: Eine Naturwissenschaftliche, Psychologische, Hygienische und Soziologiscche Studie fur Gebildete*, 1905, Munich: E Reinhardt

Foucault, M, *Herculine Barbin: Being the Recently Discovered Memoirs of a Nineteenth Century French Hermaphrodite*, McDougall, R (trans), 1980, New York: Pantheon

Foucault, M, *The History of Sexuality*, Hurley, R (trans), London: Penguin, Vol 1: An Introduction (1981a)

Foucault, M, 'The Order of Discourse', in Young, R (ed), *Untying the Text*, 1981, London: Routledge, pp 48–78 (1981b)

Foucault, M, 'The Subject and Power', in Dreyfus, H and Rabinow, P (eds), *Michel Foucault: Beyond Structuralism and Hermeneutics*, 1982, Chicago, Illinois: Chicago UP, pp 208–26

Franke, KM, 'The Central Mistake of Sex Discrimination Law: The Disaggregation of Sex from Gender' (1995) 144 University of Pennsylvania L Rev 1

Franke, KM, 'Current Issues in Lesbian, Gay, Bisexual and Transgender Law' (1999) 27 Fordham Urban LJ 279

Fraser, D, 'Father Knows Best: Transgressive Sexualities (?) and the Rule of Law' (1995) 7 Current Issues in Criminal Justice 82–7

Fraser, K, O'Reilly, MJJ and Rintoul, JR, 'Hermaphrodites Verus, with Report of a Case' (1966) 1 Medical Journal of Australia 1003

Freud, S, *Three Essays on the Theory of Sexuality*, 1962, Strachey, J *et al* (trans), New York: Basic Books

Freud, S, '"Femininity", in New Introductory Lectures on Psycho-Analysis', in Strachey, J (ed), *The Standard Edition of the Complete Psychological Works of Sigmund Freud*, 1964, London: The Hogarth Press and The Institute for Psycho-Analysis (1964a)

Freud, S, 'Psycho-Analytic Notes Upon an Autobiographical Account of a Case of Paranoia (Dementia Paranoides)', in Strachey, J (ed), *The Standard Edition of the Complete Psychological Works of Sigmund Freud*, 1964, London: The Hogarth Press and the Institute for Psycho-Analysis (1964b)

Freund, K, Langevin, R, Zajac, Y, Steiner, B and Zajac, A, 'The Transsexual Syndrome in Homosexual Males' (1974) 158 Journal of Nerv Ment Dis 145–53

Friedlander, B, *Renaissance des Eros Uranios*, 1904, Berlin: Verlag Renaissance

Fuss, D, *Inside/Out: Lesbian Theories, Gay Theories*, 1991, London: Routledge

G

GALOP, *Survey on Homophobic Violence and Harassment*, 1991, London: GALOP

Garber, M, 'Spare Parts: The Surgical Construction of Gender' (1989) 1 Differences: A Journal of Feminist Cultural Studies 137–59

Garber, M, *Vested Interests: Cross-Dressing and Cultural Anxiety*, 1993, London: Penguin

GenderPAC, *The First National Survey of Transgender Violence*, 1997, www.gpac.org/violence/HateCrimeSurvey97

Goffman, E, *The Presentation of Self in Everyday Life*, 1959, New York: Doubleday

Gooren, LJG, Zhou, JN, Hofman, MA and Swaab, DF, 'A Sex Difference in the Human Brain and its Relation to Transsexuality' (1995) 378 Nature 68–70

Gould, M, 'Sex, Gender and the Need for Legal Clarity: The Case of Transsexualism' (1979) 13 Valparaiso UL Rev 423–50

Graham, JJ, 'Transsexualism and the Capacity to Enter Marriage' (1980) 41 The Jurist 117–54

Green, D, 'Transsexualism and Marriage' (1970) 120 NLJ 210

Green, J, *Investigation into Discrimination Against Transgender People*, 1994, A Report by the Human Rights Commission, City and County of San Francisco, www.ci.sf.ca.us/sfhumanrights/lg_info.htm

Green, R, 'Mythological, Historical and Cross-Cultural Aspects of Transsexualism', in Green, R and Money, R, *Transsexualism and Sex Reassignment*, 1969, Baltimore: John Hopkins, pp 13–22 (1969a)

Green, R, 'Attitudes Toward Transsexualism and Sex-Reassignment Procedures', in Green, R and Money, J, *Transsexualism and Sex Reassignment*, 1969, Baltimore: John Hopkins, pp 235–42 (1969b)

Green, R, *Sexual Identity Conflict in Children and Adults*, 1974, New York: Basic Books

Green, R, 'Spelling "Relief" for Transsexuals: Employment Discrimination and the Criteria of Sex' (1985) 4 Yale Law & Policy Rev 125–40

Green, R and Fleming, DT, 'Transsexual Surgery Follow-Up: Status in the 1990s' (1990) 1 Annual Review of Sex Research 163–74

Green, R and Money, J, *Transsexualism and Sex Reassignment*, 1969, Baltimore: John Hopkins

Greenberg, DF, 'The Medicalization of Homosexuality', in Greenberg, DF, *The Construction of Modern Homosexuality*, 1988, Chicago, Illinois: Chicago UP, Chapter 9

Griggs, C, *S/he: Changing Sex and Changing Genders*, 1998, Oxford and New York: Berg

Gutheil, E, 'An Analysis of a Case of Transvestism', in Stekel, W, *Sexual Aberrations: The Phenomenon of Fetishism in Relation to Sex*, 1922, authorised English version from the first German edition by Parker, S, 1930, New York: Liveright, pp 281–318

H

Hale, JC, 'Transgender Strategies for Refusing Gender', presented at the Society for Women in Philosophy, Pacific Division, 20 May 1995, Los Angeles

Hasson, R, 'What's Your Favourite Right? The Charter and Income Maintenance Legislation' (1989) 5 Journal of Law and Social Policy 1

Hastings, DW, 'Inauguration of a Research Project on Transsexualism in a University Medical Center', in Green, R and Money, J, *Transsexualism and Sex Reassignment*, 1969, Baltimore: John Hopkins, pp 243–51

Hekma, G, 'A Female Soul in a Male Body: Sexual Inversion as Gender Inversion in Nineteenth-Century Sexology', in Herdt, G, *Third Sex Third Gender: Beyond Sexual Dimorphism in Culture and History*, 1996, New York: Zone Books, pp 213–40

Herdt, G (ed), *Third Sex Third Gender: Beyond Sexual Dimorphism in Culture and History*, 1996, New York: Zone Books

Herman, D, *Rights of Passage: Struggles for Lesbian and Gay Legal Equality*, 1994, Toronto: Toronto UP

Herman, D, *The Anti-Gay Agenda: Orthodox Vision and the Christian Right*, 1997, Chicago, Illinois: Chicago UP

Hiegel, AL, 'Sexual Exclusions: The Americans with Disabilities Act as a Moral Code' (1994) 94 Columbia L Rev 1451

Hirschfeld, M, *The Transvestites: An Investigation of the Erotic Drive to Cross Dress*, 1910, Lombardi-Nash, M (trans), 1991, Buffalo, New York: Prometheus

Holt, KW, 'Re-evaluating Holloway: Title VII, Equal Protection, and the Evolution of a Transgender Jurisprudence' (1997) 70 Temple L Rev 283–319

Hooley, J, 'What is This Thing Called "Gender Dysphoria"?' (1994) 2 Tranys With Attitude 6–11, Kings Cross, Sydney: The Newsletter of the Transgender Liberation Coalition Inc

Hooley, J, 'The Transgender Project', unpublished, 1996, commissioned by Central Sydney Area Health Authority, NSW, Australia

Hurley, T, 'Constitutional Implications of Sex-Change Operations' (1984) 5 The Journal of Law and Medicine 633–64

I

International Foundation for Androgynous Studies (IFAS), *Gay and Lesbian Law*, 22 April 2001, submission to the Ministerial Reform Committee, PO Box 1066 Nedlands, Perth, WA 6909: IFAS

It's Time Illinois, 'Discrimination and Hate Crimes Against Transgender People in Illinois', 5th Annual Report, 2000, www.itstimeil.org/reports.html

Iyer, N, 'Categorical Denials: Equality Rights and the Shaping of Social Identity' (1993) Queen's LJ 179–207

J

Jackman, M, 'Poor Rights: Using the Charter to Support Social Welfare Claims' (1993) 19 Queen's LJ 65

Jackson, J, *Formation and Annulment of Marriage*, 2nd edn, 1969, London: Butterworths, Chapter 8

Johnson, L, 'The Legal Status of Post-Operative Transsexuals' (1994) 2 Health LJ 160

Jones, JW, 'Discourses on and of AIDS in West Germany, 1986–90', in Fout, JC (ed), *Forbidden History*, 1992, Chicago, Illinois: Chicago UP, p 361

Jorgensen, C, *Christine Jorgensen: A Personal Autobiography*, 1968, New York: Bantam

K

Kando, T, *Sex Change: The Achievement of Gender Identity among Feminized Transsexuals*, 1973, Springfield, Illinois: Charles C Thomas

Karlen, A, *Sexuality and Homosexuality*, 1971, New York: Norton

Katz, J, *Gay American History: Lesbians and Gay Men in the USA*, 1976, New York: Thomas Y Crowell

Katz, JM, 'Transsexuals and Title VII: *Sommers v Budget Marketing Inc*' (1982) 24 Boston College L Rev 266–72

Kaveney, R, 'Talking Transgender Politics', in Whittle, S and More, K (eds), *Reclaiming Genders: Transsexual Grammars at the Fin de Siecle*, 1999, London: Cassell, pp 146–58

Keller, SE, 'Operations of Legal Rhetoric: Examining Transsexual and Judicial Identity' (1999) 34 Harvard Civil Rights-Civil Liberties L Rev 329

Kendall, C, 'Teen Suicide, Sexuality and Silence' (1998) 23 Alternative LJ 216–21

Kennedy, D, *A Critique of Adjudication: Fin de Siecle*, 1997, Cambridge, Mass: Harvard UP

Kennedy, H, 'The "Third Sex" Theory of Karl Heinrich Ulrichs', in Licata, SJ and Petersen, RP (eds), *Historical Perspectives on Homosexuality*, 1981, New York: Haworth

Kennedy, H, *Ulrichs: The Life and Works of Karl Heinrich Ulrichs, Pioneer of the Modern Gay Movement*, 1988, Boston, Mass: Alyson

Kennedy, IM, 'Transsexualism and Single Sex Marriage' (1973) Anglo-American L Rev 112–37

Kertbeny, KM, *Paragraph 143 Des Preussischen Stafgesetzbuches*, 1869, Leipzig: Serbe, reprinted in *7 Jahrbuch fur Sexuelle Zwischenstufen*, 1905

Kessler, SJ, and McKenna, W, *Gender: An Ethnomethodological Approach*, 1978, New York: John Wiley

King, D, *The Transvestite and the Transsexual*, 1993, Aldershot, Hants: Avebury

Kirby, M, 'Medical Technology and New Frontiers of Family Law' (1987) 1 Australian Journal of Family Law 196

Kogan, TS, 'Transsexuals and Critical Gender Theory: The Possibility of a Restroom Labeled "Other"' (1997) 48 Hastings LJ 1223–55

Koranyi, EK, *Transsexuality in the Male: The Spectrum of Gender Dysphoria*, 1980, Springfield, Illinois: Charles C Thomas

von Krafft-Ebing, R, 'Uber Gewisse Anomalien des Geschlechtstriebes' (1877) 7 Archiv fur Psychiatrie und Nervenkrankheiten 291–312

von Krafft-Ebing, R, *Psychopathia Sexualis: With Especial Reference to the Antipathetic Sexual Instinct*, 1965, London: Staples

Kruijver, FPM, Zhou, JN, Pool, CW, Hofman, MA, Gooren, LJG and Swaab, DF, 'Male-To-Female Transsexuals Have Female Neuron Numbers in a Limbic Nucleus' (2000) 85 Journal of Clinical Endocrinology and Metabolism 2034–41

Kuiper, B and Cohen-Kettenis, P, 'Sex Reassignment Surgery: A Study of 141 Dutch Transsexuals' (1988) 17 Archives of Sexual Behavior 439–57

L

Lasok, D, 'Approbation of Marriage in English Law and the Doctrine of Validation' (1963) 26 MLR 249

Laub, DR and Gandy, P, *Proceedings of the Second International Symposium on Gender Dysphoria Syndrome*, 1973, Stanford, CA: University Medical Center

Levay, S, 'A Difference in Hypothalamic Structure between Heterosexual and Homosexual Men' (1991) 253 Science 1034

Levay, S, *The Sexual Brain*, 1993, Cambridge, Mass: MIT Press

Lewes, K, *Psycho-Analysis and Male Homo-Sexuality*, 1995, Northvale, NJ: Jason Aronson

Lewins, F, *Transsexualism in Society: A Sociology of Male-to-Female Transsexuals*, 1995, South Melbourne: Macmillan Education Australia

Lindemalm, G, Korlin, D and Uddenberg, N, 'Long-Term Follow-up of "Sex-Change" in Thirteen Male-to- Female Transsexuals' (1986) 15 Archives of Sexual Behavior 187–210

Lothstein, LM, 'Sex Reassignment Surgery: Historical, Bioethical and Theoretical Issues' (1982) 139 American Journal of Psychiatry 417–26

Lothstein, LM, *Female to Male Transsexualism: Historical, Clinical and Theoretical Issues*, 1983, Boston: Routledge

Lundstrom, B, Pauly, I and Walinder, J, 'Outcome of Sex Reassignment Surgery' (1984) 70 Acta Psychiatrica Scandinavia 289–94

Lupton, ML, 'The Validity of Post-Operative Transsexual Marriages' (1976) 93 South African LJ 385–90

M

McClintock, J, 'Growing Up in the Surgical Maelstrom' (1997) Chrysalis: The Journal of Transgressive Gender Identities 53

McKenzie, R, 'Transsexuals; Legal Status and the Same Sex Marriage in New Zealand: *M v M*' (1992) 7 Otago LR 556–77

Marcuse, H, 'Repressive Tolerance', in Wolff, RP, Moore, B and Marcuse, H (eds), *A Critique of Pure Tolerance*, 1965, Boston: Beacon, pp 81–117

Majury, M, 'Annotation' (1990) 29 RFL 3d 258–61

Mason, G, 'Heterosexed Violence: Typicality and Ambiguity', in Mason, G and Tomsen, S (eds), *Homophobic Violence*, 1997, Sydney: Hawkins, pp 15–32

May-Welby, N, 'Spansexual; Bridging the Gender Divide' (1994) 2 Tranys With Attitude 11

Meerloo, J, 'Change of Sex in collaboration with the Psychosis' (1967) 124 American Journal of Psychiatry 263

Meyer, JK, 'Clinical Variants Among Applicants for Sex Reassignment' (1974) 3 Archives of Sexual Behaviour 527–58

Meyer, JK, 'The Theory of Gender Identity Disorders' (1982) 30 Journal of the American Psychoanalytical Association 381–418

Millns, S, 'Transsexuality and the European Convention on Human Rights' [1992] PL 559–66

Millot, C, *Horesexe: Essay on Transsexuality*, Hylton, K (trans), 1990, New York: Autonomedia

Minkowitz, D, 'On Trial: Gay? Straight? Boy? Girl? Sex? Rape?' (1995) *Out Mag*, October, p 99

Moll, A, *Die Kontrare Sexualempfindung*, 1891, Berlin: Fischer

Money, J, 'Sex Reassignment as Related to Hermaphroditism and Transsexualism', in Green, R and Money, J, *Transsexualism and Sex Reassignment*, 1969, Baltimore: John Hopkins, pp 91–113

Money, J and Primrose, C, 'Sexual Dimorphism and Dissociation in the Psychology of Male Transsexuals', in Green, R and Money, J, *Transsexualism and Sex Reassignment*, 1969, Baltimore: John Hopkins, pp 115–31

Money, J and Walker, PA, 'Counseling the Transsexual', in Money, J and Musaph, H (eds), *Handbook of Sexology*, 1977, New York: Elsevier/North Holland Biomedical Press, pp 1289–301

Moran, L, 'A Study in the History of Male Sexuality in Law: Non-Consummation' (1990) 1 Law and Critique 155–71

Moran, L, *Homophobic Violence and Harassment in Lancaster and Morecambe*, unpublished, 1995, copies available from the author, Birkbeck College, University of London

Moran, L, *The Homosexuality of Law*, 1996, London: Routledge

Moreau, P, *Des Aberrations du Sens Genetique*, 1887, Paris: Asselin

Morel, BA, *Traite des Degenerescences Physiques, Intellectuels et Morales de L'espece Humain*, 1857, Paris: Bailliere

Morel, BA, *Traite des Maladies Mentales*, 1860, Paris: V Masson

Morgan, N, 'Law Reform (Decriminalization of Sodomy) Act 1989 (WA)' (1990) 14 Crim LJ 180–89

Morgan, W, 'Queer Law: Identity, Culture, Diversity, Law' (1995) 5 Australasian Gay and Lesbian LJ 1–41

Morgan, W, 'Still in the Closet: The Heterosexism of Equal Opportunity Law' (1996) 1 Critical InQueeries 119–46

Morkham, B, 'From Parody to Politics: Bodily Inscriptions and Performative Subversions in the Crying Game' (1995) 1 Critical InQueeries 47–68

Morris, J, *Conundrum: An Extraordinary Narrative of Transsexualism*, 1974, New York: Holt

Mountbatten, J, 'Transsexuals, Hermaphrodites and Other Legal Luminaries' (1991) 16 Legal Service Bulletin 223

Mountbatten, J, 'Transsexuals and Social Security Law: The Return of Gonad the Barbarian' (1994) Australian Journal of Family Law 166–77

Mountbatten, J, 'Critique and Comment: Priscilla's Revenge: Or the Strange Case of Transsexual Law Reform in Victoria' (1996) 20 Melbourne UL Rev 871–96

Muller, V, 'Trapped in the Body – Transsexualism, the Law and Sexual Identity' (1994) 3 Australian Feminist LJ 103

N

Naffine, N, 'The Body Bag', in Naffine, N and Owens, RJ (eds), *Sexing the Subject of Law*, 1997, Sydney: LBC, pp 79–93

Nataf, Z, *Lesbians Talk Transgender*, 1996, London: Scarlet

National Coalition of Anti-Violence Programs (NCAVP), 'Anti-Lesbian, Gay, Bisexual and Transgender Violence', 1998, Washington, DC: NCAVP

Nelson, JL, 'The Silence of the Bioethicists: Ethical and Political Aspects of Managing Gender Dysphoria' (1998) 4 GLQ: A Journal of Lesbian and Gay Studies 213–30

Nicholson, J, *Men and Women: How Different Are They?*, 1984, Oxford: OUP

van Niekerk, BVD, 'Sex-Change Operations and the Law' (1970) 87 South African LJ 239–41

Nixon, E, *Royal Spy: The Strange Case of the Chevalier d'Eon*, 1965, New York: Reynal and Company

Noe, JM, Sato, R, Coleman, C and Laub DR, 'Construction of Male Genitalia: The Stanford Experience' (1978) 7 Archives of Sexual Behavior 297–303

Note, 'Transsexuals in Limbo: The Search for a Legal Definition of Sex' (1971) 31 Maryland L Rev 236–54

Note, 'Patriarchy Is Such a Drag: The Strategic Possibilities of a Postmodern Account of Gender' (1995) 108 Harv L Rev 1973–2008

O

O'Donovan, K, 'Transsexual Troubles: The Discrepancy Between Legal and Social Categories', in Edwards, S (ed), *Gender, Sex and the Law*, 1985, London: Croom Helm, pp 9–27

Oglesby, CA, *Women and Sport: From Myth to Reality*, 1978, Philadelphia: Lea & Febiger

Ormrod, R, 'The Medico-Legal Aspects of Sex Determination' (1972) Medico-Legal Journal 78–88

Ostrow, M, *Sexual Deviation: Psychoanalytic Insights*, 1974, New York: Quadrangle

Otlowski, M, 'The Legal Status of a Sexually Reassigned Transsexual: *R v Harris and McGuiness* and Beyond' (1990) 64 ALJ 67

P

Pace, PJ, 'Sexual Identity and the Criminal Law' (1983) Crim L Rev 317–21

Pauly, I, 'Adult Manifestations of Female Transsexualism', in Green, R and Money, J, *Transsexualism and Sex Reassignment*, 1969, Baltimore: John Hopkins

Pauly, I, 'Female Transsexualism: Part I' (1974) 3 Archives of Sexual Behavior 487–507

Pauly, I, 'Gender Identity and Sexual Preference: Dependent Versus Independent Variables', in Bianco, FJ and Serrano, RH (eds), *Sexology: An Independent Field*, 1990, Amsterdam: Elsevier, pp 51–62

Pauly, I, 'Terminology and Classification of Gender Identity Disorders', in Bockting, W and Coleman, E (eds), *Gender Dysphoria: Interdisciplinary Approaches to Clinical Management*, 1992, New York: Haworth, pp 1–14

Pauly, I, 'Gender Identity and Sexual Orientation', in Denny, D, *Current Concepts in Transgender Identity*, 1998, New York: Garland, pp 237–48

Pearlman, L, 'Transsexualism as Metaphor: The Collision of Sex and Gender' (1995) Buffalo L Rev 835–72

Perkins, R, Griffin, A and Jakobsen, J, *Transgender Lifestyles and HIV/AIDS Risk: National Transgender HIV/AIDS Needs Assessment Project*, 1994, Sydney: School of Sociology, University of New South Wales

Person, E and Ovesey, L, 'The Transsexual Syndrome in Males I: Primary Transsexualism' (1974) 28 American Journal of Psychotherapy 4–20 (1974a)

Person, E and Ovesey, L, 'The Transsexual Syndrome in Males II: Secondary Transsexualism' (1974) 28 American Journal of Psychotherapy 174–93 (1974b)

Plant, M, Mason, B and Thornton, C, *Experiences and Perceptions of Violence and Intimidation of the Lesbian, Gay, Bisexual and Transgender Communities in Edinburgh*, 1999, City of Edinburgh: Edinburgh

Plato, *The Symposium*, Hamilton, W (trans), 1951, Harmondsworth: Penguin

Pomeroy, WB, 'The Diagnosis and Treatment of Transvestites and Transsexuals' (1975) 1 Journal of Sex and Marital Therapy 215–24

Prince, V, *How to be a Woman, Though Male*, 1971, Los Angeles: Chevalier

Prince, V, *Understanding Cross Dressing*, 1976, Los Angeles: Chevalier

Prosser, J, *Second Skins: The Body Narratives of Transsexuality*, 1998, New York: Columbia UP

R

Randall, J, 'Transvestism and Trans-Sexualism: A Study of 50 Cases' (1959) 2 BMJ 1448–52

Raymond, J, *The Transsexual Empire: The Making of a She-Male*, 1979, Boston, Mass: Beacon

Rees, M, 'Becoming a Man: The Personal Account of a Female-To-Male Transsexual', in Ekins, R and King, D (eds), *Blending Genders: Social Aspects of Cross-Dressing and Sex-Changing*, 1996, London and New York: Routledge, pp 27–38

Reid, R, 'Psychiatric and Psychological Aspects of Transsexualism', in *Transsexualism, Medicine and Law*, Proceeding of the XXIII Colloquy on European Law, 1995, Strasbourg: Council of Europe, pp 25–50

Rich, A, 'Compulsory Heterosexuality and Lesbian Existence', in Stimpson, CR and Spector Person, E (eds), *Women, Sex and Sexuality*, 1980, Chicago, Illinois: Chicago UP, pp 62–91

Richardson, LA, 'The Challenge to Transsexuality: Legal Responses of Transsexuality: Legal Responses to an Assertion of Rights' (1983) Northern Illinois UL Rev 119

Robertson, KC, 'Note: Penetrating Sex and Marriage: The Progressive Potential of Addressing Bisexuality in Queer Theory' (1998) 75 Denver UL Rev 1375–1408

Robson, R, *Sappho Goes to Law School*, 1998, New York: Columbia UP

Ross, MW and Need, JA, 'Effects of Adequacy of Gender Reassignment Surgery on Psychological Adjustment: A Follow-Up of 14 Male-To-Female Patients' (1989) 18 Archives of Sexual Behavior 145

Rubin, G, 'Of Catamites and Kings: Reflections on Butch, Gender, and Boundaries', in Nestle, J (ed), *The Persistent Desire: A Femme-Butch Reader*, 1992, Boston: Alyson

S

Samuels, A, 'Once a Man, Always a Man; Once a Woman, Always a Woman – Sex Change and the Law' (1984) Medicine and Science Law 163

Sarat, A and Kearns, T, *Law's Violence*, 1992, Michigan: University of Michigan Press

Sawicki, J, *Disciplining Foucault: Feminism, Power and the Body*, 1991, London: Routledge

Sedgwick, E, *Epistemology of the Closet*, 1990, London and New York: Penguin

Sedgwick, E, 'How to Bring Your Kids Up Gay', in Warner, M (ed), *Fear of a Queer Planet: Queer Politics and Social Theory*, 1993, Minneapolis: University of Minnesota Press

Seidman, S, 'Identity Politics in a "Postmodern" Gay Culture: Some Historical and Conceptual Notes', in Warner, M (ed), *Fear of a Queer Planet: Queer Politics and Social Theory*, 1993, Minneapolis: University of Minnesota Press, pp 105–42

Sex Discrimination Commissioner/Human Rights and Equal Opportunity Commission, *Transgenders and Discrimination: Options for Legislative Protection: A Discussion Paper*, 1996, Canberra: Sex Discrimination Commissioner/Human Rights and Equal Opportunity Commission

Shafiqullah, H, 'Shape-Shifters, Masqueraders & Subversives: An Argument for the Liberation of Transgender Individuals' (1997) 8 Hastings Women's LJ 195–227

SHAFT, *A Handbook for Male to Female Transsexuals*, 1981, South Ascot: Berks: Self Help Association for Transsexuals

Shapiro, J, 'Transsexualism: Reflections on the Persistence of Gender and the Mutability of Sex', in Epstein, J and Straub, K, *Body Guards: The Cultural Politics of Gender Ambiguity*, 1991, London: Routledge, pp 248–79

Sharpe, AN, 'Judicial Uses of Transsexuality: A Site for Political Contestation' (1996) 22 Alternative LJ 153

Sharpe, AN, 'Anglo-Australian Judicial Approaches to Transsexuality: Discontinuities, Continuities and Wider Issues at Stake' (1997) 6 Social and Legal Studies: An International Journal 23–50 (1997a)

Sharpe, AN, 'The Transsexual and Marriage: Law's Contradictory Desires' (1997) 7 Australasian Gay and Lesbian LJ 1–14 (1997b)

Sharpe, AN, 'Naturalising Sex Difference Through Sport: An Examination of the New South Wales Transgender Legislation' (1997) 22 Alternative LJ 40–41 (1997c)

Sharpe, AN, 'Attempting the "Impossible": The Case of Transsexual Rape' (1997) 21 Crim LJ 23–31 (1997d)

Sharpe, AN, 'Institutionalising Heterosexuality: The Legal Exclusion of "Impossible" (Trans)Sexualities', in Moran, L, Monk, D and Beresford, S (eds), *Legal Queeries: Lesbian, Gay and Transgender Legal Studies*, 1998, London: Cassell, pp 26–41

Sharpe, AN, 'Transgender Jurisprudence and the Spectre of Homosexuality' (2000) 14 Australian Feminist LJ 23–37

Sharpe, AN and Moran, L, 'Challenging Violence: The Case of Violence Against Transgender People', forthcoming

Shelley, M, *Frankenstein*, Butler, M (ed), 1993, London: Pickering and Chatto

Short, S, 'Report of the Transgender Anti-Violence Project', unpublished, 1997, Sydney, New South Wales, Australia

Skidmore, P, 'Can Transsexuals Suffer Sex Discrimination?' (1997) 19 Journal of Social Welfare and Family Law 105–10

Smart, C, *Feminism & the Power of Law*, 1989, London: Routledge

Smith, AM, 'The Regulation of Lesbian Sexuality Through Erasure: The Case of Jennifer Saunders', in Jay, K (ed), *Lesbian Erotics*, 1995, New York: New York University, pp 164–79

Smith, D, 'Transsexualism, Sex Reassignment and the Law' (1971) 56 Cornell L Rev 963

Socarides, C, 'The Desire for Sexual Transformation: A Psychiatric Evaluation of Transsexualism' (1969) 125 American Journal of Psychiatry 125–31

Socarides, C, 'A Psychoanalytic Study of the Desire for Sexual Transformation ("transsexualism"): The Plaster-of-Paris Man' (1970) 51 International Journal of Psycho-Analysis 341–49

Spivak, GC, 'The Problem of Cultural Self-Representation', interviewed by Walter Adamson in Harasym, S (ed), *The Post-Colonial Critic: Interviews, Strategies, Dialogues, Gayatri Chakravorty Spivak*, 1990, London and New York: Routledge, pp 50–58

Steinach, E and Loebel, J, *Sex and Life*, 1940, London: Faber

Steiner, BW, 'From Sappho to Sand: Historical Perspective on Crossdressing and Cross Gender' (1981) 26 Can J of Psychiatry 502–06

Steiner, BW, *Gender Dysphoria: Development, Research, Management*, 1985, New York and London: Plenum

Stekel, W, *Sexual Aberrations: The Phenomenon of Fetishism in Relation to Sex*, 1922, authorised English version from the first German edition by Parker, S, 1930, New York: Liveright

Stevenson, RL, *The Strange Case of Dr Jekyll and Mr Hyde*, 1986, Der Munchen: Deutscher Taschenbuch Verlag

Stoller, RJ, *Sex and Gender*, 1968, New York: Science House

Stoller, RJ, 'Male Transsexualism: Uneasiness' (1973) 130 American Journal of Psychiatry 536–39

Stoller, RJ, *Perversion: The Erotic Form of Hatred*, 1975, New York: Pantheon

Stone, S, 'The Empire Strikes Back: A Posttranssexual Manifesto', in Epstein, J, and Straub, K, *Body Guards: The Cultural Politics of Gender Ambiguity*, 1991, London: Routledge, pp 280–304

Storrow, RF, 'Naming the Grotesque Body in the Nascent Jurisprudence of Transsexualism' (1997) 4 Michigan Journal of Gender and Law 275–334

Stuart, KE, *The Uninvited Dilemma: A Question of Gender*, 1991, Portland, Oregon: Metamorphous

Stryker, S, 'The Transgender Issue: An Introduction' (1998) 4 Gay and Lesbian Quarterly: A Journal of Lesbian and Gay Studies 145–58

Stychin, CF, *Law's Desire: Sexuality and the Limits of Justice*, 1995, London: Routledge

Stychin, CF, 'Case Note: Troubling Genders: A Comment on *P v S and Cornwall County Council*' (1997) 2 International Journal of Discrimination and the Law 217–22

Stychin, CF, *A Nation by Rights: National Cultures, Sexual Identity Politics and the Discourse of Rights*, 1998, Philadelphia: Temple UP

Sydney Gender Centre Report, *Workshop 1: Providing Services to People With Gender Issues*, 1994, Sydney: Gender Centre

T

Taitz, J, 'The Law Relating to the Consummation of Marriage Where One of the Spouses is a Post-Operative Transsexual' (1986) 15 Anglo-American L Rev 141

Taitz, J, 'Judicial Determination of the Sexual Identity of Post-Operative Transsexuals: A New Form of Sex Discrimination' (1987) 13 Am J of Law and Med 53–69

Taitz, J, 'A Transsexual's Nightmare: The Determination of Sexual Identity in English Law' (1988) The International Journal of Law and the Family 139

Taitz, J, 'Judicial Determination of Sexual Identity' (1992) Australasian Journal of the Medical Defence Union 12

Tarnowsky, B, *Die Krankhaften Erscheinungen des Geshlechtsinnes: Eine Forensisch-Psychiatrische Studien*, 1886, Berlin: Hirschwald

Terzian, H, 'Observations on the Clinical Symptomatology of Bilateral Partial or Total Removal of Temporal Lobes in Man', in Baldwin, M (ed), *Temporal Lobe Epilepsy*, 1958, Springfield: Charles C Thomas

Thornton, M, *The Liberal Promise: Anti-Discrimination Legislation in Australia*, 1990, Melbourne: Oxford UP (Australia)

Transgender Liberation Coalition (1994) 1 Tranys With Attitude, Kings Cross, Sydney: The Newsletter of the Transgender Liberation Coalition Inc

Triea, K, 'The Awakening' (1994) Hermaphrodites with Attitude 1

Truman, C, 'Lesbians' and Gay Men's Experiences of Crime and Policing: An Exploratory Study', 1994, Manchester: Manchester Metropolitan University, Department of Applied Community Studies

Trumbach, R, 'London's Sodomites: Homosexual Behaviour and Western Culture in the 18th Century' (1977) Journal of Social History 1

Trumbach, R, 'Sodomitical Subcultures, Sodomitical Roles, and the Gender Revolution of the 18th Century: The Recent Historiography', in Maccubbin, RP (ed), *Tis Nature's Fault: Unauthorised Sexuality During the Enlightenment*, 1987, Cambridge: CUP, pp 109–21

Tully, B, *Accounting for Transsexuality and Transhomosexuality*, 1992, London: Whiting

Tyler, CA, 'Boys Will be Girls: The Politics of Gay Drag', in Fuss, D, *Inside/Out: Lesbian Theories, Gay Theories*, 1991, London: Routledge, pp 32–70

U

Ulrichs, KH, writing as Numa Numantius, 'Inclusa', in *Anthropologische Studien Uber Mannmanliche Geschlechtsliebe*, 1898, Leipzig: Matthes

Ulrichs, KH, 'Vier Briefe' (1899) 1 Jahrbuch fur Sexuelle Zwischenstufen 35–70 Leipzig, reprinted in Katz, J (ed), *Documents of the Homosexual Rights Movement in Germany 1836–1927*, 1975, New York: Arno

Ulrichs, KH, *The Riddle of 'Man-Manly' Love: The Pioneering Work on Male Homosexuality*, Lombardi-Nash, MA (trans), 1994, Buffalo, New York: Prometheus, 2 Vols

V

Valdes, F, 'Queers, Sissies, Dykes, and Tomboys: Deconstructing the Conflation of "Sex", "Gender", and "Sexual Orientation"' (1995) 83 Euro-American Law and Society California L Rev 1

W

Walinder, J, Lundstrom, B and Thuwe, I, 'Prognostic Factors in the Assessment of Male Transsexuals for Sex Reassignment' (1978) 132 British Journal of Psychiatry 16–20

Walker, PA, Berger, JC, Green, R, Laub, DR, Reynolds, CL and Wollman, L, *Standards of Care: The Hormonal and Sex Reassignment of Gender Dysphoric Persons*, 1979, Galverston, Texas: The Janus Information Facility, The University of Texas Medical Branch

Walters, WAW, Kennedy, T and Ross, MW, 'Results of Gender Reassignment: Is it all Worthwhile?', in Walters, WAW and Ross, MW, *Transsexualism and Sex Reassignment*, 1986, Oxford: OUP, pp 144–51

Walters, WAW and Ross, MW, *Transsexualism and Sex Reassignment*, 1986, Oxford: OUP

Walton, T, 'When is a Woman Not a Woman?' (1974) 124 NLJ 501

Walton, T, 'Why Can't a Woman?' (1984) 134 NLJ 937

Warnes, H and Hill, G, 'Gender Identity and the Wish to be a Woman' (1974) 1 Psychosomatics 25–31

Watney, S, *Policing Desire*, 2nd edn, 1989, Minneapolis: University of Minnesota Press

Weeks, J, *Sexuality and its Discontents: Meanings Myths and Modern Sexualities*, 1985, London: Routledge and Kegan Paul

Weeks, J, *Against Nature: Essays on History, Sexuality and Identity*, 1991, London: Rivers Oram

Wein, SA and Remmers, CL, 'Employment Protection and Gender Dysphoria: Legal Definitions of Unequal Treatment on the Basis of Sex and Disability' (1979) 30 Hastings LJ 1075–129

West Australian Government Report, 'Lesbian and Gay Law Reform', Report of the Ministerial Committee, June 2001, Perth, Western Australia. See www.ministers.wa.gov.au/mcginty/gaylesbian.htm

Westphal, C, 'Die Kontrare Sexualempfindung' (1869) 2 Archiv fur Psychiatrie und Nervenkrankheiten 73–108

Wheelright, J, *Amazons and Military Maids: Women Who Dressed as Men in the Pursuit of Life, Liberty and Happiness*, 1989, London: Pandora

Whittle, S, 'Gender Fucking or Fucking Gender', in Ekins, R and King, D (eds), *Blending Genders: Social Aspects of Crossing-Dressing and Sex-Changing*, 1996, London and New York: Routledge, pp 196–214

Whittle, S, 'Gemeinschaftsfremden – or How to be Shafted by Your Friends: Sterilization Requirements and Legal Status Recognition for the Transsexual', in Moran, L, Monk, D and Beresford, S (eds), *Legal Queeries: Lesbian, Gay and Transgender Legal Studies*, 1998, London: Cassell, pp 42–56

Whittle, S, 'Transgender Rights: The European Court of Human Rights and New Identity Politics for a New Age', in Hegarty, A and Leonard, S (eds), *Human Rights: An Agenda for the 21st Century*, 1999, London: Cavendish Publishing, pp 201–16

Whittle, S, 'New-isms: Transsexual People and Institutionalised Discrimination in Employment Law' (2000) 4(1) Contemporary Issues in Law 31–53

Whittle, S and McMullan, M, *Transvestism, Transsexualism and the Law*, 1995, London: The Gender Trust

Whittle, S and More, K (ed), *Reclaiming Genders: Transsexual Grammars at the Fin de Siecle*, 1999, London: Cassell

Wilchins, RA, 'Michigan Womyn's Music Festival Controversy Grinds On' (1995) Fall, In Your Face 6

Wilchins, RA, *Read My Lips: Sexual Subversion and the End of Gender*, 1997, Ithaca, New York: Firebrand

Williams, WL, *The Spirit and the Flesh: Sexual Diversity in American Indian Culture*, 1986, Boston: Beacon

Willis, P, 'Women in Sport in Ideology', in Hargreaves, J (ed), *Sport, Culture and Ideology*, 1982, London: Routledge and Kegan Paul, pp 117–35

Wilson, R, 'Life and Law: The Impact of Human Rights on Experimenting with Life' (1985) 61 Australian Journal of Forensic Sciences 80

Wintemute, R, 'Recognising New Kinds of Direct Sex Discrimination: Transsexualism, Sexual Orientation and Dress Codes' (1997) 60 MLR 334–59

Winterson, J, *The Passion*, 1996, London: Vintage

INDEX